MICHA...
RAMS...

A LIFE

MICHAEL RAMSEY

A LIFE

OWEN CHADWICK

Oxford   New York
OXFORD UNIVERSITY PRESS

Oxford University Press, Walton Street, Oxford OX2 6DP
Oxford New York Toronto
Delhi Bombay Calcutta Madras Karachi
Petaling Jaya Singapore Hong Kong Tokyo
Nairobi Dar es Salaam Cape Town
Melbourne Auckland
and associated companies in
Berlin Ibadan

Oxford is a trade mark of Oxford University Press

First published 1990
First issued as an Oxford University Press paperback 1991
Reprinted 1991

British Library Cataloguing in Publication Data
Chadwick, Owen
Michael Ramsey.
1. Church of England. Ramsey, Michael, 1904–1988
I. Title
283.092
ISBN 0-19-282810-X

Library of Congress Cataloging-in-Publication Data
Chadwick, Owen.
Michael Ramsey : a life / Owen Chadwick.
p. cm.
Originally published: Oxford: Clarendon Press;
New York: Oxford University Press, 1990
Includes bibliographical references and index.
1. Ramsey, Michael, 1904– .   2. Church of England—Bishops—
Biography.   3. Anglican Communion—England—Bishops—Biography.
I. Title.
[BX5199.R224C47   1991]   283'.092—dc20   90-15511
ISBN 0-19-282810-X

Printed in England by Clays Ltd, St Ives plc

Preface

In 1967, while Archbishop Fisher still lived, Michael Ramsey was consulted about a future biography of Fisher. He replied by considering why the life by Iremonger of his hero William Temple was a failure. It was written too near the events. The biography ought not to be written in a person's lifetime nor too near the events. What would be most helpful, he said, would be if Fisher were persuaded to write down notes and records and impressions and leave them for subsequent use. It turned out, however, that Fisher himself wanted a life of himself while he lived so that he could provide, and others could provide, evidence which in a few years would be lost. Michael Ramsey did not think the judgement right.

During the sixties and seventies Archbishop Ramsey was on several occasions approached by authors or publishers with the suggestion that his life should be written. On this he had strong views that it was wrong to publish anyone's life while he or she lived. He therefore rejected all these applications courteously. But the experience made him realize that sooner or later his life was bound to be written.

In 1980 he approached the author with the request that he should undertake the writing of his life; with the proviso that it should not be done while he lived. I was conscious of what was said many years ago by a close friend of Ramsey who was a fellow of Magdalene College, Cambridge, Dick Ladborough the modern linguist. He said, 'No biographer, not even a Boswell, could write Michael Ramsey's life. It needs the mannerisms, the tone of voice, the unspoken humour which is not communicable.'

Ramsey was a good letter-writer, if you could read his handwriting, but he was not a diarist. His engagement-books are the least informative ever preserved. The present Archbishop of Canterbury, Dr Runcie, made available to me the correspondence and other papers in the Lambeth Palace Library. To him, and to his librarian Dr Geoffrey Bill, and to their staff, especially Melanie Barber and Dr Richard Aspin, I owe particular thanks; as to Canon Christopher Hill at the Council of Foreign Relations, and his archivist Jane Houston. Ramsey also had his own boxes of letters and papers which he passed to me. The life was treated in various books which will be found in the bibliography. Others have given me reminiscences or other evidence, and it will not be possible to mention them all; and some of them are no longer with us.

My thanks are specially due to Mrs Barcroft, who had charge of the unpublished autobiography of Ramsey's father. To Mrs Margaret Paul for memories of the home and for photographs. To Dr Michael Halls, archivist of King's College, Cambridge. To Donald Harris, who was his contemporary at King's College School as well as a friend later. To Sir Desmond Lee, who was a contemporary at Repton, and Kenneth Rose, at Repton soon afterwards. To Lord Devlin and Lord (Geoffrey) Lloyd and Lord (Rab) Butler, who were his contemporaries at Cambridge and to the trustees of the papers of Selwyn Lloyd, who was also his contemporary. To the Master and Fellows of Magdalene College for the use of A. C. Benson's diary. To Dean Eric Abbott and Professor Christopher Evans and Bishop Jim Bishop and Canon G. B. Bentley, who were his contemporaries at Lincoln. To Bishop Frank Sargeant, whose father was his server at Boston. To Charles Roach, who was his cyclist fellow-curate at Boston. To George Barlow, and Mrs R. Hurry, and Priscilla Leonard, and Lady Alice Bragg, who knew him in connection with St Benet's. To Professor Kingsley Barrett, and Dean John Wild, and Professor Hedley Sparks, who served with him during his time as professor at Durham University and later when he was Bishop of Durham. To William Baddeley and Kenneth Bradford and several others who were his pupils at Durham University. To John and Paul Lucas, who were young boys next door to him at Durham. To Sir David Hunt, who worked in Downing Street when Ramsey became Bishop of Durham. To Dr Alan Webster, who was vicar of Barnard Castle while Ramsey was Bishop of Durham. To Dorothy Daldy, who was a lecturer at Durham when he arrived as professor, and after the war became his pupil in theology. She typed his application for the Cambridge chair and when Joan was ill at Cambridge came to help out as cook and so became always known as Cook Em. (= Emerita). To Archdeacon Ron Scruby, and Canon Gordon Hopkins, and K. F. A. Parkinson, especially for his time at York. To Dr D. M. Smith of the Borthwick Institute, where are the Bishopthorpe Papers. To John Peart-Binns, who is the expert on contemporary episcopal biography. To John Pollock, who knew most about Ramsey's relation with Billy Graham. To Victor Stock, who was ordained by him and became a friend in the years of retirement. To Roland Walls, who worked with him on two missions, one to Newcastle Polytechnic and one to the university chaplains. To Ramsey's right-hand man in legal affairs, David Carey. To several of the staff at Lambeth or in the Canterbury diocese—especially Bishop Tony

Tremlett, Bishop John Satterthwaite, Bill Saumarez Smith, Barbara Lepper, Michael Nott, Philip Norwood, Michael Moore, John Miles; and above all to John Andrew his chaplain both at York and Canterbury. To Dr John Kelly, who was chairman of the Commission on Roman Catholic relations at the time of Archbishop Ramsey's visit to Rome and to Canon William Purdy who was concerned with him much over Anglican–Roman Catholic relations. To Canon Derek Ingram Hill, and to Dean White-Thomson, who worked closely with him in the Canterbury diocese. To some who served with him on the bishops' bench, especially Archbishop Sir Philip Strong and Bishop Gerald Ellison and Bishop Eric Kemp and Archbishop George Appleton and Bishop Oliver Tomkins, the last of whom knew most about his relation to the World Council of Churches. To Margaret Pawley, who worked with her husband Bernard, for several years Ramsey's representative in Rome. To Richard Rutt, the Bishop of Leicester, who while Ramsey was archbishop was Bishop in Korea. To Bishop J. K. Cavell, and Canon F. H. W. Millett, and Canon A. M. Allchin. To Archbishop George Simms for help over Irish matters. To Bishop John Howe and Bishop Edward Knapp-Fisher and Canon Samuel van Culin for help over the Anglican Communion. To Bishop John M. Allin Sr., who during part of Ramsey's time as archbishop was the Presiding Bishop of the Episcopal Church of the United States. To Dr Kenneth Greet, who in the debate between Anglicans and Methodists was one of the Methodists for whom Ramsey developed affection. To the BBC Written Archives Centre, Caversham Park, Reading, for permission to use and reproduce their archives, and to Clare Brown for her help there. To the National Sound Archives for similar help. To Prebendary Michael Saward, who was Radio and Television officer at Lambeth. To Bishop Woollcombe and Professor Leslie Houlden, who were Bishop and Principal in Cuddesdon when Ramsey retired thither, and to Bishop David Wilcox, who was Principal after he left. To Jack C. Knights, the Dean of Nashotah House, and to James Dunkley, librarian at the Episcopal Theological School, for help with Ramsey at Nashotah House. To Canon David Palmer, who was chaplain in Rome during Ramsey's retirement. To the Archbishop of York and the Bishop of Durham and the Hon. George Bruce and Peter Greenham RA and Ruskin Spear RA and Julia Sorell and Janet Soskice, then the Librarian at Cuddesdon, and Captain Peter Parry of Church House for help over portraits. To Dennis Pratley, who helped the Ramseys in Oxford. And a special gratitude to Lady Ramsey.

Contents

Contents

Illustrations

Oxford University Press would like to thank all those who have kindly given permission for reproduction of illustrations, as listed above; photographs with no acknowledgement have been provided by Owen Chadwick from Lady Ramsey's archives.

PART 1

———

THE MAKING OF A
CHRISTIAN LEADER

I

Schooling

I. CHILDHOOD

The making of Archbishops of Canterbury has been as various as the making of Popes. Since the reign of Queen Mary in 1558, when the last Plantagenet to be an Archbishop died, they did not include among their number members of the royal family. It was natural that most of them were educated at Oxford or Cambridge, since until the Victorian age those were the two places for training the clergy of the Church. From the first Protestant Archbishop Thomas Cranmer under King Henry VIII, all the Protestant Archbishops were educated at Oxford or Cambridge and a majority taught at one of those universities. For 130 years after 1558 every archbishop had been the head of an Oxford or Cambridge College. They came from almost every variety of home, from one grandson of a duke to the son of someone who survived on a small-holding. Several of them were the sons of merchants, some prosperous, some small, two ruined. In modern times differences appeared. Six of them during their career were headmasters of great schools, and this never happened before 1829, and was a sign of the rising importance which the nation gave to the teaching profession. More of them were the sons or grandsons of someone in the Christian ministry. All the five archbishops before Michael Ramsey were the sons or grandsons of Christian ministers.

Therefore, on historical precedent, in contemplating the origin of a modern archbishop we would expect him to be educated at Oxford or Cambridge; to have a good chance that he taught there; and to be the son or grandson of a Christian minister. On all three counts Michael Ramsey scored. Cambridge lay at the heart of his education and his career. On both his father's side and his mother's side he was the grandson of a Christian minister. He did even better than that. On both his father's side and his mother's side he was the great-grandson of a Christian minister.

He was a Cambridge man born and bred. He lived in the town of

Cambridge for more years of his life than in any other town, and this though he managed during his life to live in nine different towns and in one village. He was the son of a Cambridge don. He was sent to his first school there. He was sent to study at the University of Cambridge. In his student days he was happy and successful in his undergraduate career. Always he remained grateful to his college. Later he became the vicar of a Cambridge parish. Later still he became for a short time a professor at Cambridge. His aunt and sister-in-law always lived in Cambridge. It surprised some that he did not retire to Cambridge. After his retirement there was no place where he took more delight in an invitation to talk than in one of the Cambridge churches or one of the college chapels. The place always held affection for him. In the town, and in the university, he felt at home.

His father's father was a Congregational minister who came from Ireland early in life and ministered in various English chapels. While he served a flourishing chapel at Dewsbury in Yorkshire, his son, Michael Ramsey's father, won a scholarship in mathematics to Magdalene College, Cambridge, the first generation of the family to go to a university. He worked hard, which was rare among the undergraduates of Magdalene College in those days, and came out with a high degree in mathematics. Though the college was very Anglican, he retained all his family's loyalty to the Congregationalist tradition and way of worship. After a time teaching in a Scottish school, Fettes, the degree got him a fellowship in mathematics at his own college of Magdalene; where he remained the rest of his long life—teaching mathematics, holding various college offices, going every week to Emmanuel Congregational chapel, and becoming after a time one of its deacons or church officers. He was a good mathematical teacher and he wrote a number of text-books, some of which went on selling into the 1980s. To the outward eye he was austere, even bleak. Colleagues and pupils thought of him as formidable; a few found him frightening, a few found him affable. The Master of the College, Arthur Benson, said of him humorously that when roused he would become 'all eye and moustache'. But, wrote Michael Ramsey in retrospect—it is his own *but*—'he had wit and generosity and there were pupils who had deep affection for him. I was never consciously frightened of him and felt close to him and was regarded as a favourite child to him in some ways. Yet I think that at the subconscious and half-conscious levels he was a heavy weight upon me of a perhaps oppressive or repressive kind. In later life I was made unnecessarily unhappy by my religious divergence from his position.' In the long view he thought that his father's unbending moral conviction was important in his own life.

On a return visit to Fettes, Arthur Ramsey stayed with one of the housemasters and met the sister Agnes Wilson, who kept house there. They were married in 1902. They lived at first not far from Magdalene College in a house which looked across the river Cam to Midsummer Common. There the first three children were born—Frank in 1902, Michael two years later (14 November 1904), and then Bridget, the elder daughter.

His grandfather on the mother's side, that is the father of Agnes Wilson, was the vicar of Horbling in Lincolnshire. Michael Ramsey was therefore the grandson of a Congregationalist minister on one side and of an Anglican vicar on the other. He was baptized by his Wilson grandfather at Horbling. The nurse was an impostor who drugged the baby but was exposed after two days and sacked.

Michael Ramsey's mother was one of nine children and of the brothers two were schoolmasters, two were clergymen, one an organist, and one a doctor. She studied history at St Hugh's College, Oxford —early days for a woman—and knew Lewis Carroll, and was taught by one of the best teachers then in the historical school at Oxford, a future Master of Balliol, A. L. Smith, upon whom she always looked back with gratitude. Later she taught English and history at Putney High School, and before marriage published a book about Lamb's *Essays of Elia* and another book about a play by Browning.

Child of the vicarage, she did not press her Anglicanism against her husband's nonconformity. They attended the Congregational church regularly and took the children. During her too short life she never ceased to be Anglican; but she was a Socialist, and a suffragette, and religion for her came to mean, not so much creed or piety, as having a lively social conscience. She was not a violent demonstrator as a suffragette but she worked hard for the women's vote, and at times vociferously at public meetings. After the end of the first World War she was active in the co-operative movement and the Labour Party, which was not common for a woman of her background in those early years. Her son Michael's memory of her had nothing in it that was not good; a woman radiant, friendly, outgoing, understanding.

Politically she was alive. She brought Socialist thinkers or politicians into the house, like Graham Wallas or Hugh Dalton. She was a good speaker on public platforms. It was recorded that when she was speaking in the market-place she was audible by the Senate House. She paraded round the town in processions for votes for women. She also had the powerful sense of humour which her children inherited, and could be very amusing in conversation. She had other gifts which her son Michael inherited. She could hold the interest of a group of undergraduates at a tea-party and have a serious exchange of ideas with them. On Sundays she would invite a group of Magdalene undergraduates to lunch and they would stay till tea; then another group still larger came to tea. Her younger daughter remembered them clustered round her chair as she talked and, as someone said, 'toyed with the frayed edges of a bun'. She took little interest in how she dressed. One who knew her remembered a very large hole in her stocking. Her daughter could remember greenish-black wrinkled stockings, and a newspaper report of a speech, 'Mrs Ramsey—proud to be shabby'. But her face was interesting and intelligent and attractive. Her personality was magnetic.

Despite the cook and the housemaid the house gave the impression of being unloved. The dining-room was full of ugly sepia prints of old masters—mostly angels. Much of the house was painted dark brown with pale brown walls. Arthur Ramsey told his daughter that he chose this colour 'because anyone could throw a coffee-cup at the wall without it showing'. In the kitchen stood a large bag of coke. The centre-piece of the dining-room table was a bowl of electric light bulbs.

Despite the hilarious hostess, the house was a bit grim, not only in its décor. Father was convinced that his wife would not have enough to live on when he died and overworked to get money. He wrote textbooks, took lodgers, took pupils. The children saw not much of him because all day he was out at his duties and in the evenings he retired to his study to convert his lectures into books. They followed him to the study because for economy it was the only fire in the house, but he worked through their conversation and did not join it. There was a cook and a maid and he could be fierce with them. He could be stern even with his wife if something went wrong. He was liable to terrible migraines. Meal times were felt by the children to be dreary occasions. He had no real friends and was difficult. But he had a deep affection for his wife, and she for him.

They had family prayers every day after breakfast led by father. The young Michael found Emmanuel church austere, and later, when he knew what that meant, puritan. They sat in the family pew. He thought the extemporary prayer very long and hard to bear. The sermons were livelier, for the resident minister Carter was a cultivated man. Michael's younger sister found him a fidget in church and thought it was fidgeting to excess. He whiled away the time by contemplating the stained glass lancet windows behind the preacher and the holy table. They were windows of puritan worthies, including Cromwell and Milton. He liked the hymns and ever afterwards admired the Congregational hymn book.

The little boy loved toy soldiers and drafted speeches for the commanders-in-chief. The family had holidays at Perranporth in Cornwall and if the soldiers fell into a rock pool and were drowned, Michael conducted a funeral service for them. But soon he discovered that politicians were more interesting than colonels so he arranged his soldiers as though they were the House of Commons and made them harangue each other. About the age of 6 he wrote a book called 'Ways to the City Bright by the Rev. A. M. Ramsey'. Notice that at so young an age he knew that 'the Rev.' was better than 'Rev.' But the book was not orthodox in divinity because father locked it up and would not let Michael's sister read it.

When Michael was 5 the family moved house, only half a mile, to a larger house nearer Magdalene College, Howfield beyond Castle Hill. What the older Michael mostly remembered about this were the games—croquet in which the parents joined the children, tennis, a sort of squash with his brother hitting a tennis ball against a veranda wall, expeditions up the river through the Backs and then up to the village of Grantchester.

The other children found Michael to be very odd, and the girls (two sisters now) resented the oddness. This was in part due to a disability which was not realized. He had a physical clumsiness in the management of his hands. He learnt to eat tidily later than most children, and the mess down his front was hard for the others to bear. But this was not all. His younger sister remembered that suddenly he might leave the table with a wild mad look on his face and rush round the garden. In the night he might be heard running up and down his attic bedroom banging the wall at each end, and keeping other people awake. The sisters found him a loner, difficult to relate to in a normal friendly way.

The house, nevertheless, had visitors interesting to the children; a couple of famous Congregationalist laymen Frank Salter and Bernard Manning, both of whom were historians and riotous rompers with children; the Reddaway children who lived next door; the daughters of G. G. Coulton the English hammer of Popes; and the friendship between the two sets of children caused Coulton to take an interest in Michael and carry him off to the village church at Coton to see medieval graffiti. The lodgers in the house were interesting—Indian and Siamese students trying to get into the university. Michael specially liked the Siamese.

As the children grew, Michael felt himself a backward boy. This was because of his elder brother Frank, whose academic career was already starred. Michael had a sense that he pushed along behind a much cleverer creature and could not keep up. Boys who feel backward grow backward, even when they are not, for they suffer from the illusion that by nature they cannot solve the problems set to them. Ramsey was sent to two dames' schools in succession but learnt so little that his parents took him away and for a year he was taught at home by his mother. This he hated. His mother was the most important object in his life. But being taught by her made him squirm. He told his sister how it was impossible to listen, and how he felt compelled to pull horrible nervous faces all the time.

Then the parents tried the opposite method. They sent him to the King's College Choir School. This is situated on the Backs, with only a short walk across to King's College and its great chapel. It was not necessary for a boy to be musical; in addition to the choirboys there was an ordinary school. They had day-boys. Ramsey was one. The boys who boarded in dormitories despised the boys who slept at home. They denounced them as 'mouldy day-bugs'. For the rest of his life Ramsey treasured with vast amusement that once he was a mouldy day-bug.

Here the boy met the first Anglican priest who interested him in religion. The chaplain of King's College, whose work was with undergraduates, came to teach divinity to the day-boys, among whom was the little Ramsey, before breakfast on two days in the week. This was Michael Ramsey's first meeting with Eric Milner-White, whom he later came to regard as one of the big men in his life and whose photograph was on his wall when he died. When he looked back upon his short time at the Choir School of King's College, it was the meeting with Milner-White which he saw as the memorable gift from the school. Milner-White was then a charming young man of rather Anglo-Catholic opinions who was beginning to make himself an expert both on stained glass and on ways of English worship and prayer. Since he was to be the founder of the service of carols and nine lessons, he made a permanent mark on English, and not only English, life and religion. What the little boys remembered about his class was that he made divinity fun, even though it was before breakfast.

The parents continued to find Ramsey's progress too slow. They found the system of being a day-boy unsatisfactory. They had four children and not much income and in those days believed like the rest of the middle class that they could only find a good education for their boy at an independent fee-paying school. Therefore, if this backward boy was to get a good education, he must somehow be crammed up or taught up to scrape a scholarship at one of the big independent schools where most of the fees would be paid for scholars.

They now tried a boarding-school at Sandroyd in Surrey where one of the two headmasters was the brother of Mrs Ramsey. Michael was desperately homesick at first. The sufferings of the young when first they go away from home and try to hold their own with cruel contemporaries are felt to be very great even when they are not. It was the occasion of the first letter from Michael Ramsey which is preserved:

Tuesday Evening just after tea.

My dear mother,

I never were more utterly miserable. I have just had Greek before tea; It is horrid. we did translation, Xenophon, I do not know a word of it I do not think Greek alone makes me miserable, I am always miserable.

I cannot bear it any longer, I am crying now.

I cannot stand it any longer, if someone does not come to me I will give up and be miserable for ever and perhaps go home of my own accord, write or wire to Uncle C. and say you are coming at once pleas darling, and come on Saturday or I will give up altogether and always wretched.

Do not tell any about me nor anyone except father and possibly Frank, write at once if you are going to.

I am too miserable for words.

I beleive that you will take pity and come at once,

Your loving son

Michael

I am just crying like anythinke

Come at once

never mind anything else

I am utterly miserable

His mother came, but she did not take him away, and his Uncle Charlie told him that if he wrote another letter like that he would get a thrashing, so he stayed and coped. And this school, of which afterwards he could only remember that he was so homesick, must have helped the mind which was alleged to be backward and was not. For in 1918 he just missed a scholarship to Winchester College; and in those days the scholarship at Winchester was regarded as the crown for the cleverest boys in England. How to translate Xenophon and ancient Greek military manœuvres must have got into his head after all. In the same year he won a scholarship at Repton not far from Derby. It was not a scrape. He was second in the list of scholars.

One of his Wilson uncles became the organist of Ely cathedral. The boy often went to stay at Ely and at the age of 8 could be observed giving strangers a guided tour. The visitors could be seen to be bewitched at the learning about the cathedral coming out of such callow lips. Later he thought that his early affection for Ely cathedral had something to do with his interest in churches and their architecture. He began to make a collection of brass rubbings.

2. REPTON

Repton was an Anglo-Saxon town, on the south bank of the River Trent, and was at one time a chief city of the Kingdom of Mercia. Saxon remains could still be found among the buildings, there is a Saxon crypt to the church, and the setting is hauntingly beautiful. It was one of the schools that came out of the Reformation, for it was founded during the reign of Queen Mary by a landowner who sat for Derbyshire in Parliament. Like several such places it was a quiet little charity school until the railways came and boys could travel long distances to school and the Victorian needs of parents turned it over two decades into a modern and reputable independent school.

The school at Repton achieved a record by having as its headmasters two future Archbishops of Canterbury in succession. William Temple came at the age of 28 and was headmaster from 1911 to 1914. The *Dictionary of National Biography* describes this as a pleasant interlude in his life. He did not think that he judged wisely to accept, because he accepted another job only two years after he was appointed and then had to withdraw because he was found not old enough to be legal. Everyone remembered him as a big man in all senses but not as a good headmaster except that he liked everyone and everyone liked him and in chapel he was a superlative speaker. He was succeeded by Geoffrey Fisher, who was 27 when he became headmaster and pulled the school together.

In most of the seventeenth century Archbishops of Canterbury were ex-heads of Cambridge and Oxford colleges. In all the eighteenth century none of the archbishops held such a post. In the century from 1862 to 1961 six of the eight archbishops were former headmasters of public schools. That famous churchman Arnold of Rugby put a stamp upon independent education which helped to produce this consequence. Reformed universities produced able clergy whom the school could attract to their staffs; and the Victorian parent still wanted to feel that the principal educator of his child was in some way a man of God. William Temple and Fisher at Repton were among the late manifestations of this feeling. The pattern, that this was the way archbishops happened, was broken by the steady increase in lay headmasters during the earlier twentieth century. Although Ramsey himself was to be the person who altered the pattern in archbishops, he was not the cause of the change.

Therefore the little Ramsey, when he arrived at Repton in 1918, met a headmaster destined to play a far more important part in his life than is the fate of most headmasters. Fisher was quick, affable, capable. He always saw straight to the point of an argument. He could remember

Schooling 11

who everyone was. He could be a severe disciplinarian but he was not a rigid man. Despite the geniality he kept his distance.

The small Ramsey respected Fisher with that derogatory respect which schoolboys attribute to headmasters. He called Fisher 'the little snipe'. Ramsey had no sense of rapport. But it would be a miracle if a small boy felt rapport with the headmaster of a public school. He came to regard Fisher as distant, but forceful and rapid and efficient, and later as friendly. What at school he most admired about Fisher was the teacher of Latin and Greek. Fisher had zest. He rushed them along. He did not delay boringly on points of scholarship. He bubbled along with enthusiasm and humour. He made the dead languages into living literature.

The small Ramsey was not happy. His eye was not swift in pursuit of the ball, his muscles not yet co-ordinated. He did not like cricket or football. The school was very good at cricket, Ramsey was not. He resented the cult of those religions. He preferred to spend time in the school library. He liked to work away at Latin or Greek, or to pick books of history or biography off the shelves. Some afternoons he was forced onto the field and trotted around with boredom. When there were not games he disappeared into the library and found himself the only person in the building. He was not a good fielder at cricket. He would go off into a musing in the outfield. 'I had a curious strain of not attending to things which failed to grip my interest.' His father believed that he had a good eye and could have played the game well if he was not liable to slip into a trance and forget that his attention was needed.

These attitudes did not commend themselves to his colleagues. They regarded him as an oddity. Boys of 15 are not accustomed to make the lives of odd boys happy. They believe in conformity. His trousers usually fell down a bit and he was observed to be always hitching them up by peculiar digs with his elbows. Even Geoffrey Fisher decided that he was eccentric. The young society was not drawn to quaintness, or studiousness, or absence of mind in the outfield.

The three schoolmasters upon whom he looked back with gratitude tell something about the boy: (1) a clear-headed Anglo-Catholic priest with a rasp of a voice who taught classics, Henry Balmforth: (2) the librarian Burd, a true classical scholar, and the only master in the school said not to know the name of the captain of cricket: (3) a gentle teacher (Hayward), more expert at moths and butterflies than adolescents.

In his last years at Repton he was happier. By then he won the right to be an oddity. He discovered an unexpected gift which won boys' respect. He found that he could make a speech—that is, he could think on his feet, and not be at a loss for words. At the school debating society he won a name; and he quickly discovered a truth never discovered by some undergraduates nor even by some mature debaters, that you cannot speak well unless you care.

At that moment the politics of the world was exciting. The emotions of a just-ended war, with millions dead, were rampant. The general election of 1918 brought Lloyd George to renewed power on an unpleasant ticket, Hang the Kaiser. Ramsey's father and mother were nauseated by the jingoism. They resented Lloyd George for ousting his predecessor Asquith, whom they admired as a great Liberal prime minister. In the election of 1918 they could not bear it and both voted for the Labour Party.

Their young son at Repton was stirred. He turned Asquith into a private hero. He was excited by Asquith's successes, cast into melancholy by his defeats. In the school library he hunted out books on politics. Soon this hero-worship was informed. He discovered about Liberal politics in Ireland, or Free Trade, or the League of Nations. And this caused a flaming row at the school debating society. At the age of 15 this boy was blisteringly opposed to the Allied armies being sent to Russia to fight Bolshevism. An assistant master with Tory opinions spoke in favour of the need for the armies in Russia. Ramsey was very rude to him in the debate. It was not customary for boys at school to attack their masters rudely even in debate. There followed what Ramsey described as 'some unpleasantness'. He had to recite from memory in front of his headmaster fifty Greek lines from the play *Medea*—a severe punishment, for learning fifty lines of verse in a language imperfectly known would take several hours of spare time.

The severity may have had a cause hidden from the young Ramsey. Just before he arrived at the school Victor Gollancz left its staff, ejected because he tried to rouse boys' minds by heady and daring political argument. In a war for the nation's life this was held by external authorities to be provocative. The Gollancz scandal, as the blimps thought of it, was widely known. Though the war then ended, the headmaster of Repton could not but be wary of political passion expressed by boys. Gollancz was the notorious thing about Repton in 1918–19. The small Ramsey knew nothing about this controversy. Yet he had to spend hours of his time learning Greek iambic verse as a punishment for being rude to a master in a political debate.

This boyish hatred of military interference to put down Communism in Russia had a long consequence. Ramsey developed a hatred of the chief proponent of interference in Russia, Winston Churchill. For the rest of Churchill's life, Ramsey distrusted him. Meanwhile he became a regular speaker at debates. In his maturity what he remembered of his style of speaking were purple passages and a rather caustic irony. But he also remembered that by the time he left school he was 'a thoroughly political animal'.

He came into battle with the school over the obligation to parade with the Officers Training Corps. By 1920 the memory of the Great War spoke more loudly than ever. During the war military training took several hours of the school curriculum and this did not end with the armistice. To get out of the military training then given at boarding schools needed iron determination and met pressure from school-masters and unpopularity among boys.

Ramsey could not say he was a pacifist. He was nothing but glad that Britain won a war. He could not say that he had scruples of conscience for not joining in the military training. When asked by Geoffrey Fisher to explain his reasons, he found that he had difficulty in finding a reason. He said that he thought it wrong to encourage a military spirit, and that it was contrary to the ideals of disarmament. He made his headmaster admit that military training was not (strictly speaking) compulsory, armed himself with a letter from his father, and won the contest of wills.

That summer of 1920 he had conversations which affected his mind and may have been decisive indirectly for his future choice of career. In the summer of 1920, the family went on a sea-side holiday to Holland-on-sea near Clacton. His elder brother Frank was 17 and revered by Michael who was 15. Frank, at the age of 16, had already won a scholarship to Trinity College in Cambridge. But the disparity in intelligence which Michael felt or imagined made no difference to their affection. They were both ungainly. Both had huge laughs. Both were untidy. Both were thought odd by their contemporaries. And, already in adolescence, both cared for the things of the mind.

They walked together along the sands, and talked. Michael had a problem on his mind. He was the child of a religious father and a more vaguely religious mother. Yet his closest school-friend, that previous summer term, he found to be an agnostic. The quarrel between faith and unbelief touched him for the first time and unsettled his mind. On one of the walks on the beach, he told Frank about his unsettlement. He discovered to his astonishment that Frank now professed atheism. Frank said that he did not believe in God; such a belief cannot possibly be proved; the good life is possible without it; and the only faculty to judge is the reason, which tells us to say, we do not know.

This discovery of Frank's atheism was more than a perturbation to Michael. He was so worried by it that he took it, and his own doubts about faith, to his father. Arthur Ramsey gave Michael a book by a scientist (Romanes) who was once an atheist and later became a believer. When he got back to Cambridge Michael (still a boy of 15) read Romanes. The book helped him and satisfied his mind for the time.

This debate caused a reaction in the direction opposite to Frank's. He resolved to practise his religion better.

Accustomed at home to Congregational worship and at school to the Book of Common Prayer, he found that he liked the Common Prayer better. With father's leave he was confirmed in the Church of England at school. He was just 16. Father made no difficulty. He expected him henceforth to be both a Congregationalist and an Anglican. Neither father nor son realized that this was the start of a sundering between them. Geoffrey Fisher prepared him for confirmation. Afterwards he thought this course of instruction sound and sensible.

At Repton he was already interested in Anglo-Catholicism; perhaps from reaction against father's nonconformity, perhaps from reaction against his headmaster Fisher's common sense. In the school library he found a bizarre book from the Protestant underworld, Walsh's *Secret History of the Oxford Movement* (third edition 1898), which pictured Anglo-Catholics as conspirators to promote tyranny, lies, and immorality. The boy saw through the fanaticism and found that his sense of chivalry was excited. One of the nastiest pseudo-religious books of the Victorian age helped to condition the impressionable mind of a future Christian leader of the next century.

On top of all this was the constant need to defend his religion against a clever elder brother who was an atheist. The two brothers had conversation after conversation on the theme of religion, the younger one sticking to his guns. The elder said that reason dismissed religion. The younger said that religious experience was too valid to be dismissed by mere reason, that reason was not all of humanity. The argument went on and on. The elder was contemptuous when the younger replied to his crushing arguments by the reply, the reason why you think like that is that you don't say your prayers. Michael's problem was that he saw the glamour in Frank's position: the love of liberty; the excitement in the free pursuit of truth; the shaking off of convention and mere conformity; the feeling that religion was a 'stuffy valley' out of which he had grown. He also had to recognize that his brother was an unselfish person; so that the axiom, 'only religious people are unselfish' did not wash. The argument was a fire in which to test an immature faith. A school prize was offered for a study of the book *Belief in God* by Bishop Charles Gore. When Frank heard that Michael thought of going in for the prize on this set book he was indignant and sent a message to Michael, 'Who in his senses would read a book by a bishop?'

Where should he go next? Everyone took it for granted that it must be Oxford or Cambridge. Fisher saw that this mind was not the grammarian or writer of Greek and Latin prose such as Cambridge liked, but was a meditative, half-philosophical mind, which might be better suited in the Oxford school. Ramsey's father was determined to have the boy at his own university and if possible at his own college. The Master of Magdalene, Arthur Benson, encouraged the idea. In December 1922 Ramsey took the scholarship examination of a group of colleges containing Magdalene and was given the top classical scholarship.

At the time all the family rejoiced with him. It paid for a lot of education. Later in life he wondered whether it was the blessing that it seemed. Though he had won a scholarship, he would never be interested in the niceties of Greek and Latin languages. He was glad to have the equipment to enable him to read Greek and Latin. Afterwards it turned out to be indispensable to his career. But the books which he took from the shelves in those stolen hours in the school library were history and biography and political science. What he most wanted to know about was not the ancient world but modern politics with its historical background. He wondered afterwards whether his unlooked-for success in the examination caused him to read the wrong subject at the university. In old age he used to regret that he did so well in the classical scholarship because it caused him not to read history.

Ramsey went out of his years at school with a sense of contentment which in retrospect he knew to be a veneer. He pretended to himself that Repton was a gloriously happy time. He was too much of a nonconformist in his origins, too much of an individualist, at that time too much of an oddity, ever to be really happy in so tight-knit a community as a boarding-school.

Geoffrey Fisher wrote a last school report which in later years became legendary: 'A boy with plenty of force of character who, in spite of certain uncouthnesses, has done good service on his own lines'. In this report the mature Ramsey specially valued not only the word *uncouthnesses* but also the pointed description of his nonconforming character in the phrase *on his own lines*.

In September 1923 the Master of Magdalene, Arthur Benson, lunched with the Ramsey family in Cambridge. It was a few days before Michael Ramsey first became an undergraduate at his college. The Master recorded in his diary: 'Michael, a distressing object, so sharp-faced, dull-eyed, spotted'. Or, a little later, 'Michael sharp-faced, slightly priggish, friendly'. Ramsey was still 18 and had not shed the spots of adolescence. Later in life no one could have called him dull-eyed or sharp-faced. His adult eyes sparkled with amusement and vitality. His mature face was more likely to remind the observer of Friar Tuck's jollity than of Lord Brougham's long pointed nose.

3. MAGDALENE

Ramsey arrived at the university in October 1923. He remembered that at his formal entry (matriculation) the praelector of the college gave all the new undergraduates advice on their deportment: 'If a Fellow asks you to lunch, leave at 2.15 p.m.; unless the general conversation is particularly interesting when you may leave at 2.25 p.m.' His fellow-undergraduates thought of him as a gangly youth with brown hair. He had rooms in the beautiful Pepys building, at the end which looked over the River Cam and across the river to some slum-like warehouses. He found that the rooms next door were occupied by Selwyn Lloyd, whom he discovered to be like himself a strong Liberal and with whom he was therefore soon friends. He did not find it awkward that his own father was the tutor of the college and so responsible in a double sense for his pastoral care. Nor did he find it awkward that the tutor's rooms were immediately below his own in the Pepys building. Evidently he did not expect to give riotous or alcoholic parties at times when the tutor might be in. The undergraduates found him a leg-puller, and a reveller in political argument.

The chaplain of the college was a pleasant gentleman, his teacher of classics was a worthy pedant, and neither meant much to him. The person who meant a lot to him was the Master. Arthur Benson recovered from several years of mental breakdown about two years previously and was in the evening summer of his life. He wrote beautiful, at times too beautiful prose. He published at least one book a year; readers who began could not put them down, though at the end of the book they had received nothing. He kept meditating on the highest ideals and professed weakness to do anything about those ideals. He observed naughtily, subtly, wittily, passively, on occasion with a feline caress. He enjoyed well-mannered, good-looking, and well-to-do undergraduates. Michael Ramsey qualified only under the first of those epithets. Benson had what Michael Ramsey called 'romantic favourites'. But Benson drew out all undergraduates. He talked to them as equals, criticized their essays, and was liked. His mind usually stayed at the level of gossip and anecdote but not always. His diary has been well edited: to read it is like looking into a large egg-shell full of bubbles. The undergraduates of Magdalene used to say about their Master that he spent the morning doing nothing and spent the afternoon writing about what he had done in the morning.

Ramsey was fascinated by his Master. He liked him very much, and felt the enchantment, and found it almost a spell. In his first term he had to write for him an essay on the art of poetry.

Yet he also found in him a warning. He observed the introspection and its richness of imagination with a certain alarm; Benson looking into himself and finding there, as Ramsey put it, 'a huge world of fantasy', which caused him distress and yet conditioned his affection for the human race. Ramsey realized that it was possible for a mind to inhabit a partly unreal world. It was pleasant to be quiet in an armchair thinking. He decided that for him to sit back and imagine, to follow a Bensonian way and be a dilettante among refined ideas, was an actual temptation. He disliked the notion.

He kept fit at the university by playing a little hockey, in summer tennis, in winter walking and bicycling and going for runs. Twice he won the Old Boys race at King's College school. The early interest in church architecture and brasses afforded him destinations for the bicycle. On these rides, sometimes of many miles, he found things with which Emmanuel Congregational church and Repton school chapel had not made him familiar. He found Anglo-Catholic country churches. He was interested in their notice-boards and what they said. He started to pay attention to the fittings in the chancel and the ornaments. These empty country churches were not dead or cold to him. He rode his bicycle like a pilgrim on the quest for a holy city. Neither the religion of the school chapel, nor the religion of a puritan church, satisfied. He looked for signs of a faith more supernatural, less conventional, more revolutionary.

His mother was still prominent in the Cambridge Labour Party. Michael went with her to meetings and joined her when she worked for the Liberal cause because it was the next best thing to Labour.

The freshman soon made a name for himself in debates at the Union, which is the historic Cambridge debating society. His appearance, that first term, failed to impress everyone as it failed to impress the Master of his college. He was thick-set, with a moustache. He spoke with clarity, and humour, and charm, and when he felt strongly, with passion. He had a curious sing-song voice which was a handicap, but the voice had musical timbre and was attractive. Some critics thought him sonorous but the word was not uncomplimentary. He first spoke on the French invasion of the Ruhr. In March 1925 he beat a Conservative mediocrity in an election for secretary of the Union, in Michaelmas 1925 he was vice-president, in Lent 1926 president.

Ramsey's weight in debates rested upon more than his manner and his fluency and his command of words. He could be vehement in denunciation. On occasion marvellous phrases sprang out of his mouth and enthralled the audience. On off days he could sound tired, and sometimes excitement carried him away to an excess of length. He was not the cleverest speaker in the house, a palm which by general consent went to the very Tory Charles Smyth, and the house also contained Patrick Devlin and Selwyn Lloyd and sometimes Rab Butler. But he was the most persuasive speaker in the house, for he had a cause which he believed in morally. Patrick Devlin regarded him as the most effective speaker of his time:

He was not clever or epigrammatic in the Union manner and only occasionally witty, but always spoke as though he had something to contribute to the debate. He projected himself as a man who would be worth listening to. He spoke weightily—the words deliberately produced and, as it were, laid on the table. He left behind him the impression—but not as if he had ever meant to say it—that anyone who disagreed with him must really be rather stupid.

In the autumn of 1924 the general election reduced the Liberal Party to a pitiable number of MPs. Asquith lost his seat. Whether it was the unsavoury reputation of the government of Lloyd George; or whether it was the division in the party between the followers of Lloyd George and the followers of Asquith; or whether it was the aftermath of universal suffrage and the desire of the working man for a party which he could call his own—it now looked certain that the party division of the country would no longer lie between Liberal and Conservative but in a wider gulf between Conservative and Labour, with the Liberal Party on the sideline. And since Cambridge University of 1924 was hardly likely to breed recruits for the Labour Party—that took another three years—the young men and women of the university could not do much but move, or move further, towards the Conservative side.

Ramsey believed none of this. He was sure that the Liberal idea was what the country needed. He was determined to resurrect the Liberalism of Cambridge, and turn it into a force among junior members of the university. In what the Liberal idea consisted he was clear. Whether he would have been able to stick to it if he had ever risen to be national leader of the Liberal Party is not certain. It had about it the idealism of youth. But because it was idealistic it was the more persuasive when he preached it to his young contemporaries.

Conservatives and Socialists are committed to dogmas. Socialism has a dogma that private enterprise is wrong. Conservatism has a dogma that the State should not intervene. Only Liberalism is free to use State action where it is needed, to refrain where that is better. It is the Liberal idea which gives its adherents the freedom to think and enquire, and not follow a party leader like sheep. Liberals care passionately for the individual, and for the freedom of the individual. Here was Socialism putting forward irrelevant theories of class war and wanting to rule the country by a set of theories which had nothing to do with the welfare of the people. And here was Conservatism, with a do-nothing prime minister in Mr Baldwin, with an out-of-date commitment to maintaining the British Empire in a world where it had ceased to be possible or right to maintain it, so that we spént millions in building a fortress at Singapore while we spent nothing more on housing or education.

Ramsey could grip the house by pouring ridicule into whatever he hated. He could be scarifying in his abuse of imperialists. At the end of one debate there was nothing left of either Fascism or Communism when he had finished with them. But what causes them? Who will be our upstart Mussolini? To be an upper class party is to breed malcontents, that is to encourage revolutionaries. To be a Socialist class party is to encourage revolutionaries and therefore to breed reaction, which is Fascism. 'Liberalism alone is the great Lady Surgeon of a nation's maladies, and while she is temporarily abed with a broken limb, the nation is the sufferer' (Ramsey in the *Gownsman*, 6 December 1924).

He electrified the house by vituperating the way the House of Commons behaves. Members troop into lobbies at the beck of a party leader as though they have no minds to use. He spoke of the monstrous word Whip to describe the officer who marshals the privates. He spoke of the way Britain failed to take care of the environment and lamented the creeping of towns and the vanishing of the fields and hedgerows, not so much because of the animals as because of the air and the nature of man and the liberty of the soul. He had one side of him, in those days, which suspected modern science because of its part in the process of industrialization, and its philistine attitude, as he supposed, to literature. He bewildered his audience for a moment, and then moved them, when he suddenly turned a political invective about government's neglect of the environment into a lament that one of the sad losses was going to be the poetry of the countryside, the pastorals of a Vergil or a Theocritus. 'He would be keener', thought one young observer, 'upon reviving perishing literature than a perishing political party.'

In the Union he was very popular. A visitor who heard him speak long remembered how the feeling of the meeting rose towards him when he got on his legs. He could be very funny indeed. He had a gift of mimicry, and when he made a speech as though he were Asquith or Lloyd George it would raise shouts of laughter. Once he acted the part of Asquith in some amateur dramatics, and danced round the stage with 'Lloyd George', singing most comically a refrain which he wrote himself.

In the eyes of that generation of students he gave Liberalism a magic, a faith in the future. And he carried that Conservative generation to vote a motion which preferred Liberalism to Conservatism as the better future for the country.

Meanwhile he neglected his classics by engaging as a Liberal campaigner in the elections of 1923 and 1924. He toured the villages of Cambridgeshire speaking on behalf of the candidates, and spoke in several halls of the town. At one village he was the only one of the appointed speakers to turn up. Undismayed, he haled an old man out of the audience, stuck him in the chair, and then spoke himself for an hour and answered all the questions. At another meeting in the open air he spoke from a cart and was tumbled when a member of the proletariat told the horse to Gee up. He wrote 'Michael Ramsey's Monthly Message' for the Cambridgeshire Liberal Magazine, which thereafter was scattered among the villagers. The climax was on 10 March 1925.

Asquith came to speak at Cambridge—now as the Earl of Oxford and Asquith. He brought with him his wife Margot, whom Benson in his diary described as very witch-like. Ramsey was asked to meet him at dinner in Magdalene before the meeting and to second the vote of thanks in the Guildhall. At dinner the undergraduate in his second year got on well with the ex-prime minister, which is a mark up to both sides. There were queues for the meeting, many could not get in, war-songs of the Liberal party were sung, they greeted the speaker with 'For he's a jolly good fellow'. A lady chairman, horribly nervous, spent too long introducing Asquith. Asquith made a speech of forty minutes which Benson described to himself as robust but dull, and which reads dully. He spoke a message which the country has heard before—that taxation is too heavy, that unemployment (1½ million) is too high, that we spend far too much on armaments and must get disarmament in Europe, that we must stick to Free Trade . . .

Frank Salter, who was the Liberal candidate for Cambridge borough, made 'a genial solid' speech of thanks. Then Ramsey rose to second the vote of thanks. The local newspaper called his speech breezy. It is usually good to speak when the audience is bored. Ramsey spoke out about his faith for Liberalism and talked eloquently about the freedom of Liberal minds. He could say sentences which would have been preposterous if they were seen as rhetoric but which he could carry because they were delivered with uproarious humour—'Liberalism prolonged one's youth, Liberalism did not decay'. The speech, observed Benson, who thought it remarkable, was 'rapturously received' by that huge audience.

Asquith was moved. He rose to give thanks for the thanks. He publicly prophesied from that platform that this young man would one day be the leader of the Liberal Party.

Ramsey afterwards could not remember a word that he had said in his speech. He only knew that the speech had told and that he raised applause, and that he made some jokes which aroused laughter.

Not long afterwards the Liberal Party invited this undergraduate in his second year to be the party's candidate for the county of Cambridgeshire in the next election. He went to a meeting with the party caucus. 'I said that I could not commit myself as my academic time was not yet finished, but I would like to be at their disposal later.' He had decided that his career would be in politics.

As vice-president of the Union he went to the United States (September–November 1925) as part of a debating team of three, all of whom were later well-known in public life. The other two were Patrick Devlin and Geoffrey Lloyd. They went round American universities challenging the debaters. The moments which both Devlin and Lloyd remembered most clearly were the perils to Ramsey's life. He had long shown traces of absent-mindedness. If he thought something interesting, he would desert what he was doing and amble off to meditate on the new idea, muttering to himself as he walked. When he played tennis with his sister, he would infuriate her by wandering off the court to contemplate. He scared the passengers when he drove a car, if some bright idea came into his mind. So now in America his two friends had to rescue him from certain death by yanking him back, as he meditated and was about to walk in front of a fast street-car.

In American universities they poured scorn on the cult of material prosperity. The new law of prohibition of alcohol afforded them marvellous matter for the pleading of the liberty of men and women against the tyranny of majorities, and they sang or preached several eloquent perorations in praise of freedom. An agitated old lady addressed Ramsey severely and asked why he did not go back to his own country and do good there instead of stirring up trouble in the United States. They made a lot of jokes in their speeches, which pleased and shocked the Americans, for it was not then thought right in American debates. Ramsey's own preferred subjects were literature versus science as making for happiness, modern democracy, and internationalism, in which he denounced American isolationism and had an imaginative picture of the American Middle West as a lot of boors who did not know where Europe was. The Americans got them to debate the League of Nations. But Ramsey had an alarming faculty for seeing through his own utterances. As he waxed into an eloquent period, he would realize the absurdity of his situation or the humbug of his pleading and be overcome with internal laughter, a laughter so vast that on occasion it left him too weak to go on with the speech. All three speakers had Celtic blood. They let Celtic fire run, uninhibitedly.

The result of all this politics—and Ramsey's sense that he might be reading the wrong subject, because his interests were now more modern than ancient—meant that his classics did not go as might be expected of someone who won a scholarship. In the examination of that June 1925 (Classics Part I) Ramsey's name was to be found in the second class. His Magdalene friend Selwyn Lloyd was in the same class. Ramsey turned to study law, which then was regarded as the best training for a future politician. He started eating dinners at the Inner Temple. This was a necessity to qualify for a later call to the Bar.

But across this political work came another interest. A legend was afterwards believed that William Temple converted Ramsey in a mission to the university in February 1926. The truth was more complex.

The relationship with his brother Frank must not be forgotten. In private Michael still had to keep his end up against attacks, that to be religious was to be a fool, though less frequently now because Frank travelled abroad and was away much of the time.

Across the road from Magdalene College was the parish church of St Giles. It was Anglo-Catholic in its way of worship. Ramsey attended. Here for the first time he found something of what the pilgrim on his bicycle had sought: 'the sense of mystery, and awe, and of another world at once far and near . . . a sense that we were vividly in the presence of the passion of Jesus and also vividly near to heaven, to which the passion mysteriously belonged, so as to be brought from the past to the present'. His nonconformist origin found it strange, if not reprehensible, that at the main service of the day no one but the priest took the sacrament. Soon he came to value this practice very much. It left his mind free for 'pondering, adoring'.

In 1926 the Anglo-Catholics in Cambridge were strong. At Little St Mary's was the future stalwart enemy of apartheid, Geoffrey Clayton. The vicar of St Giles introduced him to the little religious group called the Oratory of the Good Shepherd, and one of those priests, Gordon Day, became a friend of Ramsey and adviser in religion. At King's was the former teacher of little Ramsey at the choir school, now a member of the Oratory of the Good Shepherd, Eric Milner-White. At Pembroke College was Edward Wynn, one of the kindest dons to grace Cambridge during the twentieth century, and another member of the Oratory of the Good Shepherd. The author of this memoir, while an undergraduate, once borrowed fourteen books about history from Edward Wynn and, on the way to return them, inadvertently dropped them all into the River Pem—and so is better placed than anyone to testify how good a man was Edward Wynn.

At the house of the Oratory of the Good Shepherd not far from Magdalene College was one of the remarkable Knox brothers, Wilfred. He earned an honest penny by teaching the New Testament to a few undergraduates, who needed to be agile to follow his paradoxes and who found themselves hoeing the weeds when they expected to study St Paul's Epistle to the Galatians. Ramsey invited his Master to lunch and invited Knox to meet him. Benson was not impressed. Benson's Diary, 25 May 1925: 'I'm not wholly at ease with Michael. Father Wilfred Knox, a nice fellow but with a horrible mirthless titter. We sparkled with energy, but I struck few sparks. He is a priest of the Oratory . . . I wonder if the Oratory is any good?'

Wilfred Knox's laugh was the highest titter most of his friends ever heard. But it was a titter far from being mirthless. He passed his life in a cacophony of amusement at the quaintness of the human race.

This meeting was one of Benson's last meetings with his undergraduate Ramsey. That 17 June 1925 he died of heart-failure following pleurisy. He was succeeded as Master of Magdalene by another Eton schoolmaster, A. B. Ramsay.

Slowly Michael Ramsey began to realize that the eternal verities were more important to him than the political excitements. He started to see that in his opinion more could be done for humanity by Churches than by political parties, even the best of political parties such as he took the Liberal Party to be; or at least that the Churches engaged at a more profound level with the predicament of humanity.

How should he express this feeling? He tried attending meetings of the Student Christian Movement, and was bored. He tried the historic evangelical society, the Christian Union, known as CICCU, and was repelled by its insistence that every word of the Bible was historically true. In spare time—between politics and classics there was little spare time—he began to read a few books of theology. By the middle of 1925 he had fairly clear convictions about Catholic Christianity. In his third year (1925–6) he went to private confession for the first time. For that purpose he went to Edward Wynn.

In February 1926 the religious groups in the university agreed, after much difficulty, upon the common organization of a mission to the university. The difficulty was that the evangelicals took a low view of the deans and chaplains of colleges, and did not expect that anything run by them would have force and challenge. The deans and chaplains of colleges were nervous lest the evangelicals bring in a firebrand of a missioner who would repel their undergraduates not only from his mission but from religion. The various parties reached agreement at last. William Temple, the future Archbishop of Canterbury, then Bishop of Manchester, fat, jolly, eloquent, and philosophical, should be the chief missioner and give his talks for a week in the university church, Great St Mary's. Norwood from London should be the missioner from the nonconformist Churches. The evangelical group, the CICCU, brought in a Northern Irish missioner, W. P. Nicholson, who was a man of fire.

The mission opened with a meeting at the Guildhall; at which Ramsey, being now president of the Union, was selected to take the chair. He read the opening prayers from the platform and spoke impressively to the undergraduates about their attitudes to the mission. Temple's address was fine, Norwood's middling, and Nicholson's embarrassing in the extreme, so that the chairman hastily closed the meeting. Coming out of the meeting, a lady was heard remarking, 'Mr Ramsey spoke very nicely but I do think he is young to be Master of a College'; for she thought that he was the new Master of Magdalene whose name was the same except for the spelling.

Nicholson was an Irish presbyterian of one of the more extreme sorts. He used to be a seaman. He worked among the poor of the Shankill Road, and later became an evangelist in America. The time of Irish Civil War after 1919 was a time of hot emotion, of many murders in Belfast, and of religious revival in Northern Ireland. Nicholson was an important piece of that revival. Shipyard workers used to march to his services. He was against tobacco, and against dancing, and against cinemas, and against going to church only once on Sundays. He was much against theologians. He was much against choirs in church. He was much against professors of theology. There were sensible men who thought him the finest evangelist of his generation. And if the committee of the CICCU be taxed with bringing in someone who did not fit the undergraduates of a university, it might be replied, first that they were desperate to find someone at short notice, and secondly, was it desirable that a missioner should fit the undergraduates?

The contrast during the week of mission was so extraordinary as to affect Ramsey's life. In the three places of mission there were on aggregate some 2,500 members of the university every night of the week. Temple talked rationally and effectively in Great St Mary's and held his audience. Norwood, despite thoughtfulness and humour, slowly lost adherents to the other two speakers. In Holy Trinity Church Nicholson abounded in anecdotes, vulgarity, rudeness, emotional appeals, a dogmatism so dogmatic as to frighten. More and more people went to hear this phenomenon in a university of the crudest fundamentalism, which horrified some of the dons as a caricature of Christianity. People who could not bear it walked out. The speaker offended by gross lapses of taste—'It is time that old bachelor on the Tiber got married',—'Nicodemus was a religious sneak'—and by forceful appeals—'Will the hypocrites please leave the church?'—and thirty or forty people walked out. He was not, commented the journalist from the local paper, 'perhaps very convincing to men and women eager to find out what Christianity really means'. Some of the young were moved by Nicholson; he was human and had pathos and they needed dogma. The university sighed with relief when he went away.

Afterwards it was said that at this mission Temple converted Michael Ramsey to decisive Christianity. No one who reads the speech of the President of the Union at the inaugural meeting of the mission, before Temple opened his mouth, can suppose that that President needed converting to Christianity. Later in life Ramsey denied that Temple had this supposed effect upon him.

Nevertheless, effect there was. Ramsey's friends thought that he was an agnostic and were surprised to see him so prominent at the mission. Chairman at the inaugural meeting, he attended Temple every night of the week and attended Nicholson once. That Nicholson evening had consequences. He was nauseated by the absurdities of the faith propounded and the way it was presented. The seven evenings under Temple gave him not much new, because he had read Temple. It was not Temple's oratory which persuaded him, for he thought it 'rather rotund'. What persuaded him were two bits of Temple's mind which he could not mistake. First, Temple confronted the life of the real world in all its complexity. Secondly, he cared about the intellectual question in religious life. He looked at the difficulties, with open eyes.

Ramsey ended the week with a conviction that Temple's quiet explanation of a Christian philosophy of life was the right way to expound Christianity in modern society and that the emotional popular mission was the wrong way because it appealed to the wrong emotions. His experience of Nicholson shocked him. 'That one evening created in me a deep and lasting dislike of the extreme evangelical style of evangelism.' Temple had neither converted him, nor given him his vocation. But, Ramsey put it, his mission 'certainly helped to clinch matters'.

Throughout his life he never lost the admiration for the mind, character, warmth, and friendliness of Temple. Into extreme old age he would lecture about Temple's mind in words rendered all the more penetrating by the obvious gratitude which the memory brought. He wanted to be buried near Temple's remains. And for the rest of his life he recoiled from the popular mission and missioner. He so disliked them that when he became archbishop it complicated his life. It made him naturally suspicious of Billy Graham, who among popular missioners was as far from William Nicholson as was possible.

In this new mood where religion was more important than politics, he thought he would like to see how the Church went in East London, at that time notorious as a depressed urban area within the national life. During the Easter vacation he spent a fortnight working in Stepney. A fortnight is not long. It was enough. At the end he knew with certainty that it was not the lawyer, nor the politician, who was the best hope for care in the country, but the Church.

Afterwards he decided that his intense preoccupation with politics and the Liberal Party had not represented his true conviction. He felt the change to be rather like 'the shedding of an adolescent enthusiasm'. The observer is sure that his memory must be wrong. The Liberal politics were too ardent to be mere intellectual exercise. We may question whether between the young Liberal Party candidate and the young Christian teacher lay such a gulf as afterwards he fancied.

4. THE ORDINAND

The best of deciding to be ordained is the knowledge that you dimly see your future and have the courage to embark on an irreversible way and feel that at least you commit yourself to help humanity in its suffering or its moral predicament. The worst is the complexity of personal relationships that ensues. Old friends who are not Christians think that you have gone fey. Old friends who are Christians in moderation think that such talents as you have could be more effective in some other vocation. Is the man becoming a fanatic? Why should a future leader of the Liberal Party throw up that possibility in order to be a curate, whose work in popular mythology (and sometimes in reality) consists in having cups of tea with elderly women? But the tenderest difficulty lies with the family if they disapprove.

His mother had seen how his mind moved. She half-expected what happened. His father had not expected anything of the kind and was disappointed. An eminent nonconformist might well have reservations about a now Anglo-Catholic son seeking holy orders in the Church of England. But his father was tolerant, and said nothing to stop him. Ramsey could feel that his resolve had a sufficient consent from his parents. The worst difficulty came with his brother Frank, whom Ramsey thought to be the cleverest person he knew. Frank did not conceal his regret.

Ramsey lost neither his sense of humour nor his power of mimicry when he became an ordinand. For party occasions he delivered a skit sermon called 'Under the Juniper Tree' which could reduce his audiences to helpless laughter by its caricature of the most platitudinous and pontificating type of preaching.

Ramsey expected that once the resolution was taken everything in the mind would be peace after doubt. He discovered that this did not happen. He found that he was now sensitive to a new series of demands and worries and was liable to be hurt in new ways, and he suffered moments with a sense of futility.

In April 1926 he abandoned the study of law and started to read theology. This was not easy to do. Universities dislike students who change courses in the middle of a year. Cambridge liked undergraduates reading theology to have two years over the work and believed that if they tried to do it in fourteen months they would do it superficially, or else they would be sure to hurt themselves by overwork. His college must have hesitated before it gave him permission. But colleges shrink ultimately from stopping a person doing what he is ardent to do and forcing him to do what he is bored to do. They gave him the leave which he sought.

The result was fourteen months of the hardest work that Michael Ramsey ever knew in his life. He lived a very retired life; gave up games, and took exercise by occasional short sharp runs; and concentrated. Never again did he remember going at anything with such concentration. He made it harder for himself, though much more valuable, by refusing to take short cuts or to mug up the subject from the textbooks: he went to the original sources. The fear on colleges of ill consequences from overwork in such circumstances was not avoided. But he found it a very happy time. He took the theological honours examination, after a preparation of only four terms, in June 1927 and was placed in the first class.

The change to theology brought a new influence into his life: Sir Edwyn Clement Hoskyns, the dean of Corpus Christi College. The coming together of Ramsey and Hoskyns was inevitable. The undergraduate was Anglo-Catholic. The teaching staff of the faculty of divinity was not—with one exception, Hoskyns.

To say that the teaching staff were not Anglo-Catholic is an understatement. The faculty of divinity at that moment was dominated by a hard intelligence, Professor Bethune-Baker, known to all behind his back as the Bath Bun. Bethune-Baker was learned and clear-headed in his writing, quick in repartee, astringent as a critic, angered by muddleheadedness in his colleagues, and willing to use sarcasm. He dedicated this formidable intellect to eradicating nonsense from the world, especially nonsense in divinity, which was a world where in those days he could find plenty of targets for his scorn. And in the faculty he was surrounded by several men of substance with much the same opinions though with less hardness in their advocacy. Since most Christian teachers are kind persons who prefer to avoid controversy when they can, and doodle anxiously during fierce argument at meetings, things tended to go the way of Bethune-Baker; partly because he was devastating, and partly because often he was devastatingly right.

To be of Anglo-Catholic opinions in this group was to be a man apart. Bethune-Baker regarded Anglo-Catholicism as part of the nonsense which it was his mission to destroy. Hoskyns, sitting at meetings of the faculty, felt alone. His sense of isolation was the chief suffering of his life in Cambridge. It was true that there were other Anglo-Catholics in Cambridge: Ramsey's helpers Milner-White and Edward Wynn, for example. But intellectually they had no weight. They taught a little easy history to the weaker students. It grieved Ramsey all his life that Milner-White of King's, whom he so admired, refused out of diffidence to play any part whatever in the work of theology.

The student needed to hear from the throne of the lecturer something which spoke to his intellectual condition and his religious condition, his mind and his soul, simultaneously. He found such a person in Hoskyns.

Hoskyns, at this moment aged 43, lectured on the thought and the ethics of the New Testament. He had studied at Berlin. 'Hoskyns', said one of the astringent colleagues who disapproved of him, 'went to Berlin and they muddled his mind and when he came back he could never get it unmuddled.'

Hoskyns was not a good lecturer. At least, he lectured in such a way that many in the audience found him impossible to understand. This was one of the reasons why Bethune-Baker, who thought that everything obscure was woolly, regarded him as useless if not bad for the young. Students were known to spend their time in his lectures counting up the number of clichés which he used. A future bishop, Launcelot Fleming, went to the lectures and was enthralled; but the class ran a sweepstake; if Hoskyns said theme it scored one mark, if he said ultimate theme it scored ten marks. A really good score could reach 100, so there were plenty of numbers to draw. Every time he said theme or ultimate theme he held up his finger and waggled it in front of his nose. He seemed to regard the New Testament as a stormy sea in which he was tossed about in a little boat as he explored. Or he gave them the impression that he wrestled, with limbs contorted, in the effort to seize hold of what truth could be found.

Ramsey found him inspiring. Hoskyns communicated enthusiasm. He infected his hearers with the sense that this search after religious truth was of urgent importance to humanity. He introduced Ramsey to modern German thought. He showed him the work of Karl Barth, who, though a Swiss, then taught at the Protestant faculty at Münster in North-West Germany, and was the leader of European reaction against the conventional liberal schools of divinity.

Ramsey always remained critical of Hoskyns. The Christian mind which he revered was then and ever after the mind of William Temple, whom Hoskyns thought to be able but superficial. Ramsey never doubted that in the formation of his mind Hoskyns was influential, and ever afterwards he was grateful. 'I learned from him, more vividly than from anyone else, that the study of the New Testament is an exciting adventure, and that while it calls for a rigorous-critical discipline, it is not made less scientific if the student brings to it his own experience of faith.'

We have now the basic ingredients of Michael Ramsey's mind. A nonconformist origin. A discovery of Anglo-Catholicism and its devotional power, originally through its fanatical critics, and then fostered by wise friends. The admiration for the mind and personality of William Temple. A desire to understand the thought and experience of the apostolic Church. A suspicion that the normal liberal interpretations of the evidence about the apostolic Church, among the leading English thinkers of the day, were clever and persuasive and yet were open to the charge of superficiality. An openness of mind to the European religious reaction against liberal Protestantism, represented especially by Karl Barth. And a belief that the Church (if it could get its message right), more than the lawyers or the economists or the political leaders, was the chief hope for society and the world. All these constituents needed fusing and moulding into a unity in his mind. He thought and meditated; filled them out by experience of pastoral care and by writing; and came to such a unity that all his later life he had a coherence of outlook, in thought and devotion and ethic, which was an anchor to the Church of England in difficult days.

Such a fusion and coherence of mind entailed certain rejections. He rejected fundamentalist ideas of the biblical evidence. History was history, and minds must be free. He rejected hot methods of evangelism by mission and believed that quiet rational exposition was the true Christian way even if its results were not spectacular. He suspected the dominant divinity of shallowness and an undue optimism. Though deeply Anglo-Catholic he rejected what the world thought of as Anglo-Catholic fuss, a mistaking of the right vestment for the right religion.

The question of questions was at bottom this: the nineteenth century, with its partial proof of evolution and its axiom that miracles do not happen, enabled the chance of historical enquiry into the life and work of Jesus through the testing of ancient documents. Since the documents are full of the supernatural, the process of enquiry must strip away subsequent accretions. The historical person was so marvellous, that legends grew round him and then doctrines were organized. The principal organizer of doctrine was St Paul. Therefore the process of finding the historical Jesus meant stripping away what St Paul was supposed to have added. There was a contrast between what Jesus intended and the Church which Paul created.

But by the middle of the twenties, when Ramsey began to study the matter, a new vision appeared. As the text of the gospels was dissected, there came indeed to appear layers or strata; some bits looked earlier than others; the documents were made up out of a weaving of stories and sayings circulating in the earliest Church and then put together by a single hand or more than one hand. But what was suddenly seen as extraordinary was that the supernatural, the miraculous, and certain doctrines were just as present in the layers now believed to be the earliest as they were in the layers believed to be later. The theory of an original simplicity about the good Galilean carpenter Jesus, which was surrounded with supernatural stories and so corrupted and made complicated, began to look far more doubtful; at least, more difficult to get out of any evidence available. Was it possible that the quest for the historical Jesus, of which Bethune-Baker was a leading representative, was based upon an illusion about the nature of the sources which were used?

Hoskyns believed that these new methods could prove that the alleged contrast between Jesus and Paul was wrong; and that there was an identity between the Jesus who lived in Palestine and the Christ who was the object of the faith of the apostolic Church.

Bethune-Baker and his school supposed that the more you strip the documents of the New Testament the more clarity and simplicity you will find. This new vision began to prove that the more you strip the documents the more mysterious they are found to be. So far from all the problems being solved, we seemed to be not far from the beginning of the quest.

This excited Ramsey. He wondered whether, before ordination, he should stay at Cambridge a little longer to do more advanced work. By the advice of his college he competed for a college research Fellowship, known as the Charles Kingsley Bye-Fellowship. The college failed to elect him to the Bye-Fellowship. They elected a man from Jesus College. Other things being equal among candidates, Magdalene College would take a Magdalene man before a Jesus man. But things were not equal. The Jesus man had a first class in history behind him, and a first class with distinction in English Literature behind him, and was president of the university mountaineering club. In his later life he became for a few months nearly as famous as Ramsey, though in a different context. For he was Jack Longland; and his name ran across the world after his experiences high on the unclimbed Mount Everest six years later. Later still he was well known for his work in education.

Ramsey was only a little disappointed at this failure. Really he wanted to get on with seeking to become a priest. Everything was happy. His mind was forming. His future way was clear. He was content to do what he would do. And he was in this mood when disaster struck.

5. CUDDESDON

A man who spent four heady years as an undergraduate was often advised to go to another place to train for the ministry. Wise men thought that he should not be too near old haunts and old friends. And this was not only a Cambridge graduate but a Cambridge resident. He needed a place of quiet, a good library, and a chapel where the worship was Anglo-Catholic and he would feel at home.

Milner-White recommended ordinands to go to Cuddesdon, his own old college; and so he advised Ramsey. It stands six miles outside Oxford, in lovely and in those days remote country, with one bus a day. Neo-Gothic in turrets and corridors and battlements, it was founded by Bishop Samuel Wilberforce of Oxford opposite the front gate of his palace, and then developed by two of the leaders of the Church of England in Queen Victoria's days into the foremost training college of that Catholic tradition.

Ramsey arrived there on 30 July 1927. He pushed his bicycle up the hill from Wheatley station in the company of another new student who had a strangely similar background: of nonconformist origins, with his father an official of a nonconformist Church; a young man who postponed his own confirmation into the Church of England because his parents might be hurt; and who swung at the university from his very Protestant background into a sense of the devotional stature in Anglo-Catholicism, and into convictions which never left him for the rest of his life; a graduate of Balliol College, by name Austin Farrer. It is pleasant to think of the two new Cuddesdon students, pushing their bicycles up the hill together from Wheatley station that July day of 1927, and so meeting for the first time. One would like to know if there was a conversation. Both of them were already known for silences.

To idealize Cuddesdon has been easy for many. They came with their ideals, found idyllic peace in the countryside, where a man could hardly fail to notice God in the quietness; said their prayers in one of the fairest little parish churches in all the land; reacted against, and then threw themselves into the orderliness of quasi-monastic life; and studied what they wanted, and thought about truth. In all these ways the place was perfectly suited to what Ramsey needed at that moment. To say prayers in the Catholic way of worship, and feed one's soul on frequent sacraments, and practise a little fasting, and use the sacrament of confession, and study Marcion and the early Church and the Bible, and to have time for quietness and silence and meditation—that was what he looked for at this moment of his life.

He did not get it.

A fortnight after he arrived at Cuddesdon his father set out in the car from Cambridge to Stamford. He carried with him the minister of the Congregational Church, H. C. Carter, and in the back seat three ladies, Mrs Ramsey, and Mrs Carter, and a Danish friend of Mrs Carter. They proceeded up the Huntingdon Road at about 20 m.p.h. or sometimes 30 m.p.h., a suitable pace for cars and roads of those days. At the top of the hill before Godmanchester Mr Ramsey felt uncomfortable with his coat and turned to pull it right. As he did not look where he was going, the car's near-side wheels started running along the grass. A telegraph pole was ahead. Mrs Ramsey and Mr Carter cried, 'Look out!' Mr Ramsey swung the wheel over violently to avoid the telegraph pole and the car careered across the road, skidded, hit the grass verge the other side, and overturned. Carter was thrown clear and escaped serious injury. The car pinned all the other four. Mr Ramsey had broken ribs, probably on the steering-wheel. The Danish lady had a fractured skull and was unconscious but alive. Mrs Carter only had a broken arm. And Mrs Ramsey was dead. She was badly injured about the head and many other bones in her body were smashed. Arthur Ramsey was found with his injuries and in a state of shock and muttering, 'It was such a little thing, I was just trying to put my coat right.'

Probably it was hardest for the husband and the two daughters. Frank did nothing but sit in the house for two days silent and with tears. But it was very hard for Michael Ramsey. The resulting turmoil, mental and emotional, ruined (the word is not too strong) his preparation to be a priest, and blotted his memory of Cuddesdon. He hardly ever spoke about his mother again. When his father died he burnt all the letters he could find.

He took a fortnight away for the funeral and to visit his father in hospital. In October he passed the first part of the examination for ordination, and afterwards could not understand how he passed. He went back to Cuddesdon for the autumn term, but the mental condition was very adverse. He was sleepless, and kept suffering from deep depressions. Other students had always found him eccentric but now they found his behaviour very odd—a lot of muttering to himself, and a total incapacity for the practical things, and sudden disappearances into silences. He hoped that a New Year's holiday in Belgium would help him but the mental turmoil came back in force.

He dreamed a lot and the dreams were perturbing. He felt as though he lived in a purposeless world. He found himself in enormous buildings, with a labyrinth of rooms, and he was lost in the pile. He wandered from room to room without aim, and without knowing whether he was on the top floor or in the basement, 'just up and up and on and on and on'. Sometimes he would be climbing up and down a cliff and he found himself stuck, unable to get higher and unable to climb down and once he was left clinging on a ledge for ever.

He put himself into the hands of a psychiatrist who passed him to another psychiatrist, Leonard Browne. He visited Leonard Browne three times a week for four months. Therefore he needed to be in London and could not be in Cuddesdon. He lived at the settlement for helping London boys, Cambridge House. He spent the mornings reading, and the afternoons visiting for two charities, one of them a school for the physically handicapped.

Once, in one of his younger sermons (Liverpool, on John 20: 21–2), he gave a hint of what it was like with the psychologist. His life was wrecked by fear, even by terror. God was cruel. Sleep failed. The doctor probed—the longer memories, the childhood. Terror of father when very small?—a fear then forgotten but driven down into the subconscious?—and yet, when this is recognized, the terror still appears again, in a new and dreadful form; and the memory must be brought to 'the touch of Jesus' and so the whole inner man is cleansed. This became a strong reason to him for the practice of private confession. You cannot cure yourself. You cannot forget. If you do, it will submerge. You need to bring it to a place where God reaches out into the secret places of the soul.

When he looked back later in life he did not think that this dark night was caused by what happened on the road at Godmanchester. He thought that its roots reached back, as the doctor thought, into earlier life. But the historian can hardly doubt the connection. Here was a student who overworked for more than a year and needed rest; who was already in an emotional condition by the recognition of the highest ideals and their obligation upon him; and then, instead of the rest which he needed, he had to endure the utterly unexpected death, in very distressing family conditions, of the person in the world to whom he felt nearest.

By Easter 1928 Michael was better. He was able to manage the May term at Cuddesdon, though he needed still to go three times a week to London to see Browne for treatment. The students at Cuddesdon still found him very odd, and very unpractical, and very absent-minded, and much given to muttering to himself. Austin Farrer watched him, and was amused at all the oddities of behaviour. But Farrer saw other things about him. First, there was no question of the power of his mind, even if that mind moved eccentrically. Second, this was not a person who bored everyone by overearnestness. On the contrary, he had a teasing humour, and a sarcasm which struck hard. Thirdly, and unexpectedly, he was a champion on the croquet pitch. Farrer decided that he was a born don.

We have another description of him at this date from a diarist who happened to meet him. 'A most curious-looking young man with a mobile white face and small red-rimmed eyes; he is said to be very clever as well as deeply religious. He seemed devoted to his little sister'.[1] It was 3 March 1928, in the middle of Ramsey's bad time.

Later Ramsey used to mock the complacency of clergymen who said that their training college gave them habits of devotion 'which they had never lost'. He attributed no such quality to his disturbed time at Cuddesdon. Nevertheless Cuddesdon was important to him. For later he also believed that the motor accident and its consequences could have destroyed his morale but for the tranquil worship of the little Oxfordshire village which for the time was his base. He did not think much of the lectures. He resented the inadequacy of the library, in which he worked long hours during such time as he was there. He regarded the chaplain as a buffoon though a dedicated buffoon. His intelligence owed nothing to the college. He felt frustrated academically. An ancient actor, with an absurd way of talking, taught elocution to the future preachers. But the place was a port in the storm.

He felt apart; withdrawn; like Newman, feeling there was nothing in the world but God and his soul. He did not find learning to pray an easy occupation. Still, he had a sense of movement; as though in the quietness they were seeking some kind of glory.

Two people helped. The principal of the college was Jimmie Seaton, a plump, cheerful, outgoing little man known as Friar Tuck, who bubbled with amusement and good sense of vitality and who liked people and gardening while he hated committees and pomposity. The second was the Bishop of Oxford, Tommy Strong; the bishop with the

---

[1] F. Partridge, *Memories* (1981), 147.

most sensitive taste and rare learning and musical apprehension of all the bishops' bench. Ramsey described him as a character, without popular appeal, donnish, with no great interest in his big rural diocese, but full of wisdom and learning, and eager for friendship with young men. If you walked round the bishop's wood shortly before you left Cuddesdon, you were likely to become aware of an elfin prelate hunting you through the shrubbery like a gaitered satyr; and when he caught up with you he would say breathlessly, 'If you ever need a bed . . . (panting) . . . don't forget I have fifteen spare bedrooms'.

During his time at Cuddesdon something happened to the Church of England, at the national level, which left an indelible mark upon many young ordinands of the time, and certainly upon Michael Ramsey. In December 1927, while he was in the midst of his darkness, and in June 1928 when he was better, the House of Commons rejected a proposal, carried by large majorities in the Church bodies, for a new prayer book, which was the old prayer book, from the age of King Charles II, modestly revised in a pastoral spirit long after the time when it needed revision. A majority in the House of Commons fancied that it possessed the training in theology, the experience of ways of worship, and the sensitivity to religious feelings, to tell a Church how it ought to say its prayers. That the House of Commons, which had its share of agnostics and non-Anglicans, should order the Church how to worship God was an interference by the State in the affairs of the Church, just where those affairs were sacred and touched the conscience. The manner of the rejection on the floor of the Chamber was unpleasant, with ranting and prejudice flaunted and loud, though it is not certain whether such sickening speeches moved sober MPs. The rejections, and the manner of the rejections, ensured that for the future the Church would take no notice of what the House of Commons thought about the way in which the Church of England worshipped.

Ramsey was a former nonconformist who had not lost the idea that Churches must be free from entanglement with the State. He was now a young Anglo-Catholic who acquired the Catholic sense of divine rights in the Church which no State can touch. He had no idea that he would ever be able to do anything about the predicament. But he formed the opinion, which he never afterwards lost, that the Church must gain its proper freedom from the State in the care for its own way of worship, if necessary by disestablishment, from which he never thereafter shrank. Whenever he thought about this in later years, his memory would go back to the Cuddesdon time and the shock of seeing a House of Commons pretending that it knew how people ought to say their prayers.

It was the one time when he doubted William Temple. Ardent for liberty, he wanted the bishops to behave fiercely, like Hensley Henson, the Bishop of Durham, and threaten the Commons with disestablishment as the answer to its unconstitutional behaviour. He expected William Temple to back Henson and was grieved to find that his hero was weak because he refused to stand up and fight. Later in life he thought that of the two, Henson and Temple, Temple was the statesman on the question. 'It was rather exasperating that the great and radical William Temple soft-pedalled. In retrospect I am glad that he did.'

But because he was in the middle of his mental stress he suffered a disaster. In January 1928 he was invited back to speak at the Cambridge Union, on the motion that the Church of England ought to be disestablished. In his horror at what happened in the House of Commons, he started to speak in favour of the motion. But a few minutes after he was launched into the speech he came to a dead stop, stared strangely at the gallery in silence, and could not go on. He found himself saying, 'In 1919 the Enabling Act was passed' and then could not remember what the Enabling Act was; although it was and still in part is the Act which defines the nature of the establishment in England. So in the middle of his speech he walked straight out of the debate and the Union chamber. The family worried about it in their different ways. His father suspected that he had a glass of wine too many at dinner. His brother said that he had been more excitable lately, and more ineffective, and running up and down more. Frank was sure that the cause was not physical but was part of the mental unsettlement. His friends on the Union committee thought that what happened was best accounted for if he saw a vision of his dead mother in the gallery watching him speak. They did not dare to ask him.[2]

Where was he to go next? The young man was an obvious don. Hoskyns wanted him in Cambridge as the chaplain of his college, Corpus Christi. The rector of Liverpool, John How, knew Ramsey from Cambridge days. He wanted a noisy, breezy curate to get at his rough teenagers. He was aware that this description did not fit Ramsey. 'I fear', said How to Ramsey, 'that you might be too retiring for the job.' It looked as though the donnish youth would go straight back to donnery and be a don for the rest of his life; perhaps he was not suitable for other kinds of clergyman.

The vacancy at Corpus Christi vanished. And on 23 September 1928 Ramsey was ordained deacon, to be the curate of St Nicholas, the parish church of Liverpool. His stipend was £200 a year.

---

[2] *Granta* (1928), 234; evidence by H. L. Elvin. Cf. Chadwick, *Hensley Henson* (Oxford, 1983), 205, note: where Henson's sermon for disestablishment is wrongly dated, though all the note is true. Fairfax Scott, later tutor of Magdalene, believed on good evidence that he and not Michael Ramsey was the culprit of the guffaw during the sermon.

2

The Parish Minister

I. LIVERPOOL

St Nicholas is the old parish church near the quay-side and the docks. The church where Ramsey ministered was bombed to bits in the Second World War. It was mostly built early in the nineteenth century with a tall fair spire topped by a ship. Near the docks the inhabitants were poor dock labourers. Many were unemployed, many had only casual work. Higher up the hill the streets were full of office buildings, so that the parishioners were caretakers. To visit his people Ramsey had to go up in lifts.

The parish had about 7,000 people. More than half the parishioners were Irish Roman Catholics, who went to two churches. Both these churches were remote and estranged. Their priests were intransigents. Ramsey felt it odd that in two Christian churches, working side by side in a crowded port, the ministers could not pray together or work together and could hardly speak together. He disliked this situation.

Moreover the diocese was not only divided between Anglicans and others. The Anglicans were divided—the stoutest of Irish Protestants versus a few stiff Anglo-Catholic parishes; and in a fight the sympathies of Ramsey's parish lay with the second. He disapproved of his bishop (A. A. David) for the tough way in which he handled three recalcitrant Anglo-Catholic priests who refused to conform to rules laid down by the bishop and yet did nothing about the radical dean of the cathedral who did things equally nonconforming in a Low Church direction. Ramsey thought this an injustice; he decided that his bishop was vague and naïve in his theology, someone who took up new ideas with enthusiasm and with very little precision of thought; and yet he saw that the bishop disliked controversy and was hurt by it, and thought him to be a friend and a man of prayer. It specially pleased him that the bishop encouraged him, in the midst of all the parish chores, to keep time for hard study.

The congregation of St Nicholas consisted of a few poor people from the neighbourhood and otherwise of less poor people from various parts of the city or from Birkenhead across the Mersey. Its congregation quite flourished. John How was a solid good preacher but not a magnet to multitudes. He was formidable, laconic, self-disciplined, earnest but not humourless, and it was said of him that he did everything with a kind of good-natured fury. Most of the time he left his two curates to get on with their thing,

Ramsey could find nowhere to live within the parish. Some distance away, only a few yards from the vast unfinished Anglican cathedral, he found lodgings (13 St James's Road) with a spinsterish landlady who by origin was a Northern Irish Protestant. One of the other lodgers was a dwarf, with whom Ramsey made friends. They called their censorious landlady IT.

The lodging was neither convenient nor happy. To get to morning service in the church he had to catch a tram at 6.50 a.m. If his work kept him late for a meal, he had satirical reproaches cast upon his head by the landlady. At the general election of 1929 the landlady could be heard telling a Tory canvasser that everyone in the house would vote Conservative and Ramsey said forcibly that he was voting Labour (there was no Liberal candidate). The air of the house turned sour. For the last weeks of his curacy he left the lodgings and hired a room in a small hotel up Mount Pleasant.

The people liked him. They are reported to have said 'The new curate's not chatty'. In later years he was once asked whether he, who was shy, was anguished when forced to go out visiting homes in Liverpool and to try to make the first touch with a strange family. He said, 'As a curate I was never frightened of visiting. I never minded being shy. I was content to be shy. I perplexed other people. I was content to be silent.'

He loved his confirmation class. He visited the sick often, in homes and in hospital. He disliked his Bible class of teenage boys because they misbehaved, but at times it was happy. He disliked the work at the boys club because the teenagers misbehaved, and because he could see no use in the work. He disliked teaching twice a week in the school because the children misbehaved. He enjoyed and admired his rector. He found his fellow-curate odious. He loved the morning hours of hard study at the Bible. He also read much else, for example a lot of Newman's sermons.

To his surprise, he discovered that what was needed to make a powerful political speech was not the same gift as that which was needed to make a powerful sermon. The technique was different. He discovered that various kinds of audience needed various kinds of utterance. He thought that he learnt a lot about preaching from this experience. Once at least he could feel that a sermon of his moved his hearers. But he told the bishop at a private interview that he was depressed about preaching, he felt the people to be so remote from the practice of religion.

An envelope of a few Liverpool sermons survived; including the first sermon which he ever delivered there (text 1 Peter 2: 9, 'ye are an elect race'). Like most first sermons it puts in too many ideas at once. He calls St John's gospel 'the most beautiful book in the world'. The collection is very biblical. It has no jokes, no digressions, nothing to lighten, except occasional quotations of poets like Tennyson. It conveys the feeling of the grandeur of the sacrament. The reader smiles when the preacher tells the people of dockland that they live 'in a garden near the slopes of the heavenly mountain'. Sometimes he wrote his sermon out in full. Sometimes he prepared summary notes. As he got on, and less nervous, the words came easily; and then he began to dislike being restricted by a written text and to prefer headings.

A little reputation outside the parish began to grow—that this was a curate who could talk. William Temple ran a mission on the Blackpool sands, preaching from a tub to the buckets and spades. He summoned a lot of helpers; among them Ramsey, who watched fat Temple on his fat tub talking profound truths in simple language. That was a compliment to Ramsey. No doubt Temple remembered that once they stood on the same platform at Cambridge. It would be pleasant to have a film of curate Ramsey talking to the young architects of sand-castles.

The curate was troubled by the conflict between his love of biblical study and the chores of the parish. He was saved from isolation of the mind by a lucky proximity. He lived hard by the cathedral. This cathedral had an exceptional canon.

Charles Raven was a fiery charismatic man with a large heart. At Liverpool he turned himself into the most powerful preacher in all England. In background he was nothing like Ramsey. Low churchman versus high churchman; philosopher of religion and science versus close student of the Bible; radical divine versus enquiring conservative; suspecter of orthodoxy versus a young man who saw the stature of the Catholic tradition. Nevertheless Raven cared passionately about things of the mind. He was forward at seeking out young people of promise and giving them encouragement.

The coincidence was extraordinary. An isolated curate who wanted knowledge found himself living a few yards from a man who at first sight was an explosive popular preacher, but who happened also to be one of the coming academic theologians of England, and an inciter of younger minds.

Raven ran a weekly class on the New Testament. Ramsey joined it.

Raven's mode of running a class was provocative. He drove Ramsey to contradict him. Never before had Ramsey run up against so formidable a Christian opponent, and never before been so forced to defend his biblical ideas. He found the experience good for his mind. Raven also had him round several times to meals at his house. After one of these lunches Ramsey recorded his affection for Raven. This was not everyone's opinion of Raven. Some good men feared his radicalism, and some good men disliked his passion, and some less good men thought him little but a rhetorician. Ramsey penetrated to the essence of the man.

During the summer of 1929, nearly a year into his curacy, and aged 24, Ramsey was attracted to a Lancashire girl. It was important to him, important enough to see that members of his family met her and that he found out what they thought of her as a possible wife for him. They were unanimous that she would not be right for him. And gradually he came to realize that there was a particular reason for the attraction which was not the empathy of the girl. She had a physical resemblance to Ramsey's dead mother. The friendship passed.

The priesthood

It was then the custom of the Church of England that a curate should be ordained to be a deacon (the lowest order of the ministry) whose duty was to help the parish priest in all his pastoral duties but who could not perform the priestly acts of celebrating the sacrament or giving absolution or blessing. After he served for a year as a deacon he was ordained as a priest. To most people coming forward to be a Christian priest, the moment when they became deacons was a bigger turning-point in the life, and more emotional, than the moment when they became priests. Truly to celebrate the sacrament for the first time, and to feel for the first time that the hands were the instruments through which God chose to nourish the souls of his people, could be overwhelming with gratitude or with penitence. But to be made a deacon was for the first time to profess before a multitude that the soul undertook the cause of God in a special ministry, and for the first time to feel sent to an apostolic work. Afterwards to wear clerical clothes for the first time, and instantly to be expected to be a confidant or soul's friend, was to many ordinands the more heartfelt turning-point.

Ramsey was unusual in that to him the priest's ordination meant much more than the deacon's ordination. He used to say that his ordination to the priesthood, in Farnworth parish church on 22 September 1929, with Raven preaching, mattered to him much the more. Why this was so we can only guess. He was a high churchman for whom the sacrament of holy communion was the supreme moment of worship. His preparation to be a deacon was disturbed by a death and by mental illness. Later in life he compared his own feelings at the two ordinations to be a deacon and a priest and his later consecration to be a bishop. He said:

When you are ordained deacon you have arrived. But being a priest—that meant far, far more. That meant far more to me than being a bishop. Becoming a bishop is an incident in the life of a priest. I sometimes forget that it is the day of the year when I was made a bishop. I never fail to remember on the day of the year when I was made a priest.

A little fold of the veil can be drawn aside to disclose his mood at that time. In September 1929, before the ordination at Farnworth, he went into retreat at Bishop Tommy Strong's Cuddesdon Palace with its fifteen spare bedrooms. During a time of meditation in that retreat, he wrote a note which survived. It is in fading pencil. Not quite all is legible:

'My grace is sufficient for thee'. How I do need to look away from self to God, I can only find satisfaction: in him.
My heart, to love him;
my will, to do his will;
my mind, to glorify him;
my tongue, to speak to him and of him;
my eyes to see him in all things;
my hands to bring whatever they touch to him;
my all only to be a real 'all': because it is joined to him.
And this will be utter joy: no man can take it away.
Self, self-consciousness, self-will, the self-centre cut away, so that the centre which holds all my parts is God.
Inquietum est cor nostrum.[1] Yes it is so because it is nostrum, cut out the nostrum, and let me give my heart to God—and all is . . . [*rest of line illegible*]
Thanks be to God for being what He is, for showing Himself to me . . .

—and then comes a list of benefactors: Carter the Congregationalist minister, and Henry Balmforth the sixth form master at Repton, and Geoffrey Fisher the headmaster at Repton, mother, father, *Frank his brother*, Jimmie Seaton the head of Cuddesdon, Tommy Strong in whose chapel he then meditated, John How at Liverpool; the institutions, Cuddesdon and Magdalene, his home, and his Bible; his special teachers William Temple and Charles Raven (Hoskyns, note well, is not mentioned); and then gratitude for his crosses: the troubles of

[1] St Augustine's 'Our heart is restless' (until it finds itself in Thee): i.e. the heart is restless because it is mine instead of God's.

schooldays, the death, 'the desolation', the anxieties and wearinesses in Liverpool, 'tiresome boys'.

And still my mind runs back to self. Cut it out, God is in me; He is my centre—let me only believe it, and His energy will flood the whole of me, and self will be drowned . . .
   Drive out, kill self, let God be then alone in me—then in God we will find (no, he-in-us will find) ourselves
> selfless
> free
> sons

Come God—my God is
      and is in me, in you
rather let God explode
      burst from within
      filling the whole of us
away from self just He He He He
Theos—no, the one—Heis.[2]

Between November 1929 and February 1930 he kept a diary. Unfortunately for the historian, it was the only time in his life when he kept a diary.

We find a man busy about his parish, up early, taking services, preaching, preparing to preach, visiting the sick, conducting funerals, running a club. Some of it was happy, some less happy. The rector was delightful, the people friendly, Raven's classes excellent. He dreaded his own Bible class and found it hard to keep teenagers in order. Two frustrations appear in the diary. The contrast between the rural peace of Cuddesdon and the noise and dirt of Liverpool was hard to bear. And an inner conflict lay between books and parish. When he studied, he was happy. When he could not study, he was miserable. He asked himself whether he was someone like Arthur Benson, the Master of Magdalene, for whom books were a form of escapism from the real world. He saw that the intellectual side of him could not be wrong, somehow he must baptize it. But when he was in this mood, fear came. During the time of desolation a year before, he suffered from fantasies. When he got exhausted from parish work, and felt unwell, a fear would darken him, that the demon, seemingly exorcized, might return. And already he knew in his heart that to be a vicar or a curate was not his vocation as a priest for the rest of his life.

[2] *Theos* = God; *heis* = one. The actual list of personal benefactors includes Vernon Johnson (an assistant at William Temple's mission), Gordon Day, uncles, sisters, grandfathers, and Bishop Vernon Smith, who conducted the retreat during which this was written.

While this internal argument reached its height, his superiors argued about him without his knowledge. From opposite ends of England the academics said that this was a born teacher who ought to be in teaching as soon as possible. Raven said it in Liverpool. Hoskyns said it in Cambridge. Bishop and rector expected him to serve his minimum engagement as a curate. Raven pushed at the bishop that he ought to be in an academic post and soon. Hoskyns found him the opening —sub-warden of Lincoln Theological College. Lincoln brought in the big guns of William Temple to get bishop and rector to release the curate before the time. Finally bishop and rector agreed, and Ramsey accepted the Lincoln work.

Later in life Ramsey believed that he learnt a lot from his short time at Liverpool. It introduced him to the human race. He met new-born babies, and said prayers in the rooms of the dying, and consoled families at the cemetery, and struggled to communicate with teenagers who did not know how to read. It introduced him to the bizarre situation that Churches treated each other worse than they treated anyone else; and to the recognition that the reason for this was not religious but racial. He met the descendants of Lascar seamen or other immigrants who settled into Liverpool and for the first time saw the need for justice to an immigrant community. Later he knew that he learnt a lot. But at the time he was glad to leave. 'It's been a great school for the temper.' He left Liverpool at Easter 1930.

Before he left, his brother Frank died very young, of a liver complaint after jaundice (19 January 1930). It was important to Michael Ramsey, not only then but much later, that before Frank's death he felt him to be less far apart over religion. In the last week of the previous October Michael stayed in Cambridge. Michael saw that his brother's mind had moved—not far, hardly at all, but still he had moved. He no longer accepted determinism and was willing to see a meaning in the words 'free will'. Instead of rejecting religion out of hand as irrational, he enquired about it. He wanted to know what are the experiences and emotions of religious people. He said that as a boy at school he had such experiences and wondered whether they were like Michael's. What struck Michael was, the enquiry was humble—as though religion might be something worth knowing about. Michael told him about the evidence of religious experience in the Christian mystics; both of what some of the great masters had said about it and of the slighter experience of simple Christians. All through this conversation he had the impression that Frank no longer sneered; and as he went back to Liverpool he was sure that he was more tolerant and sympathetic and 'was willing to grant that there was some sense in some of the things which I longed for him to share'. In mid-January 1930 he stood by Frank's death-bed and imagined his heart going out to his brother.[3]

It cannot have been easy for an ordinand or a curate to stand up to contemptuous persiflage about his religion from one of the ablest minds of the generation who happened to be his own brother. In later years he thought that twice in his life, and twice only, he seriously wondered whether Frank was right, and he wrong, about religion. The first time was when his mother died; the second time was when Frank died.

Maynard Keynes wrote an obituary of Frank in his *Essays in Biography* (1933), pp. 335 ff. We see the younger brother's personality reflected in his friend's portrait of this atheist mathematical economist: the stony heights and rare atmosphere in which his mind moved; the easy efficiency of the intellectual machine which ground away beneath his broad smiling face, his bulky Johnsonian frame, and spontaneous gurgling laugh, and simplicity of feeling, and honesty of heart and mind and purpose; and with it a common sense and practicality.

Later in Michael Ramsey's life it disturbed his conventional critics when they found a guardian of Catholic orthodoxy saying that he hoped and expected to meet atheists in heaven.

2. LINCOLN

The Bishop's Hostel at Lincoln was one of those mid-Victorian foundations intended to train future clergymen. Most of these foundations were sited in or hard by cathedral buildings because after the cathedral reforms old cathedrals had buildings or land available. The window of Ramsey's study looked out to the west end of the cathedral. The students were about forty in number, most of them not from universities. The warden to whom he was sub-warden was Leslie Owen, a man of delicate health whom Ramsey liked. His stipend was £220 a year but this was a big increase on his Liverpool pay because he had free rooms and free meals.

He gave a lot of lectures—four a week. The worst of the teaching offered in theological colleges occurs because the staff are few and the ground to be covered enormous. Therefore the few staff sit up late at night to prepare lectures on a few things they know about and a lot of things they know not much about, and spend their time keeping one page ahead of the class and depending on the textbook. This was more

---

[3] He celebrated a requiem in King's College chapel, and conducted Frank's funeral at Golders Green. He gave £100 to King's College for a prize in Frank's memory. His father doubled the sum.

educative for the staff than the students. Ramsey lectured on all the later part of the Bible and on the central Christian doctrines. Every moment therefore of his time was dedicated either to preparing or to giving lectures. Unlike some members of the staff who resented a forced superficiality, he liked the system. He enjoyed educating himself in the things he wanted to know about.

For the first time he told himself that he was fully at home in his work. He felt the teacher's rostrum to be his fit place; the place where he knew that what he had to offer was valued. He worked hard. He had to work hard. And because no knowledge is fully clear in the mind until it is explained to someone else, the time at Lincoln was further formative for his mind. 'Everything later', he said, 'was an extension. At Lincoln I built a structure of thought.'

The story got about over the years that his lectures were very obscure. That was probably the opinion of persons who found all lectures obscure. It was not the opinion of most students from those days. They found him a teacher of clarity, whose lectures were the most enjoyable and most instructive which they heard during their training.

When he had leisure he went bicycling to Lincolnshire village churches. He enjoyed the Cuddesdon-like monastic-like regularity of the daily worship. Some of the students started to use him as their confessor. He played tennis with them under the willow-trees by college, playing not well but with a brisk gusto. He went round the golf-course in 95 strokes. His shirt-tails flapping in the breeze, he faced the green at an angle of forty-five degrees and sliced every shot. He helped to reorganize the local golf course so that students could play legally and cheaply. He played the game of Murder in the dark through the vast rooms of the bishop's vast palace and told his nonconformist father that at last he found a reason why bishops should live in such large houses. In vacations he consoled his father's loneliness by taking him on holiday—Cornwall, Criccieth, the Lakes, the Black Forest and Bavaria. At other times in vacations he spent weeks doing hard reading in the library of Cambridge University and got good talks with Hoskyns. He discovered the virtues of the Gladstone Library at Hawarden near Chester, a residentiary library founded on the basis of Mr Gladstone's own books. In 1930 he went to Bavaria to see the passion play at the mountain village of Oberammergau.

The students from that time remembered a man with a sharp sense of the ridiculous; who ragged them but was too shy to be intimate with them though they liked him much for his friendliness and his humour; who was famous for long, sudden, and embarrassing silences; who was so eccentric that none of them believed that he could later be a man of distinction in England or his Church; a man who loved theology—they never met anywhere else a man who so loved theology, and who regarded theology as the highest intellectual activity for humanity; a fierce defender of liberty of opinion, for Marxists as for anyone else; whose principal theme was the glory of God, and who was evidently touched by his ideas of Plato; who did not give the impression of a mind of exceptional ability—there was not enough knife in the mind—but who gave the impression of being an exceptional person; who disturbed other people's prayers in chapel with convulsive fidgets and sudden face-rubbings—they regarded him as tense in his devotions and were afraid of a nervous breakdown; who had a manifest and rare mystical sense of the immediate presence of God, a presence so brilliant that it could almost overpower. Late at night one of the students passed Ramsey's room and heard strange sounds within, and it was Ramsey going round and round his table saying *It is fire! It is fire!* There was one occasion when he went into a café and asked for tea and then while he waited he suddenly saw a solution to a theological argument which he had with Leslie Owen the warden, and his waving of hands was so convulsive that the café refused to serve him with the tea. Once the students, not without glee, watched him celebrating the sacrament with the ends of his back braces protruding out of the top of his vestment. Sometimes he could be observed wearing some garment inside out.

Austin Farrer came on a visit to Lincoln and reported that Ramsey was a great man in the college and held his audiences spellbound and was less mad.[4]

From Lincoln days descended a story which sounds like Ramsey-legend but the truth of which he confirmed. An applicant for entry came to be interviewed. For fifteen minutes interviewer and applicant sat opposite one another. Neither said a word. Then Ramsey said, 'I think you will find Lincoln rather a quiet place.' This was the end of the interview.

In vacations he still went for interviews with his psychiatrist, who did not feel that he had quite got 'to the bottom of things'. But this no longer disturbed the even tenor of life.

A little group of letters survived which affords insight into his attitude in this earlier time at Lincoln. His Aunt Lucy came to live at Howfield in order to look after Ramsey's father and the family after Agnes Ramsey was killed. She wanted help with being prepared for confirmation and turned to her nephew for guidance. He wrote her letters. From these letters to an aunt we can gather something of his

---

[4] P. Curtis, *A Hawk among the Sparrows* (1985), 95.

habits of devotion. He taught her the words of the Angelus, the Hail Mary; though he said that he could not quite use all the words himself literally, but he respected those who could, and he did not think there was anything in it which made Mary take the place of her Son. He taught her that the sacrament of the eucharist was so big that he did not feel that he had finished with it when he came home after the service at 8 a.m. on Sunday morning. It was many-sided—worship, praise, offering, commemoration of our Lord's life and death, sacrifice, fellowship with the faithful in the unseen, all the many sides which centre in this one act. He did not need words to join in this act, he could use the words of the prayer book or his own words, but he needed no words at all. He liked incense, but he did not like an excess of ceremonial ('scarlet, lace etc') which he condemned as vulgar and intrusive. He could never be happy with morning prayer and not the sacrament as the chief morning service. He thought a procession a bore.

He began to be known. Invitations poured in. He refused to preach in St Paul's Cathedral. Offers of jobs started to come in. He refused work in London. Geoffrey Fisher went from Repton to be Bishop of Chester and invited him to be an examining chaplain; which he accepted—it would mean two or three visits a year—and was surprised to find how friendly Fisher was when they were not in the relation of boy and headmaster. At this time of his life he always called Fisher behind his back Halieus, which is Greek for fisher. Observers still thought them to be in the relation of boy and headmaster. Here were two future leaders of the Church of England, the one a man of supreme common sense, the other a mystic; the one a conservative and establishment-man, the other a liberal and a reformer—they were fated never to understand each other. After Fisher died Ramsey said that the time in their lives when they were closest in friendship was the time when he was examining chaplain to the Bishop of Chester.

As the first years passed, and the courses of lectures did not have to be prepared out of nothing, he sat at the bay window in the sub-warden's study, looking out towards the cathedral, and started to write his first book. He did not start writing the book because he wanted to write a book. He had something he wanted to say to the Christian world and the question was how best to say it. Occasionally he would descend to the students' common room immediately beneath and beg them to make less noise so that he could write. The students later believed a legend that part of this famous book was written all over the walls of his room. Longman's published the book in January 1936 at 7/6: title, *The Gospel and the Catholic Church*.

For centuries men have fought for the Church, died for it, loved it, or hated it. Now no one seems to mind about its existence. Its worship and its priests and its teaching are strange to the society in which it lives. Society is not hostile, it passes by on the other side.

Can we make the Church real to society by turning it political; by making its essence not old creeds but moral judgements on bombs, or on socialist policy? This is not the answer to which the study of the New Testament leads. There the Church's work is to point to Jesus the Messiah and his death, and to sin, and to judgement. 'In all this the Church was scandalous and unintelligible to men, but by all this and by nothing else it was relevant to their deepest needs.' The Church cannot be any easier to understand than its Messiah. And the society of his day doubted, questioned, despised. The word scandalous is repeated four times in the first three pages.

So Ramsey cried to the Church not to dilute itself, or adjust itself to what contemporary Smith or Jones can swallow. It cannot convert its gospel into social reform. Ramsey cried to the Church to be itself; to know that its being rests upon a death and an empty tomb; and to be itself whether modern Britain will listen or close its ears.

The book had a second, equally important purpose. The child of a nonconformist father learnt to drink deep of the Catholic tradition. At the centre of his mind was a fusion between the evangelical Christian and the churchman; the first, biblical, a man of gospel and of conversion, of faith and the Word of God; the second, a man with a reverence for the Christian society through the centuries, its sacramental inheritance, its order, and ministry, and continuity. And therefore this young evangelical churchman had something original to say, which was an effort to fuse the Protestant idea with the Catholic idea as they were fused within his personal history. He would show the Catholic that the Church is nothing without the Word spoken in the crucifixion. He would show the Protestant that the Church, with its order, and structure, and mission, is a necessary part of the Word spoken in the crucifixion. The book is full of the Bible, and yet is an essay in Church order.

So, on one side, the book was a Catholic churchman proclaiming the cross of Christ in a way more common among Protestants. On another side it was an assault upon the corruption of the highest truths; against turning love of the Bible into bibliolatry, or creeds into scholastic definitions, or the sacrament into magic, or Popes and priests and bishops into a bureaucracy or a rigidity where structure becomes the end instead of the means; or turning the Church into a social club.

Some people disliked this book very much. The nonconformists noted that he did not unchurch them but were not happy with his plea that they recognize bishops to be essential to the Church. Bethune-Baker and his school at Cambridge disliked the anti-rational quality in the book—the 'scandalousness' of the Church and its gospel—and took several more marks off Hoskyns for begetting such a child. When Ramsey came to read the book himself, later in life, he was astonished, and at one point burst out laughing, to discover what irrational expressions he could use. Through Hoskyns he had come for the time under the influence of the leader of anti-rational European theology, Karl Barth, who at this moment was back in Basle after being expelled from Germany by the Nazis.

But the caustic critics were not the majority. Whatever the book's faults might be, it was seen to be an original contribution of power, and that a new force in Christian thinking had appeared among the Churches in England. Here was a young man learned in the New Testament and in the early Fathers; thinking hard for himself; manifestly a lover of God and of the gospel; an Anglo-Catholic but one who spoke in tones more persuasive to Protestants than was usual among Anglo-Catholics, with tolerance, and respect, and a gratitude for all that was best in the Protestant tradition. The letter which he valued most came from the leader of English theology, who was now Archbishop of York, William Temple: 'Men ought to acknowledge their major obligations, and so I write to thank you . . .' He was also very pleased when he heard that George Bell, the famous Bishop of Chichester, took the book to read on his holiday in Switzerland.

Books of academic religion (or of any other academic subject) are not lasting because scholarship in all fields advances. If they last twenty years before being replaced they have done a good service. Yet fifty years after Ramsey's book a good judge of religious thought and literature during the twentieth century declared it to be an enduring masterpiece, which pointed forward to the road which Anglicans and not only Anglicans would follow.[5]

That year, Cambridge University advertised a lectureship. The lecturer would have to teach the history and the doctrine of the early Church. This was what Michael Ramsey knew about. Hoskyns badly wanted him for the post. But this was impossible. Before he wrote the book he could hardly get the job because he had not published a book. After he wrote the book he could not get the job because it was a Hoskynsish sort of book. Ten years later Professor Marsh was asked why the faculty refused to elect Ramsey to a lectureship. He replied

---

[5] A. Hastings, *A History of English Christianity 1920–1985* (1987), 261 and 298. Before Ramsey published the book he showed it to friends—John How, Leslie Owen, Austin Farrer, and Hoskyns's close colleague Noel Davey.

laconically, as though it was a sufficient explanation, 'He was influenced by Hoskyns.'

Moreover the book alienated the only one of Ramsey's backers who could stand up to the Cambridge establishment. In a note Ramsey criticized Raven's view of a particular question. Raven thought the criticism unfair. He protested, coldly. The note destroyed the intimacy between the two. But even if the note was deleted (and Ramsey deleted it in a later edition), Raven could not have voted for Ramsey with enthusiasm. Ramsey was now a channel for Barthian influence into England. Raven regarded Karl Barth as the worst menace to sane rational thinking. And Ramsey's book said that bishops were essential to the Church. Raven thought this nonsense. All his life Ramsey was sorry about the breach with Raven.

So Cambridge elected another person. Hoskyns, who only had another year to live, was angry at his university.

If Cambridge did not want Ramsey, others did. Suggestions of jobs kept flowing in. One of them brings us evidence of how Ramsey appeared at this time to an austere critic. St Chad's College in Durham, which was then a theological college, tried to get him as its Principal. He went to see the Bishop of Durham, who gave him tea. The bishop was Hensley Henson, who kept a frank diary: '26 November 1936. Ramsey is a heavy fellow with a fat face, and a cumbrous manner, not prepossessing, but improving on acquaintance.' After Hensley Henson's death this became one of Ramsey's favourite quotations.

There was a contrast. Inside the college at Lincoln the students thought that this teacher was a fine teacher and fun but too odd to be offered responsibilities; and outside the college were a plethora of people who were not the university of Cambridge, anxious to offer every variety of job, pastoral, academic, or administrative. Ramsey kept refusing.

This contrast was pointed by William Temple. In July 1936 he gathered in his palace at Bishopthorpe a select team of ten for the purpose of preparing for the coming ecumenical conference. There was Emil Brunner one of the two leading Christian thinkers on the Continent of Europe; there was Reinhold Niebuhr, one of the two leading Christian thinkers from the United States; there was Visser t'Hooft, the Dutchman who built up the World Council of Churches; there was J. H. Oldham, at that moment the leading thinker about Christian society in the British Isles; and there was Bernard Manning, the Congregationalist historian who was a friend of the Ramsey family in Cambridge. And there too, in this galaxy, was the sub-warden of Lincoln Theological College. He was not there only by courtesy.

Temple and Oldham pressed at him hard—he must write one of the essays, he was the only person who could do it, they told him. He thought that they were wrong to press him. He reluctantly agreed to write the essay and then did not.

It was the only time when he was intimate with his hero Temple. He found him a charming host without any touch of stiffness or pomposity; 'like a merry rollicking schoolboy'. He enjoyed Temple's huge laugh. With surprise he watched him consume a lot of macaroni. They dressed for dinner every night. The occasion hardly sounds important. But to be a young unknown among the famous, and to hear them argue, he felt to be an education. This meeting with Temple was so important to him that the photograph of the group hung on the wall of his room when he died.

The next move was strange. That spring Ramsey gave a course of addresses during Holy Week in Lincoln Cathedral. The Bishop of Lincoln, Nugent Hicks, in whose palace Ramsey played Murder, attended this course. He could not understand what Ramsey was talking about. He decided that this clergyman was in the clouds and out of the reach of the common man. He told Ramsey that his language was paradoxical and difficult. He said that what he needed was more contact with ordinary people.

Ramsey hoped now to be a teacher in a university. He needed colleagues and a bigger library. But he had a high doctrine of bishops. He thought that a priest should if possible go where his bishop sent him. The bishop gave him the extraordinary advice to go and be a curate again, at Boston in Lincolnshire. Ramsey agreed.

It was the only strange decision of Ramsey's career. For an unintelligible speaker to learn to speak intelligibly, it may not be the best training, and certainly it is not the only training, to send him to the pulpit of Boston parish church. To cure woolly-headedness it is not indispensable to inflict the woolly-headedness on the denizens under Boston Stump. And something is curious. The evidence of the students at the college is that this was a clear teacher. They told Austin Farrer that he was a spell-binder. Ramsey was asked later, were you getting unintelligible, or was it only that the bishop was a bad listener to Holy Week addresses? Ramsey replied, 'I kept saying Yes is No and No is Yes.' He was laughing when he said it.

Perhaps there was something more than coherence at stake. A theological college is a narrow world, frequently compared to a greenhouse. After only eighteen months breathing the dust of the docks, Ramsey taught for six years and a half in a greenhouse. If he went to be the head gardener of another greenhouse and did another ten years teaching among the geraniums, what species of hothouse plant might result? Perhaps this is what Nugent Hicks saw, or feared.

But we know something else about the bishop's motive which he could not or would not say to Ramsey. He told the rector at Boston that this was a person of unusual spiritual powers; that how to train him for the whole Church was a responsibility; that he was anxious that these abilities should not be confined to academic spheres. Did the bishop see, what no one else could see, that this unusual teacher had the possibility of being a great bishop?[6]

3. BOSTON

Boston Stump, a famous parish church and landmark, had a rector and four curates. The senior curate, who was Michael Ramsey, was called lecturer but his duties were no different. He lived in a little hired house five minutes from the church, on a stipend of £260 a year. At first he was melancholy at leaving the friendships of Lincoln. One of his fellow-curates was a champion cyclist, with incredible expeditions all over Europe and Asia. His fellow-curates found him liable to vast silences, during which he twisted a bit of cotton with the fingers of both hands.

Ramsey had his district to visit. He taught once a week in the primary school and felt a failure at it. He had a weekly class for Sunday school teachers, which included a Methodist headmaster and several women who taught in the nonconformist Sunday schools. This he enjoyed. From autumn 1937 he had a large class of teachers to instruct on the gospels. He was in demand as a confessor, from a few parishioners, a few neighbouring clergy, a few old students at Lincoln. He found the parish set-up conventional and that was hard to be bear; 'irksome' he called it.

Told by high authority that no one could understand him in a pulpit, he worried about sermons more than anything. He who had preached with power in Liverpool suddenly found preaching very difficult in Lincolnshire. He was sure that the bishop was right and that he was hard to follow. His struggles for clarity were painful. But they made him realize that he was getting across what he wanted to get across, and not a holy-sounding fog of words.

If the people of Lincolnshire were thought by their bishop not to understand Ramsey in a pulpit, this was not the opinion outside the

[6] Evidence of Canon A. M. Cook (Ramsey's rector in Boston) in *Boston Parish Magazine* (1961), 11.

diocese. The invitations came thick and fast. He was bad at saying no. He could not lecture for the Archbishop of Canterbury because he was already committed to lecture for the Archbishop of York. It was clear that he was no ordinary curate. He was already a member of ecumenical committees. A mind with original ideas, who wished to persuade the Protestants to be more Catholic and to persuade the Catholics to respect the truths of Protestantism, was instantly a must for those who thought about the reunion of the Churches. He started to have to attend meetings in London. William Temple got him an honouring invitation, as a delegate to the vast ecumenical conference at Edinburgh in 1937. Ramsey refused this invitation because if he were away it would be awkward for the holiday plans of the staff of Boston parish church. He afterwards thought this refusal very foolish and regretted that he did not go.

For his refreshment he played hockey vigorously in the local team or cycled in the fen country. He would walk a long distance out to some pub, often the Malcolm Arms at Anton's Gowt, and have lunch in the bar on beer and bread and cheese. On his walks he could sometimes be observed waving his hat about and talking to himself. The oddity which the fellow-curates remarked was that as he walked in the procession from the vestry up the aisle he could be heard whistling. No one minded. They took it for granted that this was Ramsey. The most famous story of Ramsey's absent-mindedness comes from Boston. It sounds like legend but there is excellent evidence of its truth. He went out without his front-door key. When he came back he rang the bell. His landlady was nervous of strangers and called through the door, 'I'm sorry, Mr Ramsey is out.' Ramsey: 'I'll return later.'

About this time he started to wonder whether he ought to be a monk. If he was not to be a lecturer at Cambridge because they did not think him academic enough, and if he was not to be a parish priest because he could not keep teenagers in order and because the adults were said not to understand him and because he felt a teaching vocation, where was his right place? He had three functions in which he knew that he was at home. The first was in prayer. The second was in teaching the truths of Christianity, not in conventional ways. And the third was as a confessor, because he knew that many souls valued him in this work. A monastery was a place of prayer, and some monks had teaching duties, and most of them had to guide souls. Was it possible that for the sake of prayer and guidance of souls he had a calling to the unmarried state? The thought that it might be right to be a monk kept coming back.

His knowledge of the Anglican religious communities, such as it was, made him think that if he decided to try this out, Mirfield in Yorkshire would be the right place; for at Mirfield many of the fathers had a vocation to teach, or to hear confessions. Once he took this far enough to discuss the plan with one of the fathers from Mirfield.

In June 1937 Hoskyns died suddenly, at the age of only 52. Ramsey felt the death to be a personal calamity. The master and the pupil had moved apart intellectually—Hoskyns willing to be more and more obscure in his wrestlings with truth, Ramsey struggling for clarity of thinking. Not till later was it diagnosed that the mental breakdown which destroyed Hoskyns crept upon him for a year or more before he died. But the death was a 'terrible blow', as he said, in the affection and gratitude of a former disciple. And it put still further off the remote vision of a lectureship at Cambridge.

The death had an unexpected consequence. Corpus Christi College provided for Hoskyns's teaching in such a way that their parish of St Benet's, on the edge of the college precinct, was vacant. They asked Ramsey to be the vicar.

The offer appealed. The parish was tiny, hardly anyone lived in it, the church was small and easy to fill; congregations select; a little Sunday school but run by a lady; some undergraduates; hardly anyone to visit; the proximity of Edward Wynn and Milner-White and Wilfred Knox and his father. If the students of Lincoln were right in thinking that he was not a good administrator, this church had less administration than any church in the land. He would have access to the great library, and some touch with the academics, and yet his pastoral instinct, and his work as a confessor, would have outlet. He then preferred the idea of such mixed work to a university lectureship. The Bishop of Lincoln thought it ridiculous that this powerful engine which was Michael Ramsey should be used in a tiny little parish, and said so, but blessed him when he found he wanted to go.

He became the vicar of St Benet's Cambridge on 6 January 1939. Corpus Christi College made the suggestion that he should sleep in Corpus but take his meals in his old college of Magdalene; a proposal so bizarre that it should be accounted for by a motive, not to have at dinner a famously silent person, imagined as a wet blanket. In those days the Fellows of Corpus were rather proud of the briskness of their conversation. Instead Ramsey moved into lodgings in Newnham (45 Owlstone Road).

4. ST BENET'S AT CAMBRIDGE

The number in the congregation did not rise. A few dons came. Ramsey's father frequently deserted his Congregational church and came to hear his son. Ramsey had a time announced for hearing confessions and some people came. The service ground its way through, because the lady organist insisted on playing the hymns *Lentissimo* and this slow pace gave torments to the new vicar.

We have a memory of Ramsey from a girl whose family attended St Benet's. She was sent to him to be prepared for confirmation. He seemed to her to be extremely ancient (he was 35). His hair was grey but with a trace of red hair remaining in his bushy eyebrows. She noticed that he walked as though he had pebbles in his shoes. 'He was very shy, and preparing teenagers for confirmation was not really his métier.' Despite this verdict, she became a faithful member of the Church. Usually a priest matters more by what he is than by what he says.

We have another memory from a girl who was then 16. She agreed with the Bishop of Lincoln rather than with the students of Lincoln, for she thought him a disaster in the pulpit; blinking, and articulating his words with difficulty, and often using the peculiar phrase 'paradoxically speaking'. Then the children were evacuated from London in fear of air raids and that made life difficult for many Sunday schools, since the London children wanted to show the local children how tough they were. But the girl remembered Ramsey taking the evacuees round him in the children's corner, and sitting on one of the low chairs meant for a child, and talking to them naturally and with an obvious pleasure.

The churchwarden Mrs Eagleston was to become a devoted friend of Ramsey. It distressed her that her vicar should be seen charging through the town with his underpants showing through his trousers. She thought that he needed a wife. She was relieved, for the sake of the parish, when he rang her up in 1940 to say that he was leaving.

He saw little of Raven. He had nothing whatever to do with the faculty of divinity. He taught two pupils from Magdalene. He studied hard at the Epistle to the Hebrews. He meant to write a book about it. The book never got written. The world moved to war. He must black out the house, and the vestry of the church. He asked the bishop to put his name on the list for an army chaplaincy.

The worst of being in a job which the world regarded as not the right place for him was that the world would not leave him alone. A month before the World War broke out, and only a few months after he became a parish priest, the Archbishop of Canterbury tried to make him head of St Augustine's College at Canterbury, which had the work of training men to be missionaries. A month after the outbreak of war the Bishop of Durham, A. T. P. Williams, wrote in his lovely handwriting a letter sounding Ramsey whether he would become the professor of divinity at the university of Durham. With the chair went a canonry at the cathedral. On 30 November 1939 the bishop converted this into a definite offer of the chair and the canonry.

Ramsey's college refused him a research fellowship. His university refused him a not lofty post in the faculty of divinity. And now he was offered a professorship at another university.

Most of the stipend at Durham came from the canonry. Therefore the university was in the habit of leaving the choice of professor to the bishop. The bishop was headmaster of Winchester College at the time that Ramsey's brilliant brother Frank was a scholar. He asked the opinion of William Temple about filling the chair. Ramsey asked himself whether if the electors had been the university officers without the bishop they would have regarded a man of one book as electable. He decided that they would not. His diffidence blinded him to the truth that the one book was already influential in modern thinking.

He was instituted to the canonry in Durham cathedral on 27 January 1940 and in mid-February settled into a gigantic house which went with the canonry. The rooms were vast. All the furniture which he possessed in Newnham furnished one half of one of the rooms. He went to an auction of a big house in Cambridge and bought a lot of cheap carpets.

He seemed born to be a professor. He arrived at this destination at the early age of 35. He looked certain to remain a professor for the rest of his life.

3

Professor Ramsey

The house had historic escutcheons on the outer walls, and unhistoric battlements on the roof, and a glorious view from its cliff over the River Wear. It poked its front door out into the green as though to challenge an equality with the deanery opposite. It had no heating, its paint was peeling, and its wallpaper obeyed the rule of the new canon's parents that it does not show the dirt when it is dark. The house was suitable for a prolific father who wore two pairs of combinations next the skin. Ramsey lived in the rooms of the bishop's chaplain at the Castle while an architect put in central heating and clothed the walls in lighter paper. Even with the new heating, warmth was hard to get: two years later the chapter struggled to find firewood for the canons since other fuel could not be got; and a defective boiler in the cathedral was made in Germany and could not be mended.

The first thing that struck the other dons who lived in the Castle was his oddness. The Warden (Vice-Chancellor) Duff assured them that he was now not nearly so odd as he was when he had known him at the choir school of King's College. The Principal of St John's declared roundly that he was a lunatic—'I saw him yesterday afternoon walking down the Bailey with one foot on the pavement and one foot in the gutter all the way'. Certainly he waved his arms about more than most men when in action. And most of the seniors had not welcomed the appointment. He was absurdly young. Some of them disliked his book.

They thought that he looked antique, when at rest. He was not yet quite bald, but nearly. He had a grey fringe round back and sides, although a few wisps that had once been fair or ginger were combed over the top. Occasionally he was referred to by those who saw him at services as 'the old canon' though he was much the youngest of the canons. They were privately amused at his clumsiness. In the college at Durham they saw him, as they thought, learning to ride a bicycle; but the truth was that whenever he rode a bicycle he looked as though he was learning to ride. They found that he was not good in processions, for the curious roll prevented him from keeping ranks like the others. They attributed this not to anything physical but to meditation on higher things.

He had no curtains but shutters and makeshift scraps for the black-out. That summer he enlisted as an air-raid warden and sat long hours of the night by a telephone doing nothing. In October 1940 the army billeted an officer in one of the numerous spare rooms. People who needed rooms came into his empty spaces. A young Roman Catholic soldier from the Lancashire Fusiliers was billeted on him for two summer months of 1941 and never forgot the joyful singing which used to accompany Ramsey's washing and shaving before he went off to the cathedral each morning. The Lucas boys kept their model railway in the house and their cries penetrated the professor's study disturbingly. Sometimes he played soldiers with them and they thought little of his plans for defence in depth. He ran races with their younger sister in the monks' dormitory. John Lucas, the future philosopher, remembered being taught Greek grammar by Ramsey and sitting on his head while reciting Greek verbs.

As a canon of Durham Ramsey was one of the custodians of a great monument of the European inheritance in architecture, at a time when bombs dropped upon Britain. The dean and canons organized their rota of fire-watching and felt helpless. They took a vow like those of the Middle Ages where someone swore to go on crusade if his wife's life was saved. They promised that if their cathedral came through unscathed, they would dedicate a window in gratitude to the Royal Air Force. The window by Hugh Easton is at the north-west corner of the cathedral and was erected in 1950. It has the text of Isaiah 31: 5, 'As birds flying, so will the Lord of hosts defend Jerusalem'; and above the city and cathedral of Durham an airman rides upon an eagle, protected from above by a winged seraph.

The Dean of Durham was Cyril Alington, a former headmaster of Eton. An assistant master at Eton reported a message from the dean's wife, a delectable woman: 'We have a new canon here at Durham. His name is Michael Ramsey. He is nice. But he has no small talk. He can talk about the Atonement. But, whether unfortunately or not, that is not the subject which is usually uppermost in our minds.'

Alington allowed him and two other canons to introduce the daily sacrament on condition that they did not expect it to be part of the cathedral's official usage. Ramsey preached in his canon's turn at the cathedral. Some people found the sing-song voice a barrier, and found the beginning and the middle easier to listen to than the end. It was soon agreed, however, that he was worth hearing. The music meant little to him, but the history, the architecture, the stones, the daily sacrament, and all the associations of the place remained with him permanently. He was in demand for the hearing of confessions and made a little chapel for this purpose on the ground floor of his house. He also took it in turns with other canons to act as verger and lock up the cathedral at night in the shortage of vergers caused by the war. He once locked two visiting American soldiers inside the cathedral one evening and promised to come to let them out in half an hour but forgot to come.

Two doors away lived his former warden at Lincoln, Leslie Owen, now the Bishop of Jarrow. Leslie Owen had a secretary who also was his chauffeur, Joan Hamilton. She visited Durham to see a friend and fell in love with the city and began to help with girls' clubs in Durham and Sunderland. Then she became Bishop Owen's secretary and driver and staff officer. The idea of becoming a monk vanished from Ramsey's heart. They announced the engagement in November 1941. The morning it was announced a vast audience arrived for Ramsey's lecture and cheered him all the way up to the dais. His eyebrows twitched and he said, 'This week we are dealing with the sixth chapter of St Matthew . . .' whereupon 90 per cent of the audience tumbled out of the room. They were married on 8 April 1942 in the Galilee chapel of Durham cathedral. It was the time of the Baedeker raids, when German bombers struck cathedral towns, and some of the guests who stayed in York the night before had sleepless hours.[1]

Joan Ramsey, open-hearted, smiling, caring, changed his life. The cold vast house became warm in atmosphere and hospitable. Since she had been secretary to a bishop (she learnt to type by trial and error), and also chauffeur to a bishop (she learnt to drive by trial and error), she knew a lot of the clergy and their wives and had visited them all over the diocese, often in the black-out, and sat with the wives while the husbands talked to Bishop Owen, so she was good at remembering about them and their children and found the wives of the clergy to be fun. She helped to create for him widening circles of friends, the cathedral community, the university, the clergy of the diocese, the students. She could not provide him with small talk, or prod him to abandon his silences. She did not cure absent-mindedness. She would send him off to some lecturing engagement with butter and other

[1] Leslie Owen married them. The dean gave the address. Eric Abbott was best man. Archie Wilson, organist of Manchester cathedral and uncle of the bridegroom, played the piano and a choir of friends sang. Leslie Owen's daughter Faith was bridesmaid. The priest behind in the photograph is Stephen Dennett. Joan's father was too lame to escort her and Dennett acted as his deputy.

rations to give his hostess, and when he came back the rations would be found as a soggy mess in his pocket. But she made him less formidable. It was also noticed that he ceased to whistle unconsciously as he walked up the aisle from the vestry. If he was in a procession the other members of the procession still worried about his inability to walk a straight line and feared that at some point he would peel off from the file. Even five years later a clergyman who came to a retreat which he conducted thought him the oddest sight, sartorially, which he had seen among academics. His high-pitched southern university voice caused amusement to North Country clergy who came. But, said one of them, 'when he began to talk about St John, all this was forgotten'. The wit which once held the Cambridge Union in thrall was again in evidence. Later in life he looked back upon the married time of his professorship at Durham as an idyll; the paradisal years of his life.

No children ever came. Occasionally they were vaguely sad about it but they never considered adopting. They were happy together and both were fulfilled in their work. And after a time they accepted it as their vocation to be childless. But they were not deprived of children. Various children, with whom both of them were very good, were about the house in profusion. There were the Lucas boys with their model railway, there were a couple of evacuees with their mothers, there was a German Jewess refugee with her adopted child, there was a friend who lived with them and helped at a school and her children were in and out a lot. Then the first 'maid' they ever had was a girl of 16 called Mollie and she had been deserted by her husband and came to live in the house with three tots. Married life was a contrast with the experience of the bachelor living solitary amid echoing halls. In the midst of all this young life it was fortunate that the house was roomy enough for the professor still to get enough quiet and space to write.

They started to run meetings in the house for the wives of the clergy, where Ramsey talked theology to them and mixed it with a lot of humour. The professor was asked out to preach in mining parishes; and he discovered that, despite the views of the Bishop of Lincoln and the teenagers of St Benet's that he was unintelligible in a pulpit, he could feel them hanging on his words. We have an eye-witness who heard him when he went to preach at Easington colliery to a large congregation of miners and their families, who felt that he himself and the other hearers were electrified. Ramsey spoke of eternal life. The witness judged part of the secret to lie in the way he seemed to think out what he wanted to say as he went along and made the audience share his struggle after truth.

2. THE DURHAM CHAIR

The faculty of divinity at Durham had as Ramsey's predecessor Oliver Quick, who with William Temple was a leading mind in the Church of England. Michael Ramsey succeeded someone famous throughout the land. The faculty could not think that a young man of 35 years, who had written one book which not everyone thought wonderful, could hold a candle to his predecessor. They felt coolly towards the newcomer.

His first achievement as a professor was to overcome and then reverse the suspicion with which his appointment was received. They found that he knew what he wanted; that he was persuasive in trying to get it; that what he wanted was good; and they suddenly realized that this new young professor dragged them into the twentieth century.

On the board of theology he was dominant, to reform the curriculum and the examinations. This was the place where there were rows about his reformation. The other members began to find that he gave the faculty coherence and a sense of purpose. This was not by drama, but by being around, and by being himself, and by an infectious enthusiasm. Whether or not he was a sound thinker, on which they could disagree, no one could doubt that they had a professor who loved his subject; he bubbled with it.

He was kept busy writing lectures for he found the faculty grossly understaffed. He had a class of thirty young men. He did not think many of them bright (but the record afterwards shows that several were very bright). He got to know them well: years later when they appeared suddenly he could remember who they were. At their request he umpired their boat-races on the River Wear. As a lecturer he was concise and audible. Though he did not dictate, he went at a pace slow enough for the listeners to take down a lot of what he said. He would end his lecture with a summarizing epigram. After a time it became known in other faculties that this was rather a special lecturer and people reading classics or history or the sciences took the trouble to go over to Ramsey's lectures and swell his class.

He managed to increase the staff in two ways; first by getting the endowment for the chair of Greek freed from the attachment to a canonry and then the endowment of the canonry used to give a second professorship of theology;[2] secondly by persuading the vice-chancellor to find money for a lectureship in New Testament studies. For this lectureship he chose (1945) Kingsley Barrett, who was a dedicated

---

[2] S. L. Greenslade, from 1943. R. R. Williams became Principal of St John's College; Alan Richardson a canon of the cathedral. Hedley Sparks was a lecturer; later R. P. McDermott came. It was a strong team.

Methodist. Since all the teachers in the faculty hitherto were Anglican, this choice of a Methodist for a key post did not go unobserved. It was destined to influence Ramsey's later career. He widened the faculty from being Anglican to being for all denominations. He widened it from a training for future priests of the Church of England to a course which anyone might wish to read for their education.

Afterwards he felt that he had a hard struggle. The teaching method which he found he regarded as spoon-feeding. He thought the lectures far too many and that he gave too many lectures for his own good. He reduced their number. He wanted more seminars and more individual tuition. He also wanted more theology. Why should a faculty of theology teach only the history of Christianity or the study of language? By the time he left it was the most respected faculty of divinity in English universities.

He hated the word *student*. In his view it divided young from old by its suggestion that only young people study. He hated the word *department* because it suggested bureaucracy. But otherwise he preferred the system at Durham, where the teaching unit was powerful, to the system he knew at Cambridge, where the social unit was powerful yet excluded the spouses. He also preferred the Durham system to the Cambridge system because it afforded the chance of more general courses of study. He did not like an excess of specialization and thought that a university should do what it could to counteract the trend, and help arts undergraduates to learn a bit of science or vice versa.

With his experience of an old university and a less old university, with two different systems, he was able to frame for himself what he valued in the English university. He thought that a lot of residence was of high importance; for he believed that the object of higher education was not just information, or preparation for a career, but a community of minds and personalities. 'It is not difficult', he would say later, 'to produce sophisticated men and women by collecting them to learn certain subjects. But it is not sophisticated men and women that a good university tries to produce. It is men and women whose knowledge goes with character, and with reverence for persons and for the things of the mind.'[3]

Young John Lucas, who lived hard by and sat on Professor Ramsey's head to recite Greek verbs, heard stories from his father of Ramsey taking on atheists in the university in public debate and wiping the floor with them. Whether the boy understood what father said, or whether Ramsey did so, is more doubtful. It was never his habit to try to wipe the

---

[3] Hansard, Lords, 11 Dec. 1963, on the Robbins Report.

floor with anyone. His experience of his brother Frank made him respectful of sincerity, and well able to hold his own against clever atheist onslaught.

The early years were war years—the horror of news, and fear of raids, and blackness at night, and poor food, and sitting up all night, and very earnest prayer. Ramsey never failed to be grateful to the young pilots who won the Battle of Britain, and always afterwards remembered Battle of Britain Sunday.

In 1943 he suffered a disaster when the stock of his now famous book was all destroyed in the London blitz. He continued to write.

The book which he spent most of the war writing was naturally about death: *The Resurrection*, published in 1945. It had large sales for a time in England and America, but it had neither the originality nor the power of his first book. The heirs of Bethune-Baker at Cambridge thought it lamentable. The *Modern Churchman* produced what Ramsey called a 'rather vehement and contemptuous' review; slightly with an air of 'we settled this question long ago, why must this young man interfere?' Ramsey was not moved and printed a reply.

Then in 1949 he published a lovely book, *The Transfiguration*. The thought of glory always rose quickly amid his devotions and the book was scholarly meditation on glory in the New Testament. In far away Haiti a young black Methodist minister, Philip Potter, who would one day be Secretary of the World Council of Churches, mulled over the book as he struggled with villainy in a very poor and very sad land. Near the end of his life Ramsey was asked which of his books he was most glad to have written. He replied unhesitatingly, '*The Transfiguration*'.

One other book came out of the Durham days, though it was not published till later. Frederick Denison Maurice, the Christian Socialist, was the most cloudy, some said most woolly, some said most profound, of the Victorian thinkers. Because of the impact of Socialism in power in Britain and of the welfare state during Attlee's post-war government, Maurice attained a celebrity not known since his death eighty years before. Lots of people wanted to know how Christians were Socialist and how Socialists were Christian. Lots of people wanted to read Maurice. They tried it and were baffled. Michael Ramsey was the son of a mother who was a Socialist and who thought that her Socialism sprang out of her Christianity. He decided to make Maurice understood by the undergraduates of Durham University. That feat could not be achieved without making Maurice more down-to-earth than he was.

Ramsey grew famous in the Churches. He got more and more entangled in committees of the ecumenical movement, which was on a rising tide of Christian hope, and which badly needed trained English academics to help. In 1947 he was well known as one of the authors—in fact he was the chairman of the group and the principal author and the person in charge of publication—of a report to the Archbishop of Canterbury, now Geoffrey Fisher, on the nature of *Catholicity*. This report made such an impact that two other groups wrote answers to it.

At such meetings he was valued. Here was an Anglo-Catholic who insisted on the apostolic succession of bishops, and thought intercommunion between the Churches, before a proper union, to be wrong, and yet refused to unchurch the Protestant Churches. Rome refused to take any part in these proceedings, except by unofficial observers. Therefore a man like Ramsey brought the argument about Christian unity up against the fundamental question of Catholicity versus Protestantism in a way which few others could.

The Protestant leaders found him far too rigid. But he was curiously persuasive. He was never tempted to see 'bishops' as a key for locking the door on dissenters. He never separated 'bishops' from an agelong body of historic Catholic devotion and prayer. He hated definitions of apostolic succession which made it sound as though a lot of laying on of hands from century to century was a bit of magic by which God preserves his Church. He once defined the Anglican doctrine of apostolic succession to several Lutherans so that at the end they could be heard saying 'Hear, Hear'. And another reason why he grew more and more weighty was his refusal to accept Guff. There was a mood, if we cloud all this up in realms of high theology then we shall all agree on what we cannot understand. Ramsey was determined on clarity. 'Seeing through a glass darkly', he once told an ecumenical committee, 'is not the same thing as an ecumenical fog.'

After the war he began to travel to meetings as a consultant.[4] The most important of these was at Amsterdam for the first meeting of the World Council of Churches 1948. Here he argued with the European leaders of Protestantism, from Karl Barth downwards, over the difference between a Catholic and a Protestant idea of the Church. At this point the old-looking young professor from Durham entered a European scene.

The Nazis created a wave of Christian feeling in Europe, almost a religious revival, in antipathy to their racialism and anti-Semitism and violence and injustice. Before 1939 the ecumenical movement was always a clerical élite within the older Churches. Its force among people

[4] He was one of the makers of a report on Christian Initiation (1946–8); was at Lieselund in Denmark 1947; at talks between the Church of Scotland and the Church of England; gave the opening lecture to the Anglo-Catholic Congress at Westminster July 1948.

lay in the missionary areas and the young Churches where Indians or Africans could not see what European divisions had to do with them. But Hitler made world Christianity something that for a moment even people in the pews could see as an expression of peace, and amity, and human rights, and the moral law in politics. The old committees where clergymen of various denominations talked in polysyllables to each other's waistcoats were given a sudden strength as they touched the aspirations of the peoples.

The meeting at Amsterdam was the focus of these hopes. It could not fulfil them. As a Cold War frustrated the yearnings which the people put upon the new organization of the United Nations, a cold war entered Christendom. Was a meeting of world Christianity a propaganda design against an atheist Soviet union? The American Secretary of State, John Foster Dulles, practically said so at the Amsterdam meeting. The Soviet government said so. Therefore the Russian Churches, at a synod in Moscow that year, said so and refused to send a single representative. The satellite states of Moscow followed this lead—no Bulgarians, nor Romanians, nor Yugoslavs. How could Christendom be represented when the weightiest part of the most historic of Churches refused to have anything to do with the meeting?

Ever since the days when Ramsey was a boy at Repton, the Pope refused to have anything to do with the ecumenical movement. The Churches said that they would try to unite—but this was nonsense, there was only one Church and he was it. Rome suspected the ecumenicals of planning a Protestant federation across the world which would be designed as a force against Rome. Some of the utterances of ecumenicals gave ground for this suspicion. An American Congregationalist, for example, saw no possibility of uniting with Rome and every reason for not uniting with Rome—let us join the Churches which teach more or less the truth, not the Churches which do not. Such speeches shocked Rome. At some meetings during the twenties and thirties unofficial Roman Catholic observers were permitted. But Rome did not merely refuse to send any representative to Amsterdam. It banned unofficial observers from attending. This rigidity shocked the ecumenicals.

How then could the meeting at Amsterdam pose as a meeting of Christendom when the largest Church in the world refused to have anything to do with it?

These strange circumstances pushed into prominence the only Catholics who were not banned from attending the meeting. The Russian revolution of 1917 drove out many Russians. At Paris Georges Florovsky taught theology and interpreted the Russian tradition to the

West. At Amsterdam he talked out of a vast tradition which otherwise was not very articulate at the meeting. His presence and influence there made him a figure in world Christendom. And the Anglo-Catholic tradition would never swallow the idea that world Christianity was a federation of Protestant Churches. Of the Anglo-Catholics the professional thinker in Amsterdam was Michael Ramsey. The cold war condemnations of Moscow and the obsessive rigidity of Rome elevated Florovsky, on that stage, into a mouthpiece of the eastern Catholic tradition, and elevated Ramsey into a mouthpiece of the western Catholic tradition.

He described his own experiences in a public article (*Ecumenical Review*, 1 (1949), 388–92). They met as a commission, under the chairmanship of the Swede Gustaf Aulén, to debate the first theme of the agenda, the Universal Church in God's Design. The commission contained Karl Barth, and Florovsky, and the American Protestant Mackay who was a man of polysyllables, and the more profound American Protestant Richard Niebuhr, and Ernst Wolf to represent the German Lutheran tradition, and a few others. Ramsey described the contrast as strange, between the hard hitting of the debate and the friendliness of the people. They quickly discovered that they could not agree. They made no attempt to cover up the disagreement with beautiful words. Any member on a committee to which Karl Barth belonged had a rough ride.

Afterwards the general meeting was disappointed and some said that this commission was unrepresentative of the Churches and ought to be disregarded. It was, they said, a set of academic hair-splitters.

But, said Ramsey, the idea that we can get Christian unity by going for a highest common factor and leaving everything else in the shadow will not work. What is vigorous and worth while in the various traditions is precisely what is not in common. The commission moved away from the idea that Christians agree on what is important and disagree only on what is trivial. They were therefore accused of putting the clock back and bringing the best hope of Christendom to an impasse. Still, despite the absence of Rome and Moscow, the antithesis between Catholic and Protestant was taken seriously by Amsterdam.

Ramsey had moved out of the Barthian influence which via Hoskyns attracted him during the earlier 1930s. The continental commentators on Amsterdam were in the habit of minuting Ramsey's name as that of the chief opponent of Barth. The recorded utterance of Barth to Ramsey at Amsterdam was, 'I am sorry you do not hate the Pope'. But Ramsey and Barth found that they shared a common sense of humour. They had instant rapport. Barth was amused and pleased when he heard how someone said that if he and Ramsey could get on so well 'the millennium must be round the corner'. Barth had never met a real Anglo-Catholic before and was excited by what he found. When he went home to Basle he showed the photographs to his family and pointed out to them 'my very good neighbour Canon Ramsay [*sic*] from Durham, an authentic Anglo-Catholic, with strange views concerning tradition, succession, ontology and so on, but also with a very convincing twinkle in his eye . . . a man with whom I more often agreed than disagreed . . . *the* outstanding figure in the picture of my first ecumenical experience!'[5]

The Roman Catholics were interested that a combination between a Russian refugee, Georges Florovsky, an English high churchman, Michael Ramsey, and a dogmatic Swiss Protestant, Karl Barth, brought the ecumenical movement to an impasse because none of them was prepared to put up with a Protestant federation, and the union of these unlikely allies was too powerful to overcome.

The nature of the meeting left Ramsey with a doubt. These meetings could not be said to be unimportant because world Christianity ought to be seen to meet. But could the discussion do any good? With such numbers, and so many set speeches, and with most of the participants having done no work beforehand, could you ever get clarity into a report produced by a mass debate? This doubt about world synods was not lessened by later experience.

By the time of the World Council at Amsterdam the question began to come into Ramsey's head what he ought to do next. He found that the canonry and the cathedral, and the administration in the university, took up a lot of time. He seemed to himself to need more leisure to pursue his studies of the New Testament and of Christian thought more profoundly. He wondered where he could find a chance of quieter work.

Some of the Scotsmen talked of getting Ramsey as Bishop of Edinburgh but not enough of the Scotsmen wanted an Englishman and no doubt there were those who wondered whether this professor who lived among clouds of glory would make a bishop who perforce lived in a too real world. Then, by an extraordinary fortune, the three Cambridge chairs of divinity which were or could be in his field of study fell vacant within three years. All of them had the attraction of fewer chores and a better library—as well as, for him, the *genius loci* of a childhood home. They also had more of a challenge than Durham. He would have to

---

[5] Barth to Ramsey, 3 Jan. 1949. The status of both Barth and Ramsey at Amsterdam was that of consultant not delegate.

move into a school where the powerful names were still Bethune-Baker (though he was retired) and Marsh and Raven and he would be, intellectually speaking, up against it in a way that he was not at Durham. That was a challenge which he would like to undertake. He thought the post 'more exposed', 'less cosy'.

He applied for the first chair and then thought better of it and withdrew the application; refused to apply for the second despite the supplications of Cambridge friends; and finally applied for the third, the chair of primacy, the regius chair made vacant by the retirement of Charles Raven.

Raven did not want Ramsey to succeed him. Although the chair was a regius chair, it was not like most regius chairs an appointment by the King. Since the reign of Queen Elizabeth I the professor was elected. In 1950 the electors consisted of a board of the vice-chancellor and eight persons of whom five were at Cambridge and three from outside Cambridge; but one of the five was away in America, and absent persons cannot vote. Elections are confidential and no one knows what happened. It is certain that the vice-chancellor in the chair gained the impression from what was said at the meeting that they were forced to elect from a weak field of candidates. It is certain that the electors discussed the name of Stephen Neill, who had had a far more brilliant academic career as an undergraduate than Michael Ramsey and had lately dazzled the university by his lecturing and preaching power. It is certain that they discussed the name of the neo-Thomist philosopher Eric Mascall, who succeeded Ramsey at Lincoln. Professor Marsh, whose superb lectures the undergraduate Ramsey attended, refused to vote for Ramsey no doubt because he disapproved of Hoskyns. The Cambridge philosopher of religion on the board refused to vote for Ramsey for he did not think his work up to standard—the Cambridge philosophers never forgave the 'irrationality' which was a streak in his first and most original book.

But in the eyes of other electors Ramsey had merits. There was nothing arid about him. He never lost sight of the religious nature of his subject, and never turned it into a boring desert. Here was a person who took a faculty in another university and turned it into the most famous faculty in the land. He was also an English thinker whose name was respected on the continent of Europe. Whether his books were or were not weighty, he thought for himself, and was no man's copy. Although a free and critical mind, he reached reasonably conservative conclusions about the New Testament—which pleased the nonconformists and the bishop on the board. And those who worked with him on ecumenical committees knew that this was nothing like so rigid an Anglo-Catholic as sometimes he was portrayed; and remembered what he did for the Methodists and other non-Anglicans in Durham. Moreover we have the proverb that no one is elected to anything except to keep two other people out—and some of Cambridge doubted whether Stephen Neill for all his brilliance was reliable, and thought that neo-Thomism, despite the quality of Mascall's mind, was a retrograde movement in divinity.

The Methodist leader Newton Flew proposed Ramsey. He worked with Ramsey on several ecumenical committees and respected his mind. The Presbyterian T. W. Manson, a leading scholar in the New Testament and capable of judging whether or not Ramsey had academic weight, seconded the proposal. And Ramsey was elected the Cambridge regius professor by the votes of five men out of seven. None of the five was on the teaching strength of the faculty at Cambridge, and three of the five came from other universities. It says something for Ramsey's person and mind and reputation that one of the two most Anglo-Catholic professors in England could be elected on the proposal of two nonconformists.

If two Cambridge electors voted against, that must mean that the faculty divided about Ramsey. A lot of people in Cambridge were disappointed at the choice. But some of the younger dons were ecstatic about the election. So were Magdalene College, and Ramsey's father, and Archbishop Fisher, and Edward Wynn who was now the Bishop of Ely. Eric Abbott prophesied falsely, 'It is to be the great work of your life'. And so it seemed. 'The iniquity of the Amorite', wrote Austin Farrer, 'is at length full, and the progeny of Hoskyns is to return on the third decade to the Promised land.'

3. THE CAMBRIDGE CHAIR

Joan and Michael Ramsey moved to a house in Newnham, not far from where he lodged when he was vicar of St Benet's eleven years before: 3 Wordsworth Grove. The house was large for their needs and soon they did not like it.

Ramsey became a Fellow of his old college Magdalene. There he was a formidable force. The Fellows were accustomed to do mostly what the Master, Sir Henry Willink, Bart., wanted. Ramsey the Liberal politician had ideas of democracy which cut across this benevolent dictatorship. He had the more force because it was, so to speak, hereditary in the college. But he liked the Master and admired the vigour of his leadership.

The faculty of divinity needed him. Marsh, the professor of Old Testament, had been a superlative teacher but his health was gone and he was now a passenger. No one except Ramsey could teach the New Testament. No one except Ramsey could teach what Christian doctrine was about. At his first lecture in the Cambridge divinity school the large room was packed. The caretaker was heard saying to the professor of Hebrew, 'It's only curiosity Sir'.

He found his work different from his work at Durham. There were fewer lectures, many more private interviews with students, many more research students to see, a seminar for graduates and lecturers, far more leisure and therefore more time for study. He gave two courses of lectures and the notes for both courses survived: one on the New Testament and one on the Christian idea of redemption. 'To the preparation of both courses of lectures I gave far more attention than I had latterly been giving at Durham.' He had a professor's room where he interviewed. He was influential on the board of divinity. It was a good time for building up the faculty. The numbers of students grew, therefore the university could justify the money for new posts.

Within a very short time several of those who were disappointed at his election swung over to gratitude for his coming and enthusiasm for what he did to the faculty. The swing from suspicion to welcome which he met at Durham he now met at Cambridge.

Ramsey missed his canonry; that is, he grieved that he no longer had a priestly connection with a church in the town. He was in demand for preaching and conducting retreats. He would appear at 6 a.m. in Addenbrooke's Hospital to celebrate the sacrament as its honorary assistant chaplain.

Bothered about Joan's health and the overspaciousness of the house, they searched and found a little terraced house almost opposite the Fitzwilliam Museum. They sold the monumental furniture suitable for the acreage of Durham canonries and moved into Fitzwilliam Street. They spent a whole day placing the furniture. Then they sank back into armchairs, thanking the Lord that never again in their lives would they move house. Never was gratitude more misplaced. Ramsey bicycled over to Wordsworth Grove to see if there were any letters. On the mat was a letter from Winston Churchill. It offered him the see of Durham.

Ramsey had been a professor at Cambridge for exactly twenty months. It is not usual for the advisers of the Crown to draw people out of important work when they have hardly had a chance to do what they have undertaken. The offer had a history behind it.

Since the days of Queen Victoria the method of choosing bishops for the Church of England had changed, not wholly for the better. Queen Victoria achieved a big improvement when she insisted that prime ministers should not choose whomsoever they liked without consulting the Archbishop of Canterbury; and in later stages she was able to insist that if the archbishop objected, the prime minister's nomination should not go forward. Her son Edward VII, though he knew far less about clergymen than his mother, continued the same trenchancy. If he found that the archbishop disliked a nomination, he coolly referred it back to Downing Street. But with the coming of Lloyd George a Celtic nonconformist began to nominate. King George V, who also knew not much about clergymen, had no desire to make trouble. The system of consulting one or both archbishops continued. But on occasion the prime minister disregarded what they said.

Lloyd George was not a person who knew little about clergymen. He knew nothing. Therefore he developed of necessity the system which Gladstone started under Queen Victoria, a little private team of sec-retaries or advisers. This was desirable. Prime ministers have various duties. If they had to be responsible for choosing the leaders of the Church, they needed information and their secretaries should be able to talk to people who had the information. Much depended upon the quality of the secretaries. One of Lloyd George's advisers was a sensible and informed man. The others were ignorant and prejudiced.

Lloyd George was driven from office. The prime ministers between the World Wars, who were mostly Conservative, ran the system with sense and responsibility. They consulted the archbishop or archbishops, took their advice, did not persist if the archbishop brought good reasons for a contrary opinion, and did not allow their 'patronage secretary' any 'independent' authority. The system ran well for the sake of the Church. Successive kings had no reason to grumble, cathedral chapters were happy to elect, and the Church of England was given good leaders—William Temple of York and George Bell of Chichester among them.

With the Second World War the system started to creak. Churchill was a sort of Anglican but was as ignorant about clergymen as Lloyd George. He was supposed to take the advice of Archbishop Lang of Canterbury but he distrusted everything Lang said because he thought him an appeaser of Hitler. The relation between archbishop and prime minister became at times very uneasy. Lang thought Churchill (from this point of view only) the worst prime minister who ever worked the system. Some of Churchill's nominations in fact were very good, that of Temple to Canterbury being the best. But it made the situation no easier because Churchill distrusted Temple as a sort of Socialist and as too outspoken a politician. One of his secretaries Colville tells us that Churchill's attitudes to clergymen had a touch of King Henry II's attitude to Thomas Becket.

After the war Attlee went back to the more responsible system. But in October 1951, when Ramsey had professed at Cambridge for exactly a year, Churchill came back to power. This was a Churchill decaying physically, slower in the uptake, less able to work long hours, less interested in the peacetime problems of the country, but still well enough to make his own decisions. He had an archbishop, Fisher, with a good judgement of men and with a lot of information about them. So the discussion, and the argument, began to develop not so much between prime minister and archbishop, as between archbishop and Churchill's patronage secretary Anthony Bevir. For the first time a civil servant, perforce, began to affect what happened.

The see of Durham was the fourth senior see in the Church. Its occupant had an instant seat in the House of Lords. When it fell vacant, one bit of history conditioned the argument. For the last seventy-three years the Bishop of Durham was a scholar; five bishops in succession ranging from one who was among the leading minds of Europe to one who was more a publicist than a scholar but who still had academic interests. During the recent years after the war the university rose in national importance and always had a close connection with the bishop.

Archbishop Fisher and Archbishop Garbett of York started to look around for scholarly clergymen and hovered over various names, all of whom taught then or had taught in universities.

On 8 April 1952 the patronage secretary went to see the Archbishop of York. Bevir's habit was to roam with a cloud of verbiage and then pop out of his hole with a startling suggestion, almost as quickly popping back. He talked of the excellence of Mortimer at Exeter, formerly a professor at Oxford. Then he started to talk about Ramsey and said 'probably the best man for Durham'. It did not seem to occur to him that Ramsey had been only eighteen months in an important job for which he was perfectly fitted.

Thus came a conflict of views. The two archbishops thought that Ramsey would be an excellent bishop but it was not right, it was bad for the Church as well as for the study of divinity, to take him out of the Cambridge chair after so short a tenure. (Notice the change which the Durham professorship, and Joan's coming, wrought—in 1940 no one could conceive of this absent-minded man as a bishop, and six or seven years later the electors to the see of Edinburgh mulled over his name and decided that it would not do, and five years after that both archbishops and the prime minister's office were agreed that he would be a very good bishop.) The prime minister hardly minded much, as yet, what was going on. His civil servant thought that Ramsey should be invited. And against the archbishops Bevir had this on his side. He had talked to the Durham people. He stayed at the deanery and talked far into the night about the needs of Durham and its diocese. The outgoing Bishop Williams wanted Ramsey to succeed him. Everyone in Durham to whom Bevir talked wanted Ramsey to come back.

The dean and chapter wanted him. Behind the scenes they may have affected the prime minister directly. For Canon Lucas, sub-dean and father of the boys with the model railway, decided while Ramsey was the professor at Durham that this was a possible Archbishop of Canterbury. This was contrary to the opinion of the world and society which thought of him as a boffin. Lucas knew Lord Halifax from his university days and now wrote to tell him that Ramsey was the man whom the diocese wanted as its bishop, and hoped that Halifax would do what he could with Winston Churchill.

Also, Bevir had another argument. Possibly, he said, this was a future archbishop. If so, it was good to give him experience as a bishop as soon as possible. And Bevir was in the strong position, that neither archbishop wished to deny that Ramsey would make a good bishop. If Churchill recommended Ramsey to the new young Queen who had never before been confronted with the situation, and the Queen asked the archbishops whether they objected, they could not say that they did.

This was a new development in the system of choosing bishops. The prime minister's secretary went down to the diocese to consult the leading churchmen. That meant, the secretary exposed his part in the proceedings. Instead of a faceless figure behind the scenes, he was obviously a person who counted. Yet he had no constitutional place in advising the Queen on the choice of bishops. That made the system look more Erastian than it ever looked before. Here was a civil servant exercising obvious power in the choice of a Church leader. On the other hand it had a large compensation. Always in English history bishops were chosen for national reasons and the diocese took second place. But now for the first time the diocese was being consulted—informally, quietly, but systematically. Under the old system, where bishops were chosen by archbishops and prime ministers who thought about the needs of the nation, Ramsey would not have been chosen. He became a bishop because, and solely because, the diocese knew him well and wanted him back. That was no small gain to set in the balance against the more obvious Erastianism of the new system.

There is a little evidence that the final choice lay between George

Chase, the Bishop of Ripon, mature in years and experience, a scholar, solid, stable, absolutely reliable, shy, and at times remote, and Michael Ramsey, without experience, untried, but one of the leaders of a party in the Church and someone who would do more to represent learning among the bench of bishops. Churchill, confronted by a choice between a totally safe appointment and an exciting gamble, would have no doubts. The new Queen approved informally. On 30 May 1952 a letter went from Churchill to Ramsey offering him the see of Durham.

The house in Fitzwilliam Street at Cambridge was in a state of shock. Someone who has accepted a leading chair at one of the universities expects to do a job and does not lightly change after less than two years. And this was more than just a professorship. It was work towards which all Ramsey's training and expectations led as the right contribution which he could make to the life of his Church and to that of Christendom. He knew that his gifts were those of a scholar rather than an administrator. He knew that he was not going to be happy if he were deprived of the chance to study.

That the letter came from Winston Churchill was a point against it. The Repton boy's horror at Churchill's anti-Bolshevist campaign had turned into a more adult and less ferocious criticism. The Liberal Ramsey thought that Churchill was totally wrong to put Britain back on the gold standard; that he was illiberal over miners in the General Strike; that he was very mistaken in resisting the advance of India to independence. He admitted the great debt which the country owed to Churchill for the Second World War. But he would have preferred Lord Halifax to Churchill as prime minister in 1940 and even in retrospect believed that the country would have fought the war better under Halifax and that the admirals and the generals would have had a less neurotic time. To receive the offer from Churchill did not raise it in Ramsey's estimation.

And something about the tone of Churchill's letter displeased Ramsey. He thought it pompous. But the actual letter survives and only a mind predisposed to suspect the sender could think it pompous: 'After the most careful consideration I have decided, if you are willing that I should do so, to recommend your name for the succession to the see of Durham.'

Did Ramsey suspect that Churchill's 'very careful' consideration was more by proxy than in person? Or dislike the ego of 'I have decided'? Anyway he did not like the tone. That was an excess of suspicion, for the letter was drafted by David Hunt, *vice* Bevir who was ill, and Hunt made it conform to precedents. And Churchill was not yet senile. He cross-examined Hunt and knew perfectly well what he was doing.

Still, Michael Ramsey, being Ramsey, had to think that this might be the will of God for him. Durham stood for an idyll of ten years. He knew the people, and the work, and a lot of the clergy. He also knew that his wife, after being secretary to a bishop and then secretary to the professor of divinity, and his hostess for eight years, was better equipped to be the wife of the new Bishop of Durham than any other woman in the country. Durham was the place where he had found happiness. But he had a fixed idea in his mind that to be a bishop was not his work.

Eric Abbott, his best man, had once begged him not to become a bishop in England. He told him that a mitre could be a candle-snuffer. Ramsey had read the life of Archbishop Randall Davidson by George Bell and found it very depressing—a noble and unspoilt man inside a sickening system—'the wire-pulling, the hedging, and energy spent on things that don't matter, and all the sitting on the fence'. But he had also read the life of Bishop Charles Gore and found it inspiring, so it was not always sickening to work as a bishop.

His first need was to find out whether Cambridge University would regard his leaving as betrayal. He went first to the then elder statesman of the faculty of divinity, William Telfer the Master of Selwyn, whom Ramsey respected. Then he went to the Master of Corpus Christi, Sir Will Spens, who was a lay Anglo-Catholic. Then he went to the head of his own college, Sir Henry Willink. To his surprise and discontent the first two thought that he ought to go. Willink thought that perhaps he should not go; but he also discontented Ramsey by treating it as a problem in how Ramsey should get the best career in a worldly sense. Nevertheless, it was clear that the wisest Cambridge leaders whom he could consult would not regard his going as betrayal if he felt it right.

On the eve of Whitsunday Joan drove him over to Ely to see the bishop, his first confessor Edward Wynn. Wynn was not a man prepared to decide anyone else's future for them.

On the Tuesday Ramsey called on his former best man Eric Abbott in London, who had urged him never to be a bishop in England. Abbott thought at first that Cambridge was bound to win. But before the end of the conversation he realized how vocation pulled Ramsey towards Durham, and talked about 'a theological bishop' and did not discourage.

From Eric Abbott he went on to Canterbury to talk to the archbishop, Geoffrey Fisher. The meeting with Fisher, in the Old Palace at Canterbury, was felt by Michael Ramsey to be odd.

Fisher, as was his way, was honest. He did not pretend that he wanted Ramsey to go to Durham. As clearly as anyone he saw what was owing to the university of Cambridge. He said that the diocese of Durham wanted him and that the Archbishop of York was now persuaded that they were right. He said that he had an open mind. He said no word to persuade Ramsey to accept the see. And then he gave what Ramsey thought a startling answer to a question which to Ramsey was a crux.

Ramsey asked how valuable it was to have scholarly men as bishops. Fisher replied that it did not matter much. But, he added, sometimes commissions were needed and then it was valuable to have a scholar-bishop as the chairman.

Ramsey had formed the view that a bishop is an apostolic teacher. His vocation is to guard the faith, to present it, expound it. He did not think that the then bench in the Church were all well qualified to this end. He had told a friend not long before, 'If you walked from Humber to Severn and dodged Derby, you would not find a bishop who can read or write'. That Archbishop Fisher treated all this as unimportant perturbed him. If the official view in the Church cared nothing about the bishop in his function as apostolic teacher, anyone who was trained to teach had a duty to join the bishop's bench if he were asked. The interview with Fisher strengthened Ramsey's feeling that he had a duty to go.

The settling blow was delivered by Archbishop Garbett, whom on the Friday Ramsey went to see at York. Garbett had a retreat for ordinands and smuggled Ramsey into the house lest one of the young men guess that something was up. He said that the Durham diocese wanted Ramsey. He said that theology among bishops was important. He said that it needed strengthening in the northern province. He was sure that a bishop was not stopped by his bishoping from going on with some scholarly work.

Thus a Dean of Durham, and an ex-Bishop of Durham, and a complicated patronage secretary who popped out of holes like a rabbit, and a doctrine of apostolic authority, and an Archbishop of York, and a desire to follow the calling of God even if it looked unlikely, winkled a professor out of a career to which he seemed to have been born. In old age Ramsey looked back and knew that this was the hardest decision of his life.

On 17 June 1952 a Fellow of Magdalene College walked down Trinity Street in Cambridge and was suddenly aware of the regius professor of divinity waddling ahead of him and throwing his arms about and muttering gloomily to himself, 'Hell! Hell!' 'Why, what's the matter?' 'The Lord works in mysterious ways! I am to be Bishop of Durham.'

Despite the advice of William Telfer that he ought to go, Cambridge was not pleased with Ramsey. Some of the younger members of the faculty of divinity were angry. The church historian Norman Sykes thought it a bad choice for the see, too party a man for a see which needed breadth of mind. Cambridge, which always assumes that anyone who leaves it passes into outer darkness, found the decision incomprehensible. They decided that it could only be because Joan's health was so poor in the fens that the professor was forced to move. This story Ramsey had flatly to deny.

Durham was very pleased. Kingsley Barrett, the Methodist, whom Ramsey had chosen for the faculty at Durham, wrote of his belief that a special providence must watch over the Church of England to give them at least some good bishops in spite of the deplorable method of their appointment.

On 8 August 1952 he and Joan gave a farewell party to Cambridge friends. On the doorstep his final words to the last guest to leave were, 'You must vote for me when next I apply for a Cambridge professorship'. Occasionally, when he came back to Cambridge in later years, and especially when he came back to help the university elect another professor of divinity, he would be nostalgic, and say, 'I should like to have another go at being regius professor'.

They went on holiday to a farmhouse at Ponsworthy in Devon and thither came a vast parcel, from the Clerical and General Tailors (Breeches Makers etc.), of Sackville Street, Piccadilly, bill £376; chimeres, wristbands, rochets, frills, breeches, gaiters, purple dress coat, black barathea breeches, patent court shoes, silver-plated shoe buckles, and other less rare articles of apparel. In the farmhouse he practised putting on the gaiters and found it a struggle. Much of the rest of the holiday he spent writing articles or reviews for publication. He also read carefully the famous book of Pope Gregory the Great, from the sixth century, on the pastoral office in the Church. He practised a new signature, Michael Dunelm. On 24 September he went into retreat at Mirfield in Yorkshire, where once he thought of becoming a monk. The retreat was a time for fear at first, and self-scrutiny. It passed 'into great peace with the help of Father Horner an old and saintly monk who gave me absolution and good counsel'.

He must do his homage to the Queen—her first bishop to do homage. The civil servants in Downing Street played it humorously. They warned the Queen's private secretary Sir Alan Lascelles that the Queen was about to meet an eccentric. David Hunt from Downing Street told Lascelles that Ramsey had been known to stop in a procession, send for a pair of trousers to replace the wrong ones which he had put on by mistake, and change them in the middle of the aisle. The Queen, he said, should not be put off by any oddity of manner but could be assured that this was a man of great learning, deep human sympathy, and outstanding pastoral gifts. (There was no truth in this legend but such legends gathered about the young Michael Ramsey and certainly he was odd in processions.)

Lascelles reported next day to David Hunt. He said that the Queen eagerly waited for the bishop to show some of his eccentricities but, 'fortunately or unfortunately' he had acted with the utmost decorum.

On 29 September 1952 Ramsey was consecrated bishop by Archbishop Garbett in York minster and enthroned in Durham cathedral on St Luke's Day, 18 October. The Marquess of Londonderry arrived with his traditional gift to a new bishop of two pheasants and a pound of butter. The Master of Magdalene asked him whether he found it uncomfortable to wear the received garments of a bishop. Ramsey replied, 'They are like false teeth. At first they irritate a bit but when you are used to them you find them serviceable.'

4

The Bishop

Both the Ramseys loved living in Auckland Castle, a historic pile eminent in the history of England and of the Church, with magnificent memorials of celebrated prelates of past centuries. 'I have never lived in a place where the past was so alive, and my great predecessors seemed like daily companions.' At first they found it very cold, especially as they moved in just before Christmas. To live in such a castle meant demands on the purse. It was the time of their lives when they found it hardest to make ends meet. It could not have happened unless the Church had helped to pay for the heating. They inherited also a historic butler, of quaint majesty, Ernest Alexander, who governed the castle since near the beginning of the century. When they arrived at Auckland Alexander asked them for the silver and his Presence was such that they did not dare to tell him that they had no silver, so Joan said that it was 'in the bank'.

Ramsey loved the many-acred park with its structure to shelter deer, though there were no deer, and its grazing cattle and its river-banks. Since the twelfth century the Bishop of Durham had a manor, and lived here except during the Commonwealth when bishops were in exile and this was the seat of the general who governed the North. In spare half-hours he would wander in the market-place and streets and shops of Bishop Auckland and talk with the people. He liked to sit on a bench in the square and talk with, or rather be talked to by, the old retired miners.

In 1954 he completed the restoration of the chapel, which was ravaged by death-watch beetle. It had once been the great hall of the castle, and is among the fairest buildings of the twelfth century which Britain possesses. Under King Charles II Bishop Cosin turned the hall into a chapel after the dilapidations of the Commonwealth general, and gave the medieval windows a clerestory. Bishop Cosin's original colours of the roof, from the seventeenth century, were discovered during the restoration and Ramsey had them brightly restored. A panelled room, which was Bishop Cosin's study, Ramsey turned into a small oratory for weekday sacraments or prayers. He liked to show parties of visitors round the house and to talk to them of Oswald, or Hild, or Cosin, or Lightfoot. The finance for the restoration of the chapel was a gamble. He asked the Church Commissioners to do it but would not wait to see whether they consented. When the head of the Commissioners, Sir Malcolm Trustram Eve, who was no man to be trifled with, arrived a few days after the Commissioners approved the expenditure, the butler Alexander showed him the restoration already complete. 'Never', said Trustram Eve, 'have I known craftsmen to be so expeditious.'

Ramsey felt the same ecstasy, of history speaking out of sanctified stones, in Durham itself. He found that in such a place present was near to past and visible near to the invisible world. He was often aware of the long tradition back from industrial Durham into the old palatinate which defended the realm of England against the Scottish raiders and then back to the Celtic saints coming out of Scotland into Northumbria.

He found that he enjoyed going to a parish to confirm the children, or to institute a new incumbent, and stay afterwards for the sausage rolls or sandwiches at the bunfight and chat up the people with a mixture of silence and belly-bumping laughter and beams all round and leg-pulling but with care and affection. Sometimes he felt desperately shy and this specially seemed to happen when titled laymen or captains of industry appeared. But mostly he did not need to talk at a bunfight, people came up and talked to him, and he would nod his head and smile benevolently and say happily, Yes, Yes, Yes. In February and March it was hard going out almost nightly but he liked it and Joan got to know the wives and children of the clergy. One Sunday in four he refused to go out and stayed at home to read and write. He was willing to go to confirm in an emergency at very short notice and this earned him some long-lasting gratitude. On a parish visit the pastor would sometimes take him to the bedside of a dying man or woman and Ramsey would sit long by the bed, saying almost nothing, but holding hands and at the end giving a blessing.

At his first diocesan conference he told them his idea of a bishop's job. He finds today unbelief, or apathy, and sometimes a collapse of the sense of right and wrong. He needs to try to see the subtler reasons for this mood. He needs not to forget that there are demonic forces in the universe whatever people say about the existence of the devil. He needs to be aware of the social reasons pulling at ordinary people, the conditions of work in an industrial society, the nature of a people's amusements. He needs continually to be at work dealing with the shifting population of a modern age, so that people who move house to a new estate shall still find a priest and a sacrament for their souls. He needs to think of how we are to find the right ministers, men and women—to let people know that there is a vocation called holy orders, of 'unique difficulty and unique happiness'; the variety of ministers, deaconesses, teachers in schools, lay preachers, monks and nuns and friars who belong to 'the praying heart of the Church', without which its mission would not have the power of God within it. He needs therefore to think about stipends and houses and church buildings. He recognized that many of the weapons were not in the power of the parish system—broadcasting, or literature, or education, or public life. But the parishes, and the parish missions, were central to the care of souls; and their ministers ought always to be refreshing themselves in the truths of the Christian faith, so that they do not slip 'into versions of it which miss its height and depth and wonder'; and those ministers ought always to make room in their lives for silence and the chance of realizing their nearness to eternity.

A special happiness was the care of those who wished to be ordained. He talked with them in his study or took them for walks in the park. He would talk not only of their vocation to the ministry but of the books which they were reading and the circumstances of their family. He usually knew their tutors and made jokes about them. He found the ordinations, three times a year, to be his happiest moments.

With his lay people he had good fortune. On 2 June 1953 the Queen was crowned in Westminster abbey. By long history the Bishop of Durham had the privilege of standing at the right hand of the sovereign throughout the coronation as her chief supporter. Since this was the first coronation to be televised to a nation, Ramsey was suddenly famous among the people of England; all the more so because the vast head, baldness girt by flowing white locks, mobile expressive eyebrows, and waddling gait drew the attention of millions of viewers. Some people thought that with the mitre on his white hair he looked like one of the effigies on the tombs of the prelates which they met recumbent in cathedrals, and fancied that here was a bishop out of the Middle Ages. The lay people of Durham were proud to have their bishop at the right hand of the Queen. This cemented their acceptance of Ramsey. He was a magnificent figure in ritual clothes. On his massive head a mitre did not appear comic, and in gaiters and apron he looked every inch a bishop, with nothing fancy-dress about him. As with William Temple, who looked equally natural in gaiters and apron, the bubbling humour and lack of pomposity heightened the effect of the personality. Ramsey thought it a protection against wrongful ceremony to understand its principles. He said, 'People who don't understand liturgical acts generally get pompous when they dress up.'

He worked mostly with secretary and chaplain. He did not hold staff meetings, and hardly consulted those who expected to be consulted, like the suffragan bishop or the archdeacons. He was reported to have said, 'I did not really know what an archdeacon does.'

Afterwards he asked himself whether he did all that he should have done about the miners and the working men. He diagnosed that his concentration on getting to know the clergy and the church people prevented him from moving among the wider community as he should. He admired what the early Methodists did for the miners and how the earliest of the miners' unions was Methodist in its inspiration. He knew what the Victorian churchmen of the north had done for the miners and how by the third quarter of the nineteenth century the Church was strong within the mining communities though it never took the place of the Methodists. No Bishop of Durham could ever forget, or was ever allowed to forget, how one of his predecessors Westcott mediated in a bitter strike; how a vast crowd stood outside Auckland Castle, seeing the owners through the windows of one room and the miners through the windows of another, waiting for five hours as they watched the bishop go to and fro between the two rooms; until he brought the parties to a happy agreement, and when he came out among the crowd he received an ovation. Ramsey knew of the bitterness engendered by the coal royalties paid to the Church, and how the miners once tried to throw a bishop into the River Wear. He believed that the nationalization of coal was a blessing both for Durham and for the Church in Durham.

He became a friend of Jack Lawson (Lord Lawson) who was a faithful Methodist, and Sam Watson the Durham miners' leader, whom he came to know intimately. He always attended the Durham miners' gala, which was the festivity and political demonstration of the mining community, and in 1955 preached them the gala sermon by invitation of the miners. There they made him sing them a song and were enchanted by the noises which came out. He thought that there was no barrier and that in time he could have done more for them.

Under the English system of parishes every diocese had variety; that is each parish had the Prayer Book but used it as it thought, with simple or elaborate ceremonial, and with variations of language sanctioned by the (illegal) Prayer Book of 1928 if it wished. The person who decided this was almost always the vicar; though of recent years he could not make elaborate changes without the support of a majority in his church council. Thus the possibility of a quarrel in the parish was still there. A parish used to simple ways of ceremony might be confronted with a new vicar who suddenly elaborated the ritual; or the opposite. These quarrels were rare. But when they came they were distressing and they particularly distressed the bishop responsible for healing; because Christians are not supposed to quarrel, and quarrelling about clothes or tinklings or perfume looked like fanaticism or obsession with triviality. But it was more than these to those in the quarrel. Were we making a Protestant Church to resemble the Church of Rome? Or were we trying to make meagre the devotions of minds which were helped to pray by colour and symbol? To mediate in such a dispute was the dreariest occupation of a bishop.

Ramsey inherited a battle like this from his predecessor. The most Anglo-Catholic parish in the diocese was in South Shields, St Mary's Tyne Dock. This had a record of superb parish priests and a full congregation. While Ramsey was a canon the chapter appointed a new vicar; and while Ramsey's predecessor was bishop, a minority of the parishioners started to protest against the vicar's innovations and were in a strong position because the vicar introduced certain ornaments without the necessary faculty to do so. When the vicar got a new bishop who was Anglo-Catholic he appealed to him for his sanction, in the hope that the bishop's approval would make up for the lack of faculty. Ramsey's first holiday in Devonshire as a bishop was made unhappy by the news of the quarrel in the parish.

He thought little or nothing about law, or jurisdiction, or faculty. What mattered were, first, to maintain the tradition of worship in the parish, and second, reconciliation. He cheerfully gave his sanction to most of what the vicar did, the use of incense, the reservation of the sacrament, the wearing of vestments, the ringing of sanctuary bells, the veneration of the cross on Good Friday, the blessing of the palms on Palm Sunday, the blessing of a Paschal candle, and the pictures of the Stations of the Cross on the walls. He only asked the vicar not to use Hail Marys with the Stations. He went into the whole ritual and found nothing open to the charge that it encouraged superstition. Meanwhile he separately interviewed the vicar, and churchwardens, and opposing groups of parishioners, and tried to get conciliation, and persuaded the lawyers to postpone the court while he tried conciliation; all to no purpose. In the judgement (Jerusalem Chamber 1 February 1954) the Chancellor mostly backed bishop and vicar; but ordered out the statue and the sanctuary bells and the tabernacle on the altar, saying that what was illegal could not be made legal by the bishop's permission. That did not settle the matter, which ran on for eight years more, long after Ramsey left the diocese of Durham. The case brought the diocese, and the parish, and its bishop, a little unwelcome publicity; but not much; for the world was tired of ritual quarrels, whereas sixty years before there would have come questions in Parliament.

On the whole Ramsey was no friend to dramatic public occasions. But he revelled in the Northumbrian past, of Aidan and Cuthbert and the Venerable Bede. On 19 July 1955 he walked barefoot across the sands of Northumbria to Holy Island, at the head of 3,000 people. On the grass in the ruins of the historic priory, surrounded by parochial banners, Ramsey told the crowd that though they were outside the modern diocese of Durham, this was their true home. He conjured before their minds a poetic word-picture of St Aidan coming from Iona in Scotland and settling there with his band of monks to pray and to spread Christianity among the heathen English; and spoke of St Cuthbert to whom on that spot the people went to seek help and comfort and guidance, until he fled across the sands and sea to be alone with God on his island—so carry the lesson back, to a county black with people and with coal, carry back the need for quiet, and separation from whirl, and silence; and so heaven will be nearer.

His predecessor but one, Hensley Henson, invented the magazine the *Bishoprick* and by the force of his writing made it a national and not only a diocesan journal. Since the heady days of Henson it had become a duller and more local object. Ramsey did not see why it should not have a wider interest as in Henson's day. He started not only to print his addresses or charges but to review books of general interest; to consider a book on diplomacy and war, and not to lose a chance of holding up the character of Asquith to admiration, or to contrast the laziness and drift of Stanley Baldwin as prime minister with the crusading fervour of a Gladstone. Some of the articles were hard for the layman to follow and quite hard for some clergymen to follow. He tried to educate them about the nature of *demythologizing*, a word of which the press had got hold, and to guide them about the best modern writing on the New Testament. He found that he could pay a compliment to Charles Raven, from whom he was so sadly sundered in spirit, for his book on Religion and Science.

The irksomeness lay in London. He attended the House of Lords but did not speak. He disliked the Church Assembly (which was the forerunner of the General Synod) and made only one speech there while he was Bishop of Durham, against the idea of *recruiting* people to come and be priests. He enjoyed the friendly little Convocation at York. But what irked him most were bishops' meetings.

Towards the ecumenical movement, as a system of vast Christian jamborees like the meeting at Amsterdam, his suspicions deepened. He attended a meeting at Lund in Sweden in 1952 and thought the atmosphere happy but the meeting useless and wondered whether the day of such occasions was not past.

But the assembly which shocked him was the next, at Evanston in the United States in 1954. He hated what he saw at Evanston.

It was too large. They sat in a place vast enough to 'house a fleet of Zeppelins'. 'I have rarely known such stultifying of the personal touch between speaker and audience.' The American media moved in. He hated the vulgarity of showing off the delegates as though they were exhibits, and the insincerity of pretending that platitudes were pronouncements of world-shaking import, and the feeling that he came a long way to greet fellow-Christians and found himself turned into a ham-actor on a second-rate stage.

A whirl of oratory for a fortnight. He liked to take ideas gently, to get time to meditate on the best modes of expressing truth. 'How futile to announce that some great lead to thought was going to emerge from the mountain of memoranda discussed at high pressure by exhausted delegates.' And he was opposed to the idea of Christian unity which dominated most of the Protestant delegates from the United States—to create a world federation of different Protestant denominations.

His frustration and boredom were at their worst in the debates on the main theme of the Conference, Christian Hope. A committee led by Karl Barth proposed a message for the Churches to adopt. But the committee was hopelessly divided on what it meant by Christian hope—whether it was hope for peace and perfection in this world, or hope for a future life, or hope only of forgiveness at the last. The document finally 'agreed' by the disagreed committee was stuffed with jargon and so incomprehensible that it was useless as an agenda for discussion; yet the meeting at Evanston had to discuss it; with results which may be imagined. Ramsey made a speech which disconcerted the managers of the conference, who thought it a bad example of English insularity. The speech led to a quarrel, soon patched up, with the general secretary Visser t'Hooft.

The meeting at Evanston clinched the sense of scepticism which Ramsey felt, not about the ecumenical movement, but about its inflated claims and its mode of organization. That scepticism and memory were to be important when he became an archbishop and was expected to be a leader in the organization.

Still, at Evanston, he allowed the personal meeting to count—with Hungarian Christians oppressed in a satellite state, with a black South African who merely by being there seemed to make the Afrikaaner defence of apartheid incompatible with Christianity. He realized, as he never realized before, how Asian and African Christianity took the lead in the world-wide Church.

Always thereafter Ramsey's attitude was consistent. He cared about Christian unity, no one more. That unity must look towards Catholics as well as Protestants. The way to find it was not by diplomacy and negotiation (though these had their part), still less by razzmatazz and public relations, but by trying to get nearer to God. All meetings were boring to him unless the participants could talk in depth and unless the debate was by a small enough number of people for personal friendships to be fostered. His principles were very strong, that the Church of England is a Catholic Church and must never compromise its Catholic principles. In those days he contemplated the idea that if the Church abandoned that inheritance he would have to resign his see.

In his family he found an unlooked-for happiness. During his twenties his father and he were sundered by religion. His father did not mind his son becoming an Anglican priest but wished that he were not so Anglo-Catholic and not so high-principled about bishops. Still, he was proud that his son should be a professor of divinity at two universities, and proud when his son became a bishop. He did not wish to desert his Congregational cause or his Church. But at the age of 86, immured by infirmity in his house, he wanted to receive the sacrament from his son. With the consent of the Bishop of Ely, who was Edward Wynn, the Bishop of Durham came to Howfield and confirmed his father and ministered the sacrament to him. The son said that this brought his father deep happiness. 'It is unusual', he wrote, 'for a bishop to confirm his own father—but it is as a great Nonconformist that I revere him.'

Ramsey was already a leader, not just in the diocese of Durham, but in the Church. He had a big personality. What he said counted. Archbishop Fisher went so far as to tell him that he was a possible future Archbishop of Canterbury. The Catholic minds in the Church rejoiced to have one of such influence, and such prayerfulness, high in the counsels of their Church.

During the autumn of 1955 Bishop Wand of London retired and the health of Archbishop Garbett of York failed. The two leading sees after Canterbury needed new occupants simultaneously. Anyone who looked round the Church of England saw Ramsey as possible for one of them. But he had been Bishop of Durham for less than three years, and was in a see which fitted his gifts perfectly.

It was a long and anxious debate about Ramsey without him knowing; between the Archbishop of Canterbury, the prime minister Eden, the prime minister's patronage secretary Bevir, Garbett the outgoing Archbishop of York, and Wand the outgoing Bishop of London. Who was the biggest person in sight? Without question—George Bell, the Bishop of Chichester. Lover of Christian unity, friend of the European leaders, ally of the Germans who stood against Hitler, courageous critic of area bombing, patron of art and theatre, compassionate over refugees, he was the only bishop in England that the world had known about since William Temple died. But he was 72 and would be 73 by the time he had to move if he moved. Is it sensible to move a man to new work at the age of 73? What is the point of moving a person who is famous through the world as Chichester to the anonymity of being Archbishop of York? There is a point in moving him to London because that is near the Houses of Parliament where he has weight. But the see of London is work for the physically strong, not for declining energy.

Who else has stature? Ramsey of Durham. He is much younger. He could manage the see of London. But he is a new bishop. And he values scholarship. Are we to kill his scholarship and make him unhappy? His wife has uncertain health, could she manage life in London? Two sees, York and London—Bell or Ramsey? If Bell is ruled out as too old and Ramsey as too new, who else has stature? George Chase of Ripon, good as gold and wise as Solomon, but even shyer than Ramsey and without his intellectual bite?

Two other circumstances entered this prolonged argument. These were hardly mentioned but underneath were not trivial. First, the York diocese had no desire for George Bell and every desire for Ramsey. Its dean was his former teacher and friend, Eric Milner-White. Dean and chapter did everything in their power to get Ramsey. And in this new structure, where the prime minister's secretary popped out of holes and asked them what they thought, they had a better chance than any previous dean and chapter. The leading layman of the York diocese was the politician whose judgement was likely to weigh with the Crown: Lord Halifax, the former Foreign Secretary, and a devout Anglo-Catholic. Halifax helped over prising Ramsey out of Cambridge. He was now likely to want the prominent Anglo-Catholic bishop. And Garbett wanted Ramsey to succeed him at York. The authorities of the York archdiocese were unanimous.

The second almost silent circumstance was Bell's reputation. He was revered in the Church of England. In Germany he was a hero. But he was resented by long memories in those who had fought a war; by Churchill's men for weakening the morale of the Air Force through his attacks on area bombing; by the school of Lord Vansittart which loathed Germans and said that Nazis were typical of that race, and hated a bishop who told them never to identify the true Germany with Hitler. The prime minister Eden was Churchill's man; a fight-to-the-limit man; an unconditional-surrender man. Suppose that Archbishop Fisher thought Bell the best person despite his age for one of these sees, could he get Bell's name past the prime minister? Or would Eden think of the air marshals, and the children who had lost their parents in a blitz, and former warriors who had seen too much blood on a battlefield, and exercise a silent veto, by going for the second preference?

Archbishop Fisher was aware of these circumstances. He had the merit of going always straight to the point—what is best for Christianity in England? and besides that the scruples of air marshals, or the wishes of the Dean of York, or the comfort of Bell, or the scholarship of Ramsey, are nothing. If York or London needed Bell or Ramsey they had a moral duty to move whether or not they wanted it. He did not think Ramsey's scholarship a weighty part of his quality as a bishop; occasionally he hinted that he thought the books were a distraction from pastoral care. And he had another point for moving Ramsey. He saw him now as a possible Archbishop of Canterbury. If we ask, how do we best train the next Archbishop of Canterbury, which see is better? Obviously (in Fisher's eyes), London.

So on 29 October 1955 Fisher recommended to the prime minister that Bell be asked to move to York because he was the biggest person in sight and—despite his age—'he might tide over for five or six years'; and that Ramsey be invited to go to London, because that huge see would 'respond to his commanding ability'. But he made the recommendation with a proviso. He, Fisher, should be allowed to ask Ramsey privately whether his wife's health would stand up to life in London.

The first Ramsey knew about these discussions between Fisher and the prime minister was when a letter arrived in Durham on 8 December 1955. The letter asked whether Joan's health would prevent Ramsey accepting the see of London if it were offered to him.

This letter horrified both the Ramseys. The aim of his life was to remain a scholar and a teacher while he was a bishop. This was of the first importance to him. He felt it a necessary part of his vocation. The London diocese was vast, difficult, rent with controversy, dotted with rebel or eccentric clergymen comic and uncomic, and needing a dedicated administrator whose time would be loaded. It would be a candle-snuffer. He did not want the job at all.

He decided only to answer the question which he was asked. He talked to Joan. He consulted Joan's doctor. He wrote to Fisher that while she might never be strong, her health did not depend upon locality. Therefore 'no personal circumstances would preclude my giving thought to coming to London'. He signed himself, not without a touch of misery perhaps, 'ever sincerely and dutifully'.

Fisher now pressed him. You are the best appointment to York. You are the best and most convincing appointment for London. I think it would be best for you also. No other bishop can meet the demands of the see of London, in statesmanship, scholarship, spiritual force, 'and the rest'. If this is right, who should go to York?

And meanwhile Garbett was still spreading doubt on whether to send him to the see of London was the best way for the Church to use the best scholar on its bench of bishops.

Fisher's next move was to consult Ramsey about the entire problem of the two simultaneous sees. On 12 December 1955 Ramsey went to Lambeth Palace. He determined beforehand that he would not mention to Fisher his longing for time to read books. But Fisher raised the question of time for study and writing. Ramsey asked the pointed question whether William Temple would have been able to write if he had been Bishop of London and not Archbishop of York. Finally Ramsey said that he would respond to any invitation provided that it had a consensus of advice behind it, and provided he was sure that the need for strength in the North was considered. Fisher thought that Ramsey at this interview was 'gloriously analytical and dispassionate' and that his point about weight in the North had force.

Ramsey's long memory always regarded the decision to leave academic life as the hardest of his life. To the observer this decision of 1955 looks as hard or harder; to agree to accept a post which he expected to hate, and for which he regarded himself as unsuitable, and in which he would have to neglect that scholarship which was essential to his happiness and to his sense of vocation and to the reason why he ever became a bishop at all, if the leaders of the Church declared that this was where he was needed. His long memory also told him that this was a moment of his life when he felt a total rapport with Fisher.

On 14 December 1955 Fisher repeated his recommendation to Anthony Eden that Ramsey should become the Bishop of London.

On the same day, knowing nothing of what Fisher was doing, Ramsey drove to Bishopthorpe outside York to see his frail and dying archbishop. Garbett said that he thought it would be right to go to London, for the sake of the Church; that he longed for him to come to York, for the sake of himself, he wanted Ramsey as his successor. 'If you go to London I shall feel it right. If you come to York, I shall be happy.' Ramsey knelt by his bedside and Garbett blessed him. Ramsey never saw him again.

For the twelve days before Christmas a black cloud hung over the Ramseys. He had no desire to move anywhere. This was not just a bishop married to the see and people of Durham, it was a love-marriage. Those years were not long enough to do what he had hoped to do for Durham, but long enough to know what needed to be done. Joan was at home both in Durham and in Auckland Castle. But from 12 December he knew that he had to move somewhere, under orders. And the fear was a burden, that he might need to move to a place which would kill his intellectual life.

On Christmas Eve among the Christmas cards he found a letter from Anthony Eden offering to recommend him to the Queen for the see of York. Whether it was the wishes of the archdiocese; or whether it was the inarticulate growls of air-marshals; or whether it was the judgement that someone of 73 carries too many years to move to big new work; or whether someone among Eden's advisers thought scholarship important for some bishops—Eden rejected Fisher's preference that Ramsey should go to London.

The relief to the Ramseys was overwhelming. Michael Ramsey took Eden's letter into the chapel but knew what his answer would be even before he put it on the altar.

In view of what was to happen, it is important to notice the situation. In 1952 Archbishop Fisher had not wanted Ramsey for the see of Durham. He thought it wrong to take him out of Cambridge so quickly. Now he preferred him at London, for Bishops of London are by geography close colleagues of archbishops at Lambeth. But Fisher was happy in accepting what happened, and glad to have Ramsey moving to York. He openly talked of him as the probable successor to the see of Canterbury. He looked forward to working with him.

The historian has a doubt. If Ramsey was to be Archbishop of Canterbury, what was wrong with leaving him in the weighty see of Durham until the day came? What higher interest of Church or nation was served by driving him to move too quickly? Did the Church of England have so obsessed an idea of hierarchy that it liked promoting people up a ladder without any snakes? Was it a mania for translating bishops—represented at its oddest in the idea that it was sensible at the age of 73 to move the revered George Bell to one of these sees? Or was it true that the Church was so short of people of stature (under the age of 73) that only one man among them had enough stature for the see of London and for that reason his scholarship must be sacrificed on the altar of a higher good? This last motive was present in Fisher's mind. It is hard to believe that it was a right judgement about all the other people possible.

Ramsey's last act for the Durham diocese was to publish a collection of his *Durham Essays and Addresses*. It is one of his best and most readable books. In it the mutual affections of bishop and diocese cannot be missed.

Ramsey felt no sense of gratitude to anyone who moved him out of Durham. He was seen weeping in the waiting-room at Durham station, and the misery was the giving up of Durham with its epic history, its Bede and Cuthbert, its beauty and its strength, his new friends and his old, the university and the mining communities. He felt it as a bereavement.[1]

The prime minister Anthony Eden was a Durham man. Ramsey felt remote from him. Soon after all this was agreed, he went to see Eden to have a talk with him about new appointments, and because Eden wanted to know him better. This meeting was a failure. Ramsey was abnormally shy about meeting the upper class and Eden's voice was the caricature of an upper class voice. But worse than this pardonable affliction was Ramsey's discovery that when they talked about his beloved Durham this Durham man showed no interest. Later he made to himself excuses for Eden; that he left Durham young and that his childhood was unhappy. Still—'I did not see him again and I did not want to'.

2. EBOR:

Ramsey's confirmation as the new Archbishop of York was held at Lambeth on 13 March 1956 and was marked by one of those protests which to the outsider are amusing and which to the subject of the

---

[1] George Bell, Bishop of Chichester, to the Bishop of Durham, 5 Jan. 1956 (Bell Papers, Lambeth, vol. 214):

Please accept my warm and affectionate congratulations on your nomination to the Archbishopric of York, together with the assurance of my prayers. You will miss Durham and its people much. But you will show the same love for the people of York as you have done for those of your present diocese, and (I am sure) win their love in a similar way. In addition to this, there are the new and great responsibilities which belong to the Primate of England. It is in their exercise, now and in the coming years, that I trust special grace will be given you for the use of your many gifts.

One of the gifts which God has given you—not too common in the Church of England today—is imagination: and I hope that it will not fail you, and that courage in its exercise will not fail you, as the Church faces the many problems, intellectual, social, ecclesiastical and international, of the times in which we live.

To me personally it has been a special joy to work with you, both in the larger ecumenical field of the World Council of Churches, in which your presence and continued interest mean and will mean a great deal, and as a fellow chairman of the Joint Committee on Relationships with the Church of South India. May God sustain and strengthen you!

Yours affectionately

George Cicestr:

protest are vexatious. Mr Kensit, a name long famous in the history of Protestant expostulations against Anglo-Catholicism, the secretary of the Protestant Truth Society, appeared at the ceremony and presented a document. He lodged what he took to be a legal objection against Ramsey being admitted to be Archbishop of York. The grounds were two. First, he had failed to do what he ought to have done when Bishop of Durham to discipline the ritualists in the parish of St Mary's Tyne Dock, although some of the parishioners appealed to him for protection against illegal practices and ornaments of a Romish character. Secondly, he had published doctrine at variance with the Athanasian Creed and the Homilies of the Church of England and his teaching was at variance with that of the Archbishop of Canterbury and other bishops. This second charge came because Ramsey had written an article in the *Bishoprick* which criticized the evangelistic work of Billy Graham, who led a mission in England a few months before. Ramsey said that the name of Billy Graham was linked with fundamentalism; and that fundamentalism was the error of regarding the Bible as so divine that the human element disappeared. Billy Graham like all such evangelists called for people from the congregation to make an immediate decision and to come out from the crowd; and Ramsey wrote that the call for an immediate decision had danger because the mind could be stifled in the process and this could bring a later revenge in scepticism and indifference. He said that at the recent mission in Cambridge Billy Graham had taught the grossest doctrines. The reader of the article remembers Michael Ramsey's experience of the missioner William Nicholson in his undergraduate years. Since many of the evangelicals shared Billy Graham's opinions and valued his methods and saw the good which he did, his article stirred wrath among them and fear about the Bishop of Durham becoming the Archbishop of York.

For this purpose Archbishop Fisher acted in his capacity as the Queen's commissioner. He ruled the objection out of order. He said that the only questions under discussion were whether Ramsey was Ramsey and whether he had been legally elected. Since no one could imagine that in these circumstances or in any other circumstances anyone could successfully impersonate Ramsey, the ritual was a piece of legal nothing which allowed a Protestant agitator the chance of publicity which might help his own cause but must also help Ramsey. If a man is worth protesting against he must be somebody.

Nevertheless, Ramsey found the experience of Kensit's protest a little frightening. For the first time he met, peeping above the surface, the force of a prejudice which had unrelenting ferocity. He would meet it, not peeping, later in his career.

Less fanatical minds of the Protestant school were not pleased with the choice for York. The editor of the *Church of England Newspaper* remarked that the overzealousness of Ramsey's friends did him a disservice by making him the representative of an intolerant school of thought and by inflating his reputation beyond what his record would endorse. Archbishop Fisher went so far as to write a very tough letter to the editor in defence of Ramsey.

The new archbishop was enthroned in York Minster on St Mark's Day, 25 April 1956. That the Dean of York was Eric Milner-White, his former teacher, gave pleasure to both parties. The dean said, 'My child in the Spirit has become my Father in God.' It was the first enthronement of an archbishop since television became a national service; and Ramsey agreed to broadcast on television on the night before his enthronement.

The diocese was larger than the diocese of Durham and more varied; industry on Teesside, moors of the North Riding, wolds of the East Riding, the plain of York, cities like York and Hull. But although it was larger his life was easier. He had three suffragan bishops and three archdeacons. By now he had discovered what archdeacons do, and did not have to do everything himself. He inherited a regular staff meeting and was penitent that he had never invented such a meeting in Durham. He now had a whole-time chaplain, Martin Kaye, whom he put in charge of the ordinands. One of them, Peter Cornwell, later published a sunlit retrospect of what it was like to be one of Ebor's ordinands, and how he valued the privilege that the bishop who ordained him was a thinker, as he put it, so profound. Martin Kaye also helped Joan to make sure that the conversation was not too oppressively silent when ordinands or clergymen came to meals. Thus Ramsey found leisure to read, and write, and make friends in the diocese. Afterwards he wondered whether he visited parishes less often than his predecessor and took the trouble to work it out. He found that he did just better than his predecessor and was pleased.[3]

Despite this diligence in the diocese he had more leisure than at Durham and much more leisure than later. At York he was able to write a weighty book, *From Gore to Temple*, which traced changes in Christian thought in England during the last eighty years.

His first problem was where to live. He had insisted on living in Auckland Castle though some people said that it was absurd for the Bishop of Durham to be saddled with such a pile. Garbett decided that no one after himself ought to be made to live in a château like

---

[3] Visits to parishes (five-year period)—Garbett 390, Ramsey 398.

Bishopthorpe. He planned to turn Bishopthorpe into a retreat house and to put the archbishop into a small house nearby called the Chantry. Ramsey instantly scrapped this plan. The Ramseys wanted a house big enough to be able to entertain the clergy and their wives in their own home. He needed room for a lot of books and wanted his chaplain and secretary to be able to live in the house. He was determined to be under the same roof as his chapel. His sense of history and of *genius loci* was potent. And the memory that William Temple used to meditate in the garden was not trivial to him. The chapel went back to the thirteenth century; in the Restoration of Charles II Archbishop Frewen gave the house a façade to the river and built a magnificent dining room; and during the eighteenth century Archbishop Drummond added a Gothic gatehouse and made the surround a charming bit of eighteenth-century Gothic. Joan had an eye which knew what to do with apparently unpromising houses. Their bachelor predecessor had no such eye and did not try to change it. Joan saw that it needed cheering up. She put coral paint in the panels of the Strawberry Hill Gothic hall. She picked out the arches in ivory white. She transformed the entrance so that it sang a welcome to the visitor. In summer she filled the great blue and white Chinese vases with the deep blue delphiniums grown from buds which Cosmo Gordon Lang originally planted. Visitors found it a lovely house, full of air and hospitality. Joan was discovered to have a genius for turning an ancient block of stone into a home. The house had not the vistas or the parkland of Auckland Castle, and its chapel could hardly compete with the chapel at Auckland, but it had good walks along the Ouse. The diocese was pleased that he lived there.

Robert Reid from the BBC interviewed Ramsey in the garden at Bishopthorpe in April 1956, with daffodils spattering the lawn. 'He's a most engaging fellow—essentially human', Reid reported as though there was something odd about an archbishop being human. 'He's a huge fellow. He looks as though he's been a footballer in his time. He's got a keen sense of humour and there's a perpetual twinkle in his eye . . . This is not a scholar emerging into the world. He's already in it . . . He will not be a rubber stamp. He already has the shape of a great leader.' In the following year a BBC man who came to Bishopthorpe to have a brains trust in the house was shocked to discover that there was no television set in the house and told him that he was cut off from the experience of millions of his countrymen.[4]

He presided three times a year at the Convocation of York, which he

---

[4] BBC Written Archive Centre (WAC) talks, microfilm T563/564; WAC Ramsey 1957–62, 18 Dec. 1957.

found a happy body. This last statement should be noticed—he disliked assemblies and places where speeches were made at length and he did not enjoy being a chairman—but he made this single exception, the Convocation of York; he always gave a presidential address, about which he took much trouble. He visited the other dioceses of his province, including a tour of several days to the Isle of Man. He preached to the World Scout Jamboree and was blamed by the *Daily Telegraph* for *reading* his sermon to a multitude of boys and that the notes were too visible when they were blown about by the wind. He went with the Dean of York and the Lord Mayor of York to interview the chairman of the University Grants Committee about setting one of the new universities in York and was glad, before he left York, to see the plea accepted. He continued to conduct retreats: the old students at Cuddesdon, clergy at Pleshey in Essex, the Franciscans at Cerne Abbas in Dorset, the nuns at Whitby; probably he was the first archbishop in the history of the see to make so much time for such days of peace, even though, for the conductor, they were days of intellectual and emotional effort.

The work dearest to his heart was the development of the Retreat House at Wydale Hall near Scarborough, for which he made money available, encouraged the nuns, Sisters of the Holy Paraclete, who ran it, and was grateful when he saw more and more people go there to say their prayers. For one who was nervous with aristocrats, it was unusual that he made a special friend in the diocese of the hereditary lay leader of the Anglo-Catholics in England: the Earl of Halifax at Garrowby, whom he would have preferred to Churchill as a war leader. They found plenty of common Church interests and then friendship; they had conversations, which Ramsey enjoyed enormously, about matters political as well as religious; Ramsey went over to Garrowby several times for meals or to stay the night and celebrate the sacrament in the morning; and he conducted Halifax's funeral at Kirby Underdale in 1959. He afterwards regarded making friends with Lord Halifax as one of the happinesses of the York years.

During his time at York he was invited to be the visitor of the House of the Resurrection at Mirfield in Yorkshire, the community of priests founded at the end of the last century by Charles Gore. He liked his association with the monastic life in this form. He conducted a visitation every five years, when he went there and interviewed each individual member of the community and finally gave them all a charge. Their work was mainly that of missions and teaching ordinands and conducting retreats, though their work in Africa was both tense and world-famous. He respected the community, valued its work, and was grateful for the friendship of its members. He shared enough of the monk's ideal to be able to help.

It was in part because of this love of the specially religious life, and in part because of the affection for the long history of the Church, that he led another pilgrimage (1959) of several thousand people to Holy Island on the coast of Northumberland and even *The Times* had a piece about the archbishop walking barefoot.

William Temple, while Archbishop of York, wrote in the *York Quarterly*, a journal which expired in the first year of the Second World War. Ramsey knew that as a bishop he had a teaching ministry, and that this needed a journal which was more than diocesan news. No sooner did he reach York than he resurrected the *York Quarterly* and kept it going for five years and nineteen numbers, with the arms of the see on the outer cover, and underneath, 'Editor: the Archbishop of York'. In some numbers he wrote half the contents; in others, especially at the time of an operation on his eyes for glaucoma, little. This operation (1960) seriously delayed him, for it left one eye permanently damaged, and he was in the Purey-Cust nursing home by the minster in York and then had a convalescence of several weeks. In the *York Quarterly* he used the services as writers or reviewers of good men about him. Here he weighed nuclear disarmament or the latest ways in the study of the New Testament or the nature of the establishment in Church and State or the Church in industrial society. He expounded to his clergy advanced books of original thinking which most of them were never likely to see or read. Two or three of his articles were hardly intelligible to some of the subscribers. It was no wonder that the journal had no easy task making ends meet. It is a well-written journal of value to the contemporary interpretation of Christian thought and life.

In the *York Diocesan Leaflet* he wrote a more popular message to his diocese. He quoted Newman's sermons, which he loved for their awareness of the closeness of the divine behind the veil of matter. He mentioned the possibility of sacramental confession at the time of Lent. He pleaded for a regular reading of the Bible, and for sermons which expounded biblical passages, and for the use of the Bible in connection with prayer. He recommended retreats in a noisy world, and gave a beautiful description of their purpose.

He begged for more laymen and more laywomen to teach in Sunday Schools. He wanted to keep the church schools and the church colleges for the training of teachers despite the large sums of money which this needed. He brought before their minds disarmament, or the plight of refugees, or the plight of countries in poverty, or the work of the Church in other lands, or murder in the Congo. He told them how morally indefensible was the policy of apartheid, and asked for prayer for Africa. He recommended to them lists of books for the better understanding of their religion, and the advice was excellent. He liked them to try one or two of the classics of Christian writing.

While he was Archbishop of York both the ancient universities made him an honorary doctor. Their different ethos was illustrated by the difference in the virtues which they celebrated. The Cambridge deputy orator of 1957 commended him for his ecumenical work, and as the tireless pastor of the northern province, and made no mention of his academic originality—perhaps the ghost of Bethune-Baker still peeped through a window of the Senate House. The orator mentioned his debt to William Temple and to Edward Wynn, and his wit, and gargantuan laugh. The Oxford public orator of 1960 commended him for all he had done in persuading Oxford undergraduates to a reasonable faith and called him a most penetrating interpreter of the New Testament and a very powerful bulwark of Mother Church. Perhaps the Oxford public orator consulted Austin Farrer.

In 1958 Archbishop Fisher assembled the Lambeth Conference of bishops. Ramsey entered this conference with a reputation outside England as well as inside it; and the proceedings of the conference confirmed the opinion of a lot of bishops that he ought to be their next leader. George Bell, retired, fatigued, soon to die, attended the conference against the advice of his doctor. He thought the agenda too large and the business too hurried. He recorded in his notes that there were not many weighty bishops at the conference but of those who were weighty Ramsey was outstanding.[5]

At the opening service in Canterbury cathedral (3 July 1958) Ramsey muddled his instructions and wandered all round the cathedral looking for where he was supposed to sit and stand.

This conference was not without hiccoughs. First, Fisher invited Archbishop Makarios of Cyprus whom some held responsible for the murder of British soldiers in the quasi-civil war in Cyprus. Makarios accepted but did not come. When the conference opened, a couple of members of the League of Empire Loyalists, one a journalist and the other a chiropodist, hired eastern bishops' flowing robes from a theatrical costumier, walked in unchallenged, and got up to make a speech against the 'archterrorist' Makarios. They left quietly when asked but their pictures gave fun to the newspapers.

The second hiccough concerned Ramsey directly. The Church

[5] R. C. D. Jasper, *George Bell* (1967), 384.

Union, organ of Anglo-Catholics, decided to hold a eucharistic congress at the Albert Hall just before the Lambeth Conference opened; a demonstration of Anglo-Catholicism at a key point of Anglican history. They invited Ramsey to give the inaugural address. He gave an address which the hearers thought masterly and was the more needed in that the succeeding speeches bumbled.

The *Observer* commented that Ramsey destroyed his chances of succeeding Fisher as archbishop by so openly identifying himself with the extreme high church party. The *Sunday Express* speculated about the next primate and thought that Ramsey probably ruled himself out by his partisan behaviour in attending the eucharistic congress. Archbishop Fisher did not approve of his fellow-archbishop being prominent in such company at such a moment of history. At breakfast together Fisher exploded and attacked the Church Union and all that it stood for and said that they had done great harm and ought to apologize. Ramsey confessed that they had done a lot of harm and ought to apologize but said that the best of them were trying to, and that the Church of England ought to apologize to the high churchmen for the way in which it sometimes treated them.

The main theme of the Lambeth Conference 1958 was the Bible. Ramsey was made the chairman of the commission on this theme. He drafted the report. The Bible and the modern world: the problem with which he had wrestled since he was an undergraduate; a Bible world-picture and a modern scientific world-picture, each hardly able to understand the other. If we take a knife to the Bible and cut out the bits which the modern world cannot understand we compromise the message which Christianity has to give to society. If we baldly declare the Bible world-picture and do not interpret it to the modern world in such a way as to make it intelligible, we are useless.

Therefore on one side we must assert the authority of the Bible over man and the Church, and not the authority of man and the Church over the Bible. It probes to the roots of moral distress and brings the remedy. While we do this we must beware of those who are so hungry for authority in our societies that they want to press the authority of the Bible over men and the Church in such a way as to lead to extravagance or to sectarianism. On the other side we must assert freedom of enquiry. We must accept that study has proved that the Bible is not historically true in all its parts; we must declare that no Christian need suppose the book of Genesis to be an accurate physical account of the making of the world, nor mind if study proves contradictions in the different accounts in the gospels. The divine spirit is at work not only in the consciences but also in the minds of humanity, and the careful study of the texts is a part of that. And we have to remember that God always remains above the possibility of human words, even when those words are the words of inspired men or women. Treated so, the authority of the Bible is not diminished but enhanced.

Thus we commend the Bible to be read by the Churches and by Christian families in their homes, as nourishment for their souls, and not to be separated from the sacrament in the liturgy; we commend modern translations, into the various languages, as a help to understanding; we commend the people who have the duty of seeking to interpret the Bible in terms of the modern scientific view of the world; and remind the Churches that all knowledge is of God and therefore that scientific discovery is also part of His work; and so the world will be brought to know God as its Maker, and the Cross as timeless.

The critics fastened upon two sections of this report. A long paragraph presented the acts of God in the Bible as like a mighty drama. This was the single part not drafted by Ramsey. The word drama, with its suggestion of a stage-play, did not please everyone. The idea of a day of creation being 'flashed upon the screen' by Genesis, as the report said, was incongruous. And at one point, showing how the books were formed into the New Testament by the early Church, the report expressed the belief that God gave the early Church its three gifts of ordering of the New Testament, creeds like the apostles' creed, and the ministry of bishops in their succession from the apostles. This did not please everyone.

The *Church of England Newspaper* said, unkindly, that the weakest part of the Lambeth Conference of 1958 was its report on the Bible; and that this would have been an excellent report for a Lambeth Conference of 1858 not 1958. But this was not a common opinion. Most bishops thought that the handling by Ramsey of this difficult theme was masterly. No Church before committed itself so decisively to the rightness of modern biblical criticism and the freedom of biblical scholarship, while it continued to maintain the Bible and the faith of Easter as indispensable to the moral predicament of humanity and of its societies.

One can picture Hoskyns looking down from the skies and being grateful for his pupil; and Bethune-Baker looking down and thinking that he always knew where Hoskyns might lead the Churches.

Those who encouraged new translations did not yet imagine what would happen. The bishops expected the hallowed Authorized Version to maintain its mastery because it was sanctified in everyone's affections and moral sentiments. They had no idea, as yet, that the coming of modern translations, and the making of English into an international language, would destroy the commonness of a single text of the Bible which was the property of the simple as of the sophisticated.

The Lambeth Conference of 1958 took other resolutions. It called for a revision of the Prayer Book—and the bishops of that day had no idea how far this call would lead the Churches. It surveyed the reunion schemes across the world. It sanctioned the ordination of men while they continued in their lay occupations. It urged the full use of trained and qualified women—and the bishops had no idea as yet how far this resolution would lead some of the Churches. It blessed the religious communities and thereby committed the Anglican Communion to an official acceptance of monks and nuns in a way which was so far unique to the Churches which came out of the Reformation. It asked governments to abolish nuclear bombs, and wished for the strengthening of the United Nations. It condemned racialism in the strongest language. It warned against the abuse of drugs and alcohol. It demanded the concern of government for the plight of refugees. It accepted that monogamy was inherent in Christianity and yet that there were polygamous societies where even the Church could not enforce the rule at once, and that the chief way forward lay in a progressive emancipation of women in those societies, especially in the sphere of education.

Those who afterwards blamed Lambeth 1958 for platitudes did not know what they were talking about.

The resolution which hit the headlines was that which approved the rightness of contraception. It denounced the idea that gratification is the end of sex, but said that parents have the duty of choosing how many children they have. They partly justified this by an eye upon the too rapid growth of population in some countries. A Jesuit instantly declared that the Anglican Communion was pandering to paganism.

Archbishop Fisher was very pleased at what Ramsey did for the conference. In particular Ramsey helped the Anglo-Catholic members of the Conference to take a more friendly attitude to the South India Church, which united a Church with bishops to Churches without bishops in a unified structure over a period of years. If the conference began with a breakfast explosion between the two archbishops, it ended with mutual gratitude for what was achieved. Yet nothing could alter the double personal difficulty—a difference of principles between a low churchman and a high churchman, and an indefinable difference of temperament.

The first problem was order in the Church of England. The legal Prayer Book was still that of 1662. Since the noises in the House of Commons in 1927 and 1928, the bishops sanctioned or winked their eyes at various modifications which were sensible and did not mind that they were illegal. For centuries the Church of England was liberal in its spirit and never pressed its clergy to conform to every rubric. But there was a difference between liberal freedom and anarchy.

State law could not provide discipline because it met resistance from consciences. Therefore church law must do it—that is, canon law. The last code of canon law, still nominally in force, was made just after the death of Queen Elizabeth I Tudor. Some of these canons were still observed (what to wear when conducting morning prayer) and some were long obsolete (rules about clergy nightcaps or yellow stockings on their legs).

It therefore occurred to the canon lawyers—a rarefied group of experts—that Church law, framed by the Church organs and then approved by the sovereign, could achieve the canons which would bind consciences. Archbishop Fisher accepted the argument and became the enthusiastic leader of the new movement. The work was hard; hard to frame, hard to get through committees, hard to get accepted. No archbishop but Fisher would have had the administrative ability or the tenacity to achieve the end.

During the discussions Ramsey grew uneasy. He had in his background two things which were missing from Fisher's background. He was a Free Churchman by origin, likely to suspect religion by law. And during his dark night of the soul while he was at Cuddesdon, part of the darkness was the behaviour of the House of Commons. Thus he had an inherent antipathy to the idea that law, even Church law, canon law, could achieve anything that was good for the Church. It should be an axiom, he thought, that the fewer the rules the better. He may have remembered St Mary's Tyne Dock, where he freely sanctioned certain things that were illegal because the parish church council wanted them for purposes of devotion. He disliked the whole idea of tidying up worship. Not that he liked anarchy. But he saw the prayers of the Church as a living and fruitful tradition which threw up new ideas, some on reflection wrong or offending and to be rejected, others the seeds of devotion. He had an inner contradiction which rose out of his background. He wanted order in the Church. But he could hardly bear the idea of law as an instrument for telling people how to pray.

This difference between the two archbishops was illustrated over the memorial requiem in York minster for Lord Halifax. As the son of a stalwart Anglo-Catholic Halifax loved the form of the first English Prayer Book, that of 1549 under King Edward VI. Naturally this order, which Halifax had in his little church, was appropriate for his requiem. But it was illegal. An order which was quietly used in some parish churches round the country without offence looked different when used on what was a national occasion with a national congregation. So Fisher knew. But Ramsey, who had come to love Halifax, wanted what Halifax wanted; in such a case, in his view, the law does not care about trivialities. Fisher objected that an Archbishop of York ought not to encourage illegality by being present at the requiem; and, painfully for himself, felt under a duty of conscience not to attend the memorial service. Nothing was going to stop Ramsey attending the memorial service for a close friend, whether it was legal or illegal.

He had a feeling that the Archbishop of Canterbury was now too powerful in the Church; that he and the other bishops were more like sheep as they sat saying yes to what Canterbury suggested.[6]

Ramsey afterwards felt that he was partly to blame that he and Fisher were not closer together. He never lost the early sense of a gulf in age, and experience, and speed of mind. He never quite got over the sense of being a boy in the presence of an adult. Fisher called him Michael, Ramsey did not yet dare to call Fisher Geoffrey. Some things he longed to talk about—he agonized over the Christians' attitude to nuclear bombs and it grieved him that Fisher did not agonize. He admired so many qualities in Fisher: the shrewdness about people, the grasp of practical problems, the ability to work very long hours, the patience under abuse from the press, the humility which went with a cocksureness that was not arrogance. And yet, despite all this, the Archbishop of York was not comfortable with the Archbishop of Canterbury except in the moments when the two powerful senses of humour coincided in laughter.

In these differences there was nothing unusual. It is orthodox doctrine that the Archbishop of York ought not to hold exactly the same opinions as the Archbishop of Canterbury. The Queen obeyed this doctrine in the choice of Ramsey for the see of York. But now, for the first time in English history, a set of circumstances existed which tested, whether this doctrine is always workable. The test came over the choice of a new Archbishop of Canterbury.

In former days this emotional moment could not arise because archbishops had little say in the choice of bishops and no say at all in the choice of their successor. But the sovereigns from Queen Victoria onwards turned consultations with the archbishop into a constitutional convention; so that now the Archbishop of Canterbury had the principal say in the choice of bishops and had a right to be consulted on the choice of his own successor; or, if he had not a constitutional right, at least he had every right to proffer advice to the prime minister whether the prime minister asked for it or not. Harold Macmillan, prime minister since 1957 and an Anglican wanting to do the best for the Church, was sure to ask Fisher for his advice and would have felt scandalous if he had not.

Fisher determined to resign from early in 1961. He was 74 that coming April and felt that he was tired mentally. And he *was* tired mentally, for once he addressed a bishops' meeting for a whole hour without stopping. By the convention in force he had the duty of suggesting the name of a successor. The biggest man in sight was the Archbishop of York. Yet the last three years made Fisher doubt whether Ramsey was possible—because of his Catholic restraint on reunion schemes and his suspicion of the ecumenical movement, because of his willingness for wide Catholic liberties in the way of worship, and because of his attitude to law. A glory of the Church of England was its comprehensiveness. It had never yet had as its leader someone who represented one of the more extreme parties in the Church—never at least since the days of Archbishop Laud which ended in the archbishop's head being cut off. Was it conscientiously possible, in such circumstances, for the Archbishop of Canterbury to recommend to the prime minister that the Archbishop of York should succeed him?

3. ELECTION TO CANTERBURY

Ramsey was told by Fisher that he intended to resign. He asked himself whether Fisher would recommend him to the Crown as his successor. He thought it possible that he would and probable that he would not. He asked himself, who else? The Bishop of Peterborough, Stopford, was an excellent administrator. The Bishop of Bradford, Coggan, was an evangelical with a quality then rare among evangelical leaders, namely learning, and was a likeable person who made himself respected by good sense at bishops' meetings. Ramsey narrowed his private short-list to three: Stopford, Coggan, Ramsey. For the first time since he was a professor at Cambridge, he began to hope, though with modesty, that he might be chosen for the work. If one is partly responsible already for the general policy of a Church or for anything else, it is better to be more responsible.

It puzzled him into the New Year of 1961 that no one asked his opinion. Five years before, Fisher drew him into the argument. This silence was marked. He assumed that this could only be because he was one of the possibles.

Without Ramsey's knowledge, Fisher came to the decision that he could not want Ramsey to succeed him, for reasons given above. He pressed Harold Macmillan not to recommend to the Queen that the choice should fall upon Ramsey. He did not think that Ramsey would be interested in the load of administration which he would have to carry. He said to one of his chaplains that Ramsey spent too much time theologizing up in York instead of tackling problems practically. He thought aspects of the Anglo-Catholic movement had danger; and that though Ramsey was not a danger, he would have such sympathy with them as not to be vigilant. He threw before the prime minister other names—Coggan, Stopford, and some more.

Harold Macmillan was perturbed. No prime minister before him had faced this exact situation. He found himself with the duty of helping to make a vital decision for the Church of England at a moment in its destiny. Like the rest of the world he could see that one possible successor was larger in stature than the others. His personal religious feelings would not make him doubt Ramsey, for he owed something in his private religion to that tradition of the Oxford Movement which Ramsey represented.

Early in his time as prime minister he asked Ramsey to come down from York so that they could meet. They talked in the Cabinet Room at No. 10 Downing Street. Ramsey, formerly put off by Eden's drawl, was at first put off by Macmillan's blear-eyed appearance and puffy eyes. 'To start with I really thought that he was asleep.' But then they talked about the North, of Stockton and Teesside, and Macmillan enquired with a warmth of feeling which Ramsey found impressive. And at one point in the conversation they touched on the kind of people who ought to become bishops. Macmillan was very frank about his personal preference. 'He discoursed about his understanding of the Church and he said that we had to hold the high and the low together but for his part his sympathies were with the high. He added that while the evangelicals had their part in the Church he did not think that on the whole they had the qualities suitable for being bishops.'

History knows a cynical law: that in all lands politicians dislike ecclesiastics who interfere and therefore, when influencing who is to be a new bishop, prefer not to have bishops too practical and too effective; and a respectable way of having ineffective bishops, the only respectable way, is to have otherworldly bishops, who live to God and spend much time in prayer and are not well informed on matters of this world.

Those who talked to Harold Macmillan at this time were sure that this cold politicking did not enter his head; that he was sincere and only wanted to do the best that he could for the Church. The kind of clergyman with whom Macmillan felt kinship was a person of spirituality and otherworldliness, not the person who was a born administrator or Church politician. Therefore he felt a rapport with Ramsey. That Fisher said that Ramsey was too Catholic would not disturb Macmillan; and that Fisher said Ramsey was not an administrator would leave Macmillan unmoved.

Yet a lay statesman ought not in such a matter to trample upon the opinions of his Church advisers. England was no longer in the days of Lloyd George or Palmerston. And the only Church adviser with a constitutional right to speak thought that he would be wrong to tell the Queen the name of the person whom his instincts told him to be the right person. There is evidence of Macmillan's perturbation of mind at this predicament.

He started by going to unofficial advisers and seeing whether they agreed with his official adviser. He interviewed, one by one, some of the other names put forward by Fisher, to see what they were like in comparison with Ramsey whom he knew already. He summoned the Dean of Westminster, Eric Abbott, to Downing Street. We do not know what Eric Abbott said but he was Ramsey's second superior at Lincoln Theological College and then his best man at the wedding. Macmillan talked to Sir Henry Willink, the Master of Magdalene. Perhaps the prime minister expected that Willink would push for a Magdalene man but he did not get a firm line out of him. Willink as a lawyer had a lot to do with the administration of the Church and saw the argument that an archbishop must be able to bear a load of administration. Macmillan consulted the Queen, who knew and liked both Ramsey and Coggan. He also took the trouble to buy and read a new book of theology which Ramsey at that moment published; an account of the development of English religious thought from the late Victorian age to the age of William Temple—*From Gore to Temple*. It is hard to imagine Lloyd George or Churchill, Disraeli or Palmerston, reading the rather obscure books which some prelate wrote about religion. *From Gore to Temple* is not an easy read for the layman. It is a study of Liberal Catholic thought in English religion. It has good things about Gore, about Hoskyns, about Temple. It mentions Bethune-Baker six times in each case with the object of dissent and in one case to imply that his opinions were obsolete. We are not aware that Macmillan had ever heard of Bethune-Baker. We do not expect that he perused every word of the book. Nevertheless we know that he liked it.

From what he was told by the Queen, by his unofficial advisers like the Dean of Westminster, and from his own conviction, Macmillan was sure that he must recommend Ramsey to the Queen. He knew that this would disturb Archbishop Fisher, which he did not wish to do. He hoped to show his respect for Fisher's advice by simultaneously recommending Donald Coggan for the see of York. He knew that he could be accused of acting like some less satisfactory prime ministers in this constitutional field, that is, choosing an archbishop of his own lay power without the approval of the Church; and he disliked that situation. But he felt that he could do no other.

Fisher announced his retirement to the Convocation of Canterbury on 17 January 1961. Ramsey, who knew the announcement was coming, delivered a public tribute to Fisher in the York Convocation. On the evening of 17 January Harold Macmillan telephoned his offer to recommend Ramsey to the Queen for Canterbury. He apologized for this method of enquiry. He asked Ramsey to telephone an answer, next morning. He said that if Ramsey accepted he had it in mind to recommend Donald Coggan for the see of York.

'How should I shirk?' Ramsey asked himself. He telephoned next morning and said Yes. Macmillan asked if he were willing for Coggan at York and he said Yes. Ramsey was sure that this was a first in history; the settlement of the choice of an Archbishop of Canterbury by telephone. All the courtesies were then observed by letter.

Macmillan made two mistakes of protocol. The Queen was about to go abroad for several weeks. Therefore this all had to be settled before Friday. This made the country talk of breathless haste. The Church likes time to say its prayers. It preferred to be allowed to say some prayers for the Queen, the prime minister, and everyone else concerned with the choice, before they reached their conclusion. Ramsey pointed this out to Macmillan in the famous telephone conversation and was overruled because of the Queen's movements. Not all the members of the Church welcomed the instantaneousness of resignation and appointment. There were protests. Some of the protests came from people who were afraid of Ramsey at Canterbury. Some came from people who longed to have Ramsey at Canterbury.

The second mistake was more technical and more secret. Without realizing it Macmillan trespassed on the modern constitutional convention. He asked the Queen to appoint an Archbishop of York without first asking the Archbishop of Canterbury. He got the sanction of Ramsey, which was important because Ramsey and Coggan would have to work together. The doctrine of dissimilarity was being observed. As Fisher pressed Coggan for Canterbury he could not object to Coggan going to the see of York. But technically, it was a breach of convention. Fisher was disturbed by it. He thought it retrograde constitutionally. He made his displeasure plain to the prime minister. London was coming vacant and London was a more important see than York and Coggan ought to go there. Thus Archbishop Fisher had two reasons for not being pleased with the prime minister. But this question was quickly resolved when it was discovered that Coggan much preferred moving to York and not London.

Macmillan said to Ramsey, 'Fisher doesn't seem to approve of you.' Ramsey defended him. 'Fisher', he said, 'was my headmaster and he has known all my deficiencies for a long time.' 'Well', said Macmillan, 'he is not going to be *my* headmaster.' Later Macmillan was reputed to have defended his decision in a sentence which is likely to be authentic because it has the Macmillan ring: 'I thought we had had enough of Martha and it was time for some Mary.'

Fisher wrote a kind letter to Ramsey, who found that in the circumstances it showed a generous spirit. 'You will add great distinction to the office in ways to which I could not aspire; but I fear you will find a great deal of the work here work which does not really interest you.' He warned Ramsey of the burden of administration and how he would need advisers.

Those who are interested in the affairs of Church and State will observe that, at two of the three crossroads of Ramsey's life, it was the State authority which secured the result. The State winched him out of the professorial chair when the ecclesiastical authority was lukewarm. The State made him the ecclesiastical head of the Church of England by trampling on the opinions of the relevant ecclesiastical authority. Thus was made an archbishop who did more than any Archbishop of Canterbury since Stephen Langton of Magna Carta to make the Church more free in its relation to the State.

In May 1961 a girl to whom Archbishop Fisher allowed a flat in Lambeth Tower when she and a husband were desperate for a place to live walked her pram round the courtyard, and observed the two archbishops also circling the courtyard and deep in conversation. She took it for granted that they talked about 'the handover'. She recorded her description. 'It was like a cock-sparrow hopping about by the side of a dinosaur. The new and younger archbishop looked twenty years older than the older archbishop.'

In June 1961 Michael Ramsey was enthroned Archbishop in Canterbury Cathedral. 'It is a macabre thought', wrote Monica Furlong in the *Spectator* (30 June), 'that if the Canterbury Special had crashed last Tuesday morning it would have wiped out at one go practically the whole of the English episcopate together with numerous foreign archbishops and bishops, most of the Orthodox patriarchs, the leaders of the Lutheran Churches in half a dozen countries of Europe and the heads of our own Free Churches.' In the cathedral she observed the new archbishop moving among the strange costumes, the rosary with purple tassles and red beads the size of pigeons' eggs, and the purple velvet fez. She expected him to keep looking over his shoulder to make sure that all the fuss was not intended for the man behind. She was moved by his address: not so much by the declaration of the reformed and Catholic nature of the Church of England, nor by his condemnation of racialism, nor by his challenge to the State to give the Church more liberty to follow its vocation in worship; but by his gratitude at the growing longing within the Church for a deeper life of prayer.

PART 2

BRITAIN AND THE
MORAL LAW

5

The Use of Time

Lambeth Palace was the home of the Archbishops of Canterbury from the end of the twelfth century. The chapel and the crypt built soon afterwards are still part of the house. The gateway was built by Cardinal Morton in 1490, and Sir Thomas More used to live there when he was young. The great hall, now the main room of the library, was built after the restoration of Charles II, for the house was used as a prison under the Commonwealth after Archbishop Laud was beheaded. By the end of the seventeenth century Lambeth House was beginning to be called a Palace. After she came to Lambeth, Joan Ramsey lamented the name. She liked people to drop in and thought dropping into a Palace was harder. She put her small desk, originally in the little house at Cambridge, into the large drawing-room and still worked at it. That is, the Ramseys, unlike the Fishers and Coggans, lived downstairs in the state rooms. She did not like to retire to what she called the aspidistra. She prided herself on being able to turn back the big room, after some state occasion, into a home within five minutes. She did not like the house so much as Auckland Castle or Bishopthorpe but came after a few years to approve of it as a plain but kindly friend. The passages of the kitchen quarters were so spacious that she once saw one of the staff ride a bicycle down one of them. They had a hole in the wall to put their personal letters down a chute but sometimes the letters got stuck halfway down the chute and then they rootled about with a stick. Joan Ramsey's heart never quite came South. Late in Ramsey's primacy a Durham diocesan pilgrimage came to a service in Canterbury cathedral; and Joan was so moved by this that she burst into the vestry at the end of the service and said, 'I hate the South' and had to be comforted by her vestured husband.

   The state rooms into which they moved were unwelcoming and cold. It took the decorative skills of Joan and John Andrew the chaplain several years before they felt hospitable. At first hens clucked outside the window. One end of the Palace was a hostel for visitors; and thirty or forty people might make a noise outside the study just when the archbishop wanted to think, and he usually wanted to think; or he might step out into the corridor and meet a stranger in his shirt sleeves and braces looking at the portraits. This was not the fault of the Church Commissioners who wanted the hostel closed because it lost them money. Ramsey asked that it be kept open because it was valued—a very ascetic act on his part. Gradually the rooms were needed for other purposes, and finally the hostel closed. But no one must think that because the archbishop dwelt in a Palace he was a sybarite. Not since his curacy at Liverpool had he lived so uncomfortably—at first.

He was the hundredth archbishop since St Augustine came from Pope Gregory the Great to Canterbury in AD 597. With his feeling for history and *genius loci*, the past of Lambeth mattered to him; and he could think about Dunstan teaching the faith to the Anglo-Saxons or St Anselm framing a philosophy for England or Cranmer writing his liturgies or William Temple 'still remembered as a prophet'. He sent off the portrait of the first Archbishop of Canterbury of Queen Elizabeth I, Matthew Parker, to be cleaned; and when it went it was cleanshaven and when it came back it had a moustache. He would remind himself that the real leaders of English religious thought and revival were never archbishops but were always the simple priests, like a Wesley or a Keble or a Maurice. He would remind himself how it was important that he should not identify too closely the institution of which he was the leader with the cause of Christianity, or run the risk that he would think, the more power to the Church, the better for society and for the cause of God. He was once asked whether someone who exercised power in a Church suffered damage to his spiritual life. He replied simply, 'God keep me from that kind of damage.'

2. THE LAMBETH ADMINISTRATION

In Convocation and Church Assembly people were interested in whether he would be a good chairman. He did not talk much. Sometimes they would have liked him to intervene more. When he talked he usually talked cogently. He liked people to have their say and preferred going to sleep to interrupting them. But he always understood the essence of the business and where the meeting was going. He said of the Church Assembly: 'It was quite remarkable how I could spend a whole morning in the chair there not knowing what anyone was talking about; and yet I would wake up and ask the right man to speak—the thing never collapsed despite this total inattention.' He found it a vast relief when a system of rotating chairmen started and the archbishop did not always have to preside.

He knew he was an academic and student of the New Testament, and that this was what he could contribute. He was bored by administration, except in vital things like the choice of bishops. He took the chair at the Church Assembly but was not only bored by its proceedings, he showed his boredom. During other people's speeches he could be seen taking notes; and the speaker might be gratified that the archbishop was following the argument so profitably. It was more likely that he was writing down the names of all the archbishops of Canterbury backwards from now to St Augustine, or all the prime ministers backwards from now to the first prime minister, as a form of doodling. It was alleged that after the Lambeth Conference of 1968 several such lists were found. The free churchman Kenneth Greet, who worked with him on the British Council of Churches and became a close friend, said that he was a chairman with an engaging disregard of the simple duties of chairmanship. Greet remembered an arid session of the British Council of Churches when the speakers went on being boring but 'the only sign that the chair was still occupied was the occasional flutter of a pale hand above a large reading-desk', behind which Ramsey could be detected scribbling on scraps of paper with a ball-point pen and with a faraway look on his face.[1] These bits of paper were not only doodling for it is proved that a letter which arrived to congratulate the mother of a newborn baby was written while he was in the chair at a meeting of Convocation. And yet, when in 1973 he tried to give up the chair of the British Council of Churches and said that it ought not to be assumed that the see of Canterbury had a right to it, everyone was determined that he should not give up the chair.

The correspondence coming into Lambeth was bulky. It came to about fifty letters a day in the post-bag. The public at large had an inflated portrait of what an archbishop can do, and imagined that he stalked the corridors of power. He was a target for cranks to protest or prophesy. There was a lady in Beirut who wished Prince Charles to marry one of her four daughters and fancied Ramsey to be the best person to arrange this. There was concern over a lady the other side of the river from Lambeth who pushed a pram with three cats in it and two dogs on leads, and it was imagined that Ramsey was the best person to cope. There was a lady anxious about the hair style of trendy curates and she thought that Ramsey was the person to see that they had nicely

[1] Greet in C. Martin (ed.), *The Great Christian Centuries to Come* (1974), 43–4.

groomed hair but she did not want their hair cropped. A college in Kansas wrote to say that they were doing research into satanic study in their Problems of Democracy class and to ask whether his administration had 'developed a policy towards Satanism'. Of the fifty daily letters 5 per cent were insane and needed no answer and were kept for a year just in case of repercussions and Ramsey would never see them unless his staff wished to amuse him. (But occasionally a crank letter would get past the staff because Ramsey would pick such a letter out of the basket at breakfast—for example one morning he picked a letter, opened it, blushed, and put it quickly back saying, 'I don't think that is of *much* value as it begins "You lying bastard"'. He was in no way outraged.) An odd crank or two afflicted him in person. An ancient Indian lady with a frock-coated Indian priest haunted the portals of the Church Assembly and tried to get at him unexpectedly and more than once he had to be smuggled out of a side-door to avoid her importunities.

Hugh Whitworth, who had the job of reading these letters, described the popular impression of the Archbishop of Canterbury as a cross between a Universal Aunt and a Court of Appeal with universal jurisdiction. Sometimes he would be asked to give a ruling on an unusual question: for example, in the marriage service the bridegroom must put the ring on the fourth finger of the left hand of the bride, what is he to do if that finger is missing? People who investigated witchcraft in Britain and discovered evidence of licking red-hot bars or of burning joss sticks or of a coven in Notting Hill thought that Ramsey was just the man to stop it all. But amid the bundles of eccentricity or triviality would be many serious enquiries or pleas which he had to attend to personally. Some people did not like a reply from the archbishop's staff officer or chaplain instead of the archbishop. One wrote grumblingly, 'I wrote to the engine-driver and the only reply I got was a wipe from the oily rag.' Nothing offended Ramsey more than the suggestion from some correspondent that he was too elevated to cope with a letter from an ordinary person. 'The greater part of my time as a Christian pastor is spent in helping ordinary people.'

He always tried to give a personal answer to the young—the school-girl, or the undergraduate, or the boy at school—and in this he counted the letters of parents asking for advice about their children. Some of the letters of this sort which he wrote are enchanting.

Many of the letters wished him to denounce some abuse or injustice in the world. Naturally he was selective in such denunciations. When he was so moved personally that he did denounce, he always received a flood of letters reviling him for interfering in politics.

The letters from one correspondent were painful to him. Archbishop

Fisher now lived in Dorset and continued to write many letters. The most important of these letters went to his successor. Fisher continued to think of Ramsey as his pupil who needed correcting. Because of boyhood Ramsey could not treat these letters serenely. The secretaries and chaplains found that on a morning when one of these letters arrived he so worried that they could not get decisions out of him on the rest of the day's post. They agonized with him. Sometimes they stole the letter so that after a time he forgot it. Later, as the letters kept coming, he stopped answering them. Fisher complained formally to the Standing Committee of the General Synod that he was not treated well by the Archbishop of Canterbury. A committee of the Synod met Fisher at the Goring Hotel in London and persuaded him to write a memorandum about the issues on which he thought it needful to speak. The memorandum was submitted to the committee, which received it, and the letters flowed thenceforth to another destination.

Fisher came to stay at Lambeth to celebrate his eightieth birthday. After he died Ramsey healed the sore place with two noble utterances, one in Canterbury on the day of the funeral, and the other in the House of Lords.[2] He spoke of his affection for Fisher, a man in the top class of administrators in any profession, a reformer who travelled across the seas and helped his scattered Church to be a family; his sternness at times and yet his lack of pomposity and his ability to laugh at himself; his kindness and the simplicity of his faith.

The responsibility was world-wide, the staff which served him was small. And there was a problem which was nothing to do with the size of the staff. Harold Macmillan diagnosed that what the Church now needed was a Mary to replace a Martha, a quiet contemplative instead of a busy servant of the people. A lot of those who knew about these things agreed with him. But the result is, we take Mary, who understands prayer, and put her into the job of Martha, and make her willy-nilly do the household chores. Church and Nation took a man with little experience of administration, and a modest reputation as a manager, and with a private conviction that administration was not his true vocation, and put him into a post which, whether religious people liked it or not, was one of the big administrative seats in the land. The result might be very good but on the way to being good it could not fail to produce friction; as the people who were used to being helped by Martha discovered that her successor did not know how to cope and might not be interested and might think some of what Martha did trivial in the perspective of what mattered.

---

[2] *Canterbury Pilgrim*, 174–5; Hansard, Lords, 18 Sep. 1972, col. 712.

Fisher was jolly with the staff, at first they desponded at the silences of Fisher's successor.[3] They found that instead of being told what to do they needed to sense what the archbishop wanted them to do—they discovered from his manner, or his voice, or the fidgeting of his fingers. One of them once said to him outright, 'The Archbishop of Canterbury never says what he wants and is always angry if he does not get it', and this utterance provoked a moment of glare and then a vast laugh, and a repeating of the saying to other people the rest of the day. Another said that working closely with him was to be reminded more and more of a deep ocean with frequent storms on the surface and an immense depth of stillness and strength underneath. These storms rarely took the form of expressed anger. Yet they knew when he was upset. One of the symptoms was silence, or fewer and fewer words. But he never minded in the least if his secretaries took it upon themselves to doubt what he dictated or to suggest an improvement. He used to complain to his secretary Barbara Lepper that she 'nagged' at him but the word *nag* was a joke and had nothing in it that was unkind. The staff had to talk to him. He hated typewritten memoranda. Sometimes he tore them up. He hated the telephone though he used it when necessary. He hardly ever needed to ask for a file, he knew the background of a case without looking it up. He hated producing texts beforehand because he did not like to speak from a full text and preferred to speak from notes; and for important occasions the secretaries had to bully him to give them a text where the press had to have it beforehand.

His power of dictation astonished the secretaries. He could dictate a long letter on a very complicated subject, like revision of the Prayer Book, and never need to alter a word before he signed it. Once he dictated seventy letters continuously and did not seem to be tired at the end. He never worked at a desk. He always sat on an armchair in his study to the left of the chimney-piece. He sat with a lap-board on his knee and a stand by the side full of letters and papers. The desk which he never used was piled high with documents. The staff sometimes found it difficult to get his attention. They needed a ruling on the answer to a letter and found that his mind was thinking about something quite different, it might be of God, and somehow they had to tug

---

[3] The staff: he inherited from Fisher Robert Beloe as lay chief of staff and Priscilla Lethbridge as head of the little team of secretaries. The senior chaplain was a clerical chief of staff. The domestic chaplain managed travel and matters touching the diocese at Canterbury. In 1966 Barbara Lepper succeeded Priscilla Lethbridge, in 1969 Hugh Whitworth from the civil service succeeded Beloe. Domestic chaplains in succession: John Andrew (he started in York), Leonard Tyzack, David Sparrow, Philip Norwood, John Kirkham. Senior chaplains in succession: Noel Kennaby, Michael Nott (1964), John Andrew (1965), Geoffrey Tiarks, who also became Bishop of Maidstone.

him earthward to think about Joanna Southcott's Box. On the other hand if they brought to him something which concerned him much, they found him two jumps ahead in the argument. He seized the important-looking letters from the basket at breakfast and took them away. Barbara Lepper, his secretary, was known to rummage around in the waste-paper basket, even in his presence, piecing together the fragments of a letter which he had torn as not worth keeping. Occasionally they found in the pocket of his cassock some letter which they wanted. This made problems for filing. One snag was that he was conscious of his wickedness and enjoyed it. 'I was very scandalous in sin', he said looking back. 'If a letter was very interesting to me I used to pinch it for my private collection and not let it go into the boxes . . . And I often used to write letters with my own hand, so that the staff could not know what I said.' This pleased the correspondent but not the staff. The leaders of the machinery at Lambeth, like Tiarks and Beloe and Whitworth and Lepper, had to be effective to make the machine run with harmony. From his staff he expected a total commitment and was hardly aware that they needed a home life, or holidays.

They needed to get at him in the middle of the morning. In the earlier part of the morning he liked to continue the religious meditation of his time before breakfast and then to consider, before the secretaries came, the more important letters. At the end of the morning he liked to disappear into the library to read for half an hour. No modern archbishop, perhaps no archbishop ever, made such goodly use of his noble library.

He was curiously bad, at times, with his staff. One of his close friends who worked with him said that he was 'hopeless at man-management'; and that in the inability to organize a team of humans he sometimes gave the impression of being ungrateful. Two of the witnesses even use the word 'callous' to describe the impression which he sometimes gave of ingratitude towards the staff. It was hard for them to realize that he did not think words important in personal relationships. He assumed that they knew him to be grateful and did not need to be told.

More than one critic of Ramsey said in print that a big fault was failure of judgement in choosing staff. A cold examination of the facts does not bear this out. A team which included Whitworth as lay chief of staff, Barbara Lepper as secretary, a bishop chief-of-staff like Tiarks, a succession of chaplains which included for example Andrew and Norwood and Kirkham, cannot be thought to lack judgement in choice of people. The opinion that he was poor at choosing rested upon headlines. There were newspaper troubles about people who were not part of his immediate staff—the housekeeper at the hostel started receiving instruction, with her husband who was a clergyman, to become Roman Catholic (false headline: Archbishop's Chaplain joins Rome); and a lay officer was believed to have printed articles holding out the possibility of sex between homosexuals. His staff told him that he must assent to the dismissal of the officer, which he did with reluctance (headlines in all sorts of papers and cartoons, Primate in Sex Magazine Row etc.). Second, there was the failure of everyone at first to realize that if you had a Mary rather than a Martha running things, you must provide a bishop to deal with some of the Martha-chores and that a priest-chaplain was not senior enough to cope with the problems of the other bishops. This difficulty was met when Tiarks became suffragan Bishop of Maidstone. Third, people had the illusion that because his eyes were fixed on heaven he failed to notice how men and women behaved.

Yet there is something more in this charge against him. He said afterwards of his domestic chaplain David Sparrow: 'He was not a good domestic chaplain. Administration was not his line. But he was a lovely man to have about. That was the way I liked it. I preferred to have as my domestic chaplain someone to whom you could talk irrelevances.'

He was not good at rebuking where a rebuke was necessary, if the culprit was his friend. But on rare occasions he could be very severe. The proprietor and editor of the magazine *Time* were shown into the study. The Vietnam war was raging. One of the two Americans made a jingoistic utterance about the war. Ramsey's face went red. He said that he was outraged by the remark which showed no compassion for the suffering innocents of that land, and he showed them the door; leaving the chaplain to cope with two self-important men humiliated.

Barbara Lepper, the secretary who worked most closely with him for longest, confessed that he was difficult to work for. The unusual nature of his method of management or non-management, could lead to exasperation among the staff. And yet, she found him fascinating, complex, and altogether big—part mystic, part genius, part eccentric.

The shyness was such as to cause secret compassion among the secretaries. They admired him because he was able to do so much, and achieve so much with individuals, in the face of this handicap. They could feel him getting tense before it was time to have an interview. They found that in Church Assembly week, where he needed to be in public and to meet many people, they felt always the same tension.

He chose good staff. But he doubted his ability to choose staff. He once compared himself with his predecessors in this matter. He said of the archbishops as judges of character: 'Cosmo [= Lang] was flawless; Temple was hopeless; Fisher was superb; I am erratic.'

In private interviews at Lambeth he was superlative with four kinds of suppliant; theologians, if they were good theologians; clergy troubled about their work, or their vocation, or their loss of faith, and in need of guidance; individual lay people troubled about their faith or absence of faith; and young people. He liked to see students. Even when they were not expected and what they wanted sounded neither urgent nor important, he insisted that they be shown in, and would give them time, and never pontificated but listened to what they had to say. His kinship with such young visitors was warming to see. Some observers thought that his obvious sense of affection might come in part because he had no child of his own. And it was so, that after they were both reconciled to having no children, they thought of young people as a special vocation.

The bishops found him a big man, as a mind, as a personality, as a religious man. But they did not think that he understood the nitty-gritty of the Church. The older among them were accustomed to Fisher's grasp of detail. One of the important measures going through under Ramsey's chairmanship was a measure to reorganize the parish system but they were clear that he never fully understood what it was about. They did not find him specially interested in ecclesiastical, as distinct from religious, affairs. Because Ramsey was not a team-player, his relationship to bishops could make them feel as though he was not interested in what they did. Eric Treacy, the train-spotting Bishop of Wakefield, is known to have preferred both Fisher and Coggan to Ramsey in the function of archbishop; even though Treacy came, not quickly, to revere Ramsey as a man. Although Ramsey's judgement on choosing bishops was excellent, his attitude to them could be critical; and there are moments when it is possible to wonder whether the old nonconformist deep in his personality affected his attitudes to bishops —they are necessary to the Church but, as it were, they ought to be suspected.

His relationship was much closer to bishops whom he consecrated personally, or whom he knew beforehand as parish priests in his own dioceses. They and their families always stayed at Lambeth Palace the night before the consecration and they always found this stay warm and affectionate. He usually told them of the *joy* in a bishop's life and work. He usually told them to make sure not to fill their time too fully so that they could find space for the unforeseen demand, and because there needed to be quietness somewhere in their lives.

Naturally the Church Commissioners had mixed feelings about him. They were in charge of the resources of the Church and worried about money and the underpaid curate and the sick clergy-pensioners and wanted an archbishop who took an interest in their work. He took a conscious decision that this was not the best use of his time. His experience in Durham and York forced him to ask the question, how can someone who is determined to keep time for study and reading and thought and teaching also find time for the pastoral care of a diocese as well as the time to take part in national affairs? He answered his own question: 'survival is only possible if there is a rigorous discipline in excluding things which do not matter and limiting painfully the things that do.' In his opinion the details of the Church Commissioners' work came into this last category. But he minded who the Church Estates Commissioners were, thanked them warmly when they retired for all that they had done for the Church, and took trouble to find a right person to succeed to the office. In 1972 he appointed the first woman ever to hold that office, (Dame) Betty Ridley.

The First Church Estates Commissioner, who is the head of the Church Commissioners, was then a tremendous tycoon, Lord Silsoe, of whom everyone was nervous. He always went straight to every point, brushed aside irrelevance, was nearly always right, was sure he was right even when he was wrong, and did not suffer fools gladly. Silsoe thought that clergymen could not understand high finance and about Archbishop Ramsey his judgement was correct. He commanded loyalty and rueful affection. Lord Silsoe discovered that the cat in the Old Palace at Canterbury was christened Silsoe.

Lord Silsoe had the idea that Lambeth Palace was not well used. He saw priceless acres in the middle of London, with a very large house in which a clergyman and his wife rattled. His plan was caricatured by the ribald as wanting to push Ramsey and his wife into a cosy little bungalow, suitable for the simple religious life, and then make money out of the site. This notion contradicted the philosophy of both the Ramseys. Ramsey did not think of size as grandeur, he thought it inconvenient. But they were both determined that 'state' visitors should be greeted not in formal rooms but into a home and they were glad that the better friendships between the Churches meant that many more visitors wanted to stay. Then Lord Silsoe suggested that the Church Commissioners themselves move their offices into the Lambeth Palace grounds. Ramsey won an easy victory over that bit of imperialism.

He did not worry about the detail of the Commissioners' work even though it was locally weighty, like the marriage of the parish of Lufton Parva to the parish of Weavertree, or the ruin of the vicarage of Gumbledown, or even the fate of the Bishop of London in a house with 82 rooms. But he cared about more than the choice of officers. He minded painfully when the committee refused to give the use of a redundant church to a reputable group of another faith. He minded when they decided to push Ian Ramsey, the Bishop of Durham, or his successor out of Auckland Castle and he made sure that the decision to push was reversed. Sometimes he tried to redraft circular letters to the clergy which he thought to sound hard or unkind. He was happy that bishops should stop calling their houses palaces or castles and thought it better if Lambeth Palace reverted to being Lambeth House; but he refused to apply this to Canterbury, where his sense of history was roused. He remembered how out of the Old Palace the martyr Becket walked to his death. And occasionally, if he were consulted, he produced a gem of drafting. They asked for his advice on whether they should invest in a firm which made contraceptive pills. He replied that he did not know the hazards, and wondered whether with so many possible investments it would be better to put the money into 'some concern which does not involve putting to me a question which I am inadequate to answer'.

He liked to go to universities. He always tried to accept an invitation to a university. He was a master at answering questions. It was the age of student rudeness and rowdiness, yet every time these occasions were successful. At the London School of Economics, where they were having a revolution, they gave him a rough time but he came out on top. At Manchester University he said that it was not the business of the taxpayer to provide contraceptive machines in university halls of residence and got some jeers but they still were fascinated to have him and gave him cheers. The ex-professor of divinity liked to be asked to give theological lectures and tried to make time to accept. Usually the question-time was more gripping than the lecture which preceded it. He could communicate a sense of excitement about the question, and a sense of enjoyment about the occasion. Such sessions of answering questions held large audiences spellbound.

What he liked least were the great State occasions. This did not apply when it was his duty to pay a tribute on behalf of the nation to someone just dead who deserved the nation's thanks—Kennedy, or Hammarskjöld, or Gandhi, or Princess Marina; and this saying thanks on behalf of the British people was happy even when he needed to choose his words with a little care, as after the deaths of Winston Churchill or Archbishop Fisher. He was happy at anyone's wedding and bestowed his affection on the pair and this applied just as much when the married couple were royal and the wedding very public. He thought of such a wedding as a family and not a State occasion. But where the State ritual had no gratitude in it, his scepticism about ceremonial made him uncomfortable. If the ritual was particularly pompous he could be heard muttering 'de dum de de doo, de dum de de dah', or humming 'Turn back O man . . .'. Monica Furlong watched him at his own enthronement, and said that he moved among the endless processions with a bewildered and abstracted air like a man who has strayed by some mistake into some thrilling and incomprehensible ceremony and finds to his amazement that he is the key figure. She talked of 'his regal but puzzled bearing like a lion who has turned vegetarian for philosophical reasons' (*Spectator*, 30 July 1961).

3. BROADCASTING

For a time the television worried Ramsey. His friends could see him sweating as he prepared. The early television appearances did not go over well to the public—the sing-song voice, the hesitation to find the right word, the touch of the academic. The wife of the head of one of the Cambridge colleges said, 'I can't believe in him as a real person. I can't believe that he means a word he says.' Experts in the medium held that his worst performance ever on television was his sermon at the consecration of Coventry Cathedral. It was described as 'rather like a sonic version of the Alps in silhouette'. But the BBC got him right from earlier days. From the time when he was a professor at Durham their private reports on his performance had perception. April 1949: 'Has a leaning to the pompous, but fortunately is aware of it. Provided this leaning does not run to excess I do not think it is a terrible crime in a man of his age and calling. His response to production is good, and he struck me as anxious to do a good job'; or again: 'Not the most effective speaker in the world to make presentable for the microphone but he was a considerable improvement on last time. He is a man with a most interesting mind . . .'. When he was early in his time as Archbishop of York, the private BBC comment was pointed:

He is a big man with probably the best mind in the Church of England and one of the best minds in the country, yet he can appear oddly foolish. He has a curious habit of grunting, nodding, and blinking while he is listening or thinking. I am sure this is now quite involuntary and sub-conscious and essential to the man—but it points to a puckishly humorous attitude to himself, which was once, I dare say, cultivated. He has always enjoyed being a man with a reputation, as he now enjoys being an archbishop, not because it ministers to his self-importance but because it really does make him laugh. So he is not a bit pompous . . . I believe him to be politically well-informed and if he were not a bishop (let alone archbishop) he would enjoy being more active politically—as a Liberal. But I think he will hedge on that subject now.

     . . . He strikes me as being more ready than the rest of his fellow-bishops to take risks with the Holy Spirit. He is not a bit of a moralist, legislator or rule-of-thumb disciplinarian. He really is sure of himself—a fruit of spirituality. Somehow you have got to get him rolling about in his chair and wagging his finger. Even at the cost of discomfiting engineers and cameramen. Allow him to wear a cassock whatever it looks like.

When the BBC felt the need of a heavyweight on a programme at that time, they turned to the Archbishop of York, though still conscious that there was a problem about his production. 'His hesitations can be edited out and he can be made to sound more fluent.'

Even as late as his last full year in the see of York the production men at the BBC were still trying to get him to use less 'homiletic' language —for example to say 'I' instead of 'we', and not to 'lapse' into Latin, and to watch out for signs of intellectual condescension. But after his first important broadcast on television as Archbishop of Canterbury in October 1961 the director of television, Kenneth Adam, wrote a warm personal letter: 'last night was splendidly successful, and a very marked improvement on the time you came to Lime Grove to talk with Archbishop Heenan, good though that was in its way.'[4]

Some of the lay nation got the erroneous impression that their new archbishop was a fuddy-duddy, or a funny old parson. A headmistress watched him at Churchill's funeral and deduced from his appalling appearance and 'sing-song voice' that he was 'an esoteric clergyman far out of touch with people'. When the row over Rhodesia was at its height, two Cambridge dons watched him on television and found him unimpressive—'like any old vicar—and with a parsonical voice—but this might be just the best line in the controversial circumstances'. The *Daily Mail* once said (2 October 1968) that his trouble was that 'he can splutter and falter his way through a question even when he knows exactly what he wants to say'. This is not the impression given by reading the transcripts of his answers to questions on radio or television. Therefore the appearance of hesitation was manner and not matter.

In October 1968—rather late, seven years after he took office—he took a crash course in the way to treat the television camera when being interviewed. Whether this helped cannot be determined. In his last years he was far more confident at his handling of the instrument. But probably that was due to familiarity with it.

It was a question whether the archbishop ought to accept invitations to appear on television. About his office was something sacred which did not go with overexposure to the media. In December 1966 he

---

[4] WHC., Ramsey 1946–62, 8 and 12 April 1949; and report from Manchester 9 December 1957 of 1 April 1957; September 1960. Cuddesdon taught ordinands to use *we* instead of *I* in a pulpit (avoid the egocentric) and did not mind occasional 'lapses' into Latin.

allowed himself to be interviewed by David Frost on the question whether Jesus existed. His answers could not have been better. The interview evidently helped a lot of people. But there were others who thought it a bad idea for the archbishop to be interviewed by David Frost, as though in some way it might lower the sacredness of his office. There was another danger, that conversations watched on television between two educated people were easy to misunderstand. Two old ladies of a village near Andover wrote a very sad letter because they had just seen the archbishop condoning the taking of drugs in an interview on television. They had understood the contrary of what he had said. Nevertheless, in moderation and in the modern age it was better to run whatever risks there were. And by about 1971 he was becoming a king on the medium. An interview of 1971 ('Chance to Meet', Cliff Michelmore presiding) was praised by the experts as a masterly performance. He knew the medium to be an opening to communicate the message which he wanted to put over to the world and did not mind if people said that the company which he kept was incongruous.

His willingness to be interviewed on television and radio had a side-benefit for the historian. Since he kept no diaries and records of his conversations were few, the BBC and ITV records of conversations made valuable evidence of direct speech. He was the first archbishop in English history for whom such evidence from television was fully available as transcript.

He had a philosophy of what television could do for religion. It ought, he thought, to be able to show Christianity as concerned with all of life and not with a particular religious department of life; not only by giving an ethical answer but by bringing onto the human scene something supernatural that alters the perspective of the soul. It ought to be able to show Christianity as something which causes people to think fearlessly and with integrity, and is not a stifling of thought. Then he thought there to be a particular danger in television—the television interview puts a premium on quick and clever and easy answers, and Christianity can never be understood by being merely clever.[5]

4. THE CANTERBURY DIOCESE

Every weekend he and Joan went to live at the Old Palace at Canterbury. This gave them the pleasure of the magnate who goes down to his country cottage to escape the noise and dirt of the city. But the pleasure

---

[5] Citations in Martin, *Great Christian Centuries*, pp. 104–5.

was more than this; for Ramsey was a diocesan bishop and when he went to Canterbury he felt that he went home, to be among the people who were specially entrusted to his care.

At first the rival pulls—between his diocese and the universal Church—troubled him. Roland Walls, on the way to Taizé, called on him in the study at Lambeth early in his time as archbishop. He said at once, 'Roland, before going into all your business just answer me a question about mine; have I to become a pope or just be a bishop of Canterbury?' Walls asked him why he asked. 'Because if you look over there on that table, you will find I'm now in the position of Pope Leo I—requests for counsel, decisions and my opinions on this and that. They come in from all quarters of the globe.' Walls said, 'Off the cuff, Father, I would recommend you to be Bishop of Canterbury'. 'Yes', said Ramsey 'that's my opinion too but it wasn't my predecessor's.'

This attitude could not survive the pressure of the business of all the Churches. But it remained an inner affection, and occasionally could be disconcerting. At a press luncheon in London a journalist sitting next to him said, 'Your Grace, with all the vast problems which face you as head of the whole Anglican Communion throughout the world, what concerns you most?' After a marked silence in which the eyebrows went up and down, Ramsey replied, 'I sometimes lie awake at night and wonder if I am acceptable to God.'

He loved to walk the streets of Canterbury and greet the people and work in the public library and read the local paper. His overcoat would be battered and his old clerical hat looked crammed on his head and he always carried a stick which he did not need. He liked to wander into the SPCK bookshop and incidentally discover how his own books were selling. (The manager sometimes took a few books off the pile to encourage him that all was well.) He liked to wander in the cathedral and chat with the visitors and even do a little guiding. He loved to preach the Easter message, very simply, in the cathedral; and to be with groups of young hikers who were pilgrims on the Pilgrims Way; and to join at a cathedral service with very handicapped people who praised God by shaking tambourines and bells and he rang his bell with as reverent a gusto as any. He was just as happy in a temporary modern heap as in a historic medieval church. He took his special pleasure in meeting ordination candidates, and entertaining the clergy to tea. The clergy liked to come but some of them did not quite know how to talk to him and he did not quite know how to talk to some of them. At parish functions he attended conscientiously but then did not know how to mix and stood apart looking lost; until he observed the young, and then he was among them, discussing what interested them and answering their questions.

The citizens voted him the freedom of the city. He was associated with the Canterbury Gardeners Society (though no one could call him a gardener) and the Canterbury Music Club (though no one could call him an eager musician) and the Canterbury Society. He was president of the Kent Association of Boys Clubs, and of the Kent Association of Change Ringers. He took an interest in and encouraged the new university of Kent at Canterbury and accepted office as one of the sponsors and was consulted about various matters of the foundation, including the name of the university (he preferred Canterbury University but Kent County Council took a big part and wanted the name of Kent to be preserved). He accepted the presidency of the Anselm Society there for the study of theology and religious studies, and tried to attend its meetings, and once had to be whisked out of a kitchen entrance to avoid a student demonstration with bowls of rice, and once, while another speaker bored the meeting, could be seen whiling away the time by counting his pound notes.

Mostly the weekend at Canterbury was a rest and half a retreat, with a good deal of reading or writing. In one quiet time at a Canterbury Christmas he wrote most of a book, published as *God, Christ and the World*. It was noticed as a special sign of his tiredness in the last two years of his time as archbishop that he began to lose interest in the running of the diocese of Canterbury.

When he arrived at Canterbury the dean was Dr Hewlett Johnson whose age was already 87 and whose affection for Stalin—it was never easy to revere Stalin but the dean managed it—produced a breach between Archbishop Fisher and dean. Ramsey pretended not to know of any breach and took it for granted that archbishop and dean were good friends and never commented on the dean's political ventures. Privately he felt incredulity that the dean at so advanced an age should wish to stay in office but he made no attempt to persuade him that it was time to retire. When the dean finally retired at the age of 89, Ramsey made sure that the new Dean of Canterbury was a quiet and uncontroversial man, Ian White-Thomson. Before the new dean even arrived, the archdeacon removed from above the door of the deanery a board three foot high with the notice in capitals, CHRISTIANS BAN NUCLEAR WEAPONS.

The man who was once so popular in little hill mining parishes in the county of Durham had not lost that art; but in the administration of the diocese there were complexities because he liked to think that he could do it and yet had not the time to do it properly. He undervalued the administrator's gift or necessity. The Bishop of Dover reported that at a staff meeting, where they were choosing between candidates for a parish, candidate A was reported to be an extremely efficient business-like priest who put the place in order and repaired the vicarage and left no debts and increased the stipend. Candidate B said his prayers and was hopeless over money and plant and absolutely no administrator. The archbishop made it clear to the meeting that he preferred the qualities of candidate B.

He was blessed with a memory for faces. He remembered names, and places, nicknames, names of children. He remembered to which saints most of the churches in the diocese were dedicated; and the names of the village pubs, and where they were; and quite a lot about the individual clergy. He often looked inattentive on expeditions but was observant.

This partly visual memory served him in good stead, for example in a pulpit if his notes went astray; and once he saved a calamity in Canterbury cathedral. Installing three new canons, he was told in the vestry that the legal papers were lost between London and Canterbury. Ramsey told the lawyer not to worry. He read out the complicated and wordy document from memory, as though he was reading out of his service sheet, and then handed the canons the service sheet as though it was the legal document.

Near the end of his time in office he asked himself in what ways the diocese had changed since the time when he became its bishop. He recorded much change, even during his thirteen years. The Church of England and the other Churches were far closer; that is, when he went to institute a new vicar to a parish, the ministers of the other denominations were now present. There was more shared worship, shared evangelism, even shared buildings.

Next, when he began everyone used versions of the 1662 Prayer Book. These were still used, but series 2 services were widely used and the series 3 services, which called God You, were growing common. He was glad about this because he thought that the services helped people to worship 'with reality and a new sense of participation' without losing the sense of reverence and mystery. But he wanted clergy to be considerate to the feelings of parishioners who valued the old 1662 rite.

Next, he noticed that he ordained fewer people; and that because of inflation money to pay stipends to those fewer people was harder to find. Therefore more parishes were in groups; more lay people helped with services. He expected therefore that in the future more lay people still would need to help and that there would be more use of priests who still worked in secular occupations. He also observed that work which was not ordinary parochial work had extended during his time—the industrial mission in Croydon and Kent, the Church's organizations for moral and social welfare. He was glad that the Canterbury diocese topped all the dioceses in the amount it contributed to Christian Aid and showed thus how it cared about the world.

He asked himself whether the fewer clergy whom he ordained were of a lower standard (he did not define that) and was confident that they were of as high a quality as ever.

He needed to think about the younger marriage of clergy. When he was young, bishops pressed ordinands and curates not to marry too young; partly because the pay of the curate was tiny and partly because they wanted the young priest to think of nothing but his vocation. The pill made the difference because it meant that young clergy or ordinands could marry without an expectation of babies at first and therefore the wife continued to work and the money was less of a problem. In 1971 the two archbishops agreed that the decision over engagement or marriage was the concern of the couple alone; but simultaneously they said that while many of the clergy are called to the married state and that blessings flow from this, the Church also needs some who find fulfilment in the unmarried state all their lives; and that candidates for ordination should be prepared to consider that as a possible vocation.

5. THE CHOICE OF BISHOPS

The Archbishop of Canterbury inherited a system of crown patronage. This system developed out of the system for choosing bishops during the earlier Middle Ages and had many centuries of prescription behind it. The axiom was that the leading churchmen were among the makers of public opinion in the State. Therefore their choice was a matter which concerned the State. The State could not choose anyone. It could only choose those whom the Church approved solemnly by ordaining them to the priesthood. And since a bishop needed to be consecrated by other bishops—three according to Catholic custom—the State could only nominate as a bishop someone whom other bishops would accept. But all over Christendom every State insisted on a right of control in some form. Sometimes it was the sole right to propose names; as, in England, the Crown insisted on the right to nominate a person for election by the dean and chapter and then consecration by other bishops; or it might be the right of veto, on political or other grounds, on names proposed by the Pope or a dean and chapter.

King Henry VIII, determined that no future Church leaders should challenge his religious policy, ensured that the deans and chapters were not troublesome; because the State chose the deans, and quite a few of the canons; and because the Appointments of Bishops Act of 1533 rendered a dean and chapter which failed to elect the crown's nominee, within twenty days after it received the name, liable to the penalties of the medieval Statute of Praemunire which could mean the confiscation of all their goods.

This statute of 1533 was still in force when Ramsey became Archbishop of Canterbury. Nevertheless, though deans and chapters were not likely to be troublesome, the possibility existed, if the Crown suggested an unworthy name, that their consciences would tell them to risk the confiscation of all their goods and so they would fail to elect. A prime minister like Gladstone was sure that the existence of the election by dean and chapter was a useful check on the Crown that it should seek to choose good men.

But the function of the dean and chapter was more a symbol than a possible way of reforming the system. The system of State nomination continued to exist; first because it had the best historic right of any system to exist; secondly because it worked on the whole well, that is, the State chose good men whom the Church liked to have as bishops; and thirdly, because the rival system seemed to be real election by a dean and chapter, which would be an unrepresentative system of choosing a bishop for a diocese. Everyone confessed that long history, and their charge of the see church, gave the dean and chapter a historic place in the election of the bishop. No one wanted to give them exclusive rights.

When Ramsey became archbishop, the only consultation with worthies in the diocese which needed a bishop was conducted by the prime minister's secretary. We saw how the argument over the sees of London and York was carried on when Ramsey was chosen for York; a private discussion between both the archbishops and the prime minister and the outgoing Bishop of London and the prime minister's secretary; with the last as the only person who made any attempt to sound opinion in the dioceses. Archbishop Fisher had no desire to change this system. But a flaming row during Fisher's last months in office, over the choice of a dean of Guildford, led to fierce demands for change, and so to a commission which reported in 1964: the Howick Report. This recommended that each diocese set up a vacancy-in-see committee to express the view of the diocese on what is needed—*what* rather than *whom*. Thereafter every diocese set up such a committee. In this way consultation with the vacant diocese, which began with Bevir's unofficial raids, was given a constitutional place in the system.

Normally the diocese asked for someone who was a good pastor and physically fit and therefore not too old. Quite often they asked for someone of an ecumenical spirit who would not disturb the good relations between the denominations in that diocese. Occasionally they referred to some special circumstance—for example that they loved their bachelor bishop but now it would be nice to have a married bishop. Occasionally they would express a preference for someone from outside their own diocese. And quite often they would ask for someone who would not be too involved in outside commitments. They wanted a diocesan pastor rather than a national figure. Ramsey accepted that this was natural but it was the business of the archbishop to ensure that some bishops sustained the role of national figures or at least played a key part in the central counsels of the Church.

Most vacancy-in-see committees preferred not to discuss names but to state in general terms what the diocese needed and then leave the archbishops to recommend a person or persons who would fulfil those needs. Those at the centre found it helpful to be told how a responsible and informed body of clergy and laity saw the needs of the diocese. They found it usually unhelpful when the vacancy-in-see committee bandied names about.

In the new conditions the archbishops needed their own adviser for appointments, and could no longer be content with using only the information gleaned for them by the secretary of the prime minister. In 1965 the two archbishops agreed to appoint Saumarez Smith, a former Indian civil servant, as their secretary for appointments. At first there was a delicacy between the consultations carried on by the secretary of the prime minister and the consultations carried on by the secretary of the archbishops. At first there were fears of offence given through interference in another's sphere. But the two men played it with wisdom and tact.

The press officer De-la-Noy thought that the most important job of an Archbishop of Canterbury was to get a strong bench of bishops and that this archbishop failed to bother much with this part of his duties. This opinion is contradicted by the archives. On no subject did the archbishop take more trouble.

The loud critic of the system was an Essex clergyman J. C. Wansey, who kept shouting to the public that the system was immoral. When Ramsey became Archbishop of Canterbury, Wansey sent him a sermon in which he thundered that because the archbishop was appointed by the State he had a permanent sense of obligation to the State which no archbishop ought to have. Ramsey replied to Wansey that this was not true. 'The fact that I was nominated for office by the prime minister in no way puts me under a sense of obligation to the prime minister or to the State, other than the obligation which any Christian has.'

Ramsey followed the custom of always writing to the prime minister about every vacancy. It made no difference to him whether the office in question was to a diocese or to a suffragan bishopric, nor whether it was in the province of Canterbury or that of York. If it was in the province of York he regarded the letter from the Archbishop of York to the prime minister as formulating the considered mind of the Church, though the Archbishop of York formulated it after consultation with himself. He always put forward three names. Sometimes he put these names in an order of preference. More usually he said that all three would in their different ways be excellent. Occasionally he made it plain that in his view the third name would be inadequate compared with the other two names. Occasionally he made his opinion clear that there was only one obvious person and that person ought to be nominated to the Queen.

The letters which Ramsey wrote to the prime minister are very good letters, kind and perceptive. They take a high view of the human race; which is not the same as to imply that in his eyes geese were swans. He combined realism with generosity. He saw the quality of humanity, and of the priests in his Church, and he saw the variety of different gifts that were needed and valued them, even when they were not gifts which were his own or which he might be expected to understand. The letters are wise, and the judgement of persons sensitive.

Mostly he knew the people from his long experience of the Church. Occasionally he needed to rely solely on the advice which he was proffered. When Douglas Feaver came to stay at Lambeth Palace on the night before his consecration to be the Bishop of Peterborough, the archbishop stood at the top of the great staircase in his purple cassock, and holding out his arms and putting all his humour into the greeting, said, 'Welcome; yes, welcome; you know, we had never heard of you!'

One of the problems which gave cause for reflection was the extent to which a bishop needed to be an administrator. An evangelist—let us say, a Fison of Salisbury—might not be an administrator. Sometimes this would not matter, for the bishop was surrounded in many dioceses by archdeacons or suffragans who could bear the administrative load. But in other dioceses, especially at times of financial stress—and all times were times of financial stress—capacity for management became a quality which it was necessary to look for. At other times the vacancy-in-see committee would state that things went very well and they had no special need of an administrator. Sometimes, as with Salisbury, Ramsey had to look for someone with rural experience, sometimes, as with Liverpool, for someone with urban experience. Quite often the vacancy-in-see committees asked for 'a man of God' or a man of prayer. But more often they took this for granted.

Sometimes Ramsey, and his colleagues, in helping to administer the patronage of the Crown, were subjected to pressure. The obvious form of the pressure was the desire of a diocese that a particular person should be appointed. This occurred on occasions when the existing suffragan made himself so respected or so beloved in the diocese that the leading clergy and laity of the diocese felt that anyone else must be a lesser appointment. In this way, for example, Bulley, suffragan of Penrith, became Bishop of Carlisle; and Treacy, suffragan of Pontefract, and the best driver of a railway engine known in the clerical profession, became Bishop of Wakefield. ('I do not think', wrote Ramsey on this latter occasion, 'that the moving of a suffragan to the diocesan post is normally a good thing'—but the diocese wanted him strongly.) Such pressure had nothing improper, it derived from affection for a sitting tenant. Such affections could not arise without experience and good reason.

Both in the choice of diocesans and in the choice of suffragans age was a consideration. Many of the most suitable men might be mature in age and wisdom. But if the bench of bishops contained no one on it under the age of 60 something would be disturbing. Ramsey did not want the bishops to become government by the old, a gerousia. He kept his eyes open for the younger people.

Sometimes he did not like to suggest the best man he could see; or if he suggested him, put in a warning that it would be better for the Church at large if he were not invited. This happened particularly with two servants of Africa: Trevor Huddleston, and Beecher the Archbishop of Mombasa. Ramsey thought their relationship to Africa so important to the Church that they ought not to be totally committed to any English diocese. From time to time he mentioned both their names to prime ministers but with this doubt, that Africa was the place which needed their care even if they were for the time in England. A prime minister did offer an English see to Archbishop Beecher but he promptly refused to leave his work in Africa. 'Leadership' wrote Ramsey to Coggan (6 October 1965), 'is so needed in East Africa and where a European leader has the confidence of both black and white he should be encouraged to stay.'

He thought much about former bishops in Africa who were ejected by their regimes. They were like confessors for the faith. They needed work somewhere in England. There came to be clashes between supporters of the exiles and Ramsey. They wanted the Church of England to do something for Africa by elevating the banished men to high office, to show how the Church in England resented the behaviour of the South African or Rhodesian governments. Ramsey had no doubt that these men suffered for conscience sake and valued them. But he did not think that people's souls in England should be used as a way of making a political point, even when the point had a tough moral tip. In choosing a bishop the first consideration was the welfare of his future people.

Vacancy-in-see committees sometimes asked not to have a particular person. Graham Leonard was prominent in resisting the proposed unity between Anglicans and Methodists. Though Leonard was a man of calibre, that made a vacancy-in-see committee, even though it was not suggesting names, say privately that the name of Leonard would not be acceptable. After Maurice Wood became Bishop of Norwich, and his uncompromising churchmanship was matter of comment in the press, a vacancy-in-see committee, though not asking for any particular person as their bishop, made it even clearer that they hoped that their new bishop would not be too uncompromising. After John Robinson became famous in controversy while he was Bishop of Woolwich, more than one vacancy-in-see committee made plain their desire that their new bishop should not be too controversial a thinker. 'South Bank Modernism totally unacceptable', said the committee of one remote rural diocese. 'Not a man of eccentric theology', pleaded the committee of another rural diocese. Mortimer, the Bishop of Exeter, was well-known as an Anglo-Catholic. When he resigned, an unofficial committee of clergy and laity in the diocese, nothing to do with the vacancy-in-see committee, petitioned that the new bishop should not be an Anglo-Catholic. And Lambeth suspected that the large size of the London committee was something to do with the jars that troubled that appointment.[6]

About 1970 pressure came to Lambeth that conservative evangelicals were so strong in the Church now that it was wrong if they were unrepresented on the bench of bishops. Ramsey considered this claim. Not himself in any ordinary sense an evangelical, he believed in the

[6] The London vacancy-in-see committee put forward three names, all of calibre: but one of the three, Graham Leonard, was a suffragan in the diocese and therefore would be unusual, another might be (and later was) needed for Canterbury, and the third had gifts that were not primarily those of an administrator. Ramsey argued that since the new archbishop was likely to be younger, the new Bishop of London ought to be a bishop of long experience; and among his three names, which included Graham Leonard, he gave a slight preference to Gerald Ellison the Bishop of Chester, who had the long experience and also the expertise in the House of Lords which was desirable in a Bishop of London; and recommended that Graham Leonard should go to the also vacant see of Truro because it would be good to have him on the bench of bishops. The prime minister (Heath) accepted the argument. Both prime minister and archbishop were bombed with outraged letters from a little group within the vacancy-in-see committee who thought it wrong to recommend to the Queen someone whom they had not mentioned. Most of the vacancy-in-see committee behaved with dignity and sense. Ramsey never afterwards regretted this controversial appointment.

comprehensiveness of the Church of England and he found the plea justified. He consulted the Archbishop of York, who though not a conservative evangelical came from an evangelical background and had a knowledge of their best men. Ramsey asked Coggan to suggest three or four names of people of this school of religion who would be capable of the office of diocesan bishop. The question was difficult; for a conservative evangelical was in the nature of the case an uncompromising person, and dioceses preferred ecumenical minds which were not too uncompromising. However, Ramsey was sure that the claim was right, and in this way Maurice Wood became the Bishop of Norwich in 1971.

The argument that ensued was interesting for the Church of England and its system.

Two of the canons of the cathedral, both good men and both known to Ramsey, protested in a joint letter. Their argument ran thus: they undertook to do all they could to make the new bishop's ministry in the diocese of Norwich happy and effective. They recognized that there was a need to strengthen the conservative evangelical voice on the bench of bishops. But that is ecclesiastical politics. And souls are more important than ecclesiastical politics. They thought that in the long run such an appointment would increase parties and division in the Church.

Ramsey replied to this doubt without compromise. This was a good man who would win the confidence of all sections of the diocese by his sympathy and spiritual qualities. It would be bad for the Church if all the bishops were central churchmen. If then we need some leaders who are to the right or to the left, it must happen that on occasion a diocese gets a bishop who is towards the right or the left. 'What matters is that the man chosen should be capable of uniting and leading the particular diocese, and I believe that in the present case that condition is present.'

Ramsey's correspondents were pleased and encouraged by this letter. All the same, they had a vote. They thought that they ought to be consulted. They said so.

Ramsey said that the prime minister can consult whom he likes but his recommendation to the Crown is his own unshared prerogative. 'It is impossible for him to submit the advice on which he decides to be vetoed by a chapter or a vacancy-in-see committee. So long as the present system continues I am sure that there cannot constitutionally be the kind of modification which you suggest.'

This last sentence was all true but in practice it was not quite the situation. The two archbishops, and especially the Archbishop of Canterbury, had a far more important part in the administration of the patronage of the Crown than that sentence implied.

The prime ministers

The constitution of Britain being what it was, the archbishop's force in choosing bishops depended upon a personal relationship to successive prime ministers. He had no admiration for any prime minister since Asquith until the time of Macmillan. And he felt a measure of distrust for three of them, Lloyd George, Winston Churchill, and Anthony Eden. In Churchill's case, but not in Lloyd George's, this distrust was coupled with admiration for the winner of a great war.

The encounters with Harold Macmillan over the choice for Canterbury left the archbishop with the sense that this was a courtly old-fashioned gentleman with whom he could have conversations about books. He found the meetings with Macmillan friendly but inconsequential (his word). Macmillan liked to enjoy the company of 'my archbishop' in what Ramsey thought of as a Victorian kind of way. Ramsey found the meetings agreeable because they talked of various intellectual interests quite outside the politics of the moment. Macmillan once said that he was reading Purcell's *Life of Manning* and knew the book to be unsatisfactory and was not sure why, and wanted his archbishop to explain. Occasionally Ramsey would send him something he had written—for example *Image Old and New*, which was his meditation on John Robinson's book *Honest to God*—and Macmillan read it and afterwards discussed it. Late in his time as prime minister he gave a dinner-party at 10 Downing Street in honour of his archbishop; and during dinner, with Field Marshal Alexander sitting opposite, Ramsey talked to him on nuclear disarmament, and it was obvious to him that Macmillan would have liked time to continue the talk; and afterwards Macmillan sent him a long letter setting out his views and trying to justify a nuclear armament on Christian as well as on practical grounds. In 1962 Ramsey forcibly criticized Macmillan's act for the restriction of immigration. Macmillan, who had quarrelled with Archbishop Fisher when Fisher denounced his premium bonds and held up to contempt his electioneering slogan 'You've never had it so good', cannot have liked this attack from 'his' archbishop. It made no difference to the friendship of the two men.

About the appointment of bishops Macmillan did what his archbishop wanted in all cases but one. The exception was Ambrose Reeves, the ejected Bishop of Johannesburg. Reeves thought that for the sake of the Church in South Africa and its witness against apartheid he ought to be made the bishop of an English diocese. Two archbishops in succession, Fisher and Ramsey, were not sure that this was the right work for his qualities. Ramsey was assailed vehemently by Canon John Collins and others for doing nothing to find work for Reeves. The charge was false, for Ramsey worried much about Reeves and how he should best be used. He came finally and after hesitation to the view that Reeves ought to be the bishop of an English see and so recommended to the prime minister. For the only time in Ramsey's experience, Macmillan refused. He refused on political grounds. He said that the relations with South Africa were difficult enough at the moment without adding to the friction an appointment which it was not necessary to make and where plenty of other good people could do the job.

Ramsey believed that this was the only time in his experience when a political motive in a prime minister's mind entered the choice or rather the non-choice of a bishop. At the time and later he was in a trouble which he could not correct publicly. Reeves' biographer (1973), unable to know what went on behind the scenes, criticized the archbishop for being hostile to the idea that Reeves should receive high office in the Church of England. Ramsey took the trouble to write a private letter of correction. 'This is contrary to the facts.'

Alec Douglas-Home, prime minister 1963–4, was an old friend of Michael Ramsey. He admired Home's character for its integrity and ability.

Harold Wilson (prime minister 1964–70, 1974–6); Ramsey found him friendly and easy to talk to. He attributed this ease of converse to the circumstance that they were both dons, and both talked like dons. Ramsey found that he had religion in him from his nonconformist days, and felt this to be a bond. But he had regrets from time to time at what he saw as the opportunism of Wilson's government, and curiously admired more Wilson's predecessor as Labour leader, Hugh Gaitskell, because though he had no religion to speak of, his parliamentary attitudes were always based on principle.

In Wilson's time, prime minister and archbishop had much to do with one another—over Africa, and race relations in Britain, and the effort to find a way out of the Vietnam war. They got to know each other well, even apart from their co-operation over the Church.

Harold Wilson took a lot of trouble about Church appointments. Ramsey thought him, on the whole, understanding and impartial. Wilson had a particular interest. He wanted to bring back Christian leaders out of Africa, whether because they were in trouble in Africa for the quality of their stands against racialism, or because they proved their leadership in difficult situations. Wilson wanted to see Trevor Huddleston a bishop in England. Leslie Brown was a scholarly archbishop in Uganda, and he was brought back when it was time for the see to be Africanized, and made Bishop of St Edmundsbury. Kenneth Skelton was the Bishop of Matabeleland and stood up to the Rhodesian prime minister Ian Smith about the Rhodesian Declaration of Independence. Archbishop and prime minister were both concerned that he should be found appropriate work in England.

Edward Heath (prime minister 1970–4). While Heath was leader of the Opposition (1965–70) they found communications difficult. It would be pleasant to possess a recording of the conversation between the most silent archbishop of the century and the most silent prime minister of the century. Heath was a Conservative and Ramsey was not and therefore some subjects were awkward in discussion, like Rhodesia. Heath invited them to lunch and gave them oysters and neither of the Ramseys knew how to eat oysters. Gradually the air got less chilly. Ramsey said afterwards, 'I felt him to be a man of integrity, an impression which I repeatedly got. He was a fairly understanding churchman, having once been news editor of the *Church Times*.'

When Heath became prime minister in 1970 he told Ramsey that he meant to do what he could for the Church. He invited Ramsey round for a talk about the kind of bishops needed, and other problems of the Church. Then he wanted to get to know the bishops, so he had dinner parties at Downing Street to which bishops came with their wives. Then controversy boiled up between them, for example over selling arms to South Africa. Heath did not allow this to affect their friendliness. And Ramsey saw that Heath was absolutely reliable on the race question.

Whether because Heath was Heath or because he knew more about the Church than the other prime ministers, he was the one minister who was likely to take someone on Ramsey's list of possible bishops whom Ramsey approved but who was not Ramsey's first choice for that see. Thereby we see the minister, for the only time among these prime ministers, affecting the kind of man chosen, though only in a small number of cases. Not himself an outgoing personality, he liked outgoing personalities in bishops. In this way George Reindorp was translated from the see of Guildford to the see of Salisbury. Ramsey may have imagined Salisbury to be a Barchester which needed a more placid prelate than the most ebullient bishop in England; so that he did not put Reindorp on his list, but was wholly content with the result. It was Heath's original prompting that finally led to the appointment of Maurice Wood to the see of Norwich; not that the prime minister chose the name but it was he who pushed that that kind of outgoing evangelist should go to Norwich. It was Heath's prompting that led to the appointment of Whitsey to the see of Chester; who was the first choice of neither of the two archbishops though they both put him on their list; a spare time bricklayer and footballer and Lancashire working man—it was not only due to Heath, for the vacancy-in-see committee asked for someone with good parish experience. Another such cheery outgoing man was Robin Woods, the dean of Windsor, who became the Bishop of Worcester; no disagreement here between minister and archbishop. In one case only Heath asked that one of the names on Ramsey's list be withdrawn. The motive for this unique request was not political.

It has already been said that in this choice of bishoprics prime ministers almost always did what Ramsey asked; unless the see was in the northern province when the Archbishop of York's preference would take a slight priority over Ramsey's, provided always that Ramsey also consented to what was done; and except in the single case of the Macmillan veto on Ambrose Reeves for reasons of the 'national interest'. All that is true. But it is not all that is true about the situation. There were two others in the process whose opinions might matter; one with a constitutional right, the other without any constitutional right. This made a concealed restriction on what Ramsey recommended to prime ministers and therefore made him less free than he looked; and made him feel less free than he wished at times to be.

The patronage secretary of the prime minister happened to be in a transitional stage in the history of the constitution. Prime ministers themselves began to wish to interfere less; either because like the Anglican Macmillan they had views that laymen might not be the best people, if unadvised, to choose bishops, or because like Harold Wilson with his nonconformist background they did not wish to intrude heavily into the affairs of a Church which was not their own denomination. This withdrawal of the prime ministers was the main reason why Ramsey could do much of what he liked. Nevertheless the system of consultation set up under Sir Anthony Bevir when he was patronage secretary, and which brought Ramsey to the see of Durham, and then the development of consultation through the vacancy-in-see committees, meant that the patronage secretary had to report on what the Church of England wanted. A man who consults a lot of people gets a lot of different opinions. Therefore it matters how he reports on those opinions, with what bias if any, conscious or unconscious. And the way in which he reported could affect the freedom of the relationship between archbishop and prime minister.

John Hewitt was the patronage secretary from 1961 to 1973. He was the son of an Anglican parson. He cared about the welfare of the Church of England, especially as a force in preserving and promoting the moral strength of the English people. These were the sixties, when in his mind, and in the mind of a lot of others, England went sleazy; with sexual freedom, and the young living together without marriage, and pornography or near it coming into television, and signs of a drug culture, and then the follies of the student revolution largely caused by the Vietnam war. Hewitt worried over this decline, which filled him with foreboding. The Church was the one body which had a chance of stemming this tide. And was it doing that job as it should? Was it standing up for righteousness in the way that the old Hebrew prophets would have stood? He lamented what he took to be its weakness in this moral fight. Left to himself untrammelled, Hewitt would have preferred bishops like Lord Longford or Mary Whitehouse or Malcolm Muggeridge, stalwart publicists for a traditional moral right; and perhaps, if Lord Longford were the right denomination and Mary Whitehouse the right sex, he could have done worse.

The archbishop had a high regard for Hewitt. Nevertheless he had two doubts about him.

The first was, he was a bottleneck to the system. He was conscientious, at times to excess. Only about half his work was to do with the Church. By 1972–3 it was clear that he was overworked. This made part of the slowness of the system which did not satisfy. It was faster than the system which followed it after Ramsey went.

As part of his sense of moral mission, Hewitt was conservative about the relations between Church and State. So far from suspecting that the Church might be freer in moral prophecy if it were less tied to the State, he believed that it was the establishment that gave the Church the right to be heard throughout the land; because it was the establishment which gave it a national quality as distinct from a denominational or sectarian quality.

Consequently there were two kinds of possible bishop about whom Hewitt had an instinctive doubt; and all who knew him are agreed that at times the feelings in him ran deep in his moral conviction. He could not bear the idea of clergymen whom he thought to compromise with sleaziness and with moral laxity. And for the same reason, though it was felt less emotionally, he could not like the idea of clergymen who wished to prise the Church away from the State. This doubt would be serious if he were allowed to apply it systematically. For many of the best radicals in the Church, radical over pastoral methods, also had radical ideas about the way in which the relation of Church and State operated. To exclude clergymen who really compromised with the sleazy was fine. To want to exclude persons who wished for disestablishment was to want to exclude some good pastors—Trevor Huddleston among them—who represented quite a body of opinion in the Church, a body to which, as we shall see, Ramsey himself was not unsympathetic. The archives show prime ministers almost always doing what Ramsey wished them to do. But what the archives do not show is that at an earlier stage of verbal discussion, Ramsey's recommendations to the prime minister might be conditioned by the omission of some name, from his list of three names, which he would have preferred to include.

Eric Kemp was a scholar who knew more about the canon law and the legal history of the Church of England than anyone else in the country. He fitted Ramsey's partiality in three important respects. He was an Anglo-Catholic of piety, but there was nothing narrow about him. He was a scholar with a profundity in his own field not otherwise seen on the bench of bishops at that moment, at least if Ian Ramsey of Durham be excepted. And his expertise was singularly useful to an archbishop trying to make head or tail of the invention of a General Synod. But Kemp, who in speech sounded the most unradical man in the world, could be radical in what he wished to happen over the relation between Church and State. Ramsey wanted him on the bench. It was impossible for Ramsey to get Kemp made a bishop until after John Hewitt retired. No one can blame Hewitt. It was not his responsibility. But unease among prime ministers persisted and Ramsey thought that he knew why. Kemp became Bishop of Chichester in 1974 shortly before Ramsey's own retirement.

The second case was a mistake on the part of Hewitt. Hugh Montefiore combined in an unusual way the scholar and the pastor. But one day he went down to Oxford with a speech to give, and the car broke down on the way with a cracked cylinder block, and there was a fluster; and by one of those moments of ill-thought out utterance he associated Jesus with homosexuals, not meaning that he had sexual feelings towards other men but meaning that he preferred not to marry and that this was a Christian thing for a male or female person to prefer to do and that among his understanding of the afflicted or the suspect to society he would also gather into his human compassion the homosexual.[7] The manner of expression let the press associate Montefiore with the slogan 'Jesus was a homosexual'. From that moment, in Hewitt's mind, Montefiore was a clergyman who compromised with the sleaziness of the age. Ramsey saw that it was ridiculous to exclude from the bench in perpetuity someone otherwise well qualified, solely because of an unusual pastoral idea in one speech.

This was the one occasion when Hewitt shocked Ramsey. In conversation Ramsey mentioned Montefiore, who was already a suffragan as Bishop of Kingston, as a possible for one diocesan see. Hewitt looked disapproving and said, 'I think the prime minister's colleagues would have something to say about it.' (The prime minister at that moment

---

[7] Lecture later published, in *Taking our Past into our Future* (1978), 77 ff.

was Heath.) This shocked Ramsey because it suggested that the prime minister's colleagues had something to do with choosing bishops, which no one had ever suggested before; and it also suggested that a Tory prime minister is expected to ask the Queen to make appointments regarded as 'decent' by his colleagues. Ramsey thought this doctrine outrageous. Hugh Montefiore became Bishop of Birmingham in 1977, three years after Ramsey's retirement.

Nevertheless, in the context of the total mechanism, the cases of Ambrose Reeves, or Eric Kemp, or Hugh Montefiore, were hiccoughs in a system which worked smoothly; where Ramsey got out of prime ministers the bishops whom he wanted. The system of appointing bishops seemed to Ramsey to work well on the whole. The Church he thought had sufficient safeguards. 'If a man were appointed bishop and were unworthy I should take very great umbrage. I should refuse to consecrate him, and would take the consequences. I should regard that as a matter of personal integrity.'

But he did not regard the system as perfect. And not long afterwards he wrote a little essay on the subject (printed in *Canterbury Pilgrim*, pp. 176 ff.). There he reported how the convention of the archbishop submitting three names grew between the wars; how the archbishop's influence reached its climax with Archbishop Lang—that is under the prime ministers Baldwin and Chamberlain—and in the early years of Fisher—that is, when Attlee was prime minister. Then the work of the patronage secretary started to grow in importance as consultation was needed until that secretary became an extra weight in the choice of bishops which had to be taken into account; and although this was much to be admired for its conscientiousness, and for its occasional inspired nominations like that of Ian Ramsey to the see of Durham, it was not the right way for the Church's chief pastors to be chosen. 'It belongs to the maturity and health of a Church that it should choose its own chief pastors . . . A Church without such powers is warped in its potentiality of growing, through whatever hazards and mistakes, in the practice of Christian wisdom.'

He also took the view that the existence of the vacancy-in-see committees since 1965 produced an effect which was unexpected and not beneficial. He valued the consultation with the dioceses and had no desire to do without those committees. But when in the winter of 1973–4, as he entered his last year of office, he reflected on what had happened, he had a doubt whether the diocesan influence on elections, which before was too weak, was now too weighty. The need of the diocese was now at the top; not the need of the Church for intellectual or political leadership.

One other person had an effect upon the system, this time with historic right: namely, the Queen. Prime ministers had to get their nominations past the Queen. As ever since the time of Gladstone in later Victorian days, prime ministers tried to make sure that they could say they had the approval of the Archbishop of Canterbury. Unlike her great-grandfather and her great-great-grandmother the Queen was not in the habit of referring matters back. But where the see was important she inevitably took a larger part in the discussion. In the filling of the see of Norwich by the conservative evangelical Maurice Wood she was fully into the discussion. Ramsey remembered that she had not then heard the expression 'conservative evangelical' and needed to have it explained. Her part in the discussions became decisive when the time came for Ramsey to advise the prime minister about the choice of his own successor.

With the Queen herself Ramsey had many friendly meetings over dinners and on other occasions, and they exchanged personal letters over important forthcoming events. Sometimes he helped her over matters of concern to her, like the choice of a Dean of Windsor. He was told that she was not content with him over his attitudes to Rhodesia and that she wondered whether he went too far for prudence in his friendliness to the Pope. But this was rumour; and when he advised her of his forthcoming visit to Pope Paul VI, she showed him how glad she was at the greater harmony between Churches and wanted the difficulties between the Churches to be further settled if possible. Doubts, if they existed, never appeared in her personal relations with him. He always felt his shyness and lack of small talk to be a disadvantage with her. He debated with himself whether it was his nonconformist origin; whether that was why, as he felt uncomfortable talking to a duke or a marquess, he never lost discomfort in talking to a sovereign. And he always kept a conscientious sense that there was only one head of the Church and that was Christ. He fell into quite an argument once with the Queen Mother because she loosely referred to her daughter as head of the Church and Ramsey felt a duty to contradict her and explain that the title 'supreme governor' did not mean head. And at a royal occasion in St Paul's cathedral, as he came out into the aisle before preaching, he bowed first to the altar and then to the Queen: and as he bowed to the altar was heard to mutter 'God first'.

During the time of her widowhood Queen Victoria loved to attend Crathie church while she was at Balmoral. One autumn she attended the service and watched her gillies and servants communicating and could not bear to remain behind and slipped quietly and unostentatiously to join them in receiving the sacrament. When this became known some of the high churchmen of England denounced her because the supreme governor of the Church of England received the sacrament in a church not in communion with the Church of England. The Queen was outraged by this comment and wrote letters which made the fiercest criticism which she ever made of the Church of England.

In the autumn of 1968 the Queen's secretary came to Lambeth to see the archbishop. The Queen had decided to attend in person the next meeting of the General Assembly of the Church of Scotland. She would be the first sovereign to do so since James I and VI. Each year she sent a high commissioner as her representative. Now she would go herself. But it was the custom that the high commissioner should receive the sacrament in St Giles with the Assembly. If the Queen did not receive, it would be unpleasant for the Church of Scotland. If she did receive, it might be regretted by some Anglicans. Personally she would like to be able to receive the sacrament. But she wanted to know what Ramsey thought and advised.

Ramsey assured the Queen's secretary that he found nothing wrong in the idea of the Queen receiving the sacrament in St Giles. He said that a majority of the members of the Church of England would see no harm; but that there might be some who did, though they would probably be fewer in number than they would have been eight years before. He undertook to sound the Primus (presiding bishop) of the episcopal Church in Scotland. Ramsey was decisive to the Scottish Primus. 'I cannot advise her not to do what other Anglicans would do without disapprobation.' The Scottish bishops, consulted informally and confidentially by the Primus, gave Ramsey the all clear.

In December 1968 there was a row about it in some Scottish newspapers. Ramsey was attacked for struggling to stop the Queen from receiving the sacrament in St Giles when she came to Scotland. The ignorance of newspapers is always a trial to good men and women who take part in public life.

To some members of the Queen's family he felt close; Princess Marina, whom he got to know well when she became the first Chancellor of the university of Kent, and afterwards through the marriage of her son and daughter, who summoned him urgently to her death-bed; there perhaps the feeling rested partly upon his understanding of the religion of the Greek Church; Princess Alexandra her daughter, and her husband, whom he married; the Duke and Duchess of Kent, partly perhaps because it was a Yorkshire wedding; Princess Anne because he confirmed her and later married her and then because his heart bled over the attempt to kidnap her with a gun. Those who knew him well were pleased, when Michael Ramsey's memorial service came, at the appropriateness that the Duke of Kent should represent the Queen.

The feeling of Ramsey that the system of appointing bishops was not yet right, for all the weight which it gave to the archbishop, was shared by others in the Church. In 1973 Eric Kemp brought to the General Synod a motion to the effect that the Church ought to choose its own bishops. The debate in the General Synod showed a mood of conservatism, with a desire to keep the Queen within the system of appointment so that bishops might remain national figures as well as diocesan, and a fear of other systems of election as they happened in other Churches of the Anglican Communion; but also a more radical feeling generally than would earlier have been found commonly among the members of the Church of England. The archbishop spoke in the debate. In his last years of office he thought that a way could be found which would make the Church's choice of leaders compatible with a continued establishment, as happened in Scotland. 'Looking at the history of Scotland as well as England, and looking at the future prospects of Christian unity, I believe that it is not only highly desirable that our Church should choose its own chief pastors, but that it is important to say that it is not necessary for such an arrangement to be incompatible with the many links with the Crown that continue and will go on continuing in this country.'

The motion to do something about it was carried by a surprisingly large majority; but nothing was achieved quickly. The subsequent change which much reduced the part of the prime minister in the choice of bishops came three years after Michael Ramsey retired. Curiously, he was not very pleased in his retirement, with the new system which he had helped to create. 'They don't get any better bishops and it takes them much longer to get them.'

This last remark shows how he valued the people whom he recommended. Once or twice one or other of his advisers said to him that there were not many good men to find. He never believed it. Occasionally someone would say to him the opposite, that there were so many good men and the pyramid was so narrow at the top and therefore lots of good men would have no chance to 'rise to the top'. Ramsey believed that there were lots of good men but he did not think bishoprics and deaneries the only offices in the Church which demanded quality. On the contrary, good men ought sometimes to be kept out of the highest jobs (in the sense of hierarchy) for the sake of the various vocations in the Church. Though he accepted the existence of hierarchy as necessary, he was free from a worldly sense of hierarchy, as if it was a ladder of promotion.

6

Parliament and the Moral Law

I. HOMOSEXUALITY

The laws about homosexuality had never received adequate discussion. Lord Boothby always claimed that it was a speech by himself in Parliament which led to the appointment of a commission to consider the subject. This commission was led by a good Anglican layman, Sir John Wolfenden, later Lord Wolfenden. It reported in 1957. By its main recommendation, the State ought to cease to make homosexual acts in private, between consenting adults over the age of 21, a criminal offence. The objects of this recommendation were (1) to help homosexuals not to feel persecuted and therefore to make them feel at home in society; (2) to avert the threat of blackmail which they suffered; and (3) to free them to seek psychiatric help without fear of consequences.

At that moment Michael Ramsey was Archbishop of York. He realized with surprise that he had never till this moment thought about the subject. He instantly accepted the argument of the Wolfenden Report, and expressed the hope that the government would give effect to its main recommendations. The Church of Scotland refused to accept the rightness of the Wolfenden Report. Other Churches which considered it accepted its plea; among them the Church of England; though not by a large majority (155 to 138, 14 November 1957, in the Church Assembly).

But though a lot of people who thought about moral issues accepted the argument, nothing was done. No government was willing to bring in a bill. Passionate feelings were aroused, irrational as well as rational. No political advantage could be gained by a bill to legalize homosexuality. Members of Parliament who might have wanted to bring in a private members' bill were afraid of the voters in their constituency. Year after year passed and nothing was done.

Those who wanted change had various viewpoints. Some thought homosexuality not merely not a crime, but neither a fault nor a disease. It was a thing that some people were born with, like a less common colour of hair. The sexual instinct expresses itself in various ways—a homosexual relationship is one of those ways. Then there were others who believed that homosexuality, though a disability for living a 'normal' life, was like an arthritic leg and certainly not like a sin; and all we need is freedom to have better treatment. We could not change men's basic desires—what we must do is to try to correct what is aberrant by psychiatric medicine. The churchmen generally held that lust is sin and a homosexual relationship if physical, and not simply a platonic friendship, is a form of lust; and therefore what was needed was the chance of pastoral care. At basis this was Ramsey's position. And when he began to speak to the point, he had no idea what he dived into.

Everyone who wanted change agreed that the young must be protected; that homosexual acts where one of the partners was a boy must still be a crime. Everyone agreed that homosexuality in the female sex could be left as it was, not a crime. Everyone agreed that certain areas of life needed special protection, where a lot of men were thrown together without women—ships at sea for example, the army, prisons. Everyone agreed that certain places, which might be contended to be private, were not—above all public lavatories, which under the existing law were infested, sordidly, with police spies in disguise.

But the opposition was formidable. The ordinary citizen of the country had little knowledge and much fantasy. Some of the opposition in Parliament had a nausea. They were against it because they were horrified, and they did not know why they were horrified. Then the leaders of youth organizations were against change. Rarely but from time to time they had to push quietly out the deviant leader who tried to interfere with his charges. They had the instinct that, if Parliament went 'weak' about homosexuality, it would make the protection of the young more complicated. These opponents included a former Chief Scout, and the president of the Boys Brigade, both peers with the right to speak in Parliament. And among these opponents we must number the most trenchant of them all though not the most persuasive: Viscount Montgomery of Alamein. He was a rare speaker in the House of Lords. But now he was roused. He spoke of the moral fibre of the youth of the nation. He begged the peers to knock a bill on the subject for six out of the House. 'One may just as well condone the devil and all his works' (Hansard, 24 May 1965, col. 645).

This was one of the not so rare cases where the hereditary peers in the House of Lords were advantageous. They had no constituents to worry about. The man with the dash and the courage to introduce the bill into the House of Lords was a journalist, and therefore not without a dubious reputation among some of the peers: the Earl of Arran.

Ramsey believed on moral grounds that the law ought to be changed in the sense which Wolfenden recommended and the bill of Lord Arran largely proposed. He never in his life ran up against a tougher opposition than that which he now encountered. This did not consist of the ex-Chief Scout nor of Field-Marshal Montgomery, who did not carry weight in the House. It consisted of two lawyers, one brilliant and one massive.

Viscount Dilhorne and Viscount Kilmuir were two of the most devastating speakers generated by a profession which trains speakers to devastate. After a long experience of the seedy side of the human race, they both had ruthlessness in their composition. And since Ramsey was on the other side, and a pillar to the other side as ex officio the chief moralist of England, they had every reason not to spare his arguments, his attitudes, or his person. They could not understand, or they pretended not to be able to understand, how those who care for the morality of the nation could support a bill bound to lead to more acts of immorality.

Kilmuir practised as a young lawyer at the bar in Liverpool when Ramsey practised there as a young curate, but they never met. As David Maxwell Fyfe he carried the load in prosecuting the Nazi war criminals at Nuremberg and won a world reputation as a prosecuting attorney. He was Lord Chancellor in Churchill's government of 1954 and carried the respect given to one who has occupied the Woolsack.

Viscount Dilhorne succeeded Kilmuir as Lord Chancellor. Before his peerage he was Sir Reginald Manningham-Buller and he was the most aristocratic person by descent ever to occupy the Woolsack. Unlike Kilmuir he was a poor lawyer and was disliked in the legal profession. He made his career by politics, not by the law. Ramsey's old friend of the Cambridge Union days, Patrick Devlin, drew a colourful portrait of Dilhorne as disagreeable, arrogant, ponderous, and a bully, though a man of integrity who only wished to serve the State.[1] This portrait by Devlin was criticized or supplemented by the reviewers of Devlin's book and by the historian of the Lord Chancellors. Those who study the antagonism between Ramsey and Dilhorne in the House of Lords will not disbelieve the essence of what Devlin had to say.

Nothing in Ramsey's previous career fitted him to cope with one lawyer of fame who was one of the best cross-examiners in the country and another lawyer of fame who was renowned as the rudest lawyer in the country. The cloth has no riposte in public debate to critics who have no

[1] Devlin, *Easing the Passing* (1985).

respect for the cloth. The mind goes back to the young student hard at the New Testament in his room overlooking the west front of Lincoln Cathedral and is amazed to think how the circumstances of life led the quiet and mystical scholar, for the sake of moral right, into this disdainful areopagus.

Ramsey took a lot of trouble to get other bishops to support him in the House of Lords. Five or six did so. But one bishop told one of his opponents that the bishops were divided whether it was right to support the bill. Those bishops who did not wish to vote for the bill held that, though the bill might do good to a few people, the psychological consequences in the country would be bad; for it would seem that Parliament did not care about moral right.

The second reading of Lord Arran's bill was carried in the House of Lords on 24 May 1965 by 94 to 49; Liberals and Labour and four bishops being among the majority, the eminent lawyers and the back-woodsmen and the youth workers being among the minority. The bill went into committee.

Here Ramsey made a mistake. At least he afterwards said it was a mistake. We beware of such an opinion for we shall meet again in him an inclination to blame himself in retrospect for things that were not his fault. However, the reader of the debates sees why he thought that he made a mistake. He was now committed to the bill; and read about the subject.

He had no regret that he knew about the subject. That was necessary if he was to form his mind. He afterwards thought that his mistake was to show that he knew about the subject. At times the matter of debate was noisome. It is better that archbishops should seem to have a general rather than a particular knowledge of sewers. It would have been better, he thought afterwards, to leave all the details to the professionals. He showed for example that he knew what was meant by anal and oral intercourse. A churchman like Quintin Hogg, who mostly agreed with what he said, thought an archbishop to be wildly imprudent if he was heard to know such unedifying detail, and that it was beneath the dignity of his office that he should be seen to tangle in such an argument with Lord Dilhorne. One peer attacked him for contributing to porno-graphy by means of Hansard (16 July 1965, col. 411). This was the most offensive utterance ever made in public to Ramsey; and would be well up in a competition for the nastiest public attack ever made upon an Archbishop of Canterbury.

All this gave Dilhorne and Kilmuir their chance. Yet these two powerful men lost the contest. Another's bill was given a third reading in the House of Lords on 16 June 1966, though not by a large majority.

Lord Dilhorne mourned that Arran's success was due to the tremendous support of Ramsey and the bishops.[2]

The letters poured into Lambeth. Three examples only: a feminine correspondent wrote to thank Lord Dilhorne for resisting 'the sanction given to sodomy by the Archbishop of Canterbury'. The *Daily Mail* accompanied an account of the bill's amendments with a photograph of Ramsey looking debauched. A retired detective wrote to Ramsey challenging him to quote in the House of Lords the text of Leviticus 20:13. But informed persons held that the legislative change contained moral gain for the State.

During the 1980s the plague of AIDS began to afflict the world and evidence was provided that homosexuals were more likely than heterosexuals to propagate the disease. This raised a question whether the liberalization of the law of homosexuality was all gain. Ramsey was asked about it, whether he now looked back on what he helped to do with any regret. He had no doubt that he was right. He had no doubt that the Churches of England, with himself as their mouthpiece, helped to make the law more humane, more Christian, and more just. He remembered that he undertook some painful reading, and that he sat through 'very snide' speeches against himself. But he did not think that he contributed in any way to 'the permissive society' nor to the decline in public morality.

In an interview of 1971 Ramsey was asked whether the Church could bless a marriage between persons of the same sex. Ramsey replied: 'I don't see the Christian Church ever giving its blessing to that. Because the Christian Church gives its blessing to the best and perfect use of sex, which is the union of a man and a woman in marriage. We confine our blessing to that.'

2. DIVORCE

During the sixties the rate of divorce continued to rise. The plan of a couple living together without marriage became more socially acceptable. The pill and other methods of contraception made a higher social class of women willing to sleep casually with men, for they had not to fear an unwanted baby; and such methods led men to expect or demand that their girl friends should sleep with them if they wished to retain their friendship. The Churches stood for family life and its sacredness.

---

[2] The bill had various vicissitudes, and a bill along its lines only went through in July 1967.

Their moral ideal was the husband and wife faithful to each other 'till death do us part' and no sexual intercourse outside the marriage bond. The casualness of modern sexual activity was to them a corruption of what was precious to humanity, and a making of a love that reflected God's love into something sleazy as well as selfish.

Still, both Church and State had to do something about the laws of marriage and divorce if they were to help preserve the better things in the traditional ideals of family life. In the conditions which prevailed in European society then, it had to be accepted that sometimes a first marriage was a calamity and a second marriage was made in heaven. Social right, and the interests of children, were often made safer by recognizing this fact than by asserting still that it was wrong. But this could only be done in such a way that the Church preserved the ideal of a permanent marriage between two people. By the time Ramsey became Archbishop of Canterbury it was well established as general custom that the Church refused to marry in church a person who had a previous partner still living—thus maintaining the ideal—but soon accepted back into its bosom the remarried couple—thus not depriving them or their children of the pastoral care which they might need.

The problem was the absurdity, still, of some aspects of the law of divorce. The Pope continued to denounce all forms of divorce and to prefer States to make no provision for divorce. This had the merit of standing for an ancient principle of the sacredness of the vow of marriage and the demerit of being irresponsible in face of the moral conditions of society. For the head of the Church of England such a stance was impossible. Ramsey thought that society was going very wrong in the matter of family life, both by the number of marriages which broke down and by the number of 'illicit unions' before marriage and after marriage. Even he could welcome the new openness with which sex could be discussed—'for sex can be a good and beautiful thing, and the wrong kind of hush-hush attitude can do harm'; yet he thought the English people preoccupied with sex, and undisciplined about it in a new and perilous way. He abhorred the desire to exploit sex for commercial purposes.

In this state of affairs various bills were brought into Parliament and the Archbishop had a duty to say what he thought.

He continued steadily to believe and teach that intercourse outside marriage and before marriage is wrong. But he accepted that two people living together, who were unmarried according to law but intended to live together till death, were not committing an offence like casual sleeping around. Still, he thought the way in which this habit grew was a sign of moral disintegration.

On 21 June 1963 he spoke in the Lords on the Matrimonial Causes and Reconciliation bill, and the speech was important in the rejection of the bill. The thing to which he most objected was a proposal that divorce should be possible after a separation of seven years even if one of the parties did not agree. But this experience of the 1963 bill made him take action. The Lord Chancellor, none other than Ramsey's harasser Lord Dilhorne, came together with him on the possibility of the Church considering what the reform of the law ought to be and then approaching Parliament. The result of this meeting between Ramsey and Dilhorne was the appointment by Ramsey of a commission on the law of divorce. He placed the commission under the leadership of the learned moral theologian among the bishops, Mortimer of Exeter, who was a conservative.

During 1966 Mortimer's commission produced its report, under the title *Putting Asunder*. The commission produced a recommendation at first sight startling. Throughout history the Church had allowed separation between married couples, where it allowed it, only if an offence against the marriage bond was committed. Mostly this was confined to adultery because that was the offence mentioned in the New Testament. By the 1920s this law produced a system for providing evidence of adultery in return for a fee. Divorce was necessary; it could not be got without adultery; morally good persons with no intention whatever of committing adultery hired a hotel and a chambermaid to prove their guilt and manufacture the evidence for divorce. Nothing was more distasteful or more ridiculous. In 1937 A. P. Herbert's bill brought a partial remedy by extending the offences which were grounds for divorce—to cruelty, desertion for three years, five years continuous insanity, or bestiality by the husband.

This was a help. But it retained the historic idea of a grave offence against marriage. People who were not adulterous, nor cruel, nor bestial still needed divorce or to be divorced. The need for evidence continued —the hotel and the chambermaid were still on occasion hired.

The report *Putting Asunder* recommended that the idea of an offence against marriage be dropped at last and that the sole ground for divorce should be that the marriage had broken down irretrievably and despite efforts at reconciliation could not be repaired. Naturally evidence was still needed. The law court must be persuaded that the break was irretrievable. But the plan had the merit of getting rid of any quest in future to decide which was the guilty party in the breakdown of the marriage. The law should cease to bother about guilt and only deal in the permanence of marriage and its possibility. Ramsey was wholly in favour of what his commission recommended. In the House of Lords on

23 November 1966 Ramsey spoke on Mortimer's report on divorce. It was a liberal and a good speech.

Almost simultaneously a report of the Law Commission appeared (Cmnd. 3123) which took much the same line. State and Church converged in their opinion of the way to reform.

The Church was not unanimous behind its archbishop. Several newspapers thought or pretended to think the idea of divorce through irretrievable breakdown to be the same as divorce by consent; so that if my wife and I do not like each other we can agree on a divorce and that will be the divorce. Ramsey was totally opposed to the idea of divorce by consent. The community has an interest in the stability of marriages and the community must have its say through the courts of the State. He was also opposed to the idea that one party could get a divorce (after ×years of irretrievable breakdown) without the consent of the other —'unilateral' divorce. He knew of the case of a wife whose husband ran away with a girl but she believed that it was a temporary infatuation and that in the longer run she could save the marriage; and Ramsey urged that she needed protecting from any kind of unilateral divorce, from the husband divorcing her without her agreement.

The Divorce Reform Bill, based upon a union of Ramsey's *Putting Asunder* plus the Law Commission's report, passed through Parliament during 1968–9. Ramsey did not like the way in which its provisions departed from *Putting Asunder* and was accused by its leading proponent in the House of Commons, Leo Abse, of a breach of faith for criticizing the divorce bill.

Ramsey said, 'I specially deplore the proposal for divorce by consent and the shortening of the period for desertion. I think it is not clear that the Bill would give enough protection to the interests of a faithful party and to his or her children.' The bill took over the idea of irretrievable breakdown, of which Ramsey approved, and the provisions for efforts at reconciliation, of which Ramsey much approved; but it also added the provision for divorce that was unilateral—after two years separation by consent of both parties, after five years without the consent of one party. Ramsey did not like it that the three years' separation should be reduced to two, or that there should be divorce merely by separation without consent. This meant that when it came to the Second Reading (30 June 1969) he could not vote for a bill which he had helped to create. Even Baroness Summerskill called the bill as it stood a Casanova's charter. Lord Longford, who was a Roman Catholic, said that parts of the bill were utterly evil.

Lord Dilhorne begged Ramsey to reconsider his refusal to vote for the bill. It was an imperfect world, and the present law was bad, and this was better; and Ramsey admitted that the present law was bad and some changes would be better. But he would not vote for it. He did not vote against it. He abstained. His bishops divided.

Between 1970 and 1986 the rate of divorce in England doubled. It does not follow that this doubling was the consequence of the new law. Under the old law there might have been a doubling of the remuneration of hotel chambermaids; such was the development of society.

If it was once accepted that in the conditions of modern society some first marriages were born to fail and that some second marriages were made in heaven, was it right of the Church to keep to its rule of refusing to remarry divorced persons in Church? And was it not pastorally better for the Church to do what it could to accept the higher ideals of couples who came to them even if one of the pair had been married before? Some thought that the old rule of no marriage in church while a former partner lived maintained the sanctity of marriage while it caused no serious hardship. But others in parishes were faced with heart-rending pleas. Some clergymen began to marry in church couples who had a partner still alive.

In 1971 an Anglican commission proposed the possibility of re-marriage of the divorced in church. The bishops divided. Ramsey was strong against the change. He always refused the archbishop's licence to marry to persons who had a partner still alive. In November 1973 the General Synod defeated a proposal that the dioceses should consider whether remarriage in church should be allowed with safeguards. But the question did not sleep. Ramsey was willing to bless with prayers a couple after a civil wedding and did so more than once. The difference between a blessing and prayers on the one hand and a marriage service on the other needed subtle distinctions. He maintained to the end that the distinction mattered.

3. ABORTION

In England abortion was criminal unless the surgeon performed the operation in good faith to save the life of the mother. This was traditional in European law and European moral codes. The Soviet Union shocked Europe, and confirmed everyone's belief in the horrors of the Bolshevik revolution, when in 1920 it allowed abortion on demand.

In an urbanized world this ancient law and moral code produced as a side-effect 'back-street abortions'; illegal operations performed for fees by criminal surgeons with dirty tools. After the second World War there were widespread demands for the legalization of abortion under proper conditions; to prevent the criminal trade; to help the health of girls endangered by the incompetence of criminal surgeons; and to recognize that there might be reasons, other than the immediate peril to the mother's life, which justified the performance of the operation.

This last idea was difficult for the Churches. To them all life was sacred. They were against euthanasia on this ground. No one could exactly say when the human foetus had the rights of a human person, but it was safest to treat it as having its rights from the moment that it could be perceived as a foetus. Therefore the Churches had an instinct to think of abortion as almost as bad as the murder of babies.

In 1964 a commission headed by Ian Ramsey, the future Bishop of Durham, issued a report on abortion which denied that abortion was the same as the murder of babies. It nevertheless declared the foetus to be sacred, and said that it was an embryo of a life capable of being God's child for all eternity, which it was right to reverence and to consider as having rights. It also recognized the right of the mother not only to live, but also not to have her health wrecked. The commission, to which the bishops generally adhered, declared that the risk to the life or health of the mother should be the sole grounds for a lawful abortion.

On 17 January 1967 Michael Ramsey gave an address to the Convocation of Canterbury, in St Margaret's Church, Westminster, in which he upheld the sanctity of the foetus. But he did not identify abortion with infanticide and held that to assert this identity was an error.

The line was hard to draw. The health of the mother—might that include the effect of another birth upon the other children of the family? They had moved beyond the idea of physical risk to the life of the mother—they accepted that in certain circumstances a birth unwanted by the mother could have devastating consequences in psychology. And now the medical methods of photography made it easier, though not easy, to predict that the coming baby would be unable to live a normal life. Ramsey had known people born severely handicapped who yet could live with happiness—would the proposal about risk prevent them living? He disliked this handing over to doctors the judgement about a future handicapped life. He disliked the idea of handing over to doctors a judgement on whether a mother would be overstrained by the birth of another child, when he knew homes and families which in the midst of the utmost difficulties produced some of the best of humanity.

Yet no bishop with open eyes—and Ramsey's mental eyes were always open even when he appeared to slumber—could think the present law good, with the consequences which it created. Something had to be done. Therefore something had to be got through Parliament. The bishops could not stick in their toes at a policy of no change. Yet they could never accept some demands which went so far as to legislate for abortion under the National Health Service on demand. Ramsey finally went far in concession. He wanted the law to allow abortion only out of consideration for the health of the mother which came under the heading of risk to life of the mother or her mental or physical health; the risk of the birth of a deformed or defective child; conception after rape; and circumstances when the bearing and rearing of the child would prove beyond the total capacity of the mother.

Ramsey spoke several times during the debates and followed them with anxiety and was mocked by Lord Dilhorne for what he said. His weightiest concession was to allow that the two doctors who were to consider the state of the mother's health, and so decide whether the foetus might be aborted, should consider her health in relation to her 'total environment' (the word 'total' was later omitted against Ramsey's vote).

The bill as it eventually passed allowed the termination of pregnancies during the first 28 weeks of pregnancy if two doctors of the National Health Service agreed that the pregnancy involved risk to the mother's life or injury to the mental or physical health of her or any of her existing children; or if the child to be born would suffer from such mental or physical abnormalities that it would be likely to be handicapped seriously. Doctors and nurses might refuse to perform the operation on grounds of conscience. In the Lords the bishops joined with others in trying to amend the bill because now it had so large a loophole. Archbishop Ramsey could not vote for the bill as it stood though he recognized that some bill was a necessity. Bishop Ian Ramsey of Durham voted for the bill because although he disliked bits of the bill it was necessary to have a bill and if this bill was the best that could be got, this bill it must be. He was not the only bishop to vote for the bill. He had to justify himself later in a letter to *The Times*.[3]

The number of abortions rose dramatically and social argument resulted. A government inquiry of Ramsey's last year in office, 1973–4, recommended no change in the law. The pressure to amend the law continued, chiefly to reduce the number of 28 weeks, perhaps to 24 weeks, or in the more rigorous school even 18 weeks.

Pastors who were consulted by women asked the archbishop for his

---

[3] Able discussion of Ian Ramsey's part in all this is by G. R. Dunstan, in *Journal of Medical Ethics* 13 (1987), 189–94.

advice, whether a woman wanting an abortion was to be discouraged pastorally. He took the view that the circumstances would vary from case to case; that rigid pressure ought not to be applied against such a woman because the moral decision must finally be left to her; but that she should be supported and helped by the pastor in every way possible.

4. EUTHANASIA

Since the medical profession kept the human race living years longer, they kept alive a lot of human beings who were vegetables because their minds had gone; and some human beings who lived but in an agony from which there was no way out. The question of when a doctor could terminate a life long troubled moralists and now troubled them more because the cases were so insistent. For a doctor to give an overdose of drugs to an agonized patient for whom no recovery was possible was murder in the eyes of the law. Everyone knew that it happened. And if it happened, ought it not to be faced and brought under some principle or legal control? The old movement for freedom to decide to die gained a fresh force. Some of its supporters were nurses who had to cope with suffering which they saw no reason for anyone to have to bear. They sent heart-rending case-histories to Lambeth.

In March 1969 a Voluntary Euthanasia Bill was brought to the House of Lords and lost by a considerable majority. Both the expert moralists among the bishops, Ian Ramsey of Durham and Mortimer of Exeter, spoke against it. Most of the medical profession was against it. It was essential to retain the confidence of patients in doctors and nurses. Michael Ramsey agreed with the negative view on the ground of the sacredness of human life and the impossibility of finding any moral system which would make it legally possible to end it.

But two years later he was asked about it at a session with the students of Aberdeen University. He then said that more 'Christian exploration was needed'. And he gave an opinion which afforded an umbrella to the doctors. 'Where a patient is lingering on in great distress,without any possibility of continuing life of happiness or purpose, it is not necessary for the doctor to continue keeping him alive.' This was reported in all the papers and had a big headline in the *Daily Express* (4 May 1971). Asked to explain he said that he did not approve of euthanasia, but he thought they should explore further into the switching off of artificial means of supporting life where a patient was in a coma or had irreversible brain damage. He was told that he was trying to interfere between God and his children and that God would call people to himself at his own time. He said that it ought to be considered further whether an artificial prolonging of a life which was not really a life was not going against what God was making plain.

5. ILLEGITIMACY

In the Middle Ages a man could not be ordained if he were illegitimate, without the Pope's dispensation. This right of dispensation was transferred to the Archbishop of Canterbury. It was always given, but Ramsey's dispensation was still needed when he became Archbishop of Canterbury. It seemed to him wrong that a man should be treated less well solely because of the behaviour of his parents. And he had the old sense of mockery at some absurd piece of ritual; for example when he was confirmed as Archbishop of Canterbury at the obsolete ceremony in the crypt of St Paul's cathedral (June 1961) and he stood before the commission whose sole job was the duty of identifying whether he was Michael Ramsey or not, he heard himself twice described in the legal instrument as 'Arthur Michael Ramsey, freeborn and no bastard'; and then he could be heard to mutter 'How do *they* know?'

The anachronism was soon remedied. A measure of 1964, passed by the Church Assembly and accepted by Parliament, provided that no person should be rejected for ordination on the ground that he was born out of lawful wedlock.

In the same year the government considered the law of illegitimacy in its relation to the right of succession. They asked Ramsey's advice; whether he thought that illegitimate children should also be given the right of succession in property. Ramsey took the view that it was only fair that any child, legitimate or illegitimate, should have the right of succession, and that if a law was not fair it was wrong. His advice to government ran, 'The Archbishop of Canterbury believes that this country could now safely embody provision in general for the illegitimate to have rights of succession. If it can do this safely, it ought so to act.'

6. CAPITAL PUNISHMENT

One of the remarkable social developments of the twentieth century was the abolition of capital punishment. In this Ramsey had a key part.

It was remarkable in more than one way. The States of abolition were democracies. Yet a majority of the population was never convinced that society was secure without the death penalty. Where, as in the separate States of the USA, government had to respond to the opinions of the people, campaigners for abolition had limited success.

Throughout western societies the change of mind rested upon three axioms. The first was ultimately derived from the religious inheritance, that human life is sacred and the State ought not to take it away. The second depended upon the experience that miscarriages of justice can happen, and the State ought not to do something too final to set right in the face of further evidence. Thirdly, better methods of social enquiry, based upon more careful statistics of longer periods of years, bred the conviction that the death penalty protected life no better than the penalty of very long imprisonment.

Until the middle of the nineteenth century society executed criminals because it had no other efficient way of keeping them out of society. But the development of the modern prison system created another way by which they could be effectively (though not always efficiently) removed from society. The feelings of ordinary men and women who wanted to keep the death penalty rested thenceforth upon something other than reason. They felt shock and anger at the violence of society. The desire for 'just retribution' could hardly be satisfied, or even slaked, by the knowledge that the committer of a brutal murder was put away for a long time. People who saw a helpless old lady battered to death for the sake of a few pounds wanted blood.

This was the problem which confronted the moralists, including the bishops and the legislators. In 1948 Mass Observation conducted a poll on the proposal that the death penalty be abolished for an experimental period of five years: 13 per cent said that it should be suspended, without qualifications; 69 per cent said that it should not be suspended, and made no qualifications.

This was not the only evidence that the people of Britain wanted to keep the death penalty. In 1948 a Labour House of Commons voted in favour of experimental abolition. In the ensuing debate in the House of Lords Archbishop Fisher spoke in favour of keeping the hangman. Of the bishops, only George Bell of Chichester spoke on the other side.

In 1956, while Ramsey was a new Archbishop of York, he was confronted for the first time with the need to vote on the issue. A Conservative House of Commons, on a free vote, passed again the motion for experimental abolition. In the Lords Archbishop Fisher made an ambiguous speech, and voted for abolition, but wanted to keep the death penalty for certain kinds of murder. Ramsey (it was his maiden speech) made an unambiguous speech and voted for abolition in the company of George Bell of Chichester and seven other bishops. The

House of Lords threw out the proposal by 238 votes to 95. They knew that they represented the opinions of the country better than the House of Commons.

The vote proved that the opinions of the bishops as a body were moving. The passing of the motion by the Commons stirred Parliament to act. The Homicide Act 1957 greatly reduced the incidence of capital punishment. It tried to distinguish killings which deserved death as a penalty (like the shooting of a policeman) from killings which did not deserve death (like a distressed mother doing away with a deformed child). It retained the death penalty for six types of killing.

The change of archbishop in 1961 made a difference. And among the bishops was now an ardent campaigner for abolition, Mervyn Stockwood, the Bishop of Southwark; who regarded the death penalty as a denial of the gospel and said that the State by practising it took what was the prerogative of God. In January 1962 Stockwood brought to the Convocation of Canterbury a motion that the death penalty should be abolished for an experimental period. Every bishop voted for abolition. Among the bishops in the Convocation of York only Ramsey's successor at Durham, Harland, voted to keep the death penalty.

This vote of the bishops gave a new impetus to the campaigners, like Sydney Silverman in the House of Commons. A unanimous vote of the bishops on a moral issue of this sort must give the campaigners a far better chance of getting the bill past the House of Lords. *The Economist* commented (20 January 1962), 'The effect of the opinion of the Anglican Church on the views of Conservative backbenchers, although it is a force that moves slowly and sometimes mysteriously, can be surprisingly decisive.' The *Daily Mail*, which did not favour abolition, hinted that some of the bishops might have slept during the debate. But it recorded Ramsey as expressing his pleasure, 'in a soft voice, as if trying to placate the ghosts of nineteenth century bishops who would have burst their gaiters in horror at the suggestions of ending the death penalty'.

The Homicide Act 1957, in intending to reform the law of murder, gave weapons to the abolitionists. Attempting to distinguish bad murder from less bad murder, it produced nonsense. If a man killed his wife with a gun he was liable to death, if with an axe he was not. If he strangled a girl and took her handbag he was liable to death, if he left the handbag he was not. Those who had to work this well-meaning act soon said that it was not workable; and at their head were the Home Secretary Henry Brooke and the Lord Chief Justice, Parker of Waddington. Some further change in the law had to happen.

The fall of the Conservative government, and appearance of Harold

Wilson's government, gave encouragement to the abolitionists because it brought as Lord Chancellor Gerald Gardiner, a joint-chairman of the National Campaign for the Abolition of Capital Punishment.

Sydney Silverman knew that with a Labour majority he could carry a bill through the House of Commons. His problem was the House of Lords. Lord Longford, leader of the House of Lords, and the Lord Chancellor first put to Ramsey an unprecedented suggestion. They said that Ramsey should himself take charge of the bill in the House of Lords and pilot it through. Silverman wrote with a formal invitation of 17 February 1965. 'It is quite certain that with the bill in your hands the chances of ultimate success would be so much greater.'

To pilot a bill through a House of Parliament requires expertise and experience. Ramsey knew that he was unqualified: 'I am only an amateur Parliamentarian.' It also required that he stand up to cruelty and rudeness from those who hated the bill. This he believed that he ought not to mind. It also required that he spend many hours in the House of Lords, and cancel many engagements. This he also felt that he must do in so good a cause, though he had to go to Australia and New Zealand in March and April. Two days after Silverman's invitation, he accepted the offer, on the assumption that the bill would not reach the Lords until after Easter. 'I know that I can count upon considerable help from the Lord Chancellor and others, and it is in that knowledge that I feel it to be a duty and a privilege to accept what you ask of me.' Lord Longford greeted this letter as wonderful news. And Ramsey left for his tour of Australasia.

It will be no surprise to the reader of these pages to find that the spearhead of the Lords' opposition to the bill consisted in Lord Dilhorne and Lord Kilmuir. Dilhorne was horrified to hear that Ramsey would pilot the bill. No doubt his motives were mixed. It could hardly do the bill other than good if the archbishop were to pilot it through, since the bill was a moral issue. Dilhorne thought it would be monstrous if the impression were given that the enemies of the bill were less moral than its advocates.

Dilhorne (26 February 1965) wrote a letter to Ramsey begging him not to pilot the bill—'frankly I do feel it would be most unwise and inappropriate for the Head of our Church to move the second reading of this bill. It is a most controversial measure on which feelings run high.' Gallup polls show that a majority of the country is against it and 'a very great number of Church people will think it inappropriate' that their archbishop should pilot the bill. 'I mentioned this rumour to an old and distinguished member of the House whom we all respect. He made the comment that if the rumour was true, it was both shocking and unwise

. . . I have no doubt that if you do it, it will give rise to very strong criticism both in the House and outside which is bound to impair your position and that of our Church.'

While Ramsey travelled in Australia, indignation among the peers mounted. On 12 March 1965 two civil servants who were experts in the passage of bills told Ramsey's chief of staff Robert Beloe that if Ramsey piloted the bill it would embitter the atmosphere instead of reducing the tension. They advised Beloe that the bill was not certain to pass. And as private citizens, they did not like their archbishop opening himself to the mercilessness which he was bound to face. Beloe sent this out to Australia.

Ramsey at first refused to give way. The matter hung fire while the Commons finished with the bill, which took much longer than anyone expected. In June 1965 Silverman begged Ramsey to pilot the bill and said what a tremendous advantage to the bill that would be. On 23 June Ramsey withdrew. He said that he would do best for the bill not by moving it. But he would do everything possible to help its passage. In the *Sunday Telegraph* (27 June) Kenneth Rose expressed his relief:

Though his qualities of saintliness and scholarship would grace any assembly I cannot see him defending the bill clause by clause, day by day, with the astuteness of an old parliamentary hand like Mr Silverman . . . For the Archbishop to emerge as the protagonist of so controversial a clause could unjustly brand opponents of abolition as less dutiful Christians.

At the second reading of the bill (19–20 July 1965) Ramsey spoke on the second day. A terrible crime deserves a terrible penalty. There has to be retribution; though not vindictiveness nor hatred nor vengeance. But Christian principle demands the possibility of reclamation; that the culprit might be alive, repentant, and different. The taking of life as a penalty devalues life. It 'derates' life. The life sentence is right, even if life is not always served. Moreover, the present act is intolerable in its working. We have either to go on or go back. There is no convincing evidence that the death penalty is a deterrent for armed thieves. No one can help feeling terribly for the victims and their families. Still more do our feelings go out to the police and the prison service, exposed to great dangers. But reason ought to prevail over emotion. Life sentences are a terrible deterrent and can issue in a wise, stern, and human penology. 'To abolish the death penalty will rid us from the wrong of a system which punishes killing by a penalty which helps to devalue human life.'

Lord Kilmuir, who had devised the Homicide Act as the minimum necessary to protect society, attacked Ramsey several times, but with courtesy. He continued to believe that the threat of the rope deterred the armed criminal. 'In over forty years in politics I never thought that I should see the day when public opinion would be sneered at from the Bench of Bishops, and every other part of this House.'

The debate was excellently argued by both sides. And at the end the House carried the second reading by 204 votes to 104. Ramsey and nine other bishops voted in favour. No bishop voted against.

The act abolished the death penalty till 31 July 1970 when it might be renewed by affirmative resolutions of both Houses. Therefore on 18 December 1969 the bishops needed to vote again. This time Ramsey and eighteen other bishops voted against hanging.

7. PORNOGRAPHY

Ramsey was not the only person to lament the squalid nature of so much of modern urbanized morals. And some Christian moralists held that a counter-campaign was necessary; to use the organs of publicity to proclaim again the traditional virtues of the family. Their leaders were as various as possible. Lord Longford, the Roman Catholic, felt it deeply; Colonel Dobbie the evangelical soldier felt it as deeply; Malcolm Muggeridge, then an Anglican and the king of satire on television and against the effects of television, felt it as deeply; Trevor Huddleston, the most celebrated missionary bishop of his generation, felt it deeply. They wanted rallies, and pressure groups. They called the movement by the name the Festival of Light. They were against all the sleaziness of what they took to be a degenerate society; against pornography now accessible to the young by new methods of photography or tape; against the standards of violence and cruelty put over into people's homes on late night films and witnessed by little children who were assumed to be in bed but were not.

Naturally they expected help from the leaders of the Church; and from none more than the Archbishop of Canterbury. They wanted Ramsey to preside at their launching rally at the Central Hall in Westminster on 9 September 1971; or, if he could not be there personally, to send a message of blessing to their campaign. They thought it obvious that he of all men must want to back their campaign to the extreme of his power.

Ramsey was troubled. He could not doubt that the aims were right. Inside himself he deplored the sleeping around, and the pornography, and the televised cruelty. But he found in himself three motives for not wanting to identify himself too publicly with the leaders of the Festival of Light.

The first was the old feeling, derived from his student years, that campaigns and rallies were not the best way to foster the good in humanity. Something about the Festival of Light was akin in mood and emotion to a campaign by some publicized evangelist. He did not doubt that such campaigns sometimes did good. But he knew that they were not his way.

The second feeling was the little fear that such campaigns might attract company with which he wanted not to ally himself too closely. Huddleston, and Longford, and Muggeridge, were all Christian men trying to do what they could for the moral welfare of the society. But he was afraid that some of their allies might identify the welfare of society with making homosexuality illegal again, or restoring capital punishment, or instituting a moral censorship of the press or the BBC. The old Liberal politician who was now the moral leader of the nation was afraid of too close a link with a movement which might attract moralists of the extreme right.

The third feeling of reluctance stemmed from his identification with the cause of justice, and racial equality, and human rights. He did not doubt the objects of the Festival of Light. But he was afraid that if he were to take too prominent a part, the Church would look as though it thought lust to be the worst sin in society; whereas greed, and oppression, and trampling on human personalities were as bad and could at times be worse.

In this mood he distressed the leaders of the Festival of Light by not sending them the blessing for which they asked. Some newspapers got hold of the item that the archbishop refused his blessing to the launching rally.

This rally brought in 4,000 people. The audience contained hostile elements like the Gay Liberation Front, and demonstrators chanted four-letter words, and three 'nuns' charged the rostrum and had to be thrown out, and a few stink bombs and tomatoes were catapulted. But on the whole the demonstrators were defeated, and Trevor Huddleston made a truly Christian speech, and Malcolm Muggeridge was given massive cheers for a speech on the way the media propagate moral pollution. A fortnight later a rally in Trafalgar Square brought in 30,000; and although Ramsey did not send his blessing, he sent them a prayer which they could use and which was used.

Malcolm Muggeridge found Ramsey's attitude impossible to understand. Huddleston backed the Festival of Light on Christian grounds, why not the archbishop? He accused Ramsey, privately, of being so obsessed with ecumenical endeavour that he was forgetting about the moral foundations of society; like a man discussing a better insurance

policy while his house is burgled and burning down. Ramsey was frank
with Muggeridge; about his feeling that rallies did harm as well as good;
about his sense that the Festival was but one among many endeavours among the Churches to do what they could for a better moral
society, and that it was a mistake to identify the important with the
spectacular. And as to not backing Bishop Huddleston—a Christian
bishop uttering the elementary truths of Christian morality could
hardly be strengthened by a bit of paper from the archbishop saying that
he agrees with these truths. 'I hope the Festival of Light will succeed in
reaching people who are not otherwise reached . . . Every intense
spiritual and ethical movement that I have known is liable to a kind of
self-righteousness, and it is not the least surprising if this Festival
is exposed to this danger.' Malcolm Muggeridge continued to find
Ramsey's stance incomprehensible.

From time to time, though not in connection with the Festival of
Light, Ramsey said the sort of things which its leaders liked. He knew
that he could not denounce a particular play by name—though he received many demands that he should do that—because he would only give
the play an advertisement. Once or twice he asked a person whom he
trusted to go and see some play and report, so that his own attitude might
be informed. He gave himself the distasteful duty of looking at examples of pornographic publications, so that if he talked he should know
what he was talking about. He sent out a chaplain disguised as a layman
to buy an armful of hard and semi-hard magazines. He had never seen
anything like them before and was nauseated. That persuaded him that
the law on pornography ought to be better framed. He got into touch
with the Home Office, to see whether anything could be done to protect
old people from pornographic pamphlets falling through their letter-
boxes, but the Home Office did not see how they could give the elderly
such protection without an unacceptable form of postal censorship.

He was pleased, unlike himself, when a group including two Anglican clergy got up on the stage in the middle of a particularly obscene
production and explained to the audience why they disliked what was
happening on that stage. He won publicity by declining to attend the
revue *Oh! Calcutta!* and was accused by a campaigner against it of
leading a sheltered life behind the walls of Lambeth Palace. He won
more publicity when he preached a sermon in the Kentish church of
Bearsted against obscenity and blasphemy in the theatre. He told the
world that the commercial exploitation of sex was *horrible*. But even
when he said this he would qualify it. We need to show the young that
Christian morality is not a series of prohibitions but an adventure of
freedom in unselfishness; and that in face of the contemporary forces

threatening the family, the Churches, if they were wise, would not concentrate on denunciation of sexual evil but would try to cope with the sickness in society which caused the evil.

The criticism of Ramsey among public moralists continued. One wrote to him to say that it was necessary to revive the Spanish Inquisition, and he replied politely that he did not think this suggestion right or helpful.

Though he disliked the pornographers very much, he was balanced about nudity. Someone wanted him to condemn topless dresses. He said that a drive of disapproval against topless dresses might have exactly the opposite effect to that which was intended.[4] Oxford University Press produced an ill-judged Old Testament in five volumes illustrated by artists of the day like David Hockney and John Bratby. Newspapers got hold of the salaciousness of a few of the pictures and noticed that the archbishop had agreed to open the exhibition. They were present in force to see what he would do and say in this predicament. He raised his expressive eyebrows at a Bratby drawing of the daughters of Job. But all he said was this: 'The Old Testament is very human and depicts life in all its crudities—warts and all.'

He received a lot of letters over *Hair* though strictly it was little to do with him. This was a doubtful production, with elements of drug-culture in it, and elements of youthful idealism. Some people got the idea that the dean and chapter of St Paul's were putting on this play in their chancel. What they did was to allow the cast to attend the sacrament and to sing songs from the musical at the evening service, in celebration of the third year of their London run. The opponents of this sort of thing were bitter against the dean and chapter and organized demonstrations at the Cathedral, and Tom Driberg from the House of Commons talked of a motion of confidence in the dean and chapter, and London churchmen voted a censure on the dean and chapter, and the archbishop's postbag was heavy, with people saying that he might at least say that he was disgusted and some of them imagining that the play was put on inside the cathedral. He did not try to interfere. The dean and chapter should defend themselves.

8. RACE

The Conservative government of the expanding fifties needed labour for the economy, and had a policy of unrestricted immigration from the

[4] This produced a remarkable headline in a Cologne newspaper: *Erzbischof von Canterbury ruft zur Toleranz auf.*

Commonwealth. In the West Indies, in Africa, and in the Indian subcontinent there were many only just at the level of subsistence who could easily find work and better pay and food if they came to Britain. Thus they saved the National Health Service and the transport system of the country. But soon the question was argued whether Britain could assimilate such numbers without racial conflict (1957 immigrants 42,400; 1961, 136,000—a number which caused Macmillan's 1962 Act to limit immigration, an act which Ramsey attacked in Parliament); whether the coming of so many non-British already produced blatant racial discrimination in certain areas of life, especially in jobs and in housing; and whether an act restricting immigration could be passed by Parliament without damaging the Commonwealth and without disturbing racial harmonies both within the nation and between the nations. In 1964 happened the race trouble at Smethwick, in 1965 at Leyton. 'It only needs', said the Lord Chancellor Gardiner, 'a bus conductor to be promoted to an inspector and trouble follows.'

Liberal minds were anxious about a rising tide of pamphlet literature which was scurrilous in a racialist way. This large immigration, without anyone expecting it, produced more than one moral problem of the first dimension in the national life of Britain. The Americans at that moment agonized over civil rights. The British found themselves in the same predicament; that of securing justice and fair treatment for citizens of their country who happened to be of a different colour, and a different cultural background, from the majority of the inhabitants. The Archbishop of Canterbury must ex officio be near the centre of the moral argument about laws or proposed laws or even local housing.

The Labour government of Harold Wilson set up a National Committee for Commonwealth Immigrants, thereafter known as NCCI. By an imaginative stroke Harold Wilson offered Ramsey the chairmanship of this committee. He aimed to show that this was not just a political difficulty but a moral one.

It was very unusual in modern times for an archbishop to be offered such State occupation. It was controversial and certain to bring him into the cut and thrust of politics; which archbishops, because they minister to the whole nation, are supposed to be above. He accepted the chair because he wanted to do all he could for racial harmony in a Britain which now was bound to be multiracial, and because he believed that his presence in the chair would help the white nation to see that it had a moral obligation about these new members of the State. The committee's secretary was Nadine Peppard, who had been a language graduate and a school teacher and from 1957 specialized on immigrants in London.

The offices of the committee were in Mayfair, not far from the Dorchester Hotel. Ramsey's first attempt to find it landed him in the Tall Girls Shoe Shop. Nadine Peppard expected Ramsey to be an ornamental chairman. At first she was bewildered and later she was pleased that he was not. Unlike many others who sat under Ramsey's chairmanship she came to regard him as a consummate chairman. In meetings that were torn apart by clashing interests, she found his sense of humour a masterly way by which to hold the company together.

Since there was only a token Race Relations Act, the NCCI had little bite in what it could achieve. Immigrant leaders of local committees suspected it of being a government stooge to cover up rather than to solve the discrimination against them. Ramsey never expected his chair to be comfortable.

He found at once that he was under fire from two fronts. On 7 December 1966 Robert Pitman in the *Daily Express* said (erroneously) that Dr Ramsey was Chief of the Race Relations Board, and that he was probably the most dangerous man of all in the racial question, and that all sorts of sloppy things went on under his aegis, because the existence of a committee like this had only one effect, not of racial harmony, but of encouraging complaints against racial prejudice.

Ramsey had a particular horror of one aspect of the word-battle. Blatant racialists claimed to be racialists on Christian grounds. A racial preservation society was founded in Sussex by two doctors and two clergymen with the aim of repatriating blacks to the West Indies by paying them money to go. Some of these founders had the interest of the black people at heart as well as the white. Naturally they attracted followers who just disliked black people in Britain. In this heated atmosphere the NCCI was accepted by reasonable men as doing useful work.

Ramsey made a few public speeches in favour of the just rights of immigrants, and these were reported in the newspapers, with respect and/or regret according to the point of view. He corresponded with and went to see the prime minister. In the House of Lords he warned of an unhealthy recrudescence of white racialist organizations in the country and begged for a tougher support for his committee. He saw with alarm that black groups, when they believed that the attitude of government had no chance of bringing them the equality which they sought, retired from backing the multiracial programme of assimilation and disappeared into their own black power organizations. He tried to attend the House of Lords whenever the subject of immigration came up. He recommended the Home Secretary to recruit members of the immigrant communities into the police force, and begged him to consider the seconding of police for a training period to a Commonwealth country. He helped ABC television to find the means of planning religious programmes for the immigrants.

Sometimes in his travels across the country he went out of his way to do what he could for the local NCCI organization. In Bristol for two days in June 1972, he had time only for one parish visit and chose the parish of St Agnes, where a play on the Exodus of Moses was to be performed by a West Indian Drama group, who saw the Exodus as a symbol of black liberation. He arrived at the church in a Morris 1000, and fell asleep in the last act, but was woken up by the goats of the escape from Egypt, real goats, bleating down the aisle. In the church hall afterwards he made a speech and said he had come because he had been the chairman of NCCI and wanted to see an inner city parish; but hardly anyone could hear what he said because of the clatter of teacups and Jamaican laughter and the babies crying; so a reporter took him outside and they sat together on the dusty steps of the church.[5]

The Kenya government of Jomo Kenyatta decided in 1967 to expel such of its Asians as had not taken Kenyan citizenship. This was bad for the country of Kenya because the Indians of East Africa provided an expertise in trade and shopkeeping and nursing which the country could ill afford to be without. Kenyatta thought it necessary because a newly independent African country must be seen to be run by Africans.

Many of the Asians in Kenya had not taken Kenya citizenship because they had British passports. Therefore a flood of Kenya Indians set off to settle in England. It happened to be a moment when the British people awoke to the size of the immigrant population, and were alarmed for their jobs and for the future unity and harmony of the country. This new flood, or the prospect of it, caused a storm. The Labour government under Harold Wilson introduced a bill to prevent most of those who had not already come from coming. If this bill was to have the desired result, and not to have the effect of increasing the numbers by encouraging people to get in before the dead-line, it would have to be carried through at once; so that even the House of Lords was under pressure to carry through all stages of the bill in a single day's debate.

Ramsey disliked all this very much. When years before he was a curate in Liverpool he had many Indian and Chinese inhabitants in his parish. He took a stance about equality then and never departed from it. He voted in the House of Lords against the proposal to carry it all in a single night; and then stayed up to an ungodly hour of the early morning to vote against the second reading of the bill.

---

[5] *Three Crowns News*, vol. 19, no. 6. The play was Christopher Fry's *The First-born*.

During February 1968 the NCCI office was pressed very hard on the Asians from Kenya. Ramsey was condemned from both sides; on the one hand from Indian immigrants in England who blamed the NCCI as weak and wanted it to explode in the face of the government; on the other hand by Conservatives, especially peers, who protested against Ramsey's attitude as unrealistic in the face of what confronted the country. As the debates grew fiercer another kind of letter began to arrive, not from peers; nastier letters, anonymous letters threatening violence against Ramsey for his attitude over immigration, some of them vile racialist letters. On 27 February Ramsey appeared on television in the programme *Twenty-Four Hours* and was uncompromising; so uncompromising that he satisfied that canon-leader of left-wing causes in Britain, John Collins of St Paul's, who wrote him a fan-letter (29 February 1968) to the effect that his stand would inspire and encourage people the world over who work for the abolition of all forms of discrimination.

Not all the letters after this broadcast were anything like so friendly. 'Would Christ be an acceptable member of the Race Relations Board? Would he even consent to be a member?' Cummings produced an amusing cartoon in the *Daily Express* (26 February 1968) of Harold Wilson and James Callaghan cowering at a desk as a warlike gaitered Ramsey battered them with a crook labelled 'Down with the Immigration Curb—Keep Britain Brown', and with Wilson saying 'Will no one rid me of this turbulent priest!' and Callaghan saying 'Mm—he's the worst residual legacy of thirteen years' Tory misrule'. Even a wise and responsible Anglican layman accused Ramsey of being under pressure from 'do-gooders, sentimentalists, intellectuals, and the rump of the Liberals'. Ramsey replied quietly that he had not formed his view under pressure from anybody.

Ramsey questioned the axiom of the bill about Kenyan Asians that the fewer the immigrants, the easier the assimilation into this country. It had a truth in it, he confessed. He absolutely accepted now that there had to be limitation on the number of immigrants if the country was to be preserved from racial conflict. But in this case of the Kenyan Asians he believed that the doctrine 'the fewer the easier' was a dangerous half-truth. For if the methods employed to keep them fewer were seen by the immigrant community to be unjust or motivated by racial prejudice, they would confirm immigrants in their suspicions, and hamper that process of assimilation which was going on.

The bill seemed to him to be open to both these objections: to the charge of being unjust, and to the charge of being motivated by a racial attitude. For the bill took away the right to come to Britain which was given when the British passport was conceded, and therefore was like a breach of a solemn undertaking; and secondly, clause 1 said that anyone who had a parent or grandparent with a specified connection with this country was not touched by the ban. This was not formally a racialist clause. But its effect was to allow white Kenyans and not allow Indian Kenyans. Some people therefore held it to be the first piece of racialist legislation ever to be proposed by a British government. Ramsey worried about the effect of community relations in Britain if this clause were seen to be racialist. He was also aware that many of the Kenyan Asians were the sort of people who would help the country—in the National Health Service, to mention the most obvious need. And as the chairman of NCCI, he resented, like all the rest of the committee, the failure of the government to consult the committee before embarking on a course of legislation which concerned its work so vitally.

He said all these things in his speech in the Lords, in a packed house, with ministers squatting on the steps of the throne. Those who heard the speech thought it to be exceedingly effective. And he ended by reminding the peers that the last time they went as a house to Westminster Abbey was for the funeral of Clement Attlee. They had at the funeral Psalm 15, and Ramsey said that he was moved by it and felt it to be a photographic portrait of the upright character that was Attlee's. And he ended his speech by quoting verse 5. 'He that sweareth unto his neighbour, and disappointeth him not; though it were to his own hindrance.' He could not have said more clearly that the government was breaking its word because it did not suit it to keep it, and that the last Labour Prime Minister was so upright that he would have kept it. The Scottish presbyterian minister George MacLeod, in a maiden speech in the House of Lords, said that Ramsey had said the ultimate words on the debate and they were the words which would last. For the readers rather than the hearers the clerks of the House ruined the point. Evidently they were not familiar with the psalms, and printed Ramsey's text as 'He that sweareth under his labour and disappointed him though it were to his own interest'; which, so far as it meant anything, said the opposite of what Ramsey said.

The speech did not please those who wanted more control of immigration. Lord Wigg said that if the bill did not pass because of speeches like Ramsey's, he would have to face the explosions which would happen in British cities. Lord Dilhorne, Ramsey's worst enemy in Parliament, loftily said that he was surprised that the primate should make such a grave accusation that this country was breaking its word, and charged Ramsey with being harsh.

The Lords carried the bill by a small majority of only 24; which showed how many people felt uneasy at what was done. Ramsey's side lost 85 to 109 though all the most persuasive speeches bar two were on the side of the archbishop.

In a sermon in St Paul's Cathedral on 3 March Canon John Collins called for support for the archbishop, and for the rejection of any political party which compromised the principle of non-racialism. The *Observer*, in a prominent article of 3 March (by 'Pendennis') said that this was Ramsey's 'finest hour. He was put on to the committee as a formal symbol of the establishment's concern; last week he turned and denounced our rulers like a medieval cleric. The Government, to its discredit, scarcely understood what he was talking about.' In a leader the same newspaper said that 'the past week has produced the nearest thing to a crisis of conscience that Britain has seen for a long time'.

The passing of the act caused a ferment for the archbishop-chairman in NCCI. Some members of the committee were outraged by the act, and all of them were angry that government had not had the courtesy to consult them beforehand. Inside the committee members pressed Ramsey to lead an act of corporate and very public resignation to prove the committee's total lack of confidence in the government. Ramsey could not think such a demo well-calculated to promote their objective, which was better community relations in this country. The act was now in force. It was not going to be repealed by any kind of pressure.

The Home Secretary, Jim Callaghan, thought it very desirable that the committee should not resign. The evening before the committee was due to meet, he sent Ramsey a personal letter begging him and them not to resign.[6] He argued that resignation would be likely to make race relations in Britain worse.

All that time the newspapers badgered Lambeth—will the archbishop resign?

The committee met on 5 March. It did not resign. Several members kept the threat of resignation up their sleeves. They all gave Ramsey their resignations and said that they would all resign if he resigned. That left him with a heavy responsibility.

Ramsey proposed that he should lead a deputation to see the prime minister to state their case. Harold Wilson received the deputation, the archbishop and eight others, on 14 March. The committee wished to make the point that the act undermined its work; that clause 1 was a clause of racial discrimination; that the committee was in these circumstances doubtful whether it could carry on. Ramsey therefore wished to suggest to the prime minister—he was too gentle a person to

---

[6] Home Secretary to the Archbishop of Canterbury, 4 Mar. 1968.

use the word demand—first, that government undertake to consult the committee before acting in the field of race relations; second that it give NCCI more money; and third that it give sharper teeth for enforcement in the coming Race Relations Bill.

The meeting lasted for an hour and a half. The prime minister gave them kind and diplomatic words. The committee thought nothing of them. They found the prime minister wishy-washy. Ramsey saw that Harold Wilson's mind was half-occupied with some other problem and the talk was interrupted by a secretary coming and conversing with him in whispers on a different matter. Wilson was struggling with a financial crisis about gold and devaluation which had to be settled within hours. He privately hoped that the archbishop did not notice how his mind was distracted. Ramsey noticed all too clearly though he never knew what the fuss was about.[7]

It was a trying month. Outside 10 Downing Street and Buckingham Palace were demonstrations and counter-demonstrations. At Lambeth Joan gave temporary beds and food to seven immigrant women and several immigrant children. The threatening letters against Ramsey arrived more copiously. In the *Daily Express* of 6 March Robert Pitman wrote a satirical article that could hurt; the homelessness of the people in Lambeth, the gardens of Lambeth Palace—could we not fill the gardens with caravans, of a suitably ecclesiastical Gothic design? 'The Primate, I am sure, would be glad to share baths etc, on a shift system.' For a time a police guard was put upon Canterbury cathedral to prevent possible daubers or hooligans.

At the end of the month, when the NCCI decided to remain in being, one member of the committee, Dr Dhani Prem, who was an Indian doctor and the chairman of the children's panel, resigned at the actual meeting, and another member resigned a day later in protest that the committee was being weak. At least ten members of subcommittees resigned. A lot of immigrants held that the committee was discredited. *The Times* even wrote a leader (28 March 1968), 'No More Resignations', saying that the crisis of the NCCI was a reflection of the dismay felt by so many liberally minded people in Britain about Britain's behaviour towards the Kenya Asians. A correspondent of the *Daily Mirror* went round asking immigrants whether the committee had done any good. Some said it had done valuable work; that it had influence with local authorities and helped to shape government thinking on the coming Race Relations Bill. The chairman of the largest West Indian

[7] Harold Wilson described the meeting in *The Labour Government 1964–70* (1971), 307.

organization, Geoff Crawford, who always refused to have anything to do with the committee, said that it had never been any good; that the immigrants on it were not representative of the immigrant community. The *Mirror* printed these findings under the heading 'Dr Ramsey soldiers on'. It implied that the NCCI was petering out with a whimper as an effective force. A group of workers from fourteen areas decided to set up a rival body to do the same work and resolved that the NCCI could no longer serve a useful purpose because it was discredited. At their meeting the Reverend Wilfred Wood, who came from Barbados in 1962 as an Anglican deacon, and was later to be the first black bishop in England but was now the chairman of the Hammersmith Council of Race Relations, said that the structure of the NCCI was set up by a government whose policy was appeasement of racialists and this meant that the NCCI was totally discredited. His assembly became stormy when four black power representatives tried to speak on behalf of 'the ghetto' and were challenged by a white speaker.

The Race Relations Bill
Now the controversy moved away from the Kenyan Asians and into a tenser phase. In April Martin Luther King was assassinated at Memphis, Tennessee. That same April the Race Relations Bill was published. And all England was thrown into argument.

In November 1967 a joint report of NCCI and the Race Relations board recommended strong legislation against racial discrimination. Quite a number of responsible people, including some good Christians, thought it bad to legislate because law was not capable of changing attitudes and to legislate was to provoke racialist feelings by forcing what was hitherto half-conscious to become articulate. Other people were against it on grounds of freedom, a virtue very precious to society, and part of freedom was the freedom of an employer to employ whomsoever he or she wished.

Ramsey did not share these opinions. He agreed that legislation by itself could not change attitudes. But he believed that it could help to change attitudes by showing that prejudice in this matter, when openly expressed in conduct, was repugnant to society; and immigrants must be made to feel that Britain is a just community which ensures equality of opportunity so far as it can. Therefore he and the NCCI welcomed the Race Relations Bill when it was published in early April, despite doubts by members whether it had teeth.

On 20 April Enoch Powell, a member of the Conservative Shadow Cabinet, made a speech at Birmingham which justified the forebodings of those who said that the Race Relations Bill would make racial feelings articulate. Powell said that the country must be mad to allow in 50,000 dependents of immigrants every year. The flow of immigrants ought to be reduced to negligible proportions. We should provide aid for them to go back home if they wished. The Race Relations Bill would give the stranger and the disgruntled the power to pillory the native inhabitants of Britain. We are in a situation where we are watching a nation engaged in heaping up its own funeral pyre. Powell turned to attack Ramsey. There could be no grosser misconception of the realities than was entertained by those who vociferously demanded legislation against immigration. These included 'Archbishops who live in palaces, faring delicately, with the bedclothes pulled right up over their heads. They have got it exactly and diametrically wrong.'

The national storm which followed contained violent speeches for and against Powell. The Conservative leader Edward Heath believed that Conservatism must not be identified with racialism and instantly dismissed Powell from the Shadow Cabinet. Some members of NCCI wanted Ramsey to add his voice to the chorus against Powell. He did not think that he could do the slightest good, but could leave it to others, and it was better to say nothing as he had been attacked personally. But he made his attitudes plain personally and in the House of Lords and, very quickly, on television.

In June police officers came round to Lambeth to say that they had received threats to assassinate the archbishop. Ramsey had to undertake to tell his staff whenever he went out of the building. Two policemen came in plain clothes and tried but failed to look inconspicuous amid a lot of colourful cassocks at a garden party on a lawn in the palace garden. They also came to formal dinners as guests and had to listen to a lot of speeches at Church Assembly.

The Race Relations Bill was passed in the House of Commons and came to the House of Lords in July 1968, on a day when Ramsey was booked to be one of the presidents at the World Council of Churches' meeting in Uppsala. He decided that he must not miss the debate and flew back from Uppsala early. This was a right decision for his speech in the debate was weighty.

He welcomed the bill as a stage in the process of education towards a multiracial society. He commended to the House what the NCCI did in preparation for this bill; and said that he would have liked its provisions against racial discrimination made tougher. He welcomed it not only for the sake of Britain. 'Race relations are a crisis in the world. What happens in one country can have immense effects for good or ill on other countries.'

It was also plain that many British workers supported Powell. There were token strikes on his side across the country. Several hundred dockers marched on Westminster, with protests against the 'victimization of Powell'; the Smithfield porters marched on Westminster. The rector of Linton in Herefordshire called Powell a saviour of his country to be compared with Queen Elizabeth Tudor or Winston Churchill. Ramsey's postbag was not small. Someone wrote to accuse him of emotional blackmail. In September a procession (about which the police were not a little perturbed—it contained a number of members of the National Front) marched from Smithfield Market on Lambeth Palace. One of the stickers waving said 'Powell for Prime Minister'. Ramsey happened to be in Canterbury.

Some Anglicans were worried by the probability of polygamy being recognized in this country, since some immigrants had up to four wives. Ramsey was approached. 'There is no question', he replied, 'of the Church altering its law concerning polygamy, or conniving at polygamy.'

The Race Relations Act, on the passing of which Ramsey congratulated Harold Wilson and Jim Callaghan as 'a splendid piece of social legislation', converted NCCI into a new committee, the Community Relations Commission. Ramsey saw this coming and realized that his position as chairman, in so impassioned an atmosphere, was not the best station for an Archbishop of Canterbury. This was going to be a red-hot seat. It is better if archbishops, whose seat is hot by the nature of their work, do not sit in seats that are bound to be red-hot and which need not be part of their job. Wilson and Callaghan wanted him to continue as chairman. He said honestly that he had not the time to do such responsible work properly. Both the Labour leaders, and several members of the committee, were very sorry indeed that he should not continue. Other members of the committee, for example David (later Lord) Pitt, believed that he was right, that he had not the time. His presence as chairman made the nation see that they were engaged not just in how to keep law and order, but in a moral principle of the first importance. 'I assure you', wrote Harold Wilson to him in a letter which the prime minister forgot to date, 'that your efforts have been very highly regarded by Her Majesty's Government, and I have no doubt at all of great value to the nation.' Ramsey told Nadine Peppard later that what he remembered about the NCCI was some very happy progress and some pretty stormy occasions.

In November Enoch Powell in a speech at Eastbourne made the same plea, in equally inflammatory language. This time Ramsey commented formally in a statement:

Mr Powell's policy is a counsel of despair. He may consider that his plans are motivated by humane principle, but they entirely rule out any possibility of harmonious racial integration . . . To leave behind a small section of coloured people, which feel that England does not really want them, can only lead to a dangerous ghetto situation. What is needed is a programme of education and the exercise of those basic Christian beliefs in the equality of man to which this country is pledged through its support of Human Rights year and the United Nations Charter.

On 11 December 1968 Ramsey went down to speak at St Martin's Church at Basildon in Essex. There was information that the event would be disturbed by the National Front. He talked for thirty minutes without interruption. Then he said that he would like to have seen a stronger Race Relations Act passed (cries of 'Shame'). He said that the Race Relations Act would help to ensure that discrimination was not practised. At that point supporters of the National Front in the gallery raised a storm of noise, with cries of 'Traitor! Villain!' and showers of pamphlets onto the floor of the church. One interrupter said, 'The National Front says Enoch Powell is right. Send them home. Take no notice of this traitor.' Ramsey went on for ten minutes struggling to make himself heard above the din. There were scuffles, and four policemen and the vicar escorted eight men and a girl from the church. (*Daily Telegraph* and *Daily Express* 10 December 1968.)

7

Parliament and the Law of the Church

1. THE BRITISH MUSEUM

For more than two centuries, the Archbishop of Canterbury was one of the three principal trustees of the British Museum and the chairman of its Standing Committee. As such Ramsey had the duty of opening the restored Duveen gallery to house the Elgin marbles properly; and he did not doubt that it was good for the Elgin marbles to be preserved in the way they were. The scholar that was in him enjoyed this ex officio function. But in 1962 a bill came forward proposing radical changes in the constitution of the museum. By these changes the archbishop, and the Speaker, and the Lord Chancellor, would no longer be ex officio trustees. Before the bill came forward Ramsey realized that the old system was an archaism and that the museum needed a chairman who could give it more constant time and attention. He welcomed the change in the House of Lords (9 April 1963). But he liked to continue as a trustee and asked the prime minister, Macmillan, to arrange that he should. Therefore he did not cease then to be a trustee. But he resigned six years later, sure that he could not to give it the time which it needed.

2. VESTMENTS

The clergy of the Church of England had a sensation that all was not well with authority in the Church because so many of them disobeyed the law of the land. A few of the laity had this feeling more strongly. The law of the land was the law of the Church and it was a Christian duty to obey the laws of both Church and State. The chief difficulty was trivial: clothes in church.

The Prayer Book of Queen Elizabeth ordered the priests when they celebrated the sacrament to wear chasubles and albs. This could not be enforced and fell at once out of use except that in cathedrals they went on wearing copes. The Prayer Book of 1662 reiterated the order that they should wear chasubles and albs. But no one obeyed the order. In the Victorian age, with the revival of older rituals, some clergy revived the chasubles and albs for use at the sacrament. Since some laity regarded this as gross innovation and not Protestant, there was trouble in parishes. There were even demonstrations which interrupted services in church.

In 1877 the Judicial Committee of the Privy Council, which was then the supreme court of appeal for the Church of England, tried to settle these disputes by ruling that the chasuble and alb were illegal. This was a well-meaning but ridiculous decision. The clergy regarded the Prayer Book as far more authoritative upon them than a verdict of a few judges who took their view from motives of policy. The judgement destroyed the possibility that the Judicial Committee would be respected as a supreme court of appeal. Bishops and clergy got on with arranging things as they thought reverent and took no notice of the Judicial Committee. By 1961, when Ramsey became archbishop, it was reckoned that some 25 per cent of churches used chasuble and alb at the sacrament; that 29 out of 43 cathedrals, and 17 out of 27 theological colleges did so; and that 90 per cent of the clergy used the coloured stole hung round the neck like a black scarf; and the coloured stole was equally illegal in the eyes of the Judicial Committee.

What was to be done? Have a measure which would reverse the judgement of 1877? The difficulty was, that this would make vestments compulsory in all churches, which no one wished to do and which in its turn could not be enforced. It was also odd to bother about reversing a decision of which no one took any notice. Therefore the leaders of the Church took the view that the right way was a simple measure to legalize the wearing of chasuble and alb in parishes where they were wished for. Such a measure would not settle all problems. For example it would not make mitres legal, which a majority of bishops wore where parishes so wished. But if it were passed it would do more than any other single act to relieve the consciences of the few clergy and laity who felt the disagreement between their Prayer Book or their way of worship and the highest judicial authorities in the land. Therefore it became a principal job of the Archbishop of Canterbury to persuade Parliament to accept the measure.

Naturally he was not comfortable. His memory of the debates over the Prayer Book in 1928 was searing. The Church took its way of prayer to Parliament then, and was scorned. Now it was about to ask Parliament to approve the wearing by the clergy of some clothes which a quarter of them already wore. He could not help asking himself, what sort of a situation was this? Had he to ask Parliament for something for which it was ridiculous that they needed to be asked?

Moreover: if the measure passed Parliament, consciences would be relieved, and a better spirit would grow in the Church. Therefore it should happen. But suppose it did not happen—suppose that Parliament threw it out—what would his own attitude be towards the establishment? What would he need to say about Church and State? Some people would be so offended in principle that they would demand disestablishment. Would he himself? He asked the question. His realism saw that clothes were not a good wicket on which to bat for disestablishment. He saw that what he wanted for the Church was to get it into a situation where it could decide such *apparently* trivial things for itself and not need to go to a House of Commons where any non-Anglican could say what he liked. But meanwhile, he had this discomfort of going to both Houses of Parliament.

He had himself worn the vestments to celebrate the sacrament ever since his ordination as priest of Liverpool, though not when he found himself in a place where that was not the custom. He valued the practice. It reminded him of the continuity of Christian history, since these were not far from the clothes of a Roman gentleman in the first ages of Christendom which therefore the early presidents at the sacrament wore. He also found colour, though with restraint, a help in worship. It was also the custom of the two largest Churches of Christendom, and was at one time the custom of the largest Protestant Church of the Reformation.

But this was not everyone's opinion. There were those who did not regard them as unimportant. Mr Kensit and the Protestant Truth Society, Earl Alexander of Hillsborough, who was a Baptist lay preacher and who unlike Mr Kensit was formidable because he was an experienced politician and because he helped to win a World War, believed that it was a shocking thing that such vestments should be made legal, a national disaster, even a national crisis. Such opponents were not weakened in their resistance by their fear that this Anglo-Catholic Archbishop of Canterbury pulled them bit by bit towards the Roman Catholic Church. And there were some who were offended by dressing up at all. A lady from Camberley asked why the clergy should appear like eastern potentates.

In February 1964 the Church Assembly passed the measure by large majorities—unanimous in the House of Bishops—and it went forward to Parliament. The government was a Conservative government under Sir Alec Douglas-Home.

During the early summer the campaign mounted to persuade either House of Parliament to throw out this measure. A factory was created for writing postcards to MPs to tell them what a national disaster this would be. Near the end of June 1964 *The Times* had a headline 'MPs fear drift to Rome'. A pamphlet was distributed which Ramsey thought very unpleasant but admitted to be clever.

The problem for the archbishop was not only the national rumour or newspaper gossip. It was the insecurity of Conservative MPs for their seats in Parliament. A general election was near. Opinion polls showed that Douglas-Home's government was not likely to retain power; or that if it retained power it could only do so by the narrowest of margins. Therefore some Conservatives would lose their seats. MPs in marginal constituencies had no desire to lose even a few voters, however quaint or fanatical, for the sake of satisfying the Archbishop of Canterbury, who could be represented as wanting them to do something that was not necessary; since, whatever happened, no one would change their custom.

The campaign began to worry Ramsey. It also worried the Conservative leaders. The leader of the House of Commons was Selwyn Lloyd, Ramsey's old friend from Magdalene College and the Cambridge Union. Prodded onward by the Chief Whip, Selwyn Lloyd went round to Lambeth on 19 June 1964. He begged Ramsey to postpone the bringing of the measure to Parliament. He said that the last weeks of Parliament were an 'overexcited' time. He recommended that the first weeks of the new Parliament would be a better time. The archbishop replied that if there were going to be more Labour members, that might mean less sympathy for a Church measure; that if he postponed the measure he would need to explain to the Church Assembly why he had postponed the measure and that he did so for purely political reasons, and then the government would look very peculiar. 'I could only do so in terms which would make an ass of myself but would make a worse ass of Parliament.' This left Selwyn Lloyd with no argument. He accepted the point and said only that the government might not find it expedient to find time for such a measure in the closing weeks of a Parliament.

The archbishop then applied formally to the prime minister that time be given to the measure. He accompanied this with a private letter to the prime minister (24 June 1964). In this letter he made the same point. 'If the Assembly were told that the measure is being postponed for lack of parliamentary time I believe that people would get the impression that the Conservative Party had acted out of consideration of electoral advantage . . . There would consequently arise a real question of principle on which Disestablishment could be demanded and the Church would be divided.'

Worried by the campaign, the archbishop started his own campaign. He wrote to all the bishops, and to all the Welsh bishops, and to some of the clergy of his own diocese, asking that they should do what they could with their own MPs to explain the true situation.

The fuss was unnecessary. The prime minister found the parliamentary time. The opponents proved to be tiny minorities. The measure easily went through both Houses of Parliament—Lords 86 to 15, Commons 205 to 23; with past and present and future prime ministers (Macmillan and Douglas-Home and Heath) in the majority.

The debate in the Lords was marked by a striking intervention from the archbishop. He had asked not to introduce the measure lest the general public or the House get the impression that he thought the subject of vestures more important than it is. He was challenged by Earl Alexander to say whether he was a Protestant. His reply was remarkable:

I am a Protestant, precisely in the way in which the Prayer Book and the Anglican formularies use that term; and when I say that in the sense of our formularies I am a Protestant, I say it without any qualification whatever. I am always, for the purposes of Christian teaching, anxious to add that, with our Anglican formularies, I believe in what those formularies call the Holy Catholic Church, and I believe in that precisely in the sense in which our formularies do, again with no qualification at all.

Earl Alexander was not satisfied and challenged him again. He said still more forcibly:

My Lords, if we started with the definition of Protestantism as understood by the National Union of Protestants (the body of which Earl Alexander was the President), I dare say I should want to make a couple of hundred qualifications; but if we start with the definition of Protestant as embodied in the Book of Common Prayer and the whole of that Book of Common Prayer, I want to make no qualifications at all.[1]

In after years this story was many times told as a special example of Michael Ramsey's jesting humour. He said he was a Protestant as the Prayer Book uses the word but the Prayer Book does not use the word and Earl Alexander the Baptist did not know that the Prayer Book does not use the word and perforce was satisfied. But this story of the jest involves an element of deception which was foreign to Ramsey's nature. It is possible that he had himself forgotten, if indeed he ever thought about it at all, that the word Protestant is not in the Prayer Book. But if he did know, he was not deceitful. Though the word is not used, the idea is not absent.

Afterwards he was very relieved. He attributed much to the quiet

[1] Hansard, Lords, 13 July 1964, cols. 49 and 52.

help of Douglas-Home and Selwyn Lloyd behind the scenes. They helped him and others to the first big step in relieving some troubled consciences; of those who in loyalty to their faith and people did things which they were not sure that in loyalty to the State they ought to do.

Yet he was sure that they ought not to be in a constitutional situation where they needed to bring such a measure to Parliament. He was already sure that there ought to be some kind of general synod which should have the power to decide such things without recourse to Parliament.

3. THE LORD CHANCELLOR

One legal survival of anti-Roman Catholic safeguards remained—or possibly remained, for the lawyers were not quite certain. The Lord Chancellor administered by law a lot of ecclesiastical patronage. He appointed to many parishes—chiefly the less well-endowed parishes where monasteries used to appoint the incumbent. Therefore when Roman Catholics were given equality of civil rights, certain offices were exempt from the operation of the Act; and because of his ecclesiastical patronage, the office of Lord Chancellor was one such office. Yet the main functions of the Lord Chancellor were nothing to do with appointing clergymen to livings. By the twentieth century it looked obsolete that the person who sat on the Woolsack in the House of Lords, and did most to appoint judges, could not be a Roman Catholic. It looked so obsolete that some lawyers argued that it no longer applied and that nothing now stopped the Lord Chancellor from being a Roman Catholic. Still, there was legal doubt. In 1974 the Lord Chancellor, Ramsey's old enemy and friend Lord Hailsham, decided to try to remove the doubt. He therefore consulted Ramsey; and found that Ramsey was wholly in favour of the removal of the doubt.

4. THE HOUSE OF LORDS

No one could think the House of Lords well designed for its work in the modern age. It was weaker in relation to the Commons because its hereditary members made it liable to the charge of not being representative of the people. Yet as business grew in the Commons its revising and redrafting power became ever more essential to the work of Parliament. This need was met in good part by the new system of life peerages which brought many political experts into the Upper House. But the new size of the House, and its average age, made a doubt on the effectiveness of the second Chamber. Its age was the chief argument (apart from history which is no trivial argument) in favour of keeping the hereditary seats; for they ensured that Parliament contained a few members who were in their twenties.

Therefore there was much discussion in Parliament and the nation on the way to improve the composition of the House of Lords as an effective instrument of government. That must ask questions about the hereditary peerages and whether history and youth were sufficient reasons for keeping them when they weakened the House by offering so dramatic an illustration that it was not representative. The discussion must also ask questions about that equally historic group, the seats of the Anglican bishops.

In February 1971 the leader of the House of Lords, Earl Jellicoe, set up a committee to examine the working of that House and to see whether it could not be improved. The committee asked for the views of the bishops. Their answers show various ways in which they regarded their function as debaters or lawmakers and what their difficulties were and what value they felt in possessing a seat in Parliament. A few of them thought that it was not their thing; whether or not they possessed a seat in Parliament, it was very improbable that they would ever take part. Then there were others who, without going so far, believed that their dioceses always had priority over Parliament; their responsibility in Parliament might give them twinges of conscience because they attended so little, but the pastoral need of their people and clergy was overriding in its demands upon their time. These bishops included at their top the Archbishop of York, Donald Coggan, who was one of those who confessed to having a guilty conscience about his neglect of Parliament but he knew where his main duty lay. Then there were the bishops who knew that they could do some good if they represented the Christian faith in Parliament, and wanted to make it easier for themselves to be there at the right times. Statistics showed that the number of bishops who valued the opportunity was more than a handful.

The difficulties which they felt in this duty were much like the difficulties felt by other peers; there was no Speaker, no control over the debates or irrelevance, only convention about the length of speeches. 'There is a lot', commented Bishop Claxton of Blackburn wrily, 'of vain repetition in this House.' The one thing that could be said on the other side was that normally the debates, despite this near-anarchy, were better as debates than the debates in the House of Commons.

Ramsey particularly wanted less irrelevance by speakers—and therefore more control by the person on the Woolsack. He confessed that gross irrelevance did not happen often, but was painful when it did.

Several bishops wanted more time limits on speeches—perhaps, suggested Ronald Williams of Leicester, a 'sweet-toned' bell should sound when the speaker had spoken for twenty minutes; but the bishops were not in a strong position to complain about the length of speeches, because one of their own number, Ian Ramsey the Bishop of Durham, out of whose mouth ideas came bubbling as in a cascade, equalled a recent record for length in a speech of 43 minutes about prisons.

A layman in this discussion called the bishops 'the moral buttress' in the House of Lords. In mere presence it was being whittled down. The size of the House of Lords had increased vastly: the number of bishops remained the same. In 1905 the House of Lords had 594 members and 75 peers was the average attendance. In the year when Ramsey became Archbishop of Canterbury there were 644 members and the average attendance was 143. Ten years later there were 770 members and the average attendance was 265. At the time of Ramsey's birth the bishops made their points in a house of 75; now the same number of possible speakers from the bishops' bench made their points in a house of 265. The reasons for this were, first, the large number of peers created under the system of life peerages since 1958; and secondly, many of these life peers had experience in the Commons or local government or the trade unions and came to the Lords intending to treat the debates like professionals and not like the old amateur aristocrats.

But for a hundred years the bishops had not exercised power in the House of Lords by the number of votes which they could muster. The Kenya Asians bill got a majority of twenty odd in the Lords on 29 February 1968. The archbishop asked himself whether a three-line whip of bishops could have thrown out what he called a 'wretched bill'. Next morning he took it up with Coggan of York; for only three bishops stayed for the vote, but Coggan had been in the House earlier and left because the debate ran into the small hours. He wrote to Coggan next morning in the gentlest form of rebuke:

I think some people will be saying that if twenty bishops had been present the bill would have been thrown out. I think, however, that it was well that that did not happen. The episode sets me thinking again about the significance of voting in the House of Lords, and I feel that the purpose of our voting is to register opinions as a kind of witness and that if we became a body which tried to influence legislation by turning up in force we should be involved in all sorts of difficulties and our position would not be tolerated. I do, however agree with those who have said in our recent discussions that if we are to maintain this kind of token voting there must be a good many of us from whom the voters can be forthcoming. Last night set me thinking about these questions again.[2]

[2] Ramsey to Coggan, 1 Mar. 1968.

Normally the bishops did not vote on political issues. Whenever there was a free vote they normally voted against the Conservative side. But moral issues could run into matters which were red-hot politics, like education, or capital punishment, or racialism in Rhodesia. And to the custom that they did not vote on politics there were exceptions. In December 1966 it mattered that the archbishops and four other bishops voted with the government about Rhodesia. The number of times that the bishops spoke went up during the sixties—because during the sixties many social questions came before the House of Lords. They spoke on private members' bills, on abortion, on homosexuality, on divorce, on capital punishment.

The vote on the Kenya Asians bill was not forgotten. Even three years later the Liberal peer, who was also an Anglican clergyman, Lord Beaumont of Whitley, attacked the bishops in the Lords for their voting or non-voting record. He said that eighteen of them voted for Rhodesian sanctions and that was with the government of the day; but only three of them voted against the Kenya Asians bill, which was against the government of the day; and if they had all turned out, and if Lord Macleod had cast his vote with his voice, the bill would have failed. Lord Beaumont inferred from this that it was permissible for the Church to support the government of the day but not permissible for it to vote against the government if there was any likelihood that thereby the government would be defeated. Ramsey was in the House and had not intended to speak. But he rose now to deny the charge flatly. 'We who sit on these benches vote according to our judgment and our conscience, which may sometimes be for and sometimes against the government of the day. I know no other principle than that which directs our action.'

During 1968 members of all the parties made a serious attempt to reform the House of Lords. This was very difficult. The Lords would be more powerful if they were no longer accused of being fuddy-duddies who were unrepresentative of the people of Britain; and no party in the House of Commons wished to make the House of Lords more powerful. Within all the parties there was a feeling, the more unreformed the House of Lords the better. But this motive was so low that in the years after 1965 various good men and women made a determined attempt to see what could be done. The Queen's speech which announced government policy for 1967–8 spoke of eliminating the hereditary basis of the House of Lords.

This was sure to affect the bishops. The bishops were members of the House of Lords since it was first summoned by medieval kings of England and therefore had a prescriptive right in the constitution. But the situation had changed. The functions of the House were different. The religion of the country was much more plural. Some of those who wished to reform the House of Lords thought that in a modern upper legislative chamber the bishops could have no place. Ramsey had to concern himself with this point of view; and since he did not mind much about establishment, he could not mind much if a reform of the House of Lords took the bishops out of the Lords. But so long as establishment existed, and there was the link between Church and State, he saw the good which could be done by Church leaders in the House of Lords and wanted to keep them there; not all of them perhaps, but some.

The committee proposing reform soon agreed on a house of two tiers: the house of hereditary right, which could only attend and speak, and the working house, of part-time politicians who would need to register at least a one-third attendance at the sessions. The only bishop who could register a one-third attendance, unless the bishops altered their habits, was Stockwood of Southwark. But it was proposed that there should be five bishops with votes, including the two archbishops; and these five should not need to attend one-third of the sessions. Ramsey and his advisers did not mind much about the votes. What they minded about was the right to speak. It seemed to be better to try to keep twenty-six bishops and then there would be a chance that ten or twelve of the bishops would make a contribution to the debates. He told Harold Wilson in a letter of 16 February 1968 that because the bishops had so many engagements there had to be a lot of bishops with the right to come so that a minimum representation of bishops could appear in the House. He told the prime minister in the same letter that he was much in favour of life peerages for selected leaders of other denominations.

Richard Crossman, who was then the Labour leader in the House of Commons, went over to Lambeth to be entertained by the archbishop to the lunch of the Church Commissioners; and was surprised that the Church drank good white wine and good red wine. After lunch he talked to Ramsey about the bishops in the Lords. Crossman understood him to say that he wanted all ecclesiastics in the Lords to be chosen by the Crown from all denominations—that is, no prelates would have seats ex officio and no denomination would have a pre-eminence. Crossman recorded Ramsey's sentence as 'The kind of cleric in future House of Lords would be Donald Soper, the Methodist minister, selected on his merits as a life peer. That's the way I'd like to see clerics chosen in the future'. Crossman pushed at him. 'So you don't want a block of seats reserved for the Church of England bishops?' Ramsey said that the bishops' pastoral duties made it impossible for them to attend regularly and that when they did attend it might not be desirable. Such was Crossman's record of the conversation.[3]

In Ramsey's papers this opinion does not appear. Obviously the plan would be necessary if the link between Church and State were broken. But in his papers on the subject Ramsey took it for granted that the link would continue and therefore that there ought to be some seats ex officio for clerics; who thereby, he believed, had the chance to do good in the nation. But it seemed very unlikely that in a general reduction of the Lords there could still be twenty-six bishops.

On 9 April 1968 Ramsey with other bishops met a strong committee of Parliament which included the Lord Chancellor (Gardiner), Shackleton the leader of the House of Lords, Callaghan, Crossman the leader of the House of Commons, Silkin the government chief whip, four strong Conservatives in Carrington, Jellicoe, Maudling, and Macleod, and the two Liberals Byers and Jeremy Thorpe. Ramsey's advisers beforehand were not sure what the result would be. Beloe thought that not many of them wanted bishops as members for the House of Lords, there would be no one on the government side strong for it and Crossman was an iconoclast; that the two Liberals still had to think what nonconformists wanted; and that the four Conservatives were friendly although they regarded the bishops as too far to the left in their politics. These predictions were deceived.

The debate in the House of Lords, on the plan as drafted in a white paper, lasted for three days of November 1968 and was the longest debate which some peers could remember: One or two speakers wanted to get the bishops out altogether but most speakers preferred to have them there. Ramsey spoke on the third day. He said that he greatly hoped that the white paper would be approved and that legislation would follow. He said that he greatly appreciated the consideration given to the bishops' bench by members of the inter-party conference, and that we would 'most heartily welcome the nomination to life peerages of members of other Churches than mine'. He thought that so long as the establishment remained it was right to have bishops in the Lords. He thought it reasonable that in a reformed House of Lords the number of bishops should be diminished.

The approval of the white paper was carried by a large majority, Ramsey and seven other bishops voting in favour.

[3] *The Crossman Diaries*, 19 Oct. 1967. When the archbishop said to Crossman (if he did say it, diarists seldom get things quite right) that some bishops who attended would be better if they did not attend, Crossman assumed that he blamed Stockwood of Southwark for being a political prelate. This is not likely. Ramsey had no blanket disapproval of political prelates. He knew that on occasion he was one himself.

Ramsey asked himself what he valued in the system by which bishops sat in the House of Lords. The question was, what are the best organs through which the Church can form moral judgements about important matters in the community and bring those judgements to bear upon the public conscience and upon the State. The answer did not seem to him perfectly plain. There were bishops who used the House of Lords for their witness—George Bell, Cyril Garbett. There were others who also wielded wide moral influence in the community but used the House of Lords little—William Temple.

What is the importance of their voting power? Is the vote one way of getting a bill through or resisting a bill? Or had it quite another function—a sort of prophetic public witness? Ramsey asked himself, is sitting in the House of Lords by a bishop a privilege—or is it a burden which had to be borne for the sake of a moral cause? When he put the question in that form he knew how to answer it. 'The House of Lords and the establishment and all that goes with it is not for me, and I think for my colleagues, a form of worldliness so much as a form of bearing the burden of history in Christ's name obediently, however painful it is.'[4]

All this work and thought on what would happen if the number of bishops in the Lords was reduced was wasted when the inter-party alliance to reform the Lords collapsed. Those who (for the sake of the Commons) preferred the House to be as unreformed as possible won the day.

In 1971 (resolution 15 June) the House of Lords behaved with generosity to retired bishops. It voted to allow them to use the facilities of the House of Lords. This invitation showed not only the courteous nature of the House, but that the bishops were a welcome element in the body.

However, the bishops had just behaved with courtesy to the peers. The peers, who were so much more numerous than formerly, and attended with more zeal than formerly, badly needed another room to talk, or to have a bar, or to smoke, or to store bottles. Some of them were former members of the House of Commons and thought it monstrous that a House in a Parliament should not have a convenient bar. They cast envious eyes upon the large bishops' robing room as though it was Naboth's vineyard. They observed that the bishops had a large room which was seldom filled because the attendance of the bishops was sparse. They found a small hole into which they suggested that the bishops might like to transfer their robes. But the bishops needed to

---

[4] Evidence to Church and State Commission, 13 Jan. 1968.

hang the robes which they wore in Parliament and they needed to wash. A quest for lavatories, and wash-basins, and cupboards, ensued.

Some on the Lords' committee suggested that the bishops should not robe at all when they attended the House. And this was a serious point for discussion with Ramsey. For Mervyn Stockwood, the Bishop of Southwark, wanted bishops not to wear robes and once appeared in the House in a lounge suit, which was much commented upon and adversely. The life peers of other denominations, like Lord Soper and Lord Macleod, did not dress up, no other peers dressed up, why should the bishops? (But this was not quite true—Lord Soper always appeared in the cassock which was his daily costume and Lord Macleod appeared in formal ex-moderator garments.) Ramsey took the view that it was better that they should appear in robes. It reminded both the peers and themselves of the purpose why they were there at all.

This little piece of parliamentary life took quite an argument and time, and was settled amicably by all parties when the bishops gave up the large robing room, and the archbishops retained their room, and the bishops moved into a smaller room which was then enlarged to meet their needs; and so the peers got their smoking-room and the peers' bottles were stored where once the bishops had washed. The non-teetotal peers were pleased with the bishops. When the works of alteration were done, some of the episcopal cupboards were found to be filled with filthy old rochets and chimeres dating back to the 1920s.

Ramsey enjoyed being a member of the House of Lords. Though his origins and his logic made him careless about value in an establishment, he found his membership of Parliament a valuable platform. He liked the place very much. He stayed often into the night, and enjoyed the debates. He was always in sunny mood if it was a day when he must go to the House of Lords. He enjoyed the friendships which he formed with some of the peers. He made attendance at the Lords a priority. The peers recognized it and gradually came to welcome him and his presence. Attendances in the chamber increased when he was known to be speaking. The Marquess of Salisbury once told John Andrew that though he was not often in agreement with the archbishop, he thought him the ablest person in the House. Curiously some peers valued him more than they valued Fisher, though Fisher had the true gift of a debater. And this was probably because Fisher used to come just to speak and then go away, and did not often stay for a long debate. Ramsey sat long, and listened to many of the other people who spoke and therefore had the feel of the place and touched its sense of courtesy. Of course this meant a bigger demand upon his time, but he thought it worth it. In his own speaking he was helped by the accurate material collected by Robert Beloe, and the clear way in which Beloe presented it to his attention.

5. PRAEMUNIRE

During 1965 there was warm feeling in the Church of England that all was not right with the relations between Church and State. Ramsey's existence helped to encourage this feeling for even in his enthronement sermon he talked of the need for more independence from the State and did not conceal this opinion thereafter. He was determined that the Church should have the necessary freedoms for its life, especially in prayer. Freedom in teaching and doctrine was what mattered to him. About freedom in the appointment of bishops he minded less; partly because he knew, as no one else knew, how much freedom the Church possessed already through its archbishops; and partly because he thought the alternative to be choice of bishops by a committee of the Church Assembly or the General Synod, which he expected to be a bad system. If the necessary freedoms could not be achieved without disestablishment he would not mind. Only, as things were, he preferred the link not to be broken; because he was afraid of the Church shrinking into a cosy ecclesiastical group and ceasing to be so involved with the world and with society. In his old age, looking back, he said, 'I've never been plain C of E like Fisher. I've been partly nonconformist and partly Tractarian. I never cared much for establishments.'

Accordingly it was necessary to have another Church and State commission—the fourth of the century.

While the Church and State commission began to sit, the lawyers achieved without their assistance an amazing change in the relations between Church and State: nothing less than the abolition of praemunire.

The statute of praemunire was first passed as long ago as 1353. King Henry VIII used the act to force cathedral chapters to elect the bishops whom he nominated for election. Since the penalties were very severe, and included the confiscation of all the culprits' goods, a majority of canons who refused to elect the crown's nominee would be liable to these penalties; and it was widely believed that the existence of this ancient act preserved the Crown's right to control the appointment of bishops. The lawyers, as they considered the reform of the law, saw that this was preposterous. No one would ever confiscate the goods of canons even if they were truculent or pig-headed. They quietly built into the Criminal Law Act of 1967 the abolition of praemunire. No one wanted the chapters to start trying to control the election of bishops. The Home Office took the trouble to point out that it was still the duty of the dean and chapter to elect the Crown's nominee within twelve days and that if they failed to do so the Crown could appoint by letters patent. This was true but the Home Office was pompous about it. They did not mention that a bishop appointed so high-handedly would not be comfortable in his diocese or in the Church.

6. THE FREEDOM OF THE CHURCH

On 13 January 1968 Ramsey went down to Greyladies at Blackheath to give his own evidence to the Church and State commission. It was snowy. Several members of the commission took the precaution of engulfing themselves in scarves and jerseys. The chairman made a note that day:

The Archbishop of Canterbury came at 10.30 a.m. bubbling with pleasure. He delivered a wonderful exposition of the whole Church–State problem; eloquent, realistic, discriminating, with a background of world-Christianity and the post-Constantine era. He sat in a chair which collapsed under him. He said 'This chair has disestablished itself'. The commission listened spellbound. Some of them had never heard him talk before. 'There's nothing to beat an academic education' said someone afterwards. He dealt with questions very well and serenely, taking a bad question and turning it into a good question before he answered it. The most interesting thing was that he valued autonomy in worship far more than autonomy in appointing bishops.'

He said to the commission:

I believe that a report from this Commission that took rather conservative lines would cause distress and bewilderment, unless it had first made a radical examination of the basic issues of Church and State. I think there needs to be a lot of sensitivity to the reasons and feelings which make Anglican establishment difficult for some people to swallow. How far is it right for the Christian Church as a divine society to be buttressed by privileges given to it by states and communities which states and communities do not give to other people . . . ?

Why has the Church of England been the slowest Church in the Anglican Communion (with the exception of the Church of Australia) to get on with the revision of public worship? But . . . on the other side . . . I think it possible that an abrupt measure of disestablishment would give the discouraging impression of a kind of repudiation of Christianity by the English State.

I believe it is a fallacy that establishment makes the Church and its leaders worldly . . . Worldliness is an influence that seeps through the whole community and a Church severed from the State can be just as worldly as a Church that has bishops sitting in the House of Lords. In my judgment the Church Assembly is as worldly a body as the House of Lords, and possibly more so!'

He said that it would be intolerable ever again (after 1928) to take a measure about a new Prayer Book to Parliament. Therefore the only alternative was to give power to Church Assembly, or General Synod its successor, to decide about prayer books without any interference from the House of Commons. What he wanted was freedom in prayer. Everything else could bide its time. He must not risk losing the looming freedom in worship by raising opposition in Parliament on other issues which were nothing to do with freedom of the Church to pray as it thought best.

When the General Synod came into existence (1970), Ramsey sent out to all the dioceses a foreword to an explanation of the measure, and a commendation of the new institution. He believed it to be a gain that bishops and clergy and laity would sit and work together in a national synod. He always believed it a gain that the General Synod should come into existence. But he had a doubt. Later experience led him to think that one result was more bureaucracy; and bishops had less time for what mattered; they had more committees to sit on instead of fewer, and must sit hours listening to discussions of questions to which they knew the answer while people who knew nothing about the problems argued. He did not doubt that synodical government was necessary and he was only sorry that it meant more words and he wondered whether all the words were necessary.

The crux was the use of the old Prayer Book. If a Church had 'freedom' in ordering its way of prayers, it must be able to abolish the use of the old Book of Common Prayer and make a new book. But if it abolished the Book of Common Prayer would it still be the Church of England?—for the Book of Common Prayer was accepted as the principal trust deed by which it held its property. A lot of people said their prayers for fifty years with the words of Thomas Cranmer and found how through the medium of those words their souls were carried up towards heaven. They could not bear the idea that their Church could deprive them of the words; and if they went to church and discovered a service which was not (more or less) in the Book of Common Prayer they hardly recognized the service to be their own. But if they were schoolboys or schoolgirls, or young people, no familiarity instilled the affections for the historic words, archaic, and rotund with the rhythms of Renaissance English. They liked it when they were allowed to talk to God in the language which they used to talk to their parents. They could not realize that prose was usually right for their parents and that there were times when poetry was a better language for God. Pastors who cared for the young hated the idea that teenagers thought the Christian message to be a fossil because it came to them in antiquated language. Though these pastors often had affection for Cranmer's words through long usage, many of them saw the pastoral need of the young as far above the feelings of the old. Such feelings they were wrongly apt to dismiss, and in their worser moods to despise, as due more to literary sensibility than to religious conviction. And if they detached themselves and looked at Cranmer critically, they saw that the sixteenth century liked longer words, and more words, than does the twentieth century.

A majority of the dioceses voted that the Synod should have power to abolish the use of the Book of Common Prayer if it judged it right. This was regarded by the doctrinaire as 'a matter of principle'. Unless the Church could abolish the Prayer Book, it could not be said to be 'free' in ordering its prayers. But before it came back to the General Synod, Ramsey and the other leaders of the Synod realized that, whatever their private views, they would never get a measure past Parliament if the measure envisaged that the use in churches of the historic book was made illegal or might at some future time be made illegal. They therefore introduced a measure which gave the General Synod the right to order the liturgies of the Church of England, and took that right away from Parliament, but which preserved the use of the historic book for any parishes that wished to keep it; not without wild accusations that in so messing the measure around, the leaders of the Synod made no proper consultations.

On 7 November 1972 the General Synod debated the point whether or not the Synod ought to have power to abolish the Prayer Book. Bishop Ellison of Chester argued that unless the General Synod had this power the Church would not be independent of the State in the matter of its prayers, and this was a point of absolute principle. Ramsey argued the contrary—he was sure that it should be lawful for a parish which wanted to have the old Prayer Book to have it whatever the Synod said. His manner of conducting this through the General Synod, in a way which meant that the Church did not lose the enormous area of independence from the State which he was just in the process of gaining for it, was masterly.

He thought it a mistake to freeze a new book of worship prematurely. It needs experience and maturity. To make a prayer book you need a committee. Authorship by a committee is the certain way to jargon and compromise and bathos. Prayers ought to be drafted by a single mind which is sensitive to the English language. In the draft services he found moments of compromise, or of banality, or even lack of taste, and he lamented. But he saw that there was no escape. You could not tell a poet to write your book of prayers and then order the professors to knock the poetry about. Nor could you tell the professors to say what they wanted and then tell the poet to put it into English that will carry the worshippers towards heaven and not let them down with a bump. You have an inescapable difficulty, for which the only cure is quiet use and quiet meditation by the Church over the years.

The Worship and Doctrine Measure was carried in the General Synod by an enormous majority on 20 February 1974 (bishops 34 : 0; clergy 170 : 2; laity 140 : 8). 'I speak', said Ramsey, 'moved by a sense of history. I was ordained deacon in the year 1928, and those of us who were ordained round about that time will never forget the deep sense of frustration with which we entered upon our ministry . . . The frustration was due to the sense of impasse in the Church's life and freedom': and now—'the State gives to the Church a degree of power that it is wonderful to think of, while at the same time the State knows the identity of the Church with which it is in partnership, an identity guaranteed by the continuing role in doctrine, and whenever desired in use, of the Book of Common Prayer . . . It is a historic day'.

By a marvellous stroke of fortune the crucial Parliamentary measure for the autonomy of the Church in doctrine and worship came to the House of Lords on Ramsey's last day as Archbishop of Canterbury, his seventieth birthday, 14 November 1974. That ensured a cheerful, not to say laudatory, passage, unopposed. Ramsey proposed it. He said that it was not a measure for disestablishing the Church of England. It was not a step towards separating the Church from the Crown. Far from being a measure for abolishing the Book of Common Prayer it gave it a secure place which could only be altered by the action of Parliament. 'If it is suggested that I am an old man in a hurry I would recall that at my enthronement in Canterbury thirteen years ago I pleaded for the necessity of a measure on these lines, and it has taken until the last few hours of my primacy for its introduction to come about' (laughter among the peers).

The Lord Privy Seal (Shepherd) said that the government was benevolently neutral. He got a lot of cheers when he paid tribute to Ramsey as an unshaken man of God in a time of theological turmoil and a wise man whose simplicity of speech and way of life remained amid all the pomp of his position. He said (untruly) that his mitre was always on straight. Lord Beaumont said that Ramsey had given a decisive answer to the dictum of Bishop Gore, who said that it was barely possible to combine the activities of being a good Christian and a good bishop. The Earl of Onslow said that this bill was disestablishment by the back door, but almost all the peers were sure that it was right and glad that they could pass it when it was so much the achievement of an archbishop who would retire at the end of that day.

The freedom of the Church in its prayers, and the looming freedom of the Church in a greater say in the choice of its leaders, was in good part the achievement of an ex-Congregationalist Archbishop of Canterbury. It rubbed out the blot upon the corporate memory which was left by a ranting House of Commons forty-six years before. It eased consciences that were troubled by the conflict of authority in the Church. It finally sanctioned a long overdue effort to match the ways of worship to the pastoral needs of modern parishes. It transformed the feeling and the morale of Church people. It was the best thing that happened to the Church of England since the Victorian revivals of religion.

With the gain came disasters. To make new liturgies is sometimes to make banal words instead of poetry. It is to deprive mature Christians of words which speak to the deepest part of their soul. Afterwards Ramsey, who fought with such tenacity to see that the rights of those who wished to pray with the old Prayer Book were preserved, was grieved in his retirement to see how the affections and past associations of many older parishioners were trampled on by parish priests and their inner ring of church people, and by some theological colleges in the way in which they trained their ordinands. But he did not doubt that despite this calamity, the sanctioning of the new liturgies was necessary to the Church and its pastoral work and its training of the young in how to worship their God. Towards the end of his life, until he could celebrate the sacrament no longer, he always used one of the newer liturgies in his private chapel.

Behind the scenes he and his helpers achieved an even bigger relief to the minds and consciences of many of the clergy.

A Church must be something; that is, it must teach something; on the basis of which it exists; and on the basis of which it owns property as a charitable trust. If the Church of England decided to teach a Muslim faith it would lose its churches and its property to those Anglicans who wished to go on in the old way; as would any charitable trust if its trustees put the money to uses which were outside the purpose of the charity.

Therefore there must be a form of doctrine to which the teachers of the Church must agree before they are licensed as teachers. In the history of the Church, and in English law, this meant acceptance by the clergy of the English Prayer Book and the Thirty-Nine Articles of Religion of 1571; the second being the document laid down by the Reformation to define the teaching of the Church; but since in any

Church teaching was inseparable from the language of worship, accepting the Prayer Book was just as important, or more important, than accepting the language of the Thirty-Nine Articles.

Language and ideas change over the years; and by the later seventeenth century Prayer Book and Articles were out of date, in some parts, if taken in their literal senses. With the Prayer Book that hardly mattered; for it was a way of prayer, and prayer is in part the words of poetry, and if the language sounded old-fashioned it could be used as poetry. But with the Articles it was troublesome. Had we to refuse to allow anyone to be a clergyman in the Church of England unless he promised to believe that Noah's flood covered all the earth, or that the wicked people are tormented in fire for all eternity, or that pacifism is unchristian, or that no one ought to have lunch with someone who has been excommunicated? If the language was understood literally we demanded this of everyone before he was ordained to the ministry of the Church.

In 1865, while Darwin and the new studies of the Bible affected minds, Church and State helped consciences generously. An act was passed which allowed the clergyman to make 'a general assent' to the Articles. That was not just a relief, it was a change without which the Church of England could hardly have survived into the twentieth century. Henceforth the young curate need only say that he agreed with the general sense or drift of the Articles and did not have to accept some particular phrases or clauses in them.

Still, the obsolete language went on disturbing minds. In the 1950s the philosopher Dean Matthews of St Paul's led a campaign to abolish the need to subscribe, even in this general way, to the Thirty-Nine Articles. And Ramsey, whose general assent to doctrine was much less loose and less vague than the assent of Dean Matthews, believed that the campaign was right. The young clergy must be helped not to be troubled in their consciences without necessity.

There were two difficulties. The first was, anyone must shrink from altering one of the trust deeds by which a charity held its property. Such an alteration could only be done with justice, if the charity secured the approval of the State. Were they to ask the State for approval about the language of Christian doctrine and endure prating from some modern Praisegod Barebones, and discourses of crass ignorance about transubstantiation, all over again?

The second was, that it is easier, and more general, to agree to an old statement of doctrine than a new; because everyone allows the older language to need adjustment. If we abolished the old Articles and wrote twenty-five new articles, might the tyranny over consciences be worse?

Who will write the new? Even though for once the Archbishop of Canterbury happens to be a learned theologian, are we to trust him single-handed with so controversial a task, sure to meet shrieks of dissent?

Ramsey was not at first sure what should be done, but was sure that something must be done. In 1967 he and Archbishop Coggan set up a commission on Christian doctrine, with Ian Ramsey as its chairman. In inviting him to be the chairman, Michael Ramsey wrote that the first task of the commission was to consider the problem of subscription to the Thirty-Nine Articles. He was pleased when in the next year the commission recommended that subscription to the Thirty-Nine Articles should cease.

But to recommend is not to do. Something must take its place —what? And are we to ask the State to approve such a change in the trust deed of the Church? As time passed it was possible to see how this could be done. If the State gave freedom in doctrine and worship to the Church, as the Church and State commission recommended, then the Church authority could alter the terms of the trust, within reason, without seeking the approval of the State authority.

As this freedom was only conceded during and after Ramsey's last moments as archbishop, he did not see its consequence while he was responsible. But he did most to cause it. During the year after he left office a canon was promulged, changing the form of subscription which the clergy must accept to something much simpler. (The clergy affirm their belief in 'the faith which is revealed in Holy Scripture and set forth in the Catholic creeds and to which the historic formularies of the Church of England bear witness'.)

This change helped in all sorts of personal scruples among those who wished to serve God in the Church. It was one of the gains which Ramsey won for English Christianity.

For thirty-seven years of his life as a priest he used a liturgy, and clothes in church, which strictly speaking were illegal. The conscience of the Church was not at ease. For the last twenty-three years of his ministry he used a liturgy, and clothes in church, which were as legal by State law as by Church law. That is one measure of what he did for the religious conscience in England.

8

Northern Ireland

Ramsey was famous for wanting to get friendliness, and perhaps eventual unity, between Protestants and Catholics. Therefore he was more unpopular in Northern Ireland than anywhere else in the world. For part of the suspicion which Ulstermen felt for the South of Ireland was fear that in a united Ireland the dominant Catholicism of the South would swamp their Protestant faith and culture. Anyone who proposed that the gulf between Catholic and Protestant was not so wide as people fancied, and ought to be narrowed, was a threat to the distance which they wished to keep from the South of Ireland. Ramsey was a political menace as well as a religious; for in this matter religion and politics were entwined.

As early therefore as his first year in the see in Canterbury, newspapers in Northern Ireland said robust things about him. They soon found plenty to say. He said things contrary to orthodox Christian doctrine. Very early in his time he said that people who led a good life on earth but found themselves unable to believe in God would not be debarred from heaven—'I expect to meet some present-day atheists there'. (No one reading this would set up the inward connection with his memory of his own brother Frank.) Then he was asked whether someone could be a Christian without believing in the virgin birth of Christ; and he said that they could; 'if you do believe Him to be divine then the virgin birth becomes congruous. I believe it is quite in order for a person to stand up in church and recite the creed, even if he has scruples about the virgin birth, provided he believes in the pattern of faith as a whole'. Among the orthodox of Northern Ireland this was declared to be Ramsey licensing deliberate lying in God's house. Then it was reported that he went to Moscow in a purple cassock and purple four-cornered hat and crossed himself frequently in St Elijah's church and later kissed the icon of St Elijah and took off his hat to kneel before the religious picture and kissed its glass twice: 'Dr Ramsey is a Baal-worshipper, his knees have bowed to the beast of Baal and his mouth has kissed Baal's lips.' But the basic charge was that he was engaged in unprotestantizing the Church of England although he was sworn to uphold the Reformed Protestant faith.[1]

In 1964 Ramsey joined the annual pilgrimage by the Church of Ireland to Saul and Downpatrick on St Patrick's Day. It was a day of incessant rain and biting wind and only three thousand people, though every diocese of the Church of Ireland was represented. Ramsey spoke and said that the relations between Catholic and Protestant were getting better; and how we ought to be grateful to St Patrick who converted Ireland to the faith; and that the mighty hymn, Patrick's breastplate, showed in the best way how the essence of the Christian creed could be put into poetry.

In 1967 he went to Dublin to give a lecture on Rome and Canterbury which was outspoken about the difficulties between Anglicans and Roman Catholics and optimistic about the new atmosphere between them. He went on to Limerick to dedicate a window in the cathedral in memory of Joan Ramsey's Irish relations by marriage, the O'Briens. He was astonished that so many Irish Anglicans arrived at Limerick to celebrate this family event and said, 'The Church of Ireland boils up in most unexpected places, doesn't it?' He lunched with an ill president, De Valera, and was excited to find that De Valera was educated on his father's mathematical textbooks.

After 1968, and the outbreak of worse troubles, such an act was more difficult for Ramsey. He had visited the Pope, with Ian Paisley and other Irishmen on his tail trying to protest noisily. And in 1968 the modern violence in Northern Ireland broke out after the march on Londonderry. Often he was appealed to—would he not intervene, or offer to mediate, or walk the Belfast streets hand in hand with the Cardinal of Armagh? He had a realistic sense of how little such drama could achieve; and he knew that he must not trespass upon the bishops who had the immediate responsibility, especially the archbishops of Armagh and Dublin. In June 1970 he discussed with Cardinal Heenan of Westminster whether a joint visit by them both to Northern Ireland could do good and they agreed that they did far better to back the efforts of the Irish prelates, Cardinal Conway and the Anglican Archbishop Simms. Nearly a year later he appeared on the Speak Easy programme, amid musical interludes from Bob Kerr's Whoopee band, and surrounded by an audience which was described as long-haired and hot-panted, and a male dancer clutched a stuffed woman to his bosom and waltzed to an ultra-sentimental gypsy melody; and Ramsey was

[1] Undated sheets issued by Free Presbyterian Church of Ulster; and *Northern Whig*, 31 July 1962.

unperturbed by this junketing environment. Jimmy Savile the disc jockey asked him whether it would not do good if he and the Pope walked together through the streets of Belfast. Ramsey said, 'It would be sensational, but I doubt if it would do much good.' A reporter remembered the proverb that you cannot fall into a pit and emerge smelling of violets, but said that the Archbishop of Canterbury had done just that.

In March 1972 the British government was forced to impose direct rule in government; which saved the situation for the moment but left the need to find some way of creating an acceptable form of local autonomy again. The discussions to this end began seriously in the spring of 1973. And Ramsey agreed to visit Northern Ireland during the spring of 1973.

In February 1973 his advisers were suddenly persuaded that he would not be safe if he went, and that in any case the visit would do more harm than good. They told him so forcibly. He felt bound to accept their advice. The Irish Press Office protested fiercely at this decision, and said that it would be understood by no one in Ireland. Ramsey then consulted William Whitelaw, who at that time was the Secretary for Northern Ireland. Whitelaw encouraged him to go. The security services took massive trouble to make sure that he would be safe.

On 30 April 1973 he flew to Belfast and was taken to see Cardinal Conway at Armagh; thereafter the visit took its usual course for a tour of an Anglican province—course of lectures to the Anglican clergy at Portrush (subject, The Holy Spirit and Christianity), dinner with the government, that is Whitelaw the Secretary of State, visit to the universities at Coleraine and Queen's Belfast, and fly home. But on the way various things happened which were not usual in visits to Anglican provinces.

On 1 May he was flown in a helicopter from Coleraine University to Londonderry to visit the army. He stood at an army post which was often the target of snipers and climbed up the sandbags and to the worry of the officers stood exposed for ten minutes looking down at the Creggan and Bogside areas. Then he spoke to the soldiers in a billet nearby and told them how many at home prayed for them and their work, and said, 'The job you are doing will help bring about order and peace.'

Ian Paisley knew that Ramsey could not approve of him. In an interview in New York in 1970 the following dialogue took place:

RAMSEY. I would not call Ian Paisley a man of God.
Q. Does he help at all?
RAMSEY. He doesn't help me. Not a scrap.

Paisley now wrote a heavy letter asking him to receive a delegation. Ramsey did not see what good could be done but Archbishop Simms advised him that it was better to receive the delegation, for the alternative was picketing and banners. Ramsey agreed to give him half an hour on 2 May on condition that there was no prior press notice and that the delegation was not more than six people. The agreement did not avoid banners. When Ramsey arrived at Portrush there was a demonstration of some thirty or forty Paisleyites outside the hotel. When he celebrated the liturgy next morning (during which he turned over two pages without noticing that he left anything out), the noise of a Paisleyite service could be heard outside.

The meeting was held at the archdeacon's home, Culfeightrin rectory. It was not happy. The archbishop offered to shake hands. Paisley refused the hand. He said, 'I have not come here to shake the hand of a man who has just shaken hands with the Pope.' He proffered a Declaration. It started with a straight orthodox fundamentalist profession of faith and of the errors of the Church of Rome. It then proceeded to abuse. You lead the betrayal of historic Christian faith. You have continually crossed yourself and kissed the icon of St Elijah in Moscow. You have attributed to the Holy Spirit your efforts to have unity with Rome. You have embraced the Pope. You have stated, 'Heaven is not a place to which we humans go in our present bodily state, nor is it a place for Christians only.'

We do not know all that Ramsey replied to Paisley for he never recorded it. He said gently that the charges of idolatry over bread and wine were 'misleading'. He said the charming sentence, 'Well, Mr Paisley, you disapprove of my Church, will you tell me a little about yours and how it is run?' But he found conversation impossible. 'So flabbergasted was he', reported Paisley's newspaper the *Protestant Telegraph*, 'that he could only interrupt the proceedings with inane comments and asides.' All experience of him proves that he would have done his best to say something to try to open Paisley's eyes. When he came out his staff saw that he was white and flattened and thought that he needed the glass of sherry with which they revived him. He said afterwards, 'I had not realized the depths of bigotry which are involved with the vocabulary about the Devil, Antichrist, blasphemy, etc.'

The Paisleyites then put a large advertisement in the newspaper placarding a sermon on the visit. The sermon said that the Archbishop of Canterbury is the emissary of the devil and Antichrist; that he thinks he knows better than God himself; that he is a Jesuit and a secret cardinal; and that it is preferable to deal with the Pope, who at least is straightforward. It was reported that the meeting had broken up when Ramsey declared himself an apostate.

One of the reasons why the archbishop liked the archdeacon's rectory as the venue for this least promising of efforts at reconciliation was that it lay near Corrymeela, which at that moment was a high symbol of the possibility of reconciliation in Ireland. He visited the community there on the same day and was warmed by what he found. It was an ecumenical community, formed as early as 1965, by young people who saw models in Taizé and the Iona community, with about 80 members who met six times a year, including two retreats, and staff of eleven; with a programme of work camps and conferences for the young. A few months afterwards he and other Church leaders in England appealed for money for the Corrymeela community. The day when he met Paisley and visited Corrymeela was a day when two Roman Catholic churches were bombed in Londonderry.

On the following day he walked the streets of Belfast, but security would not let him go far down the Catholic streets near the Crumlin Road. They were streets where only a fortnight before there were gunbattles and riots and a boy of 13 was killed in the crossfire. A Protestant woman at her front door in curlers asked why a Protestant archbishop should go visiting the Fenians when we are up here. In a street in the Ardoyne area burnt out on internment night two years before, a little Protestant woman in an old blue mackintosh shrieked and sobbed at him, 'Why are you bothering to go down there? They are the ones who shoot soldiers in the back, and killed our people. My brother-in-law lived down there and he was shot dead.' Joan Ramsey went up to her but she went on shouting till she was led away. He got among the children and they danced about him and asked him whether he enjoyed coming here and he said that he enjoyed going anywhere where he got such a nice welcome from the people (and he repeated the phrase, 'such a nice welcome') and asked them their names. One of the boys, sure that a high Christian prelate would be on his side, told him that his father had been taken by a soldier and had a heart attack and was in hospital, and Ramsey said, 'Tell him I'm very sorry about his illness and hope he'll soon be better.'

The emotional effect upon both the Ramseys came then, when they visited the hospital where the maimed were lying, both soldiers and civilians. Joan especially won an accolade from the people who followed because she did not shrink from proximity to horrors.

The quest for an agreement in Northern Ireland led to the Sunningdale meeting of December 1973 and the end of direct rule in January 1974, though the British government remained responsible for law and order. A general election in Northern Ireland of February 1974 was disastrous for the new executive government, and in March 1974 the IRA began a further vicious bombing campaign. In these conditions Ramsey agreed to go again to Belfast.

He again visited the university at Belfast, and this time preached in the cathedral. He had not preached in the cathedral last time, because it was thought that there was bound to be trouble. He discussed beforehand with the Irish office what it would be most helpful for him to do. The visit to the cathedral was on a weekend when there were two vile murders and the wounding of a judge and two big explosions in one of which a policeman lost a leg. This visit attracted the expected demonstration. When Ramsey started his sermon an ancient woman in front started shouting. He went on talking about peace in Ulster, but some ten men got up and started shouting 'rubbish' and 'papist' and then pushed their way out of the cathedral. They halted the sermon to sing a hymn and then he went on unperturbed: 'there are in this province thousands of Christians who are sick and weary of strife and bitterness. Already in many parts of this province there are Christians—Roman Catholics and Protestants—who are ready to pray together and to seek reconciliation. The future lies with those who have such thoughts in their hearts.' Outside the cathedral a larger group of about thirty waited with placards ('Protestant Ulster rejects Ramsey Arch Apostate') but Ramsey went out of a side door and never saw them. The *Sun* had a good headline: 'Ramsey in a Rumpus'.

He walked by bomb damage in Royal Avenue near the cathedral and again expressed his admiration for the soldiers and his conviction that there existed silent thousands who wanted reconciliation. At a press conference he said, 'The good gets better and the bad gets worse. But a Christian is bound to be an optimist—certain that right will one day prevail.' He said that he was in favour of power-sharing. He refused to tell Protestants who were not in favour of power-sharing that they ought to back it; he backed a plan for a provisional cease-fire; thought the withdrawal of the army would do no good; wanted mixed Protestant–Roman Catholic education extended; and said how impressed he was by the liberal minds of the students of the university of Belfast.

This cry for mixed education got him into trouble. The Catholic Church in Northern Ireland was one of the last Catholic Churches in the world, after the second Vatican Council, to be marked by the ghetto mentality. The bishops still refused the sacrament of confirmation to children sent by their parents to state schools. Therefore the Roman Catholic Bishop of Down and Connor protested to Ramsey,

vehemently, that Irish Catholics were under conscience to attend
Catholic schools.

Ramsey's reply stated his opinion (25 April 1974):

There is no question, as you suggest, of my encouraging Catholic parents to
violate their consciences. I believe that children should be taught the faith of
the Church to which they belong. I think, however, it is a tragedy that children
of different Churches, Catholic, Anglican, Presbyterian and other, should
grow up in utter ignorance of one another, and they are too often through this
segregated upbringing led to think that the members of the other Church,
Catholic or Protestant, are a kind of species of heathen. It is this tragedy which
causes me and others to hope that it may be possible to have a school system in
which children while being taught the faith of their own Church are not
segregated from the children of other Churches.

The bishop was not content with this reply.

He had more comic correspondence. A military writer wrote an
abusive letter accusing him of giving Ian Paisley a Lambeth doctorate of
divinity. A small boy of 14 from Shrewsbury wrote to him to find out
why Mr Pasley (*sic*) is aloud (*sic*) to be a presit (*sic*) in the Church of
England.

In May 1974 the plan for power-sharing in Northern Ireland, which
was far the most promising expedient for a peaceable future (and fifteen
years later was still the only expedient on the drawing-board) was
wrecked as a result of the Ulster Workers' Council strike; not a strike
like those familiar in England, but with widespread intimidation, roads
barricaded, and some murders. In Ballymena Protestant extremists
went on the rampage, wrecking three pubs and a fish-and-chip shop
that remained open contrary to their 'orders'. Then they went to
another pub and murdered at point-blank range the Catholic owner and
his brother. Electricity was down to six hours a day, garbage was not
collected and could be seen burning in bombed lots, barricades blocked
the streets, there was no petrol, and the community was at a standstill.
The British flew in more soldiers who for a time worked the petrol
stations and oil depots with surprising efficiency. But on 28 May the
strains on the Northern Irish executive pulled it apart. Direct rule was
back. Ian Paisley celebrated a paean of victory.

Among the rank and file of the Labour party were many who were
determined to get the army out of Northern Ireland. Every responsible
person who knew anything about it saw that the marching out of the
soldiers would mean civil war in Ulster, and that most vicious form of
civil war which is communal murder; that the army of the Irish
Republic could not stand idly by while Irishmen in the North murdered
each other—already on 17 May Northern Irish bombs in Dublin and

Monaghan had killed thirty innocent people and wounded 130 more; that the result would be a new partition of Ulster between Catholic and Protestant but only after a bloodbath with terrible consequences in posterity; and that communal war in Ulster would spill over into communal hatred and bombs in English and Welsh and Scottish as well as Southern Irish cities. At that moment many British people were asking, is it not better for us to wash our hands and leave them to each others' throats?

On television Harold Wilson made the most powerful speech on Ireland ever made by a British prime minister. He was furious with the extremists who defied the British government which defended them with the lives of British soldiers and paid out large sums of taxpayers' money to keep the province going; while they spent 'their lives sponging on Westminster and British democracy'. It was widely agreed, first, that these sentences rather accurately represented the mood of the British people; and secondly that the toughness of the speech made the tension worse, for it was understood to lump all the Protestants with the extremists; and even though the government said that it would not withdraw the army, the speech showed a mood of 'Why should we spend our soldiers' lives for the sake of such barbarians?'; and therefore hinted that such a decision might sooner or later be taken.

The Northern Irish moderates thought that this showed a lack of comprehension. They did not like the way the BBC broadcasts of that moment portrayed them. They decided that Ramsey could help. A delegation of churchmen from Ulster came to Lambeth. They begged him to show government that the extremists did not represent moderate opinion; they begged him to do all he could to persuade the BBC to alter the tone of its bulletins. Wilson's speech led them to think that the people in power at Westminster had very little sense of compassion for the predicament of Northern Ireland. They fiercely resented the word *sponging*. They said that they had come to the archbishop because they knew that he at least felt compassion.

Ramsey told them that he had not the power which they imagined him to have. They must go elsewhere and put their plea to the British government. He could not help them in the way which they wanted.

What however he could do for them was to make a speech in the House of Lords. His prestige in the House was now very different. He was no longer the intrusive prelate against whom Lords Dilhorne and Kilmuir made snide speeches. He was now an elder statesman whom the peers wanted to hear. And he was conscious that he was among the few members of the Upper House who had experience on the ground in Northern Ireland.

The debate in the House of Lords on 3 June 1974 showed Ramsey at his most persuasive. All over the world he had done what he could to lessen the hostilities between Catholic and Protestant. He was conscious that here in Britain was the worst failure of them all. And he was able to get across to his listeners the sense of his compassion for all the people in the province. It was a very unusual speech for an Archbishop of Canterbury, perhaps a unique speech, because it attacked both prime ministers at once. Edward Heath called an election in February at a crisis moment for Northern Ireland. Harold Wilson made his 'spongers' speech and alienated too many in Northern Ireland—'talk of that sort really must stop'. This was strong language from Lambeth to Downing Street.

He begged for three things in the policy of the government. First, it must be a policy of both the parties. This was too serious an issue to be a matter for party quarrelling. Secondly, there must be an end to all talk of withdrawing the army, an end to every threat, if you do not behave we will withdraw the troops. 'That is about as foolish a negation of statesmanship as anything can be. A part of the United Kingdom has no right to say to another part of the United Kingdom, if you do not behave better,' protection will be withdrawn. He said how much he admired the soldiers on his visits to the province. Thirdly, he told them his experience that there were moderates in Northern Ireland; not so many as they had hoped, but they must never be forgotten. And he told the peers of his experience of the Corrymeela community and its work for reconciliation. 'We as a United Kingdom are all in this and we must all persevere with the task that God has given to us. None of us lives to himself and none of us dies to himself.'

This speech did not change the hard opinions of those peers who were determined to get the British army out of Northern Ireland. But it was probably the most respected speech which Ramsey ever made in the House of Lords; in the midst of bitterness, and hardness, and turmoil of minds, a revered Christian called for moderation but with a sense of responsibility which the British ought to feel and some of them did not. A lot of peers were grateful for this utterance.

In Ireland the *Protestant Telegraph* reported in a large headline that Dr Ramsey Meets the God-King; so it misleadingly described the coming of the Dalai Lama to Lambeth.

PART 3

===

THE WORLD-WIDE
COMMUNITY

9

The Traveller

The modern air liner came into convenient use after the Second World War. This made a difference to the leaders of all the Churches. For the first time in history they could get about all the world without neglecting their jobs at home. And a far-flung denomination could for the first time find that all its parts could be visited by its head. Even Popes, so long shut up behind the walls of the Vatican, began to think about travelling to see the Catholics of the world. Archbishop Fisher was the first Archbishop of Canterbury to have airliners at his disposal and was therefore the first head of his Church to visit many of the provinces and dioceses of the Anglican Communion; to encourage, and bless, and discover what was happening, and foster the links between the mother church of Canterbury and its now very numerous and very various children. From Fisher's time onwards an indispensable qualification for the job of archbishop was willingness to travel.

Ramsey enjoyed these travels. He almost always took Joan and his chaplain, and later, after experience, a press officer as well. The Church Commissioners paid his fare and that of his staff, he paid for Joan. The journeys were arranged by his staff, but he was tireless. It was always arranged that one day in seven should be free. The programme was sifted beforehand to preserve the one day off in seven. The Americans were the organizers most anxious to squeeze every ounce of juice out of him while they had him but they respected the rule of one day off in seven. The only calamity happened in Nigeria where the bishops, after agreeing the programme, wrote an event into the free day and printed it in a beautiful programme without asking him, and Ramsey refused to go, and still refused to go after tearful pleas that mothers and children would be disappointed, and left his chaplain to cope with the consequent fury.

He enjoyed the company, the sights, the new friendships, the strength of the Churches, the help to them which he knew that his presence and his words could give. He particularly enjoyed quiet places like monasteries but he was quite at home in vast congregations or making a speech, as was once his duty, to a banquet in Honolulu attended by all the top brass of the American forces in the Pacific. He did not mind receptions in marquees. He never seemed to worry about the need to attend long liturgies, except once in New York when the music went on and on to what he thought to be an inordinate length. He specially liked meeting with students. His sessions with groups of students were extraordinarily effective. He could startle them—as when he told the students of Simon Fraser University near Vancouver, who at that time of student revolution were notorious as the most tiresomely eccentric students in the western hemisphere, that he hoped there were some eccentrics on the campus. He would consecrate a new bishop, or consecrate new buildings, or preach sermons, or give quiet days, or visit hospitals especially children's hospitals, or plant a tree, or lay a foundation stone for a new church, or lecture to every standard, from universities to the simplest meetings of laity. Because of his position and reputation in the world he was often expected to talk on the world Church, or reunion, or the mission of the Anglican Communion. Though he was feted by presidents and prime ministers and governors of states, and frequently was given honorary degrees, and occasionally inspected guards of honour, or was rushed through the streets of some capital in a limousine preceded by postilions with horns blaring, or literally trod red carpets among the flags, he was never grand. Some rather incoherent notes survived of his talks to clergy and others in various tours; to the reader they are such tangled notes as to be nearly unintelligible, but they are not so because they are complex, for they are very simple. He would conform to what his host thought would be helpful—speaking for example a little French in Montreal, or singing Cree hymns in Moosonee. He was enchanting with little children, which pleased the press photographers as well as a lot of other people. Without any practice he was a master at the walkabout, the figure so impressive and the personality so abundant. A Canadian newspaper declared that he was as typically English as Winston Churchill and resembled him in looks. Everybody felt that they expected an archbishop and were not disappointed. One Canadian newspaper declared that he was the stage model of an archbishop, 'vigorous, silverhaired with a high forehead, great shaggy eyebrows, a majestic mien, looking older than his years, but always smiling and ever ready to break into bellowing laughter'.[1] His humour seemed to be international, and funny whatever people he talked to. He tried to bring in local references or history. The *Deccan Herald* in South India (11 March

---

[1] *Western Catholic Reporter*, 22 Sep. 1966.

Arthur Ramsey

Agnes Ramsey

Howfield, the family home of the Ramseys in Cambridge

At King's College School, Cambridge. Michael Ramsey is
second from the left in the back row

The Cambridge Union Committee (Easter Term, 1925). Michael Ramsey is second from
the right in the front row

Coming out of the Galilee at Durham Cathedral after his wedding. The best man behind Joan is Eric Abbott

Michael Ramsey as Archbishop of York in the Kremlin (1956)

Michael Ramsey at his first convocation of Canterbury as Archbishop (1961)

Michael Ramsey being enthroned as Archbishop of Canterbury (1961)

Trying to save South Africa from apartheid

Daily Express 28 October 1965

Sunday Express 31 October 1965

Daily Express 26 February 1968. This was the day before Callaghan introduced into the Commons the Immigration Bill (on Kenyan Asians) of which Michael Ramsey was a doughty opponent

Michael Ramsey about to
go in procession; with Joan

Pope Paul VI and Michael Ramsey about to embrace each other
when they met in the Vatican's Sistine Chapel (1966)

The ageing servant

The meditative person

1973) said that he had a not quite Durante nose and a fringe of silver hair encircling a freckled pink pate. Quite often the reception which he received can best be described as rapturous. Crowds thronged to greet him and to hear him. The most critical of him were one or two of the heads of State or governors-general with whom he stayed. They attributed his tongue-tiedness to standoffishness. One otherwise civilized governor-general, with whom he stayed, afterwards denounced him privately in vehement language for being so remote and lofty.

He seldom took long over a tour. He knew that he was needed back in London and Canterbury. But certainly these journeys fulfilled something in his sense of vocation.

They also did something for the remote dioceses. It must not be thought that he found everything paradisal wherever he went. He worried over a diocese where a bishop was incapable, or a bishop was obsessive in believing that if his clergy disagreed with him they were possessed by Satan, or a bishop who could hardly be got into office because of the hostility of his government, or a bishop who was stopped from getting anywhere near most of his flock by the hostility of his government, or a bishop whose flock was divided racially and the mounting racial divisions in that country had calamitous effects on the Christian congregations. But the evidence does not suggest undue worry. He would do what he could to help, and left the rest to providence.

He did more by personal visits than by administrative action. Here is an example. Canterbury was then and is still the metropolitan authority for the Church in Korea, where was a young bishop, Richard Rutt. The official communications on paper between bishop and archbishop, Rutt described as painful and frustrating. When Ramsey came to Korea he was fun for Rutt and inspiring to the people. Rutt specially remembered a village confirmation, in a church about the size of his study at Lambeth, in which Ramsey preached a sermon ideally suited to the congregation. Rutt also remembered a meeting with Buddhist scholars at a university in the capital, Seoul. They asked him to explain the doctrine of creation, which they said was meaningless to them. Ramsey replied instantly, 'It means that my existence is wholly contingent' —and this was the precise idiom which was right for that academic group. But he grieved afterwards that he failed to answer one of the questions properly. They asked him how he could reconcile the Christian idea of prayer reaching out to God, who is wholly other, with their own experience of prayer as a journey into oneself. Rutt, observing him, saw that he was not used to being flummoxed and was annoyed with himself, seeing a profound question which he knew that he could answer and yet could not find the words. In the car on the way to the next engagement he kept thinking about it and repeating, 'There is an interiorizing aspect in prayer . . .'. 'It was odd', said Rutt, 'to see him stumped.'

I. THE UNITED STATES

To North America he went most frequently. Apart from the horrific visit to the World Council at Evanston when he was Bishop of Durham, and a lecture tour in the USA and Canada when he was Archbishop of York, he went to North America during nine of his years as Archbishop of Canterbury and there were only five years when he did not go, and one of those five was the year of the Lambeth Conference when the North American bishops came to Canterbury.

He enjoyed the strengths of the American and Canadian Churches and the friendliness of their clergy his hosts. He retained many warm friendships from his tours. He would usually offer them lectures on some biblical subject, like the revelation of God in the Bible, or the use of the Bible in preaching, or theology and prayer, or Christianity and humanism. Sometimes he would give a quiet day. He could vary his level of speaking according to his feel of the audience.

In 1962 it was the time of the Cuban crisis. At a household in Columbia an elderly lady attacked him, how the English never do anything to back up the Americans against the Communist menace. Ramsey was roused and talked about the year 1940 when Britain stood alone against Hitler—he asked what America was doing then? The argument started to become a quarrel and an American bishop needed to intervene. In Washington Ramsey stayed with the British ambassador Ormsby Gore, who took him to see President Kennedy. At that moment Kennedy's mind was packed with Cuba and missiles but they did not talk about Cuba. As Kennedy was a Roman Catholic they talked about the prospects for Christian reunion. It struck Ramsey how Kennedy thought that the Vatican's rigid attitude to birth control was a big hindrance to its influence and indeed to the influence of his whole Church. He took Ramsey out into the garden to meet Jacky his wife and his child and Ramsey liked his friendliness very much. At a dinner with the new Bishop of Washington they were again given oysters and hated them as much as before.

In 1962 he felt that the American Church was strong, stable, prospering in the right way. He realized afterwards, from what was to happen, that he must have been sheltered from student life. To him the universities and seminaries were quiet and orderly.

In 1967 he did a tour to attend the General Convention of the Episcopal Church in Seattle. Because in the previous year Ramsey had visited the Pope, there was an ecumenical note in this entire tour, with many interdenominational rallies. In Chicago Amphitheatre he talked to over 3,000 people among massed bands and a choir of 500 and the cardinal and the Orthodox archbishop and even the notorious Mayor Daley. In Las Vegas, famous for its gambling, a *Daily Express* photographer followed him everywhere hoping to picture him going into one of the casinos, but Ramsey did not satisfy him. Here he met Mormons for the first time, when they provided a choir. It was one of the most successful of his visits; he conducted a morning of quiet for all the diocesan clergy, Roman Catholic as well as Anglican, in the Nevada diocese. This was after a vast and overelaborate liturgy. To compete with the liturgy the English persuaded the archbishop to turn out in full fig, orders and decorations and all, and the people roared with delight as he came in floodlit. But he not only looked magnificent. It was a moment when he spoke magnificently. Then there was a dinner for the bigwigs of the town and quite a lot of the bigwigs were supposed to be the Mafia. Ramsey beamed at them, gangsters and all, and said, 'It is a very exhilarating experience to meet such lovely humanity'. The after-dinner speech had them rollicking with laughter, and the London *Daily Express* (20 September 1967) was dismayed that the archbishop, dressed in 'scarlet', told funny stories in Las Vegas. It said that though it was his duty to mix with publicans and sinners, it 'is another matter when he becomes the life and soul of a party more jocose than dignified'. It had a headline, DR RAMSEY LANDS THE JACKPOT.

The General Convention at Seattle he did not like. It made something of the same impression upon him as Evanston, 1954; 'an appalling impression', he recorded, 'the vastness of it, the separate sitting of the houses which meant that the clergy and laity did not hear the bishops discussing matters, nor did the bishops hear the clergy and laity discussing them, the concentration of power in this body meeting every few years without fuller synodical discussions in the provinces themselves.' He was agreed by the Americans to be the star of the week. He spoke to each of three houses separately—bishops, deputies, women —and preached to several thousands in the Coliseum.

The 1967 visit was special because it contained his first visit to the seminary at Nashotah House near Milwaukee; a seminary which, as we shall see later, was to become a second home. He resolved then and there that he would spend time in such a haven during his retirement. At that time the argument about 'the Death of God' raged in America and he spoke about it, three times formally, and several times in question and answer sessions with students. Moreover, it was now that he realized the deep disturbance caused to American morale by the war in Vietnam. In his sessions with students questions about the war started to be prominent; more than questions, they heckled. On any tour, and not only in America, he would always speak religiously whenever he spoke; he never failed to speak of Christ; often he talked of freedom, and of the quest for truth, and of tolerance, and of the need for religious faiths to understand each other so as to help the world. If he was challenged on controversial matters, he was direct and did not cover up with a diplomatic answer—the Vietnam war ought to stop and the Americans ought to withdraw, family planning by modern methods is right, emotional evangelism is not the right way of evangelism. Sometimes, as we shall see, such frank answers got him into trouble. At Las Vegas he was asked by a reporter, with a slant in the question, whether it was wrong to use the pulpit to denounce the Vietnam war. He said simply, 'I do it'.

The Americans were a very articulate people and had a passion for communicating ideas and did not always approve of a man with such long silences and such hesitations when at last he spoke. One of the American bishops described his own experience of being in a car with Ramsey. 'I was reminded of friends with short-wave radios in their attempts to communicate with someone via the radio waves. Like testing a frequency, I would try a subject. If it held no interest, no response came; or a word or two, and then fade-out. If it interested him, he would come in loud and clear until he finished the transmission.' Then the American would look around for another subject 'on another frequency'.

By 1968, with the student revolution and the civil rights campaign and the murder of Martin Luther King, the Churches in the United States ran into bad trouble. They put on public occasions—services or meetings—which seemed marvellous things to interrupt if you wished to make a public protest and be reported in the newspapers. A Special General Convention at South Bend, Indiana in 1969 was violently disrupted. Three months later the General Assembly of the National Council of Churches was totally disrupted. By 1970 things were better. The blacks and the young whites began to realize that all this violence was counter-productive.

The phrase above—emotional evangelism is not the right way to evangelism—now met a situation which caused Archbishop Ramsey to think more about emotionalism. His experience and his conviction led him to distrust the revivalist. Yet in America, since its foundation as an independent State, revivalism was part of the American way of life.

America was above all other countries at that time—in a few years it was to be rivalled, or even overtaken, by South America—the land of renewals, and often through the eloquent campaigner speaking to crowds. Just as the mode of electing a new president was to outside eyes an extraordinary affair of crowds and shouting and publicity, so the attempt to bring virtue and religious truth home to the people was often couched in a similar though more decorous form; and it had results which no one with open eyes could deny.

In the sixties, amid the passions of the Vietnam war, Archbishop Ramsey met it in two forms which forced him to some rethinking.

First, the civil rights movement was touched with this sense of emotional and Christian renewal. The alliance of southern blacks, usually Baptists, with liberal priests and pastors from the more conservative northern Churches, threw up a leader who in every way was attractive to Ramsey. Martin Luther King stood for justice among the races; for an appeal to Christian truth as the way of getting this justice; for a non-violent method, a Gandhi method, of persuading society that they must reorder their structure to concede this justice; and furthermore, this southern Baptist preacher was unexpectedly an American intellectual and not at all a man of mere emotionalism—the man had religious depth and social power and his eloquence to the crowds was more commanding than that of any other revivalist preacher because it was not addressed to the individual soul but to all America. When Martin Luther King was shot down by an assassin on the balcony at Memphis, Tennessee on 4 April 1968 the Archbishop of Canterbury felt it like a personal loss.

The other movement of growing power during the sixties was the Pentecostalist. It came out of the Middle West early in the twentieth century and began with the experience of 'speaking with tongues' and other physical manifestations in spirit-inspired congregations. To Ramsey such physical manifestations would never be other than misguided or perilous or in need of help in understanding the Bible. But the Pentecostalist movement grew into something much bigger than speaking with tongues: its Biblicism, its force, its concern for holiness of life, its drive to moral commitment, its conviction that Christians must listen to the Holy Spirit and act with immediacy in their obedience. It had strength and expansive power. Soon it was the fastest expanding form of religion in Latin America. And it began to affect the more traditional Churches. They asked themselves whether they neglected the doctrine of the Holy Spirit and whether they ought to listen more than they had. Their younger people started to be interested in what was now known as the charismatic experience.

During the later 1960s the American universities were the places where was fought the battle in the nation's conscience over war and civil rights. And Ramsey specially liked to go to universities and listen to the students with an open mind and try to answer their questions honestly. He, the archbishop who was afraid of revival, the critic of Billy Graham, the man who suspected emotional pressure upon crowds and believed in quiet persuasion, now started to ask himself what truth there might be in what these charismatics wanted.

Because the students were morally disturbed and the liberal society was at sixes and sevens, it became the time of drugs; even down to children at schools before the university. A curious feature of the drug culture was an interest in the mystical experience which accompanied it. A drug could send the young thing off into the empyrean where was a heaven which it was impossible to describe. He or she found in mystical language, whether of Buddhism and the religions of the east, or the Christian mystical tradition, language which spoke to the tormented soul and fitted something of the apprehension which was learnt more physically in the world of drugs. It was a rejection by youth of the rat race and the material prosperity and the American world of practical common sense. Therefore there was fresh interest in transcendence, but very little interest in the future because the cry was for present satisfaction.

The new charismatics and the new radical Christians had nothing to do with drugs. But they adopted some of the attitudes—feeling, excitement, mystical experience, dancing and other forms of physical self-expression, kisses of peace that were real kisses, and rock operas. Speaking with tongues appeared in certain churches of the Episcopal Church, that is among the Anglicans of the United States; and thereby became the concern of the Archbishop of Canterbury. Then it began to appear in certain Roman Catholic churches and among Catholic students on university campuses. Whatever oddities it produced in that tangled world, no one with eyes could deny that some sort of a revival was in progress; though it was an unusual revival in that it had little use for the Churches of the old establishments or at times for institutional religion generally.

Ramsey started to think what this movement said to the Churches. He found that a close friend among the Roman Catholic cardinals, Suenens of Malines, was thinking on the same lines. When Ramsey went to a group of young people to answer their questions, they would often ask him about the Jesus-Movement. He warmed to the simplicity and spontaneity of its affection for the human Jesus and freely confessed to his questioners that the old Churches were sometimes too cold in expressing their worship and should learn from this warmth.

With this openness he approached the two musicals playing in New York and London, *Godspell* and *Jesus Christ Superstar*. In New York he and Joan were able to see *Godspell*, and found it attractive, and full of fun and humour, and of the pointedness of the parables, and that it treated the sufferings in the gospel with reverence. *Jesus Christ Superstar* was more controversial and he did not quite like to go to see it, though he listened to it on records. But then they went to see it. He found it crude and at times blasphemous; and yet Jesus retained an unexplained authority despite the crudities, and at one point the text rose up into the conviction of the power and glory of a death. He said, 'If *Godspell* shows much of the truth because of itself, *Jesus Christ Superstar* hints at a little of the truth of Jesus in spite of itself.'

What he wanted to make sure of were two things: first that the movement always based itself on what is known from the gospels and its attitudes to Jesus were not made out of modern imagination; and second, that those who see the Spirit at work in exciting and ecstatic and emotional events should not suppose that the Spirit is not at work in the humdrum ways of ordinary life and in rational existence as well as emotional. 'Where exciting charismata are seen, there is the Spirit; but where hard work is done with cheerful and unexciting perseverance, where sorrow and pain are borne with quiet fortitude, where scholars pursue the truth with patience, where contemplatives serve us all by praying with a love beyond our own experience, here too is the Holy Spirit, here is the charismatic Christ.'[2]

On this visit to New York Ramsey made history by preaching in the Roman Catholic cathedral, where an audience of 3,000 people clapped him at the beginning and the end.

2. AUSTRALASIA

In 1965 he was in Honolulu and Fiji and Polynesia; met the prime minister of New Zealand at Wellington; and preached to a vast congregation of Maoris. In different continents he used the same addresses or lectures—Australia also was given Christianity and Humanism, and Freedom and Truth. In Townsville he was danced to by Aboriginals. In North Queensland he was bitten by gigantic mosquitoes while he was lecturing in the open air, but lectured on.

[2] Ramsey and others, *The Charismatic Church* (New York, 1973), 22, 31–2.

At Sydney he enjoyed himself much; even though as Andrew led him into the cathedral carrying the processional cross of Canterbury, a Protestant darted from the crowd and tried to snatch it from his grasp, saying that no cross should enter the cathedral. Ramsey was photographed with the Sydney beach men, wearing one of their swimming caps above his purple cassock.[3]

On that Australian tour of 1965 there was nearly a calamity. He was due to go from Melbourne to Wangaratta where he was to dedicate the completed nave of the cathedral. Joan felt ill and stayed in bed at the Governor of Victoria's house. The next day she was urgently put into the hospital run by the Roman Catholic Sisters of Mercy. A telephone call went to Wangaratta at noon that a stomach-surgeon had diagnosed a condition requiring instant surgery. Ramsey went to the chapel and prayed and wept, but went out and greeted a crowd of clergy and people as gaily as ever. John Andrew whispered to the local bishop and a fast car was laid on with police escort and he was raced back to Melbourne, with crossroads manned to let him through, and the speedometer sometimes touching 100 m.p.h. After he saw that she was perky again, he left again to carry out his tour in Tasmania and the West.

In Perth he consecrated the chapel at the theological college at Wollaston. He struck the door mightily with his pastoral staff and the college still preserves as a relic the hole which he made in the door. On the way home they were supposed to go to Singapore but everything was put out by Joan's illness at Melbourne, so for the only time they had to cancel their plans and disappoint their hosts and fly back home by easy stages through Hawaii and San Francisco and New York. They made it up to Singapore in 1973 when they made a tour of all Eastern Asia, from Madras and Malaysia to Korea and the Philippines. His gratitude did not forget the Sisters of Mercy at Melbourne. He had sent an open cheque to the Mother Superior but she refused to take a penny. Later, when he heard that the nuns' chapel needed a new roof, he paid for it.

Here is the evidence of someone who heard him give his two lectures in Sydney; evidence which could be repeated from elsewhere in the world: fifty minutes without a note on Christianity and Humanism to an audience of more than a thousand at the university of Sydney, a lecture which combined high intellectual demands with spirituality; the audience, some of which was well known for materialism and dislike of the Church, silent and rapt; then next day quite a different kind of lecture

---

[3] On the train a reporter from Sydney claimed to have heard him criticize the Sydney diocese for narrow-minded out-of-date partisanship. There was trouble. Then it turned out the report was untrue.

to all the clergy of the diocese, addressed more to the affections than the mind, on the caring of a Christian pastor; and felt by many of his hearers to be moving.

3. SABAH

Most of the archbishop's tours across the world were happy, at times inspiring. They always raised the morale of the people to whom he went, and usually raised his own optimism and faith about the state of the Churches whether they were older or younger. But sometimes this was not true. A Church, for which he might still be directly responsible, made him worry. This was true of Uganda, because of the political coups and madnesses which began to tear the state apart. It was true of the Sudan, because of the mixture of racial and religious conflict which turned into civil war. And one painful case was the Church in Sabah, which the British knew better under its older name of North Borneo.

When the British decided to get out, they thought that the society was not capable of standing on its own. The Philippines claimed it and the Indonesians had their eye on it. Since almost all its trade was with Malaysia through Singapore, the British bequeathed it (1963) as part of the Malaysian Federation. But two years later Singapore left the Malaysian Federation and the arrangement for Sabah did not look so sensible.

Nearly two-thirds of the people were still pagan or animist and many of them still lived in remote jungle. Under British toleration the Christian Churches made conversions, so that an unknown number of the indigenous Kadazans and 25,000 of the Chinese composed a strong Christian community, which could not yet do without foreign aid and expatriate clergy. The Muslims in Sabah were about equal in numbers to the Christians. But the local chief of state, trained in the British army and then the colonial service, was a Muslim and with the passive aid of the Muslim Malaysian government determined to do what he could to put down Christianity.

Two motives started the petty persecution. The leaders of the state were sensitive to the charge that they were a colonial inheritance and wanted to eradicate memories of the colonial past, which included Christian missionaries. Therefore eject missionaries, or in the more plausible jargon of a modern age, refuse to renew their work permits. Secondly, there was a political threat to the rule of a single party and of an autocrat, if Kadazans and Chinese allied. It was easy for government to say that bishops must come from Sabah. A new Roman Catholic bishop was ejected though he came from the next door State of Sarawak, as were 26 of his missionaries including a bedridden Carmelite nun who had lived there since 1930. The authorities said that they did not like persons whose first loyalty was to Rome. There began to be an impressive list of converts to Islam. By the end of 1970 the Anglican diocese was reduced to seven priests and a deacon.

The Archbishop of Canterbury had to find a new bishop. The specifications made it impossible. He must be a citizen of Sabah. He must speak Malay and English. He must be able to get on with Muslim authorities. Ramsey decided that under these conditions he could not appoint a new bishop and that the ministrations of a bishop they must receive from visitors. But this brief conclusion gives no idea of the amount of worry, prayer, consultation caused to the person at Lambeth ultimately responsible for so many souls. For a time it was not safe or wise for the Archbishop of Canterbury to write directly to the clergy in Sabah. He sent his letters to Singapore.

In December 1970 the behaviour of the Sabah government won international attention and caused western protests in Kuala Lumpur. The Sabah government denied vehemently that these stories had any truth. It said that it had police evidence that missionaries carried on activities not conducive to national unity. It then softened its policy. In March 1971 it looked better. Bishop Roland Koh of West Malaysia thought that he had found a candidate, his own Archdeacon of Penang, and that it might be possible to get the government to let him in. It seemed hardly possible for Ramsey to ask government leave for a work permit before consecrating bishops, so he asked Koh to try to achieve the result; which had the awkwardness that Ramsey could not even ask the candidate whether he would accept the job until he knew whether he had a work permit. In June 1971 the Chief Minister of Sabah provided a work permit 'subject to security clearance' and on 30 November 1971 the archbishop had the satisfaction of consecrating in Lambeth Palace chapel Archdeacon Luke Chhoa Heng Zee as the new Bishop of Sabah. He knew that he consecrated someone to a work which had superhuman difficulties that were practical, pastoral and political, and said his prayers.

Therefore when at last he felt able to visit that part of the globe, he made sure that his journey included a flight to Sabah. In such a visit as this the press saw only the State visit, and the great service, and the walkabout, and the press photographs. They did not see hidden reasons why all this was important.

He arrived at Kota Kinabalu on 15 March 1973. He called on the Chief Minister; and talked to the clergy; and preached in the cathedral;

and addressed the young people; and was given a dinner where Joan was recorded as handling the chopsticks efficiently, but no mention is made of his chopstick prowess for he had clumsy hands; and planted a tree in the cathedral compound to commemorate the visit—for the ritual record, he wielded a spade wearing cope and mitre; and inspected a guard of honour of the Boys Brigade, moving along the ranks like a benevolent field-marshal, and the press camera caught him as he looked doubtful whether this was his natural world; and was cheered away at the airport by a great crowd. They made a colour film of his visit and sent out a copy to every parish. His sermon in Sabah survived. It did not even hint at the predicament of the Church locally. It talked of God, and Christ, and eternity.

4. JERUSALEM

The holy city of Jerusalem was of the Orthodox world, in Christian history. The Anglicans, when they put a bishop into Jerusalem, were careful to reassure the Orthodox that they did not intrude into their territory, but ministered to their own people. However, in time the Anglican diocese of Jerusalem became mainly Arab in its composition. This complicated its life when the city was divided and fought over by Arab and Jew. There was another rub between the archbishop and some of the Arab clergy: the question of anti-Semitism. The Holocaust touched the conscience of Christendom as never before about the treatment of Jews through the centuries. Christian thinkers asked themselves whether modern anti-Semitism was only mob gut-reaction against a minority people, as in the Middle Ages, or whether something in Christian attitudes helped to generate the gut-reaction—for example, by blaming the Jews for their part in the crucifixion of Jesus.

In the aftermath of the second World War and the full discovery of what happened in Poland, the World Council—at Amsterdam and then at New Delhi—condemned anti-Semitism. The second Vatican Council during the sixties determined to do the same. Christianity must repudiate it as it repudiated racialism. But by the middle sixties the argument was embittered by politics. The hatred between Arab and Jew in the Middle East meant that if the Pope, or the Archbishop of Canterbury, condemned anti-semitism, that now looked as though Christianity struck a blow on the side of the State of Israel in the political conflict. And that would mean that the Arab States of the Levant would take it out on their Christian minorities whom they would regard as crypto-supporters of their enemies. These minorities were large. The Arab leaders thought that all Arabs were Muslims. Actually 10 per cent of the Arab peoples were Christians.

Consequently Roman Catholic archbishops in the Levant, whose flocks were under Arab rule, worked hard in Rome, worked even with passion, to stop the Pope from repudiating the notion that the Jewish people were to be blamed for the crucifixion of Jesus. The Vatican was accused of crucifying Christ in the year 1964. And the many fewer Arab Anglicans brought the same pressure to bear on Lambeth.

Two days before the vote in the Council at Rome, Damascus radio said that for twenty centuries Christians had regarded the Jews as the murderers of God and asked why they changed it now, at a moment when the Arabs were in a bitter struggle with the Jews and the Jews had driven a million refugees out of their homes. Why were they not so bold when the Nazis persecuted millions of Jews? Could the Church find no more propitious time to rehabilitate the Jews than the time when they had just become the persecutors of the Arabs? Five days after the vote the Jordan Parliament held a session in Amman at which both Christian and Muslim members condemned the declaration. Two bombs went off in the Christian quarter of Aleppo.

In March 1964 the Archbishop of Canterbury publicly asserted that it is wrong to blame the Jewish people for the crucifixion of Jesus. This caused a furious letter from an Arab clergyman in Palestine and a cold correspondence with the Arab Anglican bishop, Cuba'in, who told him that the statement was unfortunate and caused serious repercussions in all the Middle East. Later that year Cuba'in said that the resolution of the Vatican Council was due to the intrigues of the Zionists in Rome. He declared authentic the Protocols of the Elders of Sion, the worst anti-semitic forgery known to Europe, only accepted as authentic by tsarist police and Gestapo and anti-semitic fanatics.

Israel and the Arab States were closer to the Six Days War. The atmosphere in a Jerusalem divided between the two States grew ever more tense. Ramsey decided in the spring of 1966 to go to Jerusalem. He did not want to be political. He wanted to be a pilgrim. And he thought that the presence and the prayers of pilgrims might help to keep the fragile peace and quieten the guns. He was respected by the Orthodox in Jerusalem, and by the Roman Catholics, and he had his own Anglican flock among the Arabs. He had a chance of being welcomed by both sides, as a man of peace.

In April 1966 he trod with piety the Via Dolorosa and the Holy Places. Lately, in the better climate among the Churches, the Greek guardians made available a chapel for Anglican worship, known as the chapel of Abraham. Fisher had celebrated the sacrament there, and now Ramsey also. He paid formal calls on the heads of all the divided Christian communities—colourful events by the tradition of Jerusalem. He found the tension painful and wondered how he could help the refugees. The mayor of Bethlehem, which was still an Arab city and largely Christian, greeted him with the town band in a crowded square, among 40,000 people, outside the Church of the Nativity. While he was in what was then the State of Jordan the Arab mayors tried to get him to say something against the modern State of Israel, and the *Jerusalem Star* chastised him for 'condoning' the injustice done to Palestine by the making of the Israeli State. He said nothing political. Then he crossed by the Mandelbaum Gate into Jewish Jerusalem and saw the traditional room of the last Supper, and the Dead Sea Scrolls. Then back through the Mandelbaum Gate, and down from Jerusalem to Jericho by the road of the Good Samaritan. He said his prayers in Emmaus. What moved him most of all was Jacob's Well in Samaria.

The Anglicans in the diocese of Jerusalem had no doubt which political side the Archbishop of Canterbury should back. They wanted an Arab bishop; and the Archbishop of Canterbury, who would have to concede the request, believed that it was better to keep a Briton in charge, so that he might be an Olympian, above the conflict.

The problem was Anglican representation at the centre of Christianity. Who should be Archbishop of Jerusalem (if there should be one at all, when Jerusalem had already so many other archbishops)? Should he be an Olympian, neither Arab nor Israeli, someone big enough to be acceptable to the Anglican Communion across the world and neutral enough to be acceptable to both Arab and Israeli governments? Or should it be the bishop of the local Anglicans and therefore Arab because his people were mainly Arab (about 1,500 English speakers and about 4,500 Arabs of whom 3,000 were in Jordan)? If the see was Arab, it ought to be at Amman, the capital of Jordan, where most of the people were. But no Arab bishop would or could give up the idea of being based in Jerusalem, because to concede that would be to concede a political point to the State of Israel. The situation was strange because the bishop, Cuba'in, was the diocesan bishop in Palestine and the Lebanon and Syria, and the British archbishop—MacInnes, then George Appleton—had jurisdiction only over Jerusalem and otherwise outside Palestine. The Arab congregations were vehement against the Israeli State. Evidence was produced of books of Psalms where the number of psalms was reduced from 150 to 100 in order to omit every psalm which mentioned Israel. The Anglican Communion would never accept as their representative in Jerusalem someone who was so politically motivated against Jews and who would try to identify them with one side in the struggle.

So to succeed Archbishop George Appleton, who was one of the only people able to cross the border between Israel and the Arab States, Ramsey sent out Robert Stopford, the lately retired Bishop of London, an unemotional man who was never moved by passionate situations. Several Arabs accused Michael Ramsey of being a racialist because he would not for the moment accept an Arab archbishop.

But Stopford was sent to change the dangerous situation which contained the threat of schism. He was given the title not of archbishop but of vicar-general. He was to arrange that the archbishopric in Jerusalem, appointed from outside by the Archbishop of Canterbury, should cease, and that Jerusalem (except St George's cathedral) should be fully part of the Arab diocese.

He arranged a sort of consultative election in Cyprus where the Arab clergy should say whom they wanted to succeed the now too old Cuba'in. The votes produced in the top place a priest who five years before was arrested for placing bombs in a supermarket and served a time in prison and was now a member of the committee of the Palestine Liberation Organization. Without turning the colour of any of his sparse hairs or sleeping less well at nights, Ramsey therefore chose numbers two and three on the list, one to succeed Cuba'in and the other to be his assistant based in the State of Jordan. Of course protests came, from the first choice and a few of his backers, and from a few conservatives in England who wanted there still to be an Anglican archbishop in the cradle of the Christian world. But the consecration of the two bishops was happy. It was a dramatic change in the Christian presence in Palestine. There was no other answer to a conflict which was more nationalist and racial than religious.

While Ramsey was a boy, massacre drove the surviving Armenians out of Asia Minor and while he was an undergraduate Turkish war threw the Greeks out of Asia Minor. This made a huge difference to the Christian presence in Asia. While he was an archbishop, Islamic pressure, created by an Arab nationalism stirred to fury by the existence and the success of the new State of Israel, caused steady decline of the number of Christians in other historic Christian lands, Palestine and Lebanon. This was nothing like so grievous in numbers as what had happened to the Armenians and the Greeks fifty years before. But it was painful and sometimes wicked. In the Vatican, and in Athens, and among the informed advisers of the Archbishop of Canterbury, it caused continuous worry. There is no sign of worry in Ramsey's papers. We do what we can in these impossible circumstances, and for the rest take the long view and know that in the perspective of history, God rules.

Ramsey would have been inefficient at Stopford's work in Palestine: committees, drafting constitutions, arguing about endowments, seeing through devious clergymen. But in the general perception of what was necessary if unpalatable, he had the eye of a statesman. His doctrine told him that Christianity is international and that Jews should be willing to serve under Arab bishops and Arabs under Jewish bishops and Bermudans under Jamaican bishops and Falkland Islanders under Argentine bishops—if necessary. But his realism recognized that the world is not like this at all and that it might be his duty to make arrangements which did not wholly comply with the ideas of St Paul on how society should be run.

5. SOUTH AMERICA

South America had eleven Anglican dioceses. These dioceses had few adherents—1,000 people, 1,599, 2,000 for example, and few priests, from ten to thirty. They varied much. In some countries most of the faithful derived from English immigrants who evangelized among the local people. In others they were derived from immigrants from the United States. In Chile a majority of the Anglicans were poor Indians in the South. And, except in the Argentine, they were not more important than their numbers. Most of the people did not know that they existed. An Archbishop of Canterbury might be pardoned for not giving them time. No previous archbishop went anywhere near them; except that Ramsey went to Guyana on his tour of the West Indies and talked to a huge crowd in a park.

He felt a duty unfulfilled. They had the same claim upon him as other dioceses. And he had three motives pushing him to carry out the visit.

The first was the amazing development of religion in South America; with a once-dominant Roman Catholic Church divided between bourgeois sticks-in-the-mud unaffected by the second Vatican Council, many moderates of the centre, and radical if not Marxist priests determined that Christianity meant social revolution; with a rapid spread of evangelical groups among the people, especially the Pentecostalists but not only them, and this not just among the middle class but among the poor; and in consequence of both these movements a weightier place for all the Churches of the continent within Christendom.

It was long Anglican policy not to get involved in South America on the ground that it was a Roman Catholic continent. Lambeth 1958 realized that it could no longer be said to be a Roman Catholic continent, if it had ever been so, and that there was an urgent need for work there. Before the Lambeth Conference of 1968 the six Anglican bishops in South America wrote to the Lambeth bishops calling their attention to what was happening, and were encouraged to receive a resolution that the whole Communion ought to take an interest in the work in that continent. By going there Ramsey could do for this cause more than any other single person could do.

His third motive was personal to himself. The history of religion in South America had not left friendship between Christians. For four centuries a dominant Roman Catholic Church sought to exclude Protestants. As recently as twenty-five years before Ramsey went, Baptists were persecuted in Colombia. Modern states were more tolerant mainly because they were anticlerical. And now that evangelicals looked like a mass movement, the relationship must change for the better. But in some places evangelicals and Catholics were still very suspicious of each other; more suspicious than before because of the mass movement. The ecumenical ideals of Europe had a rough time in South America. In the Argentine there was already a friendly co-operation between the Catholic bishops and the leaders of the Anglicans, the Lutherans, and the Methodists. There the second Vatican Council already made a difference to the friendliness between the Churches. But because Roman Catholics were for so long the established religion, the various evangelical groups were anti-Catholic in their reactions.

Since his meeting with Pope Paul VI in 1966, Ramsey was the non-Roman Catholic in all the world who had the best chance of making a difference to this mutual antipathy. He was certain to be welcomed by the Roman Catholic archbishops of South America. As the bearer of independence, and as a visitor who lifted them to a public level which they never attained before, he was certain to be welcomed by the Anglicans. Whether he, the fraternizer with a Pope, would be acceptable to Latin American evangelicals remained to be seen.

Between the decision to go and the time of departure, political events made the tour more uneasy. Argentina slipped towards civil war; the reign of kidnapping, vanishing, and murder grew daily worse. All over Latin America the violence grew. This was not far from the days soon afterwards when the Ecuadorian police won a place in the book of records by arresting seventeen bishops in one meeting, and when a Jesuit who went into a Brazilian police station to protest against the torture of a girl was shot dead, and when a Brazilian bishop who befriended Indians was brutally bundled into a kidnappers' car and had all the buttons stripped off his cassock and had his face painted red and was stripped and left naked and tied up on the pavement of a suburb of his see city.

On 11 September 1973 a military coup overthrew the government of President Allende of Chile.

Allende was valued by many in the world as a kind of South American Fidel Castro of Cuba, who by the methods of radical socialism tried to bring social justice into a world where the poor were oppressed. And unlike Castro he had the democratic merit of being elected by 36 per cent of the voters. But he was an idealist in a hurry with little sense of what was practicable and less ability to control his extremists. His radical measures produced by September 1973 an inflation rate of 350 per cent; a vote of censure against him in Parliament, a vote of which he took no notice; food queues a hundred yards long and a flourishing black market; forcible expropriation of farms by unauthorized gangs in some areas of the countryside; and a near-breakdown of government.

The military coup of September 1973 was not bloodless. It was marred by the shooting of several hundred Marxists or alleged Marxists; and there were thousands of refugees. The regime which General Pinochet then established adopted the worst of police methods, arbitrary arrest and torture for political suspects. All the European left, and many moderates, were shocked at the turning of an elected social democracy, however disturbed and divided, into a nasty police state.

Ramsey had to ask himself whether, if he carried out the plan to go to Chile, he would be seen to cast a blessing on the head of a dictator who trampled upon human rights. And further, he had to ask himself whether, even if he made it plain that he cast no such blessing, the visit of so eminent a Christian leader might be misused for political ends.

In a way this was for Ramsey another reason for going. He was known to stand for human rights. He said to himself, and to several correspondents who complained about his going, that he had visited the Churches in several oppressive states, and no one had yet succeeded in challenging his integrity. Possibly, when he came to Chile, he could help those who stood up for human rights. For him this took a precedence over political scruples. The argument did not sway his determination to go.

But in March 1974 he was made to hesitate. Though the majority of Anglicans in Chile were poor Indians, the leading Anglicans were middle class. Like nearly all middle class Chileans they were relieved at the end of the anarchy and food queues of the Allende era, and welcomed General Pinochet with gratitude. They could not understand why so many in the outside world felt a moral outrage. Their bishop shared their attitude. In an interview on the BBC on 28 October 1973 he came out strongly in defence of General Pinochet and his coup. 'It is generally agreed that politics in Chile is a luxury that the country can ill afford in its state of total ruin.'

Bishop Pytches was to be Ramsey's host in Chile. Now, if Ramsey went, would he tell the world that he shared the bishop's opinions? A secret letter went off from Lambeth to the bishop in South America whom Ramsey knew best, Cyril Tucker, the Bishop in the Argentine.

In Buenos Aires Bishop Tucker already had a fall-back plan for a visit to Peru if the Argentine proved unsafe for Ramsey. He now devised a fall-back plan for a visit to Paraguay if Chile proved too red-hot for Ramsey. The archbishop's tour of South America would look rum if he got no further South than Paraguay. And in a competition between Latin American dictators for nastiness, judges of politics found it hard to distinguish the general in Paraguay from the general in Chile. However, Tucker thought that Ramsey could go to Chile, and so after hesitation did the British Foreign Office.

Before he went he did homework as usual. He read the Hansard debates on Chile; read various books on the different countries; saw a few experts personally; and got a report from Amnesty International on the evidence of the use of torture and imprisonment without trial. He asked the missionary societies in London to give him a list of 'the best revolutionaries in South America'. Whether the missionary societies were equipped to answer so unusual a question from an Archbishop of Canterbury is doubtful, but he got his list. The reign of murder in Buenos Aires made no difference to his decision; not even when Carlos Mugica, famous as the leader of the left-wing priests in the Argentine, who had survived an attempt at murder and several spells in gaol, was shot dead in the summer before Ramsey was due to go.

When it was announced that he would go, there were many protests; questions whether his journey was really necessary, and what he hoped to achieve, and whether he would bless General Pinochet. The Primate of the Canadian Church protested vehemently against the plan; so did the Chilean refugee organizations, and groups concerned with human rights.

On 17 September 1974 he flew to Colombia. At 5 a.m. in the morning Joan Ramsey woke the chaplain John Kirkham to say that the archbishop was having difficulty in breathing. Bishop Franklin, in whose house they were staying, had an oxygen bottle and Kirkham administered it to a breathless archbishop. The doctor came and said that the cause was only the high altitude. Thenceforth Kirkham had the duty of following Ramsey about with the oxygen bottle throughout a busy day, until with the weight he was carrying he was the person who needed whiffs of oxygen.

The ecumenical side of Ramsey's mission was with one exception an extraordinary success. In Colombia the cardinal-archbishop came to the Anglican church, which he had never done before, and from the pulpit gave a fine exposition of Anglican–Roman Catholic relations.

On 20 September the party flew on to Chile. On the way they landed at Lima airport in Peru. There the police separated both Ramseys from the chaplain and the press officer and then ordered the Ramseys *to run* towards the plane. Kirkham thought that they were being kidnapped and thrust past out onto the tarmac and started running after them until halted by an armed man. Back in the airport building he abused the officials with the rich vocabulary available to an English clergyman and then the Ramseys were escorted back into the building and everyone had a cup of tea.

Ramsey's arrival in Chile had its awkwardness. His critical remarks about General Pinochet reached the country. They thought him a Marxist and a new incarnation of the Red Dean of Canterbury. In the Chilean capital a sensible British ambassador advised him that it was good to call on General Pinochet and that he could do no harm; that he could say anything he liked to Pinochet in a private interview; that he ought to abstain from public criticism of the regime while he was in the country, but could be as frank as he liked when he got home.

Ramsey followed the advice. The public restraint caused a critical headline in the *Observer*, PRIMATE IN TOURIST TRAP (29 September 1974). The portrait was of an archbishop who evaded questions from the press, and went on a trip to the countryside, and had sessions of tea and biscuits with British residents, and visited General Pinochet for a short interview, and as he left Chile only remarked on the beauty of the countryside. The reporter described the circumstances of his sermon: 'The church in which he preached on humility was tightly controlled by young men in wrap-round dark glasses, commanded by Lieutenant Tovar. He beckoned me after the sermon—what was it about? "Was there any politics in it? He must stay with things of the soul, because politics is for us" said Tovar, patting the 9 mm Walther under his arm.' Dr Ramsey, said the reporter, did not see that face of Chile which was arrests and shooting. Lieutenant Tovar did not like to leave Ramsey alone. When they had a discussion for BBC television in a Chilean clergy-house, Tovar insisted on being present. They edged him along the passage because they wanted to film a talk between Ramsey and a radical young priest, Father de Sales, about social and political conditions in Chile. De Sales was already under close surveillance, and John

Miles, the press officer, got Lieutenant Tovar by guile down the passage but he could still hear everything though he could not understand everything. The priest was a brave man and said what he thought and was arrested some months later.

But Lieutenant Tovar had a use which the *Observer* reporter did not know. When Ramsey was about to land at Santiago airport, the papal nuncio received an anonymous telephone call to warn him that an attempt would be made to assassinate the Archbishop of Canterbury on his way from the airport to the city. The nuncio at once telephoned the authorities; and the result was Lieutenant Tovar and his posse. The British Embassy had hints that there might be similar attempts on him either in church or on his visit to the Embassy. This was why Tovar did not like to leave the archbishop out of his sight even when he wanted a private conversation with a brave priest.

Ramsey gave a characteristic answer to a reporter who asked him whether he minded being surrounded by so many guns. 'Guns are the ritual of Latin America . . . I noticed them as little as pipes and cigarettes.'

We have no recorded minute of what Ramsey said to Pinochet, that wife-dominated, weight-lifting unintellectual with his chic uniform and his whiffs of eau-de-Cologne and superstition. During the interview of half an hour the British ambassador was also present. Ramsey afterwards told reporters, 'I bore my testimony firmly, as I always do, specifically about human rights.' Though naturally he did not say so to the reporters, he formed the impression that General Pinochet was a very stupid man, and a totally non-political animal. He said to Pinochet words to this effect: 'From the Christian point of view Marxism is an evil thing. But Marxism is not going to be defeated by ruthlessness. It will only be defeated by justice.' Later he said, 'I was about as strong as it is possible to be without being abusive. I do not regard abusiveness as strength.'

Though we do not know what he said, except in that outline, we do know what the listening British ambassador thought of what he said.

Ramsey had a most acute political sense behind his craggy medieval features. This was apparent throughout his very tricky Chilean visit, where he had to deal with a largely pro-regime flock and anti-regime foreign media. He was specially sensitive to press photography and would compose his features according to the political circumstance. When posing for the press outside Pinochet's office, his scowl was thunderous. How important it is for an Archbishop of Canterbury to have political talent as well as religious virtue![4]

[4] The ambassador was (Sir) Reginald Secondé, whose background paper Ramsey thought to be one of the best that he ever received.

From Amnesty back home, or from private meetings in Chile, he knew of people arrested without charge, or who had vanished. He talked to the brave priest mentioned above. Soon after his arrival two doctors who were on the run from the police because of their care of the underground asked through a secret message to the Indian ambassador whether they could come to see him. His staff worried that this might be a trick to discredit the archbishop or might cause unnecessary danger to the doctors or might be an attempt by two fugitives to get asylum. It was agreed that they should meet at the embassy and come in the car of the Indian ambassador. Ramsey talked with them about the plight of their people and the poor and those who were denied human rights and who were suffering because of their allegiance to Allende. They were smuggled out by a side door.

Ramsey realized that the key to the situation, and the only way through which he personally could help the oppressed, lay in Cardinal Silva. The Church authorities had not succumbed to the regime. Cardinal Silva preached more than one sermon about human rights, and his Easter message was important in Chile—violence generates only violence, and is no way to a just society, human rights are sacred—'I would like the men of my land to get up and see the sun shining, and the mountains, and the valleys, and the oceans, without thinking that someone is hunting them, and realising that they need not be afraid.'

Cardinal Silva, whom the British ambassador described as a modest little man of moral stature, was under pressure. He received threats of assassination. He was given a bodyguard. Ramsey believed that he could do two things. First, he could encourage and strengthen Cardinal Silva, by making him feel the support and the prayers of the world-wide Church. The second was to bring him privately the names of the oppressed of whom he had been told; for he could see that in the prevailing conditions the cardinal and his committee had a better chance than anyone else of achieving something with police officers who were almost out of hand.

Archbishop and cardinal dined together at the house of the ambassador and had a long and important talk. Afterwards Ramsey believed that his private talk with Cardinal Silva was one of the chief benefits of the whole expedition to South America. They got on very well together. At dinner there was a rivalry. Ramsey boomed, 'I am the hundredth archbishop of Canterbury'. Cardinal Silva said timidly: 'I'm afraid I'm only the thirty-first Archbishop of Santiago.'

Ramsey astonished the British ambassador by his optimism. How long did he think it would take, asked the ambassador who was a Roman Catholic, before union between the Anglican and Roman Catholic

Churches? Ramsey said that it could take ten years. The ambassador was surprised and said that surely the Anglicans would also be making approaches to Protestant bodies for union and that would make ten years not a realistic hope. But Ramsey would not alter his conviction that this was the probable time which would be needed before a union.

As the archbishop flew off to Buenos Aires, the Chilean press made its capital out of the visit. 'The Archbishop of Canterbury strongly condemns Marxism.' It was true; so far as it went. But many right-wing Catholics and Anglicans in Chile still suspected Ramsey as a crypto-Marxist. He was consoled that during his time there the Anglican bishop in Chile moderated his enthusiasm for the cause of General Pinochet. He was grateful that Bishop Pytches was now disturbed by what was happening and joined with Ramsey in refusing to celebrate the anniversary of the junta, and censured one of his priests who joined in that celebration. And Ramsey was thankful to find that the Anglican bishop in Southern Chile, Bishop Bazley, was able to do a lot for political prisoners and their families.

In Buenos Aires Ramsey was invited to preach at an ecumenical service in the Roman Catholic cathedral where the lessons were read by the Lutheran leader and the Orthodox archbishop. Ramsey was embraced by the cardinal who said to him publicly, 'Está en su casa', which in the idiom is warmer than 'You are at home here'. For once the interpreter was superlative and the inspiration of Ramsey's words came through to the people. Ramsey could not remember a more warm-hearted ecumenical occasion in all his experience. Nothing like it had ever happened in Latin America. The time was 150 years since the first negotiations in Buenos Aires for the setting up of an Anglican chaplaincy and therefore was festive to the Anglicans of the Argentine.

The occasion impressed the city. The visit was given maximum coverage on radio and television and in the press. One of the newspapers ran a headline UN OBRERO ECUMÉNICO, which means 'a worker for the ecumenical cause', but worker in the sense of 'working man', 'one of us'. Another, *Gente*, was more impressed that he was Lord, and was appointed by Queen Elizabeth II, and wore Pope Paul's ring, and 'captained' 66 million Christians, and yet was unpompous, and passed jokes on good Argentine steak and enjoyed the young when they played guitars, and sat on the grass with them, and waved his arms conducting their song, and played with his panama hat saying that it was the best and most practical cardinal's hat that he had ever known, and thought non-violence an efficacious way of meeting violence, and admired Mahatma Gandhi because he was Christlike though not a Christian and admired Dom Helder Camara, the Brazilian bishop, who by non-violence resisted the oppressions of his government. And as he conducted the guitar music of the young he started singing very softly the heart-rending song of longing which the blacks of the United States sang, 'Kumbayah, Señor, Kumbayah' (Come here Lord, come here). *Gente* interviewed him and asked him about the ring. He said, 'I wear it and take care of it and cherish it, as a symbol of hope'. 'Hope in what?' Ramsey: 'Hope for the union of all the Christians in the world; hope for understanding, for dialogue, and for love.'

In a country where a married archbishop was so strange, they asked him whether marriage is a good thing for an archbishop. He said only, 'It is a good thing. It is a good thing.'

In an Argentine where priests were murdered on suspicion of sympathy with the political left, Ramsey went out of his way to praise the most famous priest of the left in all Latin America—Archbishop Helder Camara of Recife in Brazil. Helder Camara was in Europe at that moment and Ramsey did not meet him when he went to Brazil. That year Helder Camara received a sort of Norwegian substitute for the Nobel Peace Prize, and made a speech about the seven deadly sins of our age, which are racism, colonialism, war, paternalism, pharisaism (= especially clergy who think sexuality a worse sin than capitalism and exploitation), evasion (= the old palming off of the young, especially in universities), and fear—for two-thirds of the human race is afraid of arrest and afraid to talk. The Argentinian journalists did not sound surprised that their visitor should admire Helder Camara.[5]

The Roman Catholic leaders had realized that the problem of South America was too vast to be coped with by any one Church and therefore they wanted far more co-operation from leaders of other Churches which they felt to be willing to co-operate and willing to understand them. Some of them also thought that the Anglicans might help them to be reconciled with the anti-Catholic prejudices in some of the evangelical groups. Michael Ramsey happened to be in South America at a time of opportunity.

He handed over his authority as metropolitan and established an autonomous South American Church. The single insoluble problem lay in the Falkland Islands. Argentine anger at British rule in the Falklands grew noisier. The inhabitants of the Falklands liked being under the Archbishop of Canterbury and had no wish to be under a bishop in Buenos Aires elected by Argentinians. Ramsey held on principle that Christianity transcends nationality and that the Falklanders ought not

[5] *Gente*, 3 Oct. 1974. Ramsey had met Helder Camara in Brussels the year before.

to mind being under a bishop elected by Argentinians. But he recognized that they did mind, and promised that they should keep a special relationship to the see of Canterbury, perhaps by means of a bishop who visited occasionally. The deed which he handed over was wrongly drafted and contained Argentine jurisdiction over the Falkland Islands and had to be unscrambled.

Rio de Janeiro

On the way (1 October 1974) his plane was grounded by fog at São Paulo and he was due in Rio that evening for a service. He was not perturbed. He sat on his suitcase in the airport lounge reading a book, with the world hurrying by, and apparently unaware of his surroundings. He reached the service in Rio three-quarters of an hour late.

To Brazil also Ramsey carried lists of imprisoned and vanished people. While he was there he kept receiving private notes, supplications that he should do what he could for some individual. Here also he used the cardinal as a lever to get enquiries pursued in such cases.

In Rio de Janeiro happened the most unusual of the ecumenical occasions. This time it went awry.

The evangelical groups and sects made amazing headway in Brazil. Mostly they were not in the traditional Churches but in the Pentecostalists or in other more independent communities; simple, biblical, often charismatic, usually anti-Catholic. For the first time in history a religion that was not Roman Catholic was a force in Brazil.

Billy Graham agreed to conduct a crusade at Rio. It was held in the Maracana stadium, which could seat vast numbers of people. It was due to begin on the evening of 2 October 1974 at 8 p.m.

Billy Graham learnt that Ramsey was due to arrive in Rio the night before. He could hardly take no notice and was not the man to take no notice. A message went to Ramsey, which asked whether he would care to share the opening of the crusade.

Ramsey's attitude to Billy Graham had changed since the days when Kensit objected to the new Archbishop of York because of his hostility to Graham. He never ceased to believe, to the end of his life, that Graham's methods were not the best. But personal experience of Graham—meeting at the World Council in Delhi 1961, dinner at Lambeth 1964, shared platform in Hawaii 1965, dinner at Lambeth 1966—transformed his feelings. '*Personally* I respect Billy Graham very much as a humble and thoughtful Christian who is wonderfully unspoilt by years of evangelism which so often "goes to the head".' From that year they were friends. He was still sure that Graham's methods were not the best, but evidence forced him to admit that every time Graham came to England on a mission, more young men had vocations to be priests.[6]

Therefore he now accepted Graham's invitation to the stadium on condition that he was allowed to address the meeting. Billy Graham wrote him a warm-hearted letter of gratitude—'overwhelmed with joy . . . we come from such diverse religious backgrounds and yet . . . this glorious unity'.

This agreement pleased and bothered the Anglican bishop, Edmund Sherrill. It pleased him because it was certain to cause a stir of no modest proportions. It bothered him because he talked to the local organizers of the crusade. He found that they were enthusiastic about Ramsey coming and speaking. But he also found that they were afraid of what he might say. It was the opening of the crusade. Time was of the essence, in the psychology of a vast crowd. They preferred Ramsey to commend Graham briefly and make way. They asked Bishop Sherrill to make it clear to Ramsey that what was wanted was a greeting of three or four minutes. And they were nervous of what he might say. To a high proportion of the audience, anyone who had anything to do with a Pope was a traitor. And anyone prominent in the ecumenical movement was a traitor. Many of them thought ecumenism an invention of the Pope to deceive true believers. The organizers at Rio were afraid that Ramsey, if he spoke, would speak what was wrong.

Ramsey did not believe in crusades. In a country of the poverty which he had been seeing, he doubted a vast expenditure on such enterprises. But Billy Graham's kindness and humility dissipated all his scruples. He had received an invitation from an evangelist, the only evangelist of such a type in all the world whom he now respected, to speak to a vast crowd. No one had less idea that his sole job was to commend Billy Graham to the multitude and stand aside. He met the organizers and thought them 'bossy', as though they wished to tell him what he was to say, and realized that they were disquieted at what was to happen. He had a message to deliver, and he would deliver it. He understood—it was a bit of a misunderstanding but in good faith—that Billy Graham generously invited him to talk about anything he liked for as long as he liked.

The people were astonished to see coming onto the platform someone who was evidently a cardinal, in a red robe, and with flowing white hair. A wave of dismay ran through the assembly.

The interpreter was an old presbyterian pastor. Before they came onto the platform Ramsey explained to the interpreter the areas which

[6] Cf. Alec Douglas-Home, *The Way the Wind Blows* (1976), 77.

he wished to cover; and the interpreter said that he could not translate all that on grounds of conscience. They took the problem to Billy Graham, who said that the archbishop was his guest and that the translator would interpret every word. Then the interpreter asked Ramsey if he could add to his translations to make them clear. Ramsey of course said that he could; thus the effect was long-winded.

The crowd in front of him was variously estimated at anything from 40,000 to 80,000. This was smaller than expected but was an astonishing achievement for Billy Graham; for the night happened also to be the night when another religious event, of even greater popular appeal, Brazil's famous footballer Pele playing his final game, was televised throughout the country.

Ramsey's South American experience made it important to him to say two things. First, he realized how anti-Catholic some of them were; and he believed that this attitude, so far as it rested upon prejudice, was less than Christian. 'You cannot come to Christ unless you bring your Roman Catholic brother with you.' This was not a popular message in that stadium. He went on to another message only in part more acceptable to his audience. 'Christ is with the poor and the under-privileged . . . You cannot come to Christ unless you take far more seriously than you appear to be doing the question of poverty, especially when we are spending a lot of money on evangelistic campaigns. If you are asked to come forward to testify to Christ, don't come unless you bring with you a resolve to be charitable to your Roman Catholic brothers. Don't come unless you resolve from now on to be doing something about poverty.' In the context of Latin America Ramsey was not far from the liberation theologians who held that the gospel means social transformation as much as individual conversion.

Ramsey was heard to say things which he did not get round to saying. When he talked of the need for Christian unity, the interpreter explained that he did not wish all Protestants to submit to the Pope. When Ramsey talked about the duty to help the poor, the interpreter explained that he did not mean the 'social gospel' but meant that the fruit of conversion would be help to all that suffer. The organizers minded the length and did not know how much of the length was the interpreter's. One of the officials at first thought that this wrecked Billy Graham's crusade. Coming to hear Billy Graham, the audience found it alarming to be talked to by a cardinal. They grew restless.

When Billy Graham rose, he took Ramsey's message into his own message; and all was well.

Ramsey was astonished to find himself speaking from one of Billy Graham's platforms. He felt a breath of private amusement at standing where he was incongruous. He was grateful to Billy Graham for giving him such a chance. He never spoke, face to face, to a larger audience. He never afterwards knew what dismay he caused among the multitude and the organizers of the crusade.

So ended this last eventful tour. The British Foreign Office was pleased with him. The state government of Rio Grande do Sul in Brazil awarded him a medal for his efforts for universal peace.

Ramsey thought afterwards that he had never seen such extremes of wealth and poverty except in India. He saw a lamentable shortage of priests everywhere in the Roman Catholic Church. He saw the small numbers of Anglicans and yet that in several places they were taken seriously by the Catholics. He worried about their predicament nevertheless. He said in the aircraft on the way home that he would have liked to send out twenty Franciscans to help them.

Asked whether his journey was productive or counter-productive, he said that he had encouraged the Anglican Christians of Latin America; encouraged friendship between the widely sundered denominations in Latin America; gained a knowledge of the world which was a help to a leader in the Church; and was able to give a little strength to Cardinal Silva in his struggle for human rights in Chile.

IO

Africa

I. EAST AFRICA

The visit to Africa in April to June 1960 was the longest visit abroad which Ramsey ever made. He was still Archbishop of York. It was a centenary. In the heyday of Victorian exploration David Livingstone, who sailed up and down the Zambezi and Shire rivers, found there little but death and disease and the slave trade but imagined how different it might be. He appealed to the universities of England to send a mission to settle up country, in what is now partly Malawi and partly the inland upcountry of Mozambique. His appeal was powerful but naïve and sent men to their deaths. The mission went out with enthusiasm under Bishop Mackenzie, as the Universities Mission to Central Africa (UMCA). They found in the region nothing but death and disease and slave-raiding; and after heroic endeavours in impossible conditions, which brought several deaths including that of the bishop, had to be withdrawn. But this failure was the seed of work based in Zanzibar and working eastward into the Malawi country and what is now Tanzania, with astonishing success, with a considerable contribution to the destruction of the slave-trade, and with the eventual growth of flourishing African Churches.

It was a hundred years since Bishop Mackenzie had arrived at the mouth of the Zambezi. The mission by tradition was mainly Anglo-Catholic in its ways of worship. The Archbishop of York was the obvious person to go to celebrate the centenary. He flew to Northern Rhodesia, now Zambia, where he met the clergy of the Copper Belt, and had supper at the Ecumenical Centre with 800 people under fairy lights dangling from the trees. He was driven by car to Lusaka, 200 miles, and had to get out and help push the car at one point and at another point to help change the wheel. He commemorated the centenary to 600 on the site of the future Lusaka cathedral. At Mponda's, which was the Nyasaland headquarters of UMCA, he was surrounded by singing people wanting to kiss his hand, and one of the men danced in front of him all the way to the house. On Sunday 1 May he led a pilgrimage to

Magomero where Bishop Mackenzie had his sanctuary for the pathetic humans rescued from the slave-raiders. It looks across to the towering Milanje mountain, and has a sharp curve in the little river as a moat against marauders. Under the shade of blue gum-trees was the marked grave of one of Mackenzie's first missionaries. The almost illegible notes of what the archbishop said at Magomero are preserved. He took as the text John 12:24, 'unless a corn of wheat fall into the earth and die, it remains of itself alone. But if it die, it bears more fruit'. This was a special text for that moment, because it was the text which nearly a hundred years before John Keble wrote in the end page of the book that was with Bishop Mackenzie when he died. Ramsey dedicated a twenty-foot high metal cross on the site to the memory of all who served Christ in that part of Africa during the last century. Those who followed him all round his tour found this moment at Magomero the most moving of the expedition.

In Nyasaland he found himself in the thick of that nationalist movement which turned Nyasaland into Malawi and at that moment it was hostile to the European and the white missionary, with effects in the Churches. The Presbyterian leader in the country could not safely visit some of his outlying churches because he was European and associated with a policy they repudiated. Ramsey found all this tragic, that Europeans who gave so many lives to help the peoples of that country, should now be regarded with suspicion when they wanted, or ought to want, nothing but the independence and freedom of the peoples. Paradoxically he saw that in this crisis they needed more European money, more European teachers, and more European priests instead of fewer. The principal trouble was the plan of the British government to turn Rhodesia (Zimbabwe), Northern Rhodesia (Zambia), and Nyasaland (Malawi) into a federation, and the Africans of Malawi were determined not to be married to the Rhodesians. At one mission station in the country Ramsey could not stop because they heard a rumour that he was a 'Federation Archbishop'—whatever, he said, that might mean. Yet he admired the Christianity of Nyasaland. He tried to get to the island of Likoma in Lake Nyasa where was the historic cathedral, with huge cracks in the walls and the wooden window-frames moth-eaten and the stained glass perilous and a great congregation assembled to meet him; but big storms on the lake forced his launch to turn back twice. He said he would risk it but the captain would not and the archbishop was unable to reach the island, disappointing congregations of thousands at Likoma and Liuli, with their gardens kempt and school bands rehearsed and mountains of food waiting. The food was not wasted.

His addresses were interpreted as he spoke. Africans travelled miles across difficult country to sit or kneel at his feet. He was moved by the African hymn-singing and specially seemed to enjoy it when some of the congregation sang in English and others in Swahili.

Then he went by a little chartered four-seater plane flying low, northward up Lake Nyasa to Tanganyika, which was not yet quite Tanzania, but which seemed to him to be developing happily under self-government and not to suffer the same nationalist tension. He watched the country clergy and catechists at work, and went to places which a priest could only rarely reach to give the sacrament, and talked in their schools and preached in their churches with people sitting on the floor of the aisles as well as crammed into the pews; he would sit in the shade of a great tree and watch a display in his honour of dancing or dumb-bells. He found it a place of strict Church discipline, to protect the convert from a relapse into polygamy or witchcraft, and therefore of long preparation before baptism. It interested him that the Africans much used sacramental confession, because there was a tribal custom which resembled it.

Then on to the diocese of Masasi, which was shortly to elect Trevor Huddleston as its bishop; as he drove along the road to Masasi he was presented with ten chickens and 100 eggs but we are not told what he did with them; he confirmed 80 candidates in Masasi cathedral. They gave him an ebony carved crucifix, which, unlike the ten chickens, he valued and kept with him the rest of his life. ('I will find for this crucifix', he told them, 'a special place in my chapel at home and whenever I see it it will tell me again that the Lord Jesus died for the people of Africa and loves the people of Africa still and seeing that I will pray again and again for you before this crucifix.' When he got home he did just that.)

And so on to Dar-es-Salaam and then to Zanzibar, where he called on the Sultan. He preached in a dark floodlit cathedral and was moved to do so, because he knew that it was built on the site of the old slave-market and the building was a symbol of everything good that Christian endeavour brought to Africa. Nevertheless he found Zanzibar sad; it was dominantly Arab, and the Africans seemed to him to feel themselves second-class citizens.

He came back feeling that this was the most dangerous and the most creative moment in the history of Christianity in that part of Africa and that the home Church ought to be much more aware of the needs than it seemed to be.

2. RHODESIA

In unloading the British empire, British governments obeyed a healthy principle. They would hand independence only to a government which could claim, by a reasonable constitution, to represent the majority of the people in the territory from which the British withdrew their power.

This principle was often modified in the face of facts. Where it must lead to civil war, as in India, the British refrained from carrying it into practice. Instead they divided the country into two and then gave power in the smaller state to what was the minority in the big state. Where it might lead to civil war because the country was divided racially—as in Uganda, or the Sudan, or Nigeria, where racial or tribal divisions ran deep—they handed over power to a majority, hoping that liberal democratic processes would obviate the need for shooting between the peoples; and they did not at first realize how hard it would be for tribal peoples to take to liberal democratic process. In Uganda and the Sudan and Nigeria civil war followed inevitably, though not at once. When the British handed over power to a unified people, more or less of one people or tribe, the handover was almost painless; and it could be almost painless even when the people were divided into tribes.

Southern Rhodesia made a special case. The colony had had self-government since 1923. They thought that they did not need a transfer of power. That had been transferred long before. They thought that they only needed their independence recognizing.

British sense of justice, and British need to be seen to be just among the newly independent states of Africa, could not be content with this plea. In Rhodesia lived 200,000 whites and over four million blacks. The 200,000 whites ruled. The British could not hand over power to a minority even though they were British. At least they must insist that blacks had a way of progress towards equal rights.

Public order in Rhodesia grew more difficult in the face of demonstrations and the beginning of guerrilla bands in the bush. When Ramsey became Archbishop of Canterbury the Rhodesian government was in the middle of a train of measures enacted for the sake of public order, measures which stank in the nostrils of British liberals; among whom, it must never be forgotten, was the Archbishop of Canterbury.

In 1961 Britain conceded a new constitution to Rhodesia. It ended Britain's powers in Rhodesia; except that the British Parliament still had power to revoke this almost independent constitution. The first election under this constitution produced a government of the right wing which wanted Rhodesia to remain permanently under white rule. The British gave them most of the army and air force which they had stationed in Zambia and Malawi and Rhodesia. The force was effective and well equipped.

Rhodesian demands for final independence kept running into British demands for changes in the constitution. In April 1964 the Rhodesian United Front put in as head of government the ex-Air Force officer Ian Smith. Smith kept saying that in his lifetime there would never be rule in Rhodesia by the majority of blacks. This was what most of his constituents wanted to hear.

Harold Wilson as prime minister of Britain had evidence which made him afraid of a seizure of total independence by white-ruled Rhodesia. On 27 October 1964 he issued a statement warning of the consequences of such a rebel act. It would be treason. Southern Rhodesians would no longer be British. Trade between the two countries would peter out.

On the very day of this statement there was talk in the Rhodesian Parliament that Britain intended to use force to suppress rebellion in Rhodesia if there was rebellion. A government did not talk about rebellion and treason unless it intended to use force. But soon it was clear that this was not true. It was soon obvious that the Labour government had very little mind to use force.

In May 1965 the Rhodesian Front won all the white seats in the Rhodesian Parliament. Business men in Rhodesia were not at all in favour of a seizure of independence. They were afraid of bankruptcy. But Ian Smith now had the mandate, and the power, to declare an independent Rhodesia if he judged that he could get away with it. He possessed, and began to use, draconian methods of imprisonment without trial. He suppressed the newspaper *African Daily News*. He slowed the pace of African advance in education, which would have the effect of delaying the time when Africans could gain a majority of votes. Academic freedom in the university was under threat. The teaching of anthropology was touched by a political slant. Some members of the Rhodesian Front wanted a system of apartheid on the South African model.

In Rhodesia the Churches were influential in society. They had close links with their mother-organizations in Britain. From the summer of 1965 information out of Rhodesia began to pour onto the desk at Lambeth at which Ramsey never sat: information from the two Anglican bishops in Rhodesia, from the Archbishop of Central Africa (whose see was in Zambia), from the secretaries of missionary societies, and from other denominations.

The advice which reached Lambeth was almost unanimous. Its near-unanimity may be summarized thus: the government of Ian Smith is not to be trusted. It is almost certain that he will throw off British power. If then Britain does nothing, all Africa will regard her as an accomplice in setting up a racialist state. Failure to resist Ian Smith would set back the cause of African development in Rhodesia, and hamper the work of the Churches not only in Rhodesia but in all black Africa. Therefore, if rebellion comes, it must be resisted, in the last resort by force.

Ramsey was the President of the British Council of Churches. It held its October 1965 meeting at Aberdeen. Its international committee brought there a resolution, which proposed Christian backing for the use of British force in Rhodesia in the last resort.

By act of the Conservative government Rhodesia possessed a modern little army and air force. It was not certain that this force, British trained and British led, would be willing to fire on the forces of the Queen. But it was also certain that the forces of the Queen would not be enthusiastic in risking their lives or in firing against people whom they regarded as other British soldiers. There was the danger of bloodshed between 'kith and kin' from which everyone shrank with horror. Harold Wilson had a majority in the House of Commons of only four. His party, almost unanimously against Ian Smith, was also against the use of force. But some informed people believed that the British only had to threaten force, and the force was so overwhelming that the rebellion would collapse or even not begin. This was how Kenneth Skelton, the Bishop of Matabeleland in Rhodesia, saw it. He advised Ramsey in this sense.

But another opinion came out of Rhodesia to Lambeth. The other Rhodesian bishop was Cecil Alderson of Mashonaland. He had served longer years in Africa than Skelton. Though against the policy of Ian Smith, he thought about the white congregations of his diocese. He had no desire to alienate them, which Bishop Skelton was in danger of doing. Alderson was convinced that a British use of force would be fatal. On 8 October 1965 he wrote a vehement letter in this sense to Lambeth.

The British government looked weaker than the Church leaders. Harold Wilson said tough things against rebellion but publicly renounced force if the rebellion rose. That was a way to encourage rebellion. The government looked to be in need of more backbone. Possibly the Churches could encourage backbone.

In face of all the advice which he received at Lambeth, Ramsey was sure that the British government would co-operate in injustice unless it was prepared, in the last resort, to use force against a rebellion which had as its aim the making of a racialist state; provided, that is, the force could be used without war and as a police action. Morality was usually stiff on the side of peace. But, he believed, this was a case where morality, except among pacifists who regarded the use of force as wrong always, demanded the use of force if all else failed.

He decided to tell the prime minister what he thought, and wrote him a letter to this effect (10 October 1965).

The noises made by Ian Smith in Rhodesia sounded daily more alarming. In New York the United Nations General Assembly (enormous majority, 107:2, Britain abstaining) demanded that Britain take 'all possible measures' to prevent Smith declaring Rhodesia independent, or, if he did, to suppress him by force (12 October)—the two votes against were those of South Africa and Portugal. The organization of African Unity, in which the heads of African States met at Accra, demanded that Britain take over the running of Rhodesia, if necessary by force. If Britain failed, said the African heads of state, whose language in those days often passed beyond the political possibilities, they were prepared to use force themselves.

On 18 October Ramsey tried a desperate idea of appealing to Ian Smith personally. With the Baptist leader E. A. Payne, who chaired the executive committee of the British Council of Churches, he sent a telegram to Ian Smith. He begged him to refrain from a Unilateral Declaration of Independence (UDI). He begged him to continue to seek agreement with Britain through negotiations. The telegram said that UDI 'would endanger the very values you seek to defend and the future of all races in Rhodesia and her neighbours'.

There is no evidence of any reply by Ian Smith to this telegram.

At this crux, and amid all the tension that Rhodesia would go into rebellion at any minute, the British Council of Churches met at Aberdeen, 26–27 October 1965, with Ramsey as its president. The Council had 130 members. Only 72 of them attended.

By 60 votes to 5 (no abstentions recorded) the Council adopted a resolution about Rhodesia. They said that *Christian faith demands* that the four million Africans have a share in deciding the government of their country and the ordering of their lives; that the British government was right to insist on this before conceding independence; that any 'Unilateral Declaration of Independence' must be resolutely opposed; that measures, including 'economic measures' must be concerted with the United Nations. 'Even if this should necessitate the British government being prepared to resume responsibility for government, the nation should have the wisdom and moral courage to take an action which is required by justice and compassion for all the peoples of Rhodesia.' That is, unlike Harold Wilson and the Labour party, the representatives of the British Churches were prepared to face up to war.

Ramsey did not think the resolution tough enough. The object of this resolution was not a cry for abstract justice but to strengthen the hand of a prime minister in a weak situation and in a mood of weakness; and just possibly to influence public opinion in such a way that Ian Smith would see at last that he travelled on a dangerous road, and so to help him to draw back. Ramsey would have preferred tougher wording.

He was a Liberal politician at the heart, and he was always a Liberal on what he took to be moral grounds. At Aberdeen he made a speech which showed the strength of his feeling. He did not expect anyone to mind. He did not expect even to be reported except in the minutes.

He said that the resolution said what was true and necessary and right, 'though it says it in a rather peremptory kind of way'. But there was a glaring omission. 'What are Christian people to say and do if Rhodesia goes over the brink? And already Mr Smith has declared a good many times his intention to go over the brink.'

It is not for us as Christian Churches to give the government military advice as to what is practical or possible. That is not our function. But if the British government thought it practicable to use force for the protection of the rights of the majority of the Rhodesian people, then I think that as Christians we have to say that it will be right to use force to that end.

The British Council of Churches can say what it likes because no one listens. The representatives of the Methodists can say what they like because only Methodists listen. The organization of African States can say what it likes because hardly anyone, even in Africa, listens. The United Nations General Assembly can say what it likes because only the converted listen. But if the Archbishop of Canterbury says what all these bodies have agreed in saying, that is different. Suddenly Ramsey was at the centre of the windiest political storm endured by an Archbishop of Canterbury since the revolution of 1688.

Archbishops of Canterbury are always in bad trouble at least once during their pontificate. Temple was in trouble over doubtful economics, Lang over the abdication of King Edward VIII, Davidson because he cared for the workers in the General Strike of 1926. It was much to Ramsey's credit that by far his worst trouble hit him because he wanted justice in Africa.

Measured by inches of headlines, the *Daily Sketch* of 27 October won. WE BACK WILSON IF HE USES FORCE. It was a correct headline, and did not mislead. The *Daily Telegraph* won a prize for the least sensational headline, *Dr Ramsey backs use of force*—but it could mislead. The *Daily Express* said that the British people may all be appalled over Ramsey's tirade. And so the press built on its own headlines next day—storm, shock, cartoons of bishops in uncomplimentary postures, and of prelates armed to the teeth. In the *Daily Mail* Ramsey was portrayed wearing a grenade hanging from his neck where the pectoral cross ought to hang.

Ramsey offended three groups in the nation. Pacifists were against him. The most comic condemnation came from Canon John Collins of St Paul's, who spent much of his life working for Africans—he called the archbishop ham-handed. Lord Soper, as a leading pacifist, said that he was shocked. The people with relatives in Rhodesia, and associated with the right wing Rhodesian Front in England were offended; and with these were often associated Tories of the right wing of the party. In the *Daily Sketch* there was a long article on how we could prise Ramsey out of his see by any means short of the way in which we got rid of Thomas Becket. The Earl of Southesk invited Ramsey to resign and to submit himself for re-election by universal suffrage.

The worst of being the centre of the storm is the discovery of one's allies. The Communist party backed Ramsey, a group of atheists at Oxford telegraphed their support, and not all the other public allies were consoling. But in Parliament he had backers with names of substance—Michael Foot, Shirley Williams, David Steel—whom no one could dismiss as cranks. In the House of Lords Lord Arran called him 'perhaps the most courageous man I know'. Edward Heath sent a private message that he regretted some of the Tory attacks on Ramsey and would like a talk.

In accordance with the proverb *episcopi Anglicani semper pavidi*, the bishops of the Church of England were not impressive. In a storm their instinct was to put their heads below the parapet. It left Ramsey more exposed and isolated than was right. Mervyn Stockwood of Southwark the most urban and the most radical of bishops, came out resolutely for Ramsey, as did Gresford Jones of St Albans and Mark Hodson of Hereford, the most conservative and most rural of dioceses. A few others later joined these ranks. For the most part the silence was deafening enough to be discreditable to the bench of bishops. Ramsey noticed it. He thought his bishops must be vexed and embarrassed.

On the Cenotaph appeared a placard: Ramsey Warmonger and Traitor. In Rhodesia silly men started burning Bibles to send the ashes to Ramsey. On 29 October a vandal took an aerosol paint gun and sprayed the high altar of Canterbury Cathedral with the word PEACE, and red and blue paint on the chairs, and at a Bible open on the lectern, and the tomb of the Black Prince, and St Augustine's chair. Next day someone sprayed more paint over the archbishop's chair and the lectern in York minster. That Sunday the police gave Ramsey protection during the services at Canterbury.

Outwardly he did not seem to mind the hurricane. Liberal-minded men of every description rallied to his aid. He was surprised when he only echoed the General Assembly of the United Nations, more gently than they. But he looked serene; except that when in the House of Lords Lord Brocket and Lord Dilhorne launched an irrelevant personal attack upon him (28 October) it was observed that his beetling eyebrows beetled more formidably.

Inside he was not serene. Many years later he told a friend that the most grievous trial of his life was to find himself, when feeling ran so high, cut dead by once-courteous peers in the corridors of Parliament. One of those peers proved that to be a lord it is not necessary to be a gentleman, by abusing him, as he passed in the corridor, with the curse 'bloody bugger'. All this was a grievous trial to Ramsey; the sense that former friends were foes. He afterwards said that he felt frightened; the fear that he could not approach someone lest he be repulsed and insulted. He expected to come out in pimples and did not. He noticed himself shrinking back into his envelope of shyness.

The press attack he minded most was that from Quintin Hogg, formerly Lord Hailsham. Hogg was one of the Conservatives whom Ramsey respected, and whom he rejoiced to find a faithful Christian. In the *Sunday Express* for 31 October Quintin Hogg came out with a whole page against Ramsey. It was cast in the form of a plea for a change in the mode of choosing bishops. His reason was the 'monumental' blunders of bishops chosen under the present system; blunders which would ruin the career of any politician. He cited a couple of less fortunate occasions in the career of Mervyn Stockwood; Archbishop Fisher anathematizing Macmillan's premium bonds; John Robinson, giving evidence in the case of *Lady Chatterley's Lover*; and now we have Ramsey. Let bishops be elected; and for fixed terms. Then 'they would cease to make such asses of themselves'. This less than statesmanlike article was adorned by the cartoonist Cummings with ridiculous pictures of Fisher, Robinson, Stockwood, and Ramsey. These pictures made the article nastier. Quintin Hogg, who was pugnacious but not malicious, probably never intended such an effect. Ramsey was very sorry to feel a breach with Quintin Hogg. He was never quite content until, a few years later, the friendship was re-established.

Other comments he did not mind; that he was 'a political innocent' (John Grigg in the *Guardian*). The *Observer* said that prudence is not necessarily the most desirable virtue in a Church leader. Paul Johnson in the *New Statesman* (29 October) wished that Harold Wilson saw the moral issue as clearly as Ramsey. 'I think', said Kenneth Kaunda, the prime minister of Zambia, 'that the Archbishop is simply being Christian' (*Daily Telegraph*, 30 October).

In this speech at Aberdeen Ramsey compared Britain's moral obligation in Rhodesia to use force if it should prove right, to Britain's 1939 obligation to help Poland against Hitler. He only meant, morality sometimes demands the resort to force. Some people took him, or pretended to take him, as meaning a comparison between Ian Smith and Hitler, between the Rhodesian Front and the Nazis. No sensible person thought that he meant this. But it was the single sentence of his Aberdeen speech which he afterwards wished that he had not said.

He never perceived what is very evident to anyone reading the papers of that time. The people of Britain were gloriously ignorant of Rhodesia. They fancied it a happy colony, run well by their kin. A prelate, stepping out of his office, recommended the overthrowing of this Shangri-La for the sake of a doctrine which everyone knew not to work in a country with a high rate of illiteracy, namely the doctrine of one man one vote. Ramsey continually received reports out of Rhodesia, and from the officers in London of organizations in Rhodesia. He was served with memoranda on them by his chief of staff Robert Beloe. He knew far more than the people of England about conditions in Rhodesia.

Nevertheless there was a snag to the use of force; even apart from the risk of bloodshed by Britons firing on Britons. It would mean the imposition of direct rule from Westminster, at least for a period. In 1966 Edward Heath was sure that direct rule in Rhodesia would delay and not advance the progress of Rhodesia towards independence. The Labour party was against force because it was against force. The moderate Conservative was against force because it could set back all that was good in Rhodesia.

In retrospect Ramsey wondered how he survived the year 1965. 'I think I was helped a good deal by the kind of interior peace which I had learned at Cuddesdon. I think the year made it clear that I was a person who stood for certain things and was not a mere talker of platitudes.'

In November Ian Smith declared Rhodesia to be independent of Britain.

Public attitudes in Britain swung overnight. Ramsey regained some of his reputation, and with a new stature. He spoke in the consequent debate in the House of Lords, 15 November 1965. He said that the moral issues were clear. It was a question of progress in education, of civil rights, of freedom from racial discrimination. We need to impose sanctions on Rhodesia not because we want to protest against Ian Smith, or to punish Ian Smith. We need them to bring an illegal regime to an end. And when he spoke of sanctions, he meant tough sanctions. He spoke of the danger of watering down sanctions. They were not to be a polite gesture to world opinion. They must bite. Harold Wilson stated that the measures would bring the rebellion to an end 'within a matter of weeks'.

For the next nine years the argument between Britain and Rhodesia rumbled on with ill-feeling and recrimination. Sanctions troubled the Rhodesian blacks but hardly the whites and their petrol and whisky flowed as freely. Ramsey was steady, in being resolute that Britain should never be seen to be helping to set up a racialist state and therefore that the argument, better settle for a compromise than not settle at all, was a worthless argument. Consequently Ramsey backed sanctions against Rhodesia whenever they were proposed by the government and were controversial in the House of Lords. In this capacity his backing was weighty, and some of his speeches were memorable.

Naturally he came in for a lot of criticism, about being a political parson. The Marquess of Salisbury, who had historic and family reasons for caring much about Rhodesia, blamed Ramsey for giving the impression that anyone of moral principle would be bound to accept his line, and described Lambeth Palace as an ivory tower out of which he invited Ramsey to descend into the real world (Hansard, 8 December 1966, cols. 1261–2). (Lord Wells-Pestell—'The most reverend Primate of All England does not live in an ivory tower. He just faces facts'.) Lord Coleraine challenged Ramsey to find any evidence in the New Testament that our Lord wanted the Romans to give majority rule to Palestine, and to say whether there was not plenty of historical evidence to show that majority rule was frequently a form of tyranny. Lord Grimston attacked Ramsey for an unchristian lack of generosity to the predicament of Ian Smith and his colleagues, and said that his references to moral issues were only a smokescreen to cover political mishandling. Lord Saltoun asked how Ramsey could support sanctions when that meant thousands of starving black children.

Ramsey, though not moved by his critics, did not take his line easily. He did believe, and said loudly, that Britain was in danger of moral disaster. He repeatedly reminded everyone that they were not just dealing in tactics, reason of state, and diplomacy, but in morality also. Yet he felt it a dreadful moral dilemma, to be faced with the plea—if you vote for a moderate racialist regime in Rhodesia you will avert the coming of an extreme racialist state with apartheid. In 1970, as we shall see, he visited South Africa. The visit left him with an abhorrence of apartheid and the idea of its application to Rhodesia. In November 1971, Sir Alec Douglas-Home, a believer in the human race, with whom

Ramsey was on terms of friendship, was on the verge of agreement along lines which tried to safeguard African development but left Ian Smith with too much power to frustrate what would normally happen if the proposals were carried out. (This was the so-called 'Salisbury Settlement'.) Ramsey talked in the debate (2 December 1971) of a tragic country, born out of British colonial enterprise, now with a racialist police state constitution, and they were discussing an agreement which might modify it a bit here and there, in the hope of some African advancement. He said that it must be an act of faith that these proposals would help Africans, and he was willing to make that act of faith— and therefore he declined to vote against the proposals because the Rhodesian peoples might give their consent to them and he could not be one who, by prophesying doom, encouraged the worst to happen. Yet he could not vote in favour of them.

The Rhodesian black leader Bishop Muzorewa came to Lambeth to see Ramsey in February 1972. Like everyone else who did not know, he imagined Ramsey to be much older than he was. He reported after the interview: 'I felt encouraged as I left his office, yet surprised that one as old as he could sound so militant.' No room ever looked less like an office than Ramsey's study at Lambeth.[1]

The situation began to change only a few months before Ramsey retired from his see and was never settled during his time as archbishop. The guerrilla war in Rhodesia became impossible for Ian Smith's government to control. Then in April 1974 everything changed with the revolution in Portugal and the decision of the new left-wing regime to give independence to Mozambique. One of Rhodesia's supply lines was cut. More and more white Rhodesians started to leave. South Africa realized that it could not be in its interest to prop up white Rhodesia. London no longer had any control of the situation. Ian Smith could do nothing but accept the coming of Zimbabwe.

3. BIAFRA

In 1965 Ramsey went to Nigeria and laid the foundation stone of the cathedral at Ibadan (7 January) and consecrated the newly finished part of Onitsha cathedral at Benin; he went to the Oji River leper settlement and wearing a white cassock and a white panama hat blessed 400 lepers and attended a meeting of the committee of the World Council of Churches at Enugu. The visit had an unplanned gain. Soon Nigeria fell

[1] Muzorewa, *Rise up and Walk* (1978), 107.

into civil war. And it happened that the Archbishop of Canterbury already knew some of the best Church leaders on both sides in the war.

Nigeria was a creation of the British. When the British left, they left a country which liked its unity and yet was divided into a Hausa Muslim North and a Christian South; and the Christian South was divided into a number of tribes of which the biggest were the Yoruba to the West and the Ibo to the East. Because the British had agreed to exclude Christian missionaries from the Muslim North, there was a wide difference in standards of education, between a westernized South and a feudal North. The Ibos were an able and energetic race who largely controlled the trade and the transport and supplied most of the clerks in the civil service.

The Nigerians sensibly tried to solve their disunities by a federal constitution. The first President was an Ibo, the first prime minister a Hausa. But the tensions could not be brushed aside and there were rigging and intimidation at elections. A general election of 1965 was marred by blatant ballot-rigging and fraud, many refused to accept it, and there was near-anarchy in the country which caused the inevitable army coup, January 1966, by Ibo officers. It was not bloodless. In July 1966 there was a Northern coup and that September some 30,000 Ibos in the North were massacred, and thousands more fled southward and eastward. In Eastern Nigeria were two million refugees.

So came the civil war. The Ibo East seceded in July 1967 and called itself Biafra. Its head was General Ojukwu. Since both armies were of raw and undisciplined recruits, atrocities were inevitable.

In a civil war, who should supply weapons? The Russians supplied Federal Nigeria with fighter aircraft. The French and the Portuguese supplied Biafra with arms. What should the British do? The British government were in a predicament. They created the Nigerian army. It used their weapons. Should they stop supplying them? If they stopped would Federal Nigeria turn against Britain and destroy its interests? If they went on with the supply did they encourage murder and war? Harold Wilson's government took the decision to continue to supply arms, though only at the level which they had attained before. They said they were bound to help the 'legal' government in Nigeria.

The Biafrans found the attitude of the British government incredible. And since they were a Christian country and the majority of their opponents were Muslim, some of them expected a world-wide Christian crusade in defence of Biafra against Muslim enemies. They found the failure of the British Churches incredible; and especially the failure of the Archbishop of Canterbury, whom they imagined to be a powerful personage, to stop the Queen letting her ministers commit this crime of supplying weapons to fight a war against a Christian nation. For a year or two the abusive cry 'the silence of the Archbishop of Canterbury' was as common in Biafra as the cry 'the silence of the Pope' was common among Jews during and after the Holocaust.

In July 1967 the Biafran chief justice Sir Louis Mbanefo, who was a devout Anglican and passionately pro-British, went to Lambeth with Archbishop Patterson of West Africa, whose see was inside Biafra. They explained to Ramsey the feelings and needs of the Biafran people and talked of the rising tide of resentment in Biafra against England and its Church. Six months later (12 February 1968) Mbanefo wrote from Biafra to Archbishop Patterson: 'Lives of Christians, and members of his communion, are being lost on both sides; what has he said? Not a word of concern or condemnation . . . The Church of England could at least throw its weight for peace . . . It is the apparent unconcern and disinterestedness which irritates our people . . . Unless Canterbury speaks out our people here will identify him with the British government policy.'

On the day after this letter was written Fenner Brockway took a motion to the House of Lords that the supply of arms to Federal Nigeria ought to cease. The Archbishop of Canterbury was his seconder. Ramsey said that there were immense differences between the peoples and that the only hope lay in agreement and tolerance; that the Biafran people must be given secure guarantees for their future safety; that the thesis that one side was the 'legal' government and the other side rebels was false. He hoped that the Commonwealth might provide a force to keep the peace. This speech received backing from powerful peers like Lord Goodman. It made no difference to the attitude of the British government.

Ramsey did not find it an easy situation for himself. The facts were (1) that Nigeria prospered economically if it held together and was not divided; (2) this was not a war of Muslim versus Christian, nor even of tribe versus tribe, for many Yorubas and some Ibos fought on the Federal side; (3) anything he said could be twisted into a statement which sounded totally pro-Biafra and he did not believe that a Christian leader could be politically on one side when there were many Christians on both sides. Nevertheless he thought it the moral duty of the British government to be neutral and that meant not supplying weapons. And he thought that the supply of weapons in any case would prolong the war and multiply the killings. Therefore he had a moral duty to keep pressing on government that they stop sending weapons; but in such a way that he did not seem to be only a political ally of Biafra. The road was full of holes.

In March 1968 he consented, though not without a feeling that he did something which was a bit papal and rather unanglican, to send out two delegations of churchmen, one to each side; three people in each, and each of the three from a different denomination. His choice for Biafra was Leonard Wilson, the Bishop of Birmingham. His choice for Federal Nigeria was Bishop Sansbury, secretary of the British Council of Churches. Each delegation took a message to the Churches from Archbishop Ramsey. The message had to be differently worded to fit each side in the war. Both messages assured the Nigerians and Biafrans of prayer—(which was true, for he and others were doing much to awaken the needs of all the Churches to the sufferings and bloodshed in Nigeria). The message to Federal Nigeria asked for a negotiated peace to bring the war to an end. The message to Biafra said that they had been pleading in England that the Biafrans should receive guarantees of their future safety, and asked for negotiations to secure a just settlement.

Early in March 1968 the two delegations arrived in Nigeria. In Biafra Leonard Wilson saw that he was taken for a ride. The government of Biafra took him over and pushed him around as if to prove that the British were now on the Biafran side. He was hardly allowed to meet the Churches in Biafra. The ears of the delegation were assailed with accusations against the British government and the British Churches. They did not try to defend the British. They tried to explain that the British Churches and the British government were not the same thing. No one believed them. Archbishop Ramsey's speech in the House of Lords was circulated widely in Biafra and caused much gratitude.

The Biafran delegation on their government tour saw bombed hospitals and refugee camps and schools; and they were taken to public meetings where they were welcomed but faced with placards like BRITAIN JOINS MUSLIMS TO EXTERMINATE CHRISTIAN BIAFRANS. SHAME!; or EIGHT MONTHS' SILENCE IS GODLESS! One placard said, THE CHURCH OF ENGLAND IS THE GOVERNMENT OF ENGLAND. They kept being told that if the Church had delayed any longer they would have lost many of their people. They found an intense brooding resentment produced by the siege mentality.

The Archbishop of Canterbury was very grateful to Leonard Wilson. But to him the need seemed to be not so much politics or pleading for negotiation, which others could do, as supplies, especially medical supplies, but any supplies to the starving and the refugees, except weaponry. He did what he could to this end. He had an eminent Biafran to stay at Lambeth, and dined with the Nigerian High Commissioner, and approached the Commonwealth office about ways in which Oxfam could get food into Biafra and successfully got an assurance that RAF planes could be used if that became possible; and on 15 July 1968 had another go in the House of Lords: 'Are Her Majesty's Government aware that the continuance of the supply of arms to Nigeria is proving a hindrance to the acceptance of relief by starving people in the Biafran territory?' The government voted a quarter of a million pounds for relief. But it went on supplying weapons.

There now happened one of the most moving episodes in Ramsey's career.

On 25 July 1968 the Lambeth Conference opened. It was the Archbishop's duty to invite the bishops of the Anglican Communion. Federal Nigeria expected only the bishops of Federal territory to be invited. Ramsey also invited the Biafran bishops. Since by then Biafra had hardly any communications with the outside world, as the Federal armies advanced, the journey of the Biafran bishops was roundabout and risky. But they came.

The history of past wars proved that Christianity was hardly strong enough to bridge the gulf between competing nationalisms and that the bishops of both sides were taken up as enthusiasts each in his own national cause. Would the Federals and the Biafrans speak to each other, and if they were willing would they dare in view of what their governments might say?

The Archbishop of Canterbury was determined that they should. He made sure that the collection at the opening service in Canterbury cathedral should go to Christian Aid to help the sufferers in Nigeria and Biafra and commended the cause to all the parishes. He was supported by the stalwart Archbishop of West Africa Patterson, who as an expatriate supporter of Biafra would only be able to return to his see for a short time. And they found among the black bishops on both sides a mood which proved how deep-rooted was Christianity among the African peoples and how they could teach Europe a lesson. During the Conference a delegation of African women came to tell Ramsey that he must understand that this was a religious war of Muslim versus Christian and to blame the Church of England for 'toeing the policy line of the British government'. But the Nigerian and Biafran bishops met and prayed together. On 16 August they agreed (!) a communiqué. It thanked Christians for all they had done for the work of reconciliation. It especially thanked the Archbishop of Canterbury 'for his message to us when war broke out', for sending the delegations to both sides, and for 'his persistent work for peace'. They called on the governments to work for peace and to look with pity on the sick and starving and to consider a further delegation to work for a negotiated peace.

Three days later Lord Brockway drafted a public letter asking for an international force, the ending of the supply of arms, and an effort to save the starving. He asked the Archbishop of Canterbury to sign. Ramsey hesitated. He owed his influence in Nigeria to the respect which he won from both sides and did not wish to jeopardize his influence in Federal Nigeria. But since he agreed with the letter in all respects, he got over his hesitation and signed.

Towards the end of the year Biafra had obviously lost the war. Yet the war went on. The French government still supplied the Biafrans with weapons. General de Gaulle's attitude was that federations do not work and that it was better for Biafra to be allowed to secede. Archbishop Patterson, back in Biafra, had two of his white missionaries murdered by Federal soldiers and started to ask that Biafra should now be given weapons, though he still wanted an international force. Various people asked whether Ramsey could do anything to help dissuade the French from supplying arms. Was it possible that the Vatican could influence the French? And if it were possible, some English Roman Catholic bishops thought the Vatican more likely to heed an appeal from Ramsey than from themselves. The Church leaders in England tried to persuade the Archbishop of Canterbury to join a delegation to the prime minister against the supply of arms but he thought it had all been said before several times and that they would do better with a public letter; which he redrafted (10 December 1968).

On the evening before, he went down to Basildon in Essex and made that speech on race relations which caused him to be barracked by demonstrators. In the speech he demanded in the name of humanity that British stop supplying weapons, and press for a cease-fire, and create a peace force, and make a more massive effort to relieve the starvation. On 20 December he asked that the bells should ring out for the sake of the suffering in Nigeria and Biafra and himself pulled one of the ropes in Canterbury cathedral.

In May 1969, with the war over and Biafra beaten, the Nigerians threw out Archbishop Patterson with insult—'he has done everything with malice and hatred in his heart to hurt Nigeria'. Ramsey thought this to be the fate of the true Christian confessor and hero. He said so to Patterson's successor.

4. SOUTH AFRICA

Ramsey was invited to South Africa for the centenary of the first provincial synod of the Church of the province of South Africa. Everyone agreed beforehand that he could not refuse, and that for him to visit South Africa was tough, and that he would be forced to walk a tightrope. If what he said was prudent, he would compromise himself and the Church of England. If what he said was imprudent, it could envenom a poisoned situation. *The Times* (leader, headline 'A Hard Trek for Dr Ramsey') said that he seemed to be heading into a gale and could not turn back.

He wanted to be seen as religious and not political. He knew perfectly well that religious things are political.

During the late autumn of 1969 the South African rugby team, famous in rugby history as the Springboks, toured Britain. Violence occurred at their matches in demonstrations against apartheid. Bishops joined a demonstration against them. Naturally the Archbishop of Canterbury was appealed to by all sides. It was British tradition that sport is above politics. Suppose that you take the view that in this case a demonstration on political grounds may do such good that it overrides this rule of non-political sport, may you encourage the demonstration? And if you join the demonstration, what is to happen if you find yourself, as so often in demonstrations, with violent men on your side?

Ramsey held that a sports team selected upon a basis of racial discrimination was very undesirable; that the citizens of Britain there-fore were right to protest; but that the violence of demonstrators is counter-productive and Christians ought to be careful that their protest is non-violent.

The next controversy was a decision by the committee of the World Council of Churches in Geneva to include among its grants of relief to organizations in the Third World a small number of grants to bodies which claimed to be guerrilla forces against South Africa or Rhodesia. It was made a condition that this money should be used only for medical aid; but no one could afterwards control how the money was used and whether it might not end up in the purchase of a Kalashnikov rifle. That the highest representative body of Protestant and Orthodox Christians should send money which, it was said, could be used to help what in international law was murder, cast down the reputation of the World Council of Churches in middle class Europe in such a way that to this day it has not recovered its former reputation; whereas in the Third World its repute rose.

Ramsey was sure that to subsidize guerrilla movements against South Africa was wrong. There could be a just rebellion. Rebellions against Hitler, he said, were just. But 'we have to be very certain who is planning them, that they know what they are doing, and what is the likelihood of a just kind of society emerging from the rebellion'. He saw no truly organized and responsible body of resistance in or outside

South Africa. To help 'guerrillas' was to try to help something too vague, too disorganized, and at times too murderous. He told the General Synod in England that here was a case where passionate concern ran ahead of clear thinking (16 February 1971). Not all the General Synod shared this view. One of his bishops, Patrick Rodger of Manchester, publicly criticized Ramsey for not giving the wider context of all the good done by the World Council when he criticized its grants; and warmly defended the grants (letter to *Church Times*, 20 September 1971). Such defences did nothing whatever to pull up again the reputation of the World Council among the European Churches. Ian Paisley from Northern Ireland produced a motion for the House of Commons: 'that this House deplores the Archbishop of Canterbury's identification with the World Council of Churches, of which he is president, in subscribing moneys to certain African terrorist groups which are armed with Chinese and Russian weapons . . .'. Naturally the House of Commons took no notice of this motion. Apart from all the other errors in the motion, Ramsey was no longer a president of the World Council of Churches.

The next controversy blew up over the British government selling arms to South Africa. Ramsey wrote to the prime minister Edward Heath, on behalf of himself and a hundred other bishops, asking him not to sell arms to South Africa. Edward Heath rejected the plea. This made Ramsey a political fact from the moment he set foot in South Africa.

He left Heathrow on the evening of 12 November 1970. Preaching and lecturing as usual on tours, he moved across South Africa; to the provincial synod at Cape Town which was the main Church purpose of his visit; to Stellenbosch which was the leading Afrikaaner university; to Port Elizabeth and to Grahamstown; to the Federal Theological Seminary at Alice, the chief place for training black clergy of several denominations, and at that time a hopeful and exciting venture, unaware of the fate that was in store; to Umtata in the Transkei, where he saw something of his first Bantustan or black homeland about to be created; to Pietermaritzburg and Durban, and then into Zululand; and so to Johannesburg and Pretoria and Soweto, the most testing time of his tour.

The notes of several of the addresses survived. Wherever he went he tried to be religious rather than political; and yet to speak of society. He would talk of Christ and humanity, of all men and women as children of God, of Christianity as brotherhood between peoples, of the way in which Christian doctrine does not recognize racial separations of individuals or groups. He stuck to the truths of the Bible, and left his hearers to apply them to their condition. But afterwards journalists got at him and pressed him and then he would answer frankly—apartheid is unchristian, the World Council is wrong to give money to guerrilla fighters, Britain is wrong to sell weapons to South Africa. He was asked whether he would back violent rebellion in South Africa. He said that he would not. He believed that violence would come unless the white people did more than they were doing for social change. But he would do nothing to encourage that violence.

At the theological college in Alice, which was already under the pressure from government which would end in its closure and transfer, some of the African students, backed by a little group of white teachers, pressed him about violence in a question and answer session. 'Should we not fight? Have we got to wait and endure until the Lord returns?' For once Ramsey found it not easy to answer a question from students. The questions on the theme went on and on until he had to say that he had said everything he could say on the question and would say no more. He cheered them up in other ways—that there ought to be more black bishops in South Africa when so many of the Christians there were black; that it was possible that black Churches could make new advances both in Christian thinking and in the union of the Churches; that if the Dutch Reformed Church would only have a dialogue with other Calvinist Churches it would see that it is possible to be both Calvinist and not static; that South African Churches showed a lot of parallels with the state of the Christian Churches under Hitler and that piece of history should be studied. He was asked whether it was desirable for Britain to trade with South Africa. He said that it depended. He was himself a manufacturer. 'I do a bit of trade with South Africa.' He manufactured books. Since his books were edifying he hoped that South Africans would buy them. He knew that there were other forms of product which were undesirable (e.g. weapons). But where the lines should be drawn, that needed an expert in business. They all believed him when he said he was not an expert in business.

There were a few incidents. Outside the provincial synod at Cape Town, where he gave an address variously described as low-key, or diplomatic, and which received a standing ovation, stood pickets of black clergymen, handing out leaflets protesting that the Anglican Church in South Africa practised apartheid. At Stellenbosch University the programme said a question and answer session with students, but the authorities would not allow this so it became a lecture. Just before he arrived the officials threw three black students out of the hall; and as Ramsey began to speak, two whites, a man and a woman, rose to protest—'we understand the Archbishop is against apartheid—two blacks have already been kicked out'. The Archbishop of Cape Town in the chair took no notice, the two protesters clattered out, and Ramsey did not know till afterwards. We shall see later the repercussions which this was to cause.

The pilgrimage through Zululand was like a medieval progress; halts on the road to greet little waiting crowds or to hear choirs sing; pause at a hospital to plant a milkwood tree; stop at Isandhlwana to see the battlefield of British defeat by a Zulu impi. The Zulus were astonished. They were specially astonished when they heard an Archbishop of Canterbury singing in Zulu. They told him so. He said, 'I thought you said this language was difficult. It is not nearly as hard as Welsh.' He found Zululand, where black and white races worshipped together, inspiring.

In Johannesburg cathedral on 29 November 1970 a congregation of more than 2,000 of all races crammed into the building and closed circuit television carried service and sermon to the crowd outside. He disliked the atmosphere; he could sense the police scattered among the audience; he smelt the air of strain; he smelt what he described as 'evil in an unusual way' and found it rather frightening. He said to them: 'Some believe that violence is the answer but this is not the Christian calling. Yet the alternative to violence in our contemporary world is not to be resting in the status quo but to be growing together in togetherness, to the establishing of human dignity for every man.' 'It is our good will that is the alternative to violence. Christ did not call to violence. He called his followers to be ready to suffer with Him.'[2]

The South Africans admired his coolness. Battered by television and newsmen at every step, he went on serenely, talking when he thought he had something to say, refusing to talk when he thought it the wrong moment, but seemingly unperturbed and always in command. The pressmen found him mellow and good-humoured. He was learning at every step.

On 27 November he went to see the prime minister, Vorster. Everyone wanted to know what happened. Neither Vorster nor Ramsey would say a word about what was said at the meeting. Ramsey's friends could see that he was upset. He asked to be driven home by a circuitous route so that he could have time to adjust to civilized society. Late that night he went into the chaplain's room in his dressing-gown on the way to the bath and said, 'The worst day of my life is over.' He told the

[2] This was how he was reported. But the address as printed in *CP* 145–7 has a less resigned sentence 'the alternative to violence is the making of considerable changes . . . while there is still time'.

Bishop of Pretoria, 'It was like a meeting between heads of States of two nations at war.'

Nothing was ever published about the conversation with Vorster. Ramsey made rough notes of what was said. Later he worked this into a formal minute of the meeting. He sent copies to the British prime minister and the British high commissioner. As the interview lasted forty minutes the record cannot be of all the words that were spoken. It shows that Vorster spoke the sentence 'I do not agree' four times and in every other sentence was blunt, dour, and aggressive.

Here is Ramsey's record, slightly shortened by the omission of inessentials:

The secretary took me into the prime minister's room. A lot of photographers came in and we stood side by side being photographed. I deliberately looked as grim as I could, because I did not want cheerful pictures of me with the prime minister to reach Uganda where in any case my meeting with the prime minister would be criticised [and where he was to go next].

Arms.
v. Before you left England you told Mr Heath that you were against the sale of arms to this country. That was a most unfriendly act. Why do you not care to protect Africa from Communism? Communism is a terrible danger.
c. I and all churchmen are concerned about the Communist menace, but it is my sincere view that there are parts of Africa where Africans are put off Christianity when Christianity appears to go with white supremacy and discrimination against Africans.
v. So you accuse our policy of encouraging Communism. Is there any evidence of that?
c. There is a good deal of evidence from experienced missionaries, such as leaders of the Church Missionary Society which has long worked in many parts of Africa, the policies of discrimination by Christian countries do put Africans off Christianity and therefore make them more vulnerable to Communist propaganda.
v. My Church the Dutch Reformed Church, has done more missionary work than all the rest of the churches put together.
[c. thought it best to change to another subject.]

The Anglican Church in South Africa.
c. I have been in the last weeks seeing a lot of the Churches and their work, especially of course the Anglican Church. I have seen the work amongst white, coloured and black people, in hospitals and schools, and also something of the cooperation of the Churches together. Much is being done quite apart from controversial matters to bring people to Jesus Christ.
v. I do not agree. The Anglicans meddle in politics and condemn our policy.

c. I am speaking of the work of ordinary parish priests and pastors who bring the gospel to the people.

v. I do not agree. I object to Michael Scott.[3]

c. Michael Scott has not been in this country for a long time now. He is not here now. I am talking in a friendly way about the ordinary ongoing work of the Churches.

Marriage.

c. I want to ask you about one matter of great difficulty for the work of the Churches. It is a matter on which members of the Dutch Reformed Church are concerned as well as other Churches. It is the frequently long separation of men from their families on account of migratory employment. The Churches are concerned about the strain on family life and marriages and are trying to face the pastoral problems.

v. We did not invent migratory labour. The British practised it. It has been for many years the way of life of the Bantu, the way which they prefer. When Italians go and work in Switzerland you Anglicans do not complain. The complaints about this are unjust.

c. But I am speaking about the pastoral problem. How do you think the Church should best help with the personal and moral problems which are involved? I ask this in an entirely friendly spirit.

v. The Church should preach the gospel and not pass judgments.

c. Certainly they must preach, but they must also care for people and families and lead them in the Christian way.

v. That is not my province. We did not invent this problem. It happens in many countries and you do not complain.

c. But is not migratory labour here a compulsory system?

v. No.

c. It is voluntary?

v. Yes.

Dutch Reformed Church.

c. I have had some very friendly contacts with members of your Church. I hope there may be more contact and dialogue between them and Anglicans and others.

v. I do not agree. It simply means your people criticising our policy of apartheid.

c. No, there is much that the churches can discuss about theology and evangelism. It is possible in my experience.

v. I do not agree.

The Anglican Church again.

v. As long as your Anglican clergy preach the gospel they can stay here. But

---

[3] For Michael Scott (ordained 1930) and his career in South Africa and Namibia see now Mary Benson, *A Far Cry* (1989).

when they are subversive like Trevor Huddleston and Ambrose Reeves they must leave the country.

c. Hundreds of them are striving to bring people to Jesus Christ. I have seen something of their work in very different congregations.

v. Some of them advocate violence. We are in a continuing state of war with Communism and violent tendencies.

c. Do you not think that people are likely to turn to violence when they have no freedom for political association, discussion, and peaceful influence?

v. The Black people have complete freedom for political association so long as it is not Communist.

c. Are you really saying that Africans throughout the country have complete freedom for political association?

v. Not of course in those areas which Providence has assigned to the white people. In their own areas they have complete freedom.

Further Points.

v. The police methods in South Africa and laws concerning detention and questioning which are much abused are also practised by the British and resemble the law now in force in Northern Ireland.

c. I want to ask about two Anglican priests who were expelled from Stellenbosch. I have read the article which was the ground of complaint and I see nothing subversive in it. It does in fact criticise the World Council of Churches grants.

v. No. It was a subtle article showing a Nazi mentality which said one thing and hinted at another. If other priests are subversive I will see that they are expelled too.

[Vorster rose to show Ramsey the door.]

c. May I ask you about one personal matter? The Anglican province has given me a gift of money from white, coloured and black people, and asked me to use it solely for missionary work in some other part of the world. What step do I take about permission for money to leave the country?

v. It is unlawful for such money to leave the country without the donor clearing it with the Department of Finance.

c. Goodbye prime minister. I am glad to have had this talk with you.

v. Goodbye.

The record of this interview is the record of a meeting between a courteous man who wanted to suggest ideas of care and compassion and the ruler of a country who showed not a sign of care or compassion, still less of courtesy.

Ramsey called the interview very stony. He afterwards told Edward Heath that Vorster was very grim, and the 'most totally rude man I had ever met, as there was not the slightest attempt to be pleasant at the beginning or end of the interview'. When they emerged to be photographed they looked hostile towards each other. Looking hostile was unnatural to Ramsey. He preferred to look hostile because of the coming visit to Uganda and so he needed to look hostile. Later in London he was rash enough to say in public that he looked grim on purpose, and allowed the anti-Ramsey press in Southern Africa to mock him for putting on an act. He said that Vorster looked unpleasant because he could not help it and Ramsey looked unpleasant because he meant to.

On 1 December 1970, his last full day in South Africa, Ramsey met Helen Joseph, who had been under house arrest for eight years. Helen Joseph came to the bishop's house, and they had coffee together, and a talk, and Ramsey gave her his blessing. Two could talk, three was a meeting and illegal. Joan had to go in separately.

Later he gave a last press conference. He warned of violence to come unless the white government made radical changes. He urged white South Africa to speak out whenever possible against the system of pass laws for the migratory labour, with the effect of disrupting African family life. He flatly denounced the scheme for African independent homelands, and called the Parliament in the Transkei 'a dummy parliament'; which was what it was. He talked of leaving in 'a state of deep pain at the human tragedy of South Africa'.

As he left, *Die Burger*, the official organ of the Cape Nationalist Party, said in a leader that his visit had been fairly disastrous. 'He heads a State Church which, for its own vitality, is too closely equated with British imperialism.' Ramsey, it said, was admirably fitted to be the agent of British imperialism as the Anglican competition for the souls of the newly freed, and to set out South Africa and apartheid as a universal scapegoat.

On 9 December he gave a press conference in London. What the reporters seized upon was his conviction that South Africa was a police state; with a system of salaried informers and spies; and that this got him down. He was rash enough to say that occasionally he wondered on his tour whether his room was bugged. They found him disturbed about the break-up of African families under the pass laws. Would there be violence? 'If there is not going to be violence there must be very considerable change.' Did he want a boycott of South Africa? He did not. He believed in 'contact'—provided it was with all races. But he was glad that the South African cricket tour to England was cancelled.

The comment on bugging gave good material to anti-Ramsey media in South Africa. Salisbury radio in Rhodesia, where Ramsey was not the favourite clergyman of the government of Ian Smith, said that he was talking through his mitre, and decided that he might be an avid reader of the books about James Bond.

Some radicals thought that he should have gone much further in the ferocity of his condemnation of the South African system. Some black radicals in South Africa blamed him for refusing to back violent resistance. This forgot that he was also the head, in honour, of the most important influence for good within South Africa, namely the Church of the Province of South Africa, with a numerous membership both white as well as black. And to it the wisest comment was an editorial piece in the *New Statesman* for 11 December.

> He looked tired, and clearly relieved to be back among the home-made biscuits at Lambeth Palace. Though he has, of course, a mound of correspondence from church members to deal with, asking why he is 'meddling with politics'. I think he has 'meddled' very skilfully, and find the charge that he pussyfooted over the question of violence somewhat foolish. He went further than most liberals, a year or so ago, would have believed it possible for any Primate to go. A step further and he would have fallen off the tightrope. He does have a duty to keep his balance.

All the liberal minds of South Africa and Britain were grateful to Ramsey and admired the surefootedness with which he trod so narrow a path. The Archbishop of Cape Town spoke for many when he said that Ramsey raised the morale of their people amid all their frustrations.

Thirty-three Labour MPs tabled a Commons motion applauding the stand taken against apartheid by Ramsey while in South Africa. Edward Heath, the prime minister, invited him to describe his experiences at a private interview (27 January 1971).

Because he spoke out to discourage civil war in South Africa, and yet was so stout an enemy of the South African government, he was on occasion declared by reporters to be a pacifist. But Ramsey was never a pacifist. He thought the war against Hitler right; he thought the Korean war right; he even thought the origins of the Vietnam war right in intention, though wrong in its course. Then what about the right to rebellion against injustice? He thought much about this question. And his view was decidedly against, under the conditions that prevailed. 'Rebellion in South Africa would probably bring about the most appalling suffering among those it is supposed to be helping. But there can be such a thing as a just rebellion. For it to be just, there has to be a good likelihood of its succeeding in bringing about justice.'

For the remainder of his time in office Ramsey had anxious care over the acts of the South African government towards Anglican churchmen. Shortly after he preached in Johannesburg cathedral the South Africans put on trial its dean, ffrench-Beytagh; and after a dubious trial and a five-year sentence reversed on appeal, expelled him; Ramsey was concerned in how best to use him in England. In February 1972 Bishop

Colin Winter was expelled from Ovamboland in Namibia, and Ramsey, both publicly and privately, did what he could for him; even approaching on his behalf the government in Pretoria. When the heroic Afrikaaner pastor Beyers Naude came under attack as head of the Christian Institute in South Africa, which helped persecuted blacks in ways that were often legal but were sometimes illegal, Ramsey did what he could to ask public prayers for him and to raise money to help defend him, and stopped the business of the General Synod to draw their special attention to his plight, and contributed a preface to the published account of his trial.

The expulsions of English bishops and priests, and his desire for more black bishops, led Ramsey to think it important that the leadership of the South African Churches should be in South African hands. In 1974 the Archbishop of Cape Town retired. Cape Town invited Reggie Cant, canon of York, to allow his name to go forward for election. Cant asked Ramsey for his opinion. Ramsey loved Cant for his person and revered him for his spirituality, for they worked closely together when Ramsey was Archbishop of York. But now he was frank. 'I do not see you in the post'—probably he meant Cant's quietness —and in addition, 'it would be a very big mistake for the South African Church to import a priest from England to the see of Cape Town rather than choose someone from within the province . . . It would be a real blunder.'[4]

During 1973 the Church argued over investment in South Africa. Ramsey recognized that total disinvestment for international companies was impossible. And he did not think that a policy of boycott achieved anything that would help the people they were out to help. But he did not like investments where exploitation of Africans by the company was proven. There was an awkwardness over shares in Consolidated Gold Fields, where enquiry pointed to exploitation of the African worker in that lesser part of the company's activity which lay in South African mines. The Church financiers did not buy shares in the company, they bought shares in a company which Consolidated Gold Fields took over. Ramsey was not pleased, when this was argued about, because the chairman of the Church's central board of finance said that the only guide on how to invest was the financial benefit of the Church of England. Ramsey was still less pleased when the chairman of the board of finance said that how the board of finance behaved was nothing to do with the Archbishop of Canterbury and implied that he had no business

---

[4] Ramsey to Cant, 10 April 1974. A letter from Bishop Colin Winter of Ovamboland shows the good that Ramsey could do even in remote Namibian villages which he would never see (22 January 1974).

to interfere, and when one of his investment colleagues refused to do anything about it and accused Ramsey of being misinformed. It was not long before the shares in Consolidated Gold Fields were sold.

5. UGANDA

On the way back from South Africa he visited Uganda. That made an awkward juxtaposition.

On 3 December 1970 Ramsey was photographed with the rascal president Milton Obote, who lent him an enormous Rolls-Royce. With Obote he had four talks. He preached in the cathedral, and installed a new bishop at Mbarara. He laid a foundation stone at the memorial at Namugongo where the Uganda martyrs were murdered ninety years before. Despite the awkwardnesses, the reception was as crowded, as beflagged and as vocal with enthusiasm as anywhere. Joan Ramsey, unlike herself appearing in public without him, laid the foundation stone of the Mothers Union building in Kampala. She even made a little speech about motherhood.

But this visit to Uganda was not comfortable. Ugandans disapproved of him going to South Africa. The more radical were angered at his continued, and restated, opposition to grants from the World Council of Churches to guerrilla organizations. They kept asking him, 'why don't you support our freedom fighters, as the World Council of Churches does?' Ramsey was uncompromising. He said, 'The World Council grants are in this context encouraging a sort of emotional belligerence, which does not face the serious questions about what a just war or a just rebellion would involve.' The Students Guild of Makerere University, no less silly than the committee of the students guild of most universities on occasion, issued a preposterous document. They accused Ramsey of condoning apartheid in his speeches in South Africa and said that he went 'all out in support of racialism as a way of life'. They noted that he did not protest at Stellenbosch when a black student was torn from his audience; that he condemned the grants of money to guerrillas; that he condemned the use of force even under intolerable racist conditions and thereby told the world not to fight against capitalist exploitation, imperialism, and racialism; and he insulted Uganda by offering it money given him by the students of the racist Stellenbosch University. The Makerere Students Guild said that Christianity was always among the first and most effective agencies of imperialism. We have to build a socialist anti-imperialist ethos and among the first things we must look to are religious institutions with their headquarters in the west, 'extending their *tentacles* to squeeze us and keep us subservient'.

In physical structure Ramsey was not at all like a tentacle. But he was like a Greek bearing gifts. He wanted to help the Ugandan churches with a gift of £2,700 which was brought to him by African children and was 'multiracial money'. He said that he had not seen the expulsion of the black student at Stellenbosch. 'Had I done so, I would have called them back—of course I would.' However Archbishop Sabiti thought it better, amid the ill-feeling, not to accept South African money for his Church. Sadly, Ramsey took it back and looked for another need.

What to do with the money? Ramsey had in Uganda a young lay Christian worker, by name Terry Waite. At that time there was a murderous civil war in the Sudan, fought between the North and the South, the North being largely Muslim and the South being largely Christian. Many Sudanese Christians, including two of their bishops, fled over the border into Uganda. Terry Waite was engaged in trying to do what he could for them. Ramsey saw that this would be a use of his money still in Uganda and yet not open to refusal by the Ugandan Church. In April 1971 he sent Terry Waite £2,200 with instructions that he was to say nothing whatever about the origins of the money and that he was to use it for the Sudanese bishops, especially by the purchase of cars.[5]

After his visit to Uganda President Obote was evidently grateful because he sent him the cumbrous present of two elephant tusks six feet high and a zebra skin. It was one of Obote's last acts in a corrupt regime.

Not long after Ramsey's visit the northern Muslim soldier Idi Amin overthrew Obote's regime, with the killing of about a thousand people. In June 1971 Amin, who liked to make anti-British speeches which would have been bloodcurdling if they had not been absurd, attacked the Archbishop of Canterbury publicly for not doing what he could to help the Ugandan Church in its troubles. Bishop Luwum, a northerner who was close to Obote and therefore at risk under the murderous regime which now developed in Uganda, called at Lambeth in August 1971 to consult the archbishop about the tension in the Ugandan Church; and Ramsey was insistent that the record of the conversation be kept confidential lest it increased the danger to Luwum's life. The divisions in the State exacerbated the existing tribal tensions within the

---

[5] Ramsey to Terry Waite, 14 April 1971. Two years later he gave Terry Waite a fine reference for a new job: much intelligence, and knowledge of the overseas Churches, and of the ecumenical scene. Ramsey to John Howe, December 1973.

Ugandan Church and at one point in the winter of 1971–2 Ramsey was coping with two Ugandan dioceses trying to secede from the Ugandan Church and make a new Church of their own; and was for a moment pleased with the ogre Amin because he summoned all the Church leaders to the presence and told them brutally not to be so unchristian as to fight each other. This pleasure with Amin did not last.

Amin threw out the Ugandan Asians. Some of them had the right to come to Britain on British passports. Ramsey was strong that this was a moral obligation and Heath's government was of the same mind. The archbishop denounced in a BBC broadcast Amin's 'dreadful racialist policy'. He gave a Lambeth Palace cottage to a homeless Ugandan refugee family till they should find something better, and this charitable act brought him a pile of some of the most vitriolic post he ever received. Someone tried to accuse him of racial discrimination before the Race Relations Board. Enoch Powell talked of 'prelates and others who, as the Pharisees of old caused a trumpet to be sounded when they distributed their alms, were careful to be seen doing their works of charity in full view of the press and television cameras'.

And President Amin said that he wanted all Ugandans to attend church and so to get discipline in the home and so to make his job easier. In 1974 a military coup against Amin failed, with more bloodshed. Luwum that year became Archbishop of Uganda. Just before Ramsey retired from his archbishopric, Amin summoned Luwum and told him that he would not kick out the British missionaries who taught in schools and worked in hospitals, he loved them very much. But before long Luwum was to be murdered brutally, the next in a long line of African martyrs.

6. SUDAN

The Sudan became independent in 1956 after many years of Anglo-Egyptian sovereignty. Like so many states which went independent, it had the trouble that it was divided between two peoples. In the North round Khartoum, which was the headquarters of the state, the people were mostly Arab and Muslim. In the South, divided from the North by the barrier of the huge Nile marsh, the people were mostly negro and either primitive animist or Christian.

Like the ruler of Sabah, the rulers of Khartoum, or some of them, had the idea that they could unify their divided State by making it Islamic; which meant, to discourage the Christians of the South and encourage their conversion to Islam. In 1962 was passed the Missionaries Act, which expelled all expatriate missionaries from the South. Government ruled that the Churches could not build new buildings for worship nor could they repair their old buildings. They could not exhibit church posters. They ruled that clergy must have a permit from the police to move about. They provided money for the building of mosques. Many did become Muslims. Christian services, where there were no buildings, continued under trees.

But the gulf between North and South was deeper than a religious divide. The political conflict erupted into civil war, where the army got out of hand, and atrocities happened and the cleavage between the two parts of the State was incurable. In a state of civil war some of the Northern politicians, and ignorant or savage commanders in the field, identified the Christian leaders of the South as the chiefs among rebel propaganda.

In July 1965 mobs burned down the Roman Catholic seminary; and one night at 3.30 a.m. burned down Bishop Gwynne College, which was the only Protestant college serving the Sudan. No one was killed because the students were forewarned and fled into the bush and though the staff was not forewarned they escaped into the bush as the cordon drew round the buildings; and an assistant bishop lay under a hedge for three hours.

For a time anyone who was a prominent Christian in the South was likely to have a short life. The two Sudanese assistant bishops and many of their clergy fled over the border with their people, to Uganda or Congo or Ethiopia, and tried to minister to them in their refugee camps. By the middle of 1966 the only churches functioning in the South were the cathedrals at Juba and Wau and a big church at Malakal. The United Nations estimated the Sudanese refugees from the South at that time as about 100,000.

The bishop of the diocese, with his headquarters in Khartoum, was still an Englishman, Oliver Allison. Repeatedly he asked leave to visit his clergy and people in the South, and repeatedly the leave was refused by the government. He knew where his assistant bishops and some refugee clergy were but he had no idea of the whereabouts of some thirty clergymen and had a fear that they might have been massacred.

In August 1966 the Minister of the Interior at Khartoum summoned the heads of the denominations and frankly recognized the tragedy of the previous year and begged them to persuade the refugees to return and asked that Islam and Christianity should work together to convert the animists of the South. Allison said that they longed to return and only waited to be sure that they would be safe.

Throughout this tragedy Lambeth was kept informed. The

Archbishop of Canterbury continually asked himself what if anything he could do to help. At first he thought that any attempt by himself would only irritate the Sudanese and make matters worse. But later he saw that he could do good by seeing the Sudanese ambassador in London.

In the last week of August 1966 the Sudanese ambassador went round to Lambeth Palace to see Ramsey. The ambassador said that it was not a case of the Sudanese State versus the Christians, but a general uprising in the South which the State could not control. Ramsey asked, then why had the government stopped Bishop Allison from going to see what happened in the South? He told the ambassador that most of the churches were burnt and asked who would pay for their rebuilding. He did not imagine that the Sudan would expect England to pay, for that money would be suspect as 'colonialist'. He asked, how could the refugees in Uganda and Ethiopia be persuaded to return after the way in which they had been treated?

The ambassador seemed 'almost' ashamed of what had happened in the South. He thought it possible that government money would help to rebuild the churches. He suggested that the two refugee assistant bishops should be given a safe-conduct to Khartoum to talk with the present prime minister.

It was evident that the Sudanese, or some Sudanese, now regarded the Church not as a mischief-maker but as an agent of reconciliation. Ramsey went off to Canada much cheered; and ten days later Bishop Allison was given permission to visit the South. He spent ten full and exciting days in and near Juba, and confirmed 107 people, and returned much encouraged to Khartoum. He asked the assistant bishops if they would go back but they refused. They said that they were with their people in the refugee camps.

Yet the bloody civil war went on. When in December 1970 the archbishop arrived in Uganda on the way home from South Africa he saw Terry Waite, who was helping the Sudanese refugees in Uganda. In Kampala he made a speech which the Foreign Office disliked. He talked of the 'terrible and relentless persecution of Christians' in the Sudan. 'I feel very greatly for the sufferings of persecuted Christians both within that country and as exiles. We want to do our utmost to help and befriend them and to protest against that very great injustice.' The Foreign Office disliked this because they struggled to keep friendship going with Khartoum; because they preferred to pretend that the war in the South had no element of a religious war; and because a lot of Britain's oil flowed out of Libya, which backed Khartoum. The Foreign Office complained about the speech and denied that there was a religious persecution. Since in Uganda Ramsey met the two exiled Sudanese bishops he had plenty of eye-witness evidence of religious persecution and was not moved by the Foreign Office. He also had evidence that a few months before a Sudanese army unit raided across the border into the Congo and locked a hundred refugees into their church and burnt it to the ground. The Sudanese ambassador in Uganda, Osman Mahgoub, disliked the speech even more than the Foreign Office. He said that Ramsey's statement was intended to divert attention from his failure to condemn apartheid in South Africa and his opposition to the World Council grants to guerrilla movements. He said that Christian missionaries in the Sudan were expelled because they fomented hatred between North and South.

But for the archbishop, and for Terry Waite in Uganda, and for anyone else whom he sent out to Uganda, like George Appleton, what could be done was very limited and had to be done delicately. At all costs Khartoum must not see Anglican leaders as the principal agents in helping rebels in the bush of the South. By September 1972 there looked to be hope. Allison was able to hold a bishops' meeting in Juba which included even the two refugee bishops from Uganda. They were hunting for the ruins of their old churches and vicarages in the bush and found temporary churches erected and filled to overflowing. It was less good in Khartoum, where government closed the cathedral and built a wall round it. When the cathedral was empty a few experts at cracksmanship broke into the crypt where the valuables were stored and got them away and ripped out the choir stalls and the ceiling fans. There were again a few ordinations in Juba, mostly of deacons to serve in the bush. The main roads were still impassable for fear of mines. But everyone had a vast feeling of relief after so many years of suffering.

Allison retired from the see in February 1974 and was succeeded by the first Sudanese bishop, Elinana Ngalamu, who had spent some time as a refugee in Uganda. He was able to be enthroned at Juba that month and was the first bishop to be called Bishop *of* the Sudan. Even before his consecration Ramsey was advised that it was not safe to write to him direct. Though his southern region had been deprived of expatriate clergy for ten years, except for Allison's visits, the time was one of Christian expansion despite all the horrors. In the bush was a flourishing Christian Church growing with almost the speed of a mass movement—with little log-huts or huts of mud-and-wattle for chapels and schools, and wandering deacons or catechists to teach them hymns and negro spirituals and to write down the names of the baptized in some old exercise book, and a flowering of indigenous Christian lyrics in the forests.

When Ramsey retired from his see he was able to feel reasonably heartened. He could not foresee that another and worse civil war was soon to follow.

I I

The Lambeth Conference

I. LAMBETH 1968

Ramsey was not enamoured of multitudinous conferences. He did not look forward to his turn at presiding at a Lambeth Conference. But he knew that it was important for the Anglican Communion. The number of bishops invited was doubled, with representative suffragan and assistant bishops; 462 delegates accepted. Hence the meeting lost the relics of the intimacy which had once reigned. They needed to meet in Church House at Westminster. It was a sign how the conference moved away from its historic origins of being a lot of personal guests of the archbishop who should therefore gather in his private house. Many found discussion easier in a chamber built for discussion. But not all the bishops found such a chamber easier, some of the bishops from Africa and the East felt embarrassed at speaking in a formal Parliament. After the second afternoon they decided that the press should be allowed into all the plenary sessions. The presence of the press, and the right of the observers and consultants to speak from the gallery, made a difference to the feel of the debates. The size of the assembly, and the anti-colonialist attitudes of that age, and a radical streak among some of the American bishops, made the English bishops less important within the whole meeting than in the past.

In Westminster the bishops felt less dominated by the archbishop. But that was also because the archbishop had changed.

1968 was the first Lambeth Conference to receive a message of greeting from the Pope. It was the first Lambeth Conference where bishops were not in gaiters. Archbishop Fisher turned up at the garden party in Lambeth in gaiters, and one bishop turned up in gaiters to register. Ramsey's cassock was now the model for costume for the platform party; most bishops were in lounge suits. Everyone agreed in gratitude to Joan as a hostess to the bishops and their wives; small parties of sherry or dinner at Lambeth and at weekends in Canterbury.

The fathers of the conference condemned racism; accepted that violent revolution was in some circumstances a possible Christian option but preferred non-violent ways of changing injustice and specially commended the non-violent methods of Martin Luther King. They accepted that the wording of the Thirty-Nine Articles was obsolete as a fundamental statement of Anglican doctrine, except in their historical context, and suggested to all the Anglican Churches that subscription to them should not be required of ordinands; backed the movement for conservation of the natural environment; accepted that deaconesses are deacons (big vote, carried 221 to 183); voted that the arguments for or against the ordination of women to the priesthood are 'inconclusive', but asked the various provinces to study the question. It created an Anglican Consultative Council to meet more frequently and guide the Anglican Communion during the ten years between Lambeth Conferences. The conference reached out to the civil war in Nigeria, and the civil war in the Sudan, and the civil war in Vietnam, and to what the Churches could do for world hunger; and during one morning came the news of the Russian invasion of Czechoslovakia, which to Ramsey was shocking. He summoned the bishops to prayer in Westminster Abbey for Czechoslovakia. 'I salute the brave and faithful people of Czechoslovakia and may God be with them until deliverance comes.'

Only once did the arguments of the bishops pass into ferocity. Some wanted to preserve all that was good in tradition, others wanted openness to the world and intelligibility. This argument was not academic. It affected attitudes to old prayer books and new, old translations of the Bible and new, historic statements of Christian truth and new, tried pastoral methods and new. Some wanted the Church to be more of a praying Church, a community of quiet, that encouraged the nun and the contemplative. Others wanted the church to be more committed to action, in the fight against racialism or poverty. Some called on the Church to retire to be near its Master, others kept crying for it to go out into the world and, as the phrase went 'be involved'. Some blamed the men of prayer as quietists; and the men of prayer saw the danger that too impassioned a demand for a political Church would become only a sentimental way of trying to do good to society and neglect the help which Christianity was to bring to individual men and women. Yet the one big quarrel came over none of these varying tugs at the Christian conscience, but over an internal ecclesiastical debate, the different attitudes to the proposals for unity between the Anglicans and the Methodists.

The bishops, somewhat to their surprise, quite liked Ramsey as a chairman. He did not speak much. He spoke seventeen times, which was more than anyone else, but these were mostly brief, chairman's interventions. He once intervened, at a point of frustration, with a speech which everyone regarded as masterly. Once he intervened, about Christian unity, to quote 'a wisdom infinitely greater than my own', which was that of William Temple, with whom (he said) he exchanged letters on the subject when he was young. Once he was blamed for high-handedness towards an American bishop but mostly his fault as chairman was as usual the other way. They liked his sense of humour and enjoyed it that he enjoyed his own jokes as much as they. They admired his stamina—that at the end of so exhausting a series of debates, sometimes on very hot days, he was still buoyant in spirit. They respected his interventions not only because of his office but because they regarded him as a theologian. What came over to them above all was the religiousness of the man. His stature grew during the weeks of the conference.

One of his critics among the English bishops, Treacy of Wakefield, who dismissed the debates as dull, swung over in his attitude to Ramsey by sitting under him at a 'day of recollection' for the bishops (26 July 1968). He suddenly perceived that this was a simple lover of his Lord who would be willing to die for his faith if it were necessary. For Treacy this sudden perception remained in the memory as the best thing about the conference.

He did not have to keep order much because the bishops passed a resolution limiting drastically the length of speeches. Once they passed the resolution he was firm with the bell. But he did not like to stop people when they spoke totally off the point. He always expected that somehow they would come round to it sooner or later. During boring speeches he could be seen writing busily. Occasionally, at the end of such speeches, his attention might be needed and then a secretary told him what everyone was talking about. He rarely expressed his own opinion on what was being discussed. But the bishops thought that his private opinion could easily be read from his face.

John Macquarrie was an Oxford theologian who attended the conference as an observer. He had a surprising observation about its members and its chairman. He said that he was astonished to find so many of the bishops being swept along among the fashions and the slogans of the popular thought of the sixties. And he felt in retrospect, that Ramsey's achievement, not only at this conference but throughout that unsettled age, was the intellectual stance—not his books but his attitude—open to new ideas but not being swept along by fashion, at once critical and respectful of tradition.[1] The press officer De-la-Noy, who had reasons

[1] Macquarrie in Martin, *Great Christian Centuries*, 157; for Treacy, Peart-Binns, *Eric Treacy* (1980), 192.

for being critical of Ramsey, watched him in the chair and thought that he could seldom have been happier. He thought him the best mind there.[2]

Archbishop Fisher did not think much of this Lambeth Conference. He told two eminent Anglicans that the conference had less moral authority than its predecessors; that it was too large; that it took over from Rome the idea of collegiality without understanding it; that it imperilled the future of the Anglican Communion. Some of those who experienced both 1958 and 1968 preferred 1958 because it was easier to organize a smaller number of people in debates. The Bishop of London is known to have preferred the masterful chairman of 1958 to the chairman of the loose rein ten years later. But this was not everyone's opinion. Philip Strong, the primate of Australia, said that he much preferred Lambeth 1968 to Lambeth 1958 because the atmosphere was more truly religious.

Ramsey was asked five years later whether the Lambeth Conference was obsolete. He denied the suggestion with vigour.

2. LIMURU

The Anglican Consultative Council, appointed by a two-thirds vote of the provinces of the Anglican Communion, had 51 members. It first met at Limuru in Kenya, high on the Rift escarpment not far from Nairobi, at the end of February and beginning of March 1971. Its conclusions were controversial. Its members were criticized afterwards as lightweight. Even the secretary thought half the members lightweights. But a meeting where only half the members are lightweights is heavy. The 51 members from all the 21 Anglican provinces contained about equal numbers of Europeans and non-Europeans. Ramsey was president. The chairman was Sir Louis Mbanefo, former chief justice of Biafra; not a good chairman but a respected layman.

The World Council of Churches at Geneva, which began to be under the leadership of Africa and Asia, sanctioned grants of money to various bodies fighting against 'racialism'; and among the bodies to receive grants were guerrilla organizations fighting, or planning to fight, in Angola, Mozambique, Namibia, Rhodesia, and South Africa. This was reiterated at a committee meeting of the World Council at Addis Ababa early in that year, 1971. The grants were given under the stipulation that the money should not be used for military purposes. When divided

[2] M. De-la-Noy, *A Day in the Life of God* (Derby, 1971), 25.

by nine, £83,300 would not buy many bullets for each guerrilla even if every penny were misused.

This divided the world morally. Many of the British people identified guerrilla movements with the IRA. The decision also strained relations between the Vatican Secretariat for Christian Unity and the World Council, far more than was ever allowed to appear in public pronouncements.

To the growing Christianity of Africa and Asia and Latin America, Christianity was also liberation. So it was proposed at Limuru that the Anglican Consultative Council should back the decision of the World Council of Churches.

Ramsey argued against the resolution. Guerrilla wars bring terrible suffering. The time of violence might come, but it was the duty of the Christian to try every other road first. The Bishop of Cape Town tried to get the resolution moved out of order, but in vain. The resolution was carried by the very large majority of 'over 40' to six; that meant, five abstainers. The Bishop of Mashonaland, Paul Burrough, walked out of the conference in protest at the resolution. Afterwards Ramsey said that he had a good deal of sympathy for the Bishop of Mashonaland; no doubt because he lived in Rhodesia, a country then facing guerrilla war and its consequences.

The more far-reaching decision at Limuru touched the question of women priests; of which more later.

Ramsey took the opportunity to preach, and meet students, in Nairobi; and was very happy with the students. Among them were refugees from South Africa who asked him for money for football boots so as to be able to set up a team; and with his cheque of £100 they bought twelve pairs of football boots and two footballs and put the rest of the money into the bank. He met Jomo Kenyatta, the president of Kenya, who gave him an ivory stick and a monkey-skin cloak, in which he looked bizarre but beaming; no more bizarre, however, than President Kenyatta in his rival costume. It was a compliment to a chieftain. Terry Waite came down from Uganda to get Ramsey's advice about the dangerous relief work on the Uganda–Sudan border. John Howe made a note in his Log Book on 5 March 1971 that the archbishop seemed to have enjoyed Limuru—'Told me the Council was "creative".'

Ramsey much enjoyed Limuru. It was such a contrast, this relatively small group where real discussion was possible, with the vast meetings which ever since Evanston he distrusted. His first reaction was to think that the meeting was valuable. Later on reflection he changed his mind. 'I quickly came to think that it was not the right way to run the Anglican Communion and that it was a poor substitute for a meeting of archbishops.' 'I think that Lambeth 1968 erred in giving power to the Anglican Consultative Council.' Father William Purdy attended as an observer all the meetings of the Anglican Consultative Council from 1971 to 1981 and thought that Limuru was the worst—the most incoherent and most unorganized—too incoherent for a real vote on the crucial issues which faced the Churches.

St Augustine's College, Canterbury

It had historic buildings and during the Victorian age was a college for training missionaries. In a post-colonial world this looked out of date. After the Second World War it was turned into a college for priests from overseas to study in England. In this capacity it was valued. But it ran into difficulty over money. The expense which fell on the various overseas provinces had to be justified. The kind of postgraduate study which the Americans or the Canadians wanted was not the same, usually, as the kind wanted by the young priest out of Africa or Asia. In 1966 the archbishops under Ramsey's chairmanship, meeting in Jerusalem, refused to put up the money to cover the large deficit; and in 1967 the college closed.

To this day there is disagreement on whether this was a disaster. With the world-wide ties weakening in liturgy or organization, personal friendship between the leaders was ever more important; and they had often acquired it as fellow-students at St Augustine's. This criticism suggests that the closure of St Augustine's was like the Anglican Consultative Committee, a way of weakening the bonds which held together the world-wide denomination. If the financial papers are read, and the practical problem faced, it is hard to see how any other decision could have been taken. But we note only that to this day Ramsey is blamed by some critics for not standing up to his fellow-primates at their meeting in Jerusalem of 1966, or for not finding other money to replace what other archbishops refused to give.

3. WOMEN AND ORDINATION

Lambeth 1968 left a problem unresolved which had to be settled.

Under the conditions of the second World War, where Hong Kong was isolated and a prison, the then Bishop of Hong Kong ordained a woman deaconess, Florence Li, as a priest at Macao in order to get sacraments to the people. When the emergency was over she was persuaded to withdraw into lay life. But meanwhile the women's movement everywhere and especially in the United States made headway.

That it became a matter for discussion during the fifties was shown when a question about it was asked of Ramsey in the moment after he became Archbishop of York. In the garden at Bishopthorpe he was asked by a correspondent whether he had any objection to women ministers (note the wording). He said that the question ought to be fairly weighed. Christianity had enhanced the status of women. But Christ only chose men as his apostles; and as the Church on earth has the analogy of the family the priest is like the father in the family. Still, 'I'm very ready to have a good look at the possibility of change, knowing that God does reveal new truth to us after the lapses of time.' But it is important to consider it in relation to the whole cause of Christian unity—that is with Methodists, and with Roman Catholics, and in the links with the other Anglican provinces overseas.

During the early years at the see of Canterbury Ramsey saw no possibility that women could become priests. This was on the traditional Catholic grounds. The Church had always insisted on males as priests. It was a universal tradition of the centuries. If it could be changed, it could be changed only by an ecumenical council of the whole Church. As lately as 1967 in the Church Assembly he said, 'I am not in sympathy with the ordination of women because I think that if God had meant his Church to have women priests, He would have made it known rather sooner than He has done.' For this sentence Monica Furlong wrote a column in the *Daily Mail* (7 March 1967) to attack him; and he wrote her a charming private letter: 'I agree that the sentence of mine which you quoted was silly and your comments on it were fair. I usually get caught when I say something silly, though not always by someone as charitable as you are.'

In his later years Ramsey came to believe that some time it could happen and probably would happen, though not in his time as archbishop. This change was due to his perception of the way minds moved in the Lambeth Conference of 1968. That conference asked all the Churches to study the ordination of women to the priesthood and to report the result to the Anglican Consultative Council. It agreed that theology was neither clearly against, nor clearly in favour of, the ordination of women to the priesthood. The committee on the question wanted a clear statement that there was no theological objection to the ordination of women as priests but this was opposed and amended to the inconclusive resolution.

The question came to the meeting at Limuru (1971) because the Bishop of Hong Kong sent it thither. Hong Kong was the only diocese to have experience of a woman priest (if she was a priest). In the sacramental work of Florence Li they had seen nothing to regret and much to commend. The diocesan council at Hong Kong approved the principle and the bishop asked the meeting at Limuru for guidance.

A feminine co-opted member of the Council, Miss I. F. Jeffreys from Australia, asked for a practical answer to the question whether women might be ordained priest. And John Mbiti, the first black lecturer in divinity at the university of Makerere in Uganda and an observer at Limuru (for he was an Anglican) said that in certain parts of Africa the matriarchal system made it more appropriate that women should be priests, as women were the leaders of society.

In the debate Ramsey spoke against the resolution to approve, and expressed grave doubts on the principle. The resolution was carried only by a narrow majority, 24:22; with Ramsey and the chairman, Mbanefo, and Bishop Williams of Bangor, voting against. The resolution, proposed by an American black and seconded by an American woman teacher at a seminary, said that if the Bishop of Hong Kong, or any other bishop acting with the approval of his province, decided to ordain women to the priesthood, his action would be acceptable to this Council; and that this Council would do what it could to encourage all other provinces to continue in communion with the dioceses where this happened.

The Anglican Consultative Council was only consultative. It had no deciding authority. It would have been better if such a thorny issue could have been decided by a synod of the whole Anglican Communion. But on this issue people, and time, pressed. Lambeth Conferences did not meet often. The American Church was in turmoil. The slender majority of Limuru began at once to be treated, by those who wished for women priests, as though it was a decision of the Anglican Communion. Even before he retired from his see, Ramsey was brought up against the trouble which ensued.

Ramsey voted against both the crucial resolutions at Limuru. For an archbishop and a primate to be in the minority on two crucial issues led the *Daily Telegraph* to ask who now led the Church of England. But in voting against the resolution about women, the archbishop was still with a mind that was not closed. For as he came out of the meeting-room at Limuru where the vote was taken, he said to the Roman Catholic observer William Purdy, 'I think your Church may well be doing it twenty years from now.'

At home again from Limuru, Ramsey was asked why he was against women priests. He said that he was not against women priests. He was against our Church doing something so unusual without reference to other Churches. He said that he could picture a woman Archbishop of Canterbury. 'It might be a bit of time ahead.'

Meanwhile the pressure for women priests mounted. In the spring of 1971, soon after Limuru, Bishop Baker of Hong Kong made it clear to Ramsey that he wanted to ordain women as well as men. Ramsey wrote (10 June 1971) that he ought to be very hesitant, for the Lambeth Conference wanted all provinces to report before any decision was taken, and the resolution at Limuru, being carried by so small a majority, where a change of one vote would have changed the result, could not be regarded as committing the whole Communion.

During the summer Bishop Baker came to see Ramsey, who reiterated his scruples. But during the following months, Baker thought a lot about it and eventually decided to go it alone and not to wait for more consensus. On 9 November 1971 he told Ramsey that he would ordain two women as priests. Ramsey reiterated his warning (Ramsey to Baker 12 November 1971)—the South East Asia Council advised against it; we need the views of all provinces; Bishop Baker is wrong in claiming that Limuru spoke for all the Anglican Communion; and he, Ramsey, was concerned about the consequences in the ecumenical movement. He asked that if Bishop Baker went ahead he should not say that the Archbishop of Canterbury approved.

Bishop Baker went ahead. He said that for centuries the clergy were a club for men and so lost something of their representative character. He spoke of Christ raising the status of women, not least in China. He did not expect that what would be suitable for Hong Kong would be suitable for everywhere; but someone has to start. This was no deviation in Christian moral standards, no change in the creed, no radical break with liturgical order; they were loyal to the holy Catholic Church; and their people had a great pastoral need, in which half of the industrial workers were women. 'I believe we are impelled by the Holy Spirit to make better provision for the needs of men and women alike through a ministry more representative of humanity as a whole'; after which words he ordained to the priesthood Jane Hwang, a Cantonese who had an MA at Columbia University in New York, and Joyce Bennett, who had a BA in history from the university of London and was head of a Hong Kong school and a deaconess.

Naturally this gave some comic headlines to the English press —priests-in-skirts, and whether mitres would sit comfortably on feminine hair-dos.

Then in 1972 a surprising new pressure came in England. Parliament debated a bill against discrimination against women, especially in their applications for jobs. Powerful peeresses, who had no or little religion but concern about women's rights, like Baroness Summerskill and Baroness Gaitskell, did not see why the Churches should be exempt from the bill. Lady Summerskill was tremendous—use women by all means, exploit their services, far from giving them equal pay give them nothing—that is the norm in the Church—the churches are empty, decrepit, crumbling, waiting to be demolished—she would not urge intelligent women to give the kiss of life to the unintelligent organized Church as it is today—men have destroyed it, let men reconstruct it—the established Church has made a life study of keeping women in their rightful place according to its own lights (Hansard, 14 May 1973). The peers were as nervous of forcing the Pope to ordain women as priests as they were of forcing the Archbishop of Canterbury. Ramsey did not even like to speak in the Lords because he thought his presence would be a red rag to provoke Lady Summerskill. He received a lot of letters abusing him for saying things which he had not said. The act when it passed exempted the Churches.

In America the results achieved for civil rights by the campaign of civil disobedience affected also the Church. In 1972 the American bishops (74 to 61) agreed to ordain women to the priesthood but also agreed not to act independently. It was therefore still illegal to ordain women to the priesthood in the Church of the United States. Nevertheless, on 29 July 1974, in defiance of church law, eleven women were ordained to the priesthood in Philadelphia. They had no regular bishop to ordain, so they were ordained by three retired bishops and a bishop from Costa Rica; one of the ordinands was the daughter of one of the retired bishops. The rector of the church was black, the preacher was black, and the mood of the congregation of 2,000 smelt of the atmosphere of the civil rights campaign. The crucifer was Barbara Harris, who fourteen years later would be elected the first woman bishop in the Episcopal Church. A public protest was called in the church at the moment for lodging objections. This caused deeper turmoil in the American Church into which Ramsey was drawn. He thought there was no excuse for such indiscipline and was glad that the American bishops felt the same.

In face of such an event the problem would not disappear. Ramsey went to Nottingham and was asked about it and said, 'I rather wish the theological arguments against it were stronger'. When he passed through Hong Kong next year he was photographed by the press smiling at Joyce Bennett, one of the first two whom Bishop Baker of Hong Kong ordained.

He was content to be retired as it developed into a problem for the Church of England. His attitude in retirement may be summarized thus: there is no evidence in the New Testament against women as priests. I rather wish there was. There is nothing to stop the Church ordaining women as priests now—except the feeling that it ought to be an act of the whole Church. There is nothing in women which makes them incapable of becoming priests. I expect it will happen sometime. If it happens we should all accept it because we should accept what the Church decides. But I hope it will not happen quite yet because I much value the Catholic inheritance and the links with Catholic Christendom East and West. I expect that the Roman Catholic Church will do it sometime, perhaps before long.

At that date this last expectation was not naïve. The Pope's pastoral constitution of 1965 rejected all discrimination against women on the ground of their sex. While Ramsey was archbishop the Roman Catholic Church began to use women as pastors of parishes in areas where there was no priest—which the Anglicans did not; and they began to use women, chiefly nuns, as the ministers of the sacrament, though from the reserved sacrament. In 1970 Pope Paul VI made St Teresa of Avila of the sixteenth century and St Catherine of Siena of the fourteenth century into Doctors of the Church. This rank in the calendar of saints was hitherto reserved for men. Women were not excluded from the teaching office of the Church. The Pope said that this did not mean that women could have a magisterium in the Church, but the distinction was subtle because he went on to say that some women's words and writings had become a light to guide their brothers. And the practice of the Church began to conform in a way which its theory was slow to follow. In parishes in Salvador for example, where a woman was the parish pastor and could administer the sacrament and marry the people and baptize and bury, to perceive the difference between a priest and a woman doing the work of a priest required a microscope. In the same year the Dutch Roman Catholic bishops were given a resolution that their Church should consider whether women could become ordained. The resulting quarrel was discouraging. Yet three years later one of the two or three most respected theologians in all the Church, Karl Rahner, said that the practice of the Church in not ordaining women had no decisive theological reasons. He did not expect any quick change in the practice of the Church, but the practice was not a dogma and was based simply on a social structure which used to exist and was changing fast. If the next decades made Ramsey look naïve in expecting that the Pope would soon change, he then had reason for his expectation.

He long valued an American priest whom he first met as a seminarian at Nashotah House. In 1977 this priest joined the dissident movement in the United States because he believed that the American Anglicans corrupted their Catholicity by allowing women to be priests. Ramsey thought him wrong to go into schism and made his opinion plain. Later the priest saw that for him this was no way forward and was received into the Orthodox Church. That touched something in Ramsey's soul. He sent a happy message.

When the American Church decided to go ahead and ordain women as priests he was confronted with a new question. On his last visit to America in his retirement he stayed in New York with his friend, the Presiding Bishop John M. Allin. He went to the sacrament in the chapel of the Church Center building and there found to his surprise that the celebrant of the sacrament was a woman. He asked himself what to do. To withdraw from the service or to appear to slight the woman celebrant was a likely cause for confusion, distress, and pain to the small congregation. He needed therefore, whatever his private uncertainty, to do an act of charity and he received the sacrament. Allin asked him about it afterwards. He said, 'I decided I must receive. Had I still been the Archbishop of Canterbury I don't believe I would have received. But somehow I felt I should today amid these present circumstances.'[3]

[3] Allin's evidence, 21 Nov. 1988.

PART 4

CHRISTENDOM

12

Eastern Christendom

I. THE AFFECTION FOR THE EASTERN WAY

Michael Ramsey's love of the Christian East started while he was a student at Cuddesdon. To the college came another student, Derwas Chitty, who had just spent a year in Jerusalem and was full of its religion. Chitty had a high-pitched voice, rapid limbs which contorted themselves in the effort to say something that was too mystical for words, an infectious enthusiasm, and a religious love of everything eastern, from icons and tall black hats to the beards of the clergy. He was also a natural scholar who later turned himself into an expert on the earliest of the Christian monks. His enthusiasm infected the young Michael Ramsey, who had never been to the lands of the Eastern Church and had no experience. Chitty talked about *glory* as the leading idea of Eastern religion; and this fitted a perception which was already strong in Ramsey's soul.

Ramsey was not drawn further until he became a teacher at Lincoln. To that college came exiled Russians as visitors and lecturers. It was these Russians who drew Ramsey further into his affection of the heart for the religion of the East.

The Russian revolution of 1917 set up a curtain between religion in Russia and the rest of the world. The English hardly knew what was going on in the Russian Church, except that they knew it had a bad time and that many priests were murdered. Many Russian churchmen fled. They turned up in Paris, or London, or New York. The emigration produced Russian congregations in the western countries. They wanted to explain themselves to the West, and the British had a chance as never before to understand what Eastern religion was about. The Easterners succeeded in communicating, especially to the disciples of the Oxford Movement, the beauty within their heritage; the sense of a living way of worship; the affection for the quiet meditative prayer of the heart; the sense of mystery in the universe and of God as too high for human definition; and the powerful sense of the communion of the saints, fostered by the icons and by a stylized tradition of art and ornament.

To Lincoln, while Ramsey was sub-warden, came two very different expounders of that faith. Nicholas Zernov was an open and charming layman who was persuasive in his speech in interpreting the Eastern tradition so that the West could see its strengths. People found Zernov's person so attractive that they thought they ought to like his religion. After him came Georges Florovsky, a priest and a theologian and a man who used much longer words than Zernov, and the ordinands could not understand what he said; but he was formidable, well capable of holding his own against western critics of his faith. At Lincoln Florovsky and the young Ramsey struck up that alliance which, as we saw, produced international consequence at the World Council meeting in Amsterdam. Ramsey joined the society which arose out of this movement, the Fellowship of St Alban and St Sergius. He spoke at its meetings and wrote articles for its journal (the first as early as 1935).

Ramsey passed into what he later described as a honeymoon with Orthodoxy, an excited honeymoon, with new insights into the nature of worship and the nature of religious thinking.

Then he gained in knowledge until he was a professor. He felt all the time that the centre of his thinking was the New Testament as understood by the early Greek Fathers; together with such Anglican divines as were themselves influenced by the Greek Fathers. He found modern Greek and Russian religion to be in direct continuity with much of this old Greek thought. More than once, later, Ramsey said that while he was a professor he was more an eastern Christian thinker than a western; or once, that he was more an Orthodox thinker than an Anglican.

This second phase of his affair of the heart with the East ended when he became a bishop and carried the responsibility for a Church in good part Protestant. Then he realized fully that he was part of the western tradition and could never be otherwise. But he continued to think that his Church ought to share that experience of his own which he went through with the help of Derwas Chitty—that is, whenever the western Church was in trouble, it could help itself by turning to the riches of faith and worship and thinking in the Churches of the European East.

His experience, even after he became a bishop, was nil; except that it was much to have worked with Zernov and Florovsky in English groups at home and at World Council assemblies abroad. In 1956, just as he became Archbishop of York, he went for the first time to an Orthodox country, Russia. Among the Russian congregations and services his heart found itself at home. He admired them the more because they practised their faith under a Marxist government which publicly regarded all religion, and especially their religion, as ridiculous.

2. CONSTANTINOPLE AND ATHENS

The head of the Orthodox Churches by a primacy of honour was the Patriarch of Constantinople, called the Ecumenical Patriarch. He was Athenagoras, and well-known in the west, and very sympathetic to western Christianity and to Anglicanism in particular.

Athenagoras was born under the Ottoman Empire but got himself a good education at school and the college at Halki in the sea of Marmara and learnt to love the novels of Dostoyevsky, who became important to him. His early career was troubled by the frequent changes in frontier through wars, and he did a short spell as a monk on Mount Athos. Even in old age he said, 'I feel myself to be a little a monk of Mount Athos.' Through the YMCA he learnt English and made his earliest visit to the west. In 1922 after thirteen years as a deacon and only a few days as a priest, he was made the metropolitan of Corfu; and instantly was a hero in all Greece because of what he did when an Italian admiral criminally shelled the fort at Corfu which was packed with 7,000 Greeks and 350 sick Armenian children, all refugees from Asia Minor. He sailed out to the Italian flagship to protest and ended up with some compensation to the refugees. His popularity grew because of what he did for the refugees, as later for Greek refugees from Albania.

In 1930 he was sent off to the Lambeth Conference to represent the Greek Church and then to be Archbishop of North and South America, a large enough diocese; and in the United States, where most of the Greek Orthodox were. It was the hottest seat in his Church outside Istanbul, for they were split several ways. He had charm and magnetism and tact, and he kept the monastic rule in his private life. He had good relations with Presidents Roosevelt and Truman; and it is possible that this last friendship helped him to be elected Ecumenical Patriarch at Constantinople at the time of the Cold War when Turkey badly needed American help. He flew to Istanbul in Truman's private plane. The Americans had the idea, in their plans for the Cold War, that harmony between Greece and Turkey must be got for political reasons against Russia and that this ex-Turkish citizen in the supreme post of the Greek Church could do a lot to achieve it. They also had the idea that a personage of such a stature could counter the growing influence of the Patriarch Alexei of Moscow, and therefore of the Russians, in the Balkans and the eastern Mediterranean. Alexei had a persecuted

Church but even in persecution he probably had 50 million Orthodox and was rich. The Patriarch of Constantinople had a persecuted Church but a few tens of thousands of Orthodox and was poor. All he had was the historic prestige of his see, much declined in the modern world, and his personality.

Athenagoras was exceptional. His knowledge of French and English, his acquaintance with the western world, his openness to international ideas, his range of friendships in the world-wide Church, his earlier experience with the seamier intrigues of Balkan politics, his deep learning in the Greek Fathers and some modern writers—it is safe to say that Constantinople had never seen an archbishop like him in the long line of ecumenical patriarchs.

In Istanbul he did not have an easy time, though it was easier than in the time of his successor. Turkish pressure on the Greek minority in Istanbul was steady and the numbers of Greeks fell rapidly. He lived in seedy but historic buildings in the Phanar which were partly burnt in a fire of 1941 and no adequate restoration was yet allowed. He had to become a Turkish citizen before his enthronement, and as he was born in the Ottoman Empire this was easy for him. He tried to have easy relations with Turkey. 'I am a Turk', he would say, in refusing to have anything to do with Greek nationalism. A large picture of Ataturk, the founder of modern Turkey, hung above his chair where he received visitors.

But the quest for harmony was hopeless. In September 1955 the row between Greece and Turkey over Cyprus caused a disgraceful renewal of the old anti-Greek rioting. Mobs in Istanbul and Smyrna destroyed 78 churches and looted thousands of Greek shops, and many Greek shopkeepers or residents were forced to hoist Turkish flags, and the police stood and watched, except that the patriarchate was saved by a police guard. Athenagoras got the churches rebuilt and a small amount of compensation for the shopkeepers. But the emigration began again, and by the time he died he had lost nearly 60,000 of his people. In 1966 prayers were being said among the Orthodox Churches that he might not be expelled from his see and that his people might not be uprooted. The Turkish President made a speech accusing the Patriarch of political activity which was banned to him under the conditions of his residence in Istanbul. Parcels of books sent to him as gifts from the West never reached their destination.

Turkish crowds clamoured for his expulsion from Turkey. A Turkish deputy in Parliament produced a bill to eject him from Turkey and to close his college at Halki. It was one of the tragedies of the modern world, and was helped to be a bit less tragic by the stature of the best of all the ecumenical patriarchs. It was the biggest protection for the ecumenical see, that its occupant, with a now tiny flock and under constant threats, had a world stature. He needed the West to help save himself and his Church. He was the only person capable of being accepted as talking on equal terms to a Pope.

Archbishop Ramsey visited him in 1962 and they became close friends, especially on a day out together to the island of Halki in the sea of Marmara where in those days, before Turkish pressure closed it, was the Greek seminary, and where after this visit they liked to help train some Anglican students. Athenagoras was a giant of 6 feet 4 inches in height, with a face and a voice and a beard which were authoritative, and with the warmest of hearts. The patriarch fed the birds from a window with his own hand, and a mouse in his bedroom, and when he walked in the garden he took care not to tread on the insects.[1]

On the way home Ramsey called upon the Metropolitan of Athens, Chrysostom. Indeed, though it could not be said publicly, the real purpose of his journey was to help the Church of Greece in grave trouble and the first reason to call on the Ecumenical Patriarch at Istanbul was to make himself more influential among the Greeks. The situation in Greece was not comfortable. The previous Metropolitan of Athens, Iakovos, was unacceptable to the government and was accused by the press of unmentionable crimes, and resigned after only twelve days in office so that the case could be tried. He was acquitted of all the charges but did not get back the see which by then his rival from the last election, Chrysostom, occupied.

Into this situation Ramsey arrived out of Istanbul. He pretended to know nothing about it. He took it for granted that all was well. He visited a Greek monastery, and gave a lecture at the university about Anglican affection for the Orthodox tradition; because, he said, it represented Greek thought which helped Anglicans to understand themselves, and because they had found Orthodoxy not just in books but as a living tradition and a living way of worship in its liturgy.

The Patriarch Athenagoras came to visit Ramsey at Lambeth in 1967 and some observers thought this the most moving of all the visits of Orthodox heads of Churches to Ramsey. Indeed it was the first time that an Ecumenical Patriarch came to London. Never since Theodore of Tarsus in the seventh century was there an Archbishop of Canterbury so capable of penetrating and valuing what the Ecumenical Patriarch

---

[1] On this visit Ramsey also met the head of the Armenian Church, and greeted the people in the Armenian Cathedral. In July 1962 he preached at the Armenian church in London. Later there was a plan that he should visit Soviet Armenia but it came to nothing.

stood for, and never before was there an Ecumenical Patriarch so capable of penetrating and valuing what the Archbishop of Canterbury stood for. Ever since Ramsey went to Istanbul in 1962 the Ecumenical Patriarch read the London *Times* every day and specially looked for news of what the Archbishop of Canterbury did or said.

But underneath the visit was less comfortable than it looked. Outwardly this was a visit of two non-political leaders of the Christian Church. Underneath there were politicians who minded.

The Archbishop met him at Heathrow, with a lot of very enthusiastic Greeks. In the car on the way to Lambeth he told Ramsey that henceforth he proposed to call him Beatitude (which is the title of the Patriarch) because that expressed the place of the see of Canterbury in the Church. When Athenagoras arrived at Lambeth (9 November) he went straight to the chapel and said that he felt at home; partly because Lambeth was bound up with the history of the Anglican Church, and partly because it was linked with the history and progress of relations between the Orthodox and the Anglicans. Privately he talked to Ramsey of the joy of his own meetings with Pope Paul VI, and of his admiration for the Patriarch Alexei of Moscow. All his private references to Turkey and its President were full of charity. He made no criticism of the Turkish government. The only doubt he half-expressed was when Ramsey said that he had heard from the President of Turkey that the college of Halki would be able to continue. Athenagoras talked of his love of the English liturgy, what a great liturgy it was, so beautiful, he said, and so relevant, 'it is in spirit the same as ours'.

He was taken to see the Queen, and interested her by his love of England and his belief that Britain could do much for keeping the peace in the Mediterranean and the world. He did not seem to be conscious that Britain then had its own political difficulties and frustrations. Nor did he seem to think theology important. Ramsey thought him rather naïve about theology—his attitude was, you theologians can settle the difficulties over reunion, the real difficulties are not in theology. He said, 'We are already united. It is only the theological questions that need solving.'

In Westminster abbey and Canterbury cathedral he spoke of his love of the Anglican Communion and of Archbishop Ramsey and of his high hopes for the future. In Westminster abbey each presented the other with a chalice as a prophecy, as Ramsey described it, 'of the time when we shall drink of one cup'; the English gift was an inscribed chalice of the seventeenth century, the Orthodox gift was a Byzantine chalice. Athenagoras spoke English, or a sort of English; talking for example of Ramsey's visit to Halki as 'a forerunner of the good spiritual summer, rich in euphoria and plenitude of spiritual fruits'. Despite this high language, no one who listened could doubt that he meant every word of his praise and gratitude to the British and to the Anglicans. At Canterbury the archbishop led the patriarch to sit in the chair of St Augustine during the singing of the Te Deum.

This visit was the most fertile in its results of all the Orthodox visits to Lambeth because the two of them signed the communiqué which recommended the setting up of an Anglican–Orthodox dialogue.

But meanwhile the politics meant that Lambeth had to tiptoe a delicate line. The Turks resented that Athenagoras should be taken to see the Queen. They resented it that the Greeks should be such enthusiasts at London airport and at the Greek cathedral, where the liturgy lasted two and a half hours and the patriarch then spent two hours more in the cathedral receiving the queue of those who wished to kiss his hand. John Satterthwaite at Lambeth Foreign Relations persuaded the Greek metropolitan in London not to hang Greek flags all about his cathedral when the patriarch came to the liturgy. But still the Turks disliked what happened.

The Turkish president happened to be on a State visit to London only a fortnight before. Ramsey had the chance to talk with him at Buckingham Palace (1 November), and was conscious that the Turk was embarrassed whenever the patriarch or his Church were mentioned. He said to Ramsey what he must have known not to be true though it was supposed to be true. He said, 'Turkey is a secular State in which Christians have the same rights as anyone else. Unfortunately difficulty is made by propagandists outside Turkey and misleading statements are sometimes made. This does not help matters.' Ramsey was not as fierce as he was when he met Russian liars. He said, 'I entirely understand but friendly relations between the Patriarch and Turkey matter much to us.'

The Turks disliked it that the visit of Athenagoras should happen at all, but if it was going to happen he should not follow so closely on the heels of their president. They demanded beforehand that the visit of Athenagoras be postponed. The Foreign Office tried to 'smooth the feathers' of the Turkish ambassador. But he refused an invitation to the Lambeth banquet which Ramsey gave for Athenagoras. The Greek ambassador accepted.

To the Turks this was not a non-political mission. To them it was Greek propaganda in London at a time when Greece and Turkey were in dispute over Cyprus and the British government was necessary in deciding what was to happen to Cyprus.

In London were three members of the Greek royal family, of whom the most important for the patriarch was the widow of the Duke of Kent, Princess Marina, whom Michael Ramsey knew well and admired. She asked privately if she could see the Ecumenical Patriarch alone. That could not be done publicly. It was arranged that she should call privately at Lambeth Palace after tea on the Sunday of the Patriarch's visit.

While the patriarch was in London messages arrived that if he postponed his return to Istanbul there was danger that he would not be allowed to re-enter Turkey. The Cypriot government arrested the Turkish leader Denktash. In retaliation the Turkish government sent a secret message to London that they would not readmit the patriarch to Turkey. This caused a flurry of diplomatic argument in London, for the patriarch was due to be the guest of the Austrian government in Vienna on his way home and there to receive an honorary degree. Athenagoras went straight from St Paul's cathedral to the Turkish embassy where he was ordered to cancel the journey to Vienna and was told that he should give the excuse of illness. The Greek metropolitan who escorted the patriarch said that they were not going to tell diplomatic lies. But the patriarch could do no other, under this bullying, but 'postpone' his visit to Vienna. On the day before he was to leave Lambeth, the visit to Vienna was cancelled so that he should not imperil his chance of being allowed to re-enter Turkey. Lambeth advised him to leave Heathrow quietly without a large delegation to see him off.

Two days after he flew back to Istanbul (Ramsey was relieved that he was let in) the British consul-general called on him at the Phanar. The atmosphere was tense, and the police were more protective even than usual, and the patriarch appeared to be worried, but cheered up when he described the warmth of his reception by the Queen and by the archbishop. He said that Britain had a great role to play in the world and he hoped that the British fleet would soon be back in the Mediterranean. He did not mention Cyprus. The consul-general did not encourage these ideas.

After Athenagoras left London the Turkish ambassador complained to Lambeth that the archbishop and others called him the Patriarch of Constantinople. He received a sharp reply. He was told that whenever the city was mentioned the archbishop and his staff were strictly correct and called it Istanbul. But since for fifteen centuries the patriarch had been called the Patriarch of Constantinople, they would continue to call him that in prayers and addresses because they could not undo history.

The Greek colonels made a coup in 1967 and overthrew the parliamentary government in Greece and deposed their Metropolitan of Athens, Chrysostom, the former host of Archbishop Ramsey, and invented some new Church laws to get into bishoprics the people whom they wanted. They suspected Athenagoras of being pro-Turkish and tried (vainly) to abolish his jurisdiction over the northern Greek sees. They started to treat dissentients in the Greek Church badly.

Ramsey could not protest against the removal of Chrysostom, because Chrysostom, who was already 87 years old, blessed the colonels' choice of his successor Hieronymus Kotsonis, from his hospital bed. He could not protest because he and his advisers knew that Chrysostom had lost all control of the situation and that Kotsonis, who had studied at Mirfield and Lincoln and served on the central committee of the World Council, was a man to be wished for. But Ramsey could and did protest when the colonels forced an ecclesiastical tribunal, in a trial behind closed doors, to depose the Metropolitan of Salonica, Panteleimon, whom Ramsey respected.

What with these political afflictions of the Orthodox Church, Ramsey was disappointed how long it took to set up the conversations between the Anglicans and the Orthodox. The first meeting was at Oxford in 1970 and the second not till 1972. The full Joint Commission, representing all the Orthodox Churches and all the provinces of the Anglican Communion, did not meet until July 1973. By then it was hampered by the question of women's ordination. But he was grateful that before he retired he saw a start to what he had worked for.

At Christmas 1970 a bottle of brandy suddenly appeared at Lambeth as a present from the Patriarch of Constantinople. Brandy was not Michael Ramsey's drink. In the February after that some presents arrived from Istanbul for Joan. In Greek Athenagoras spelt her name RAMSEU, and called her the Most Generous First Lady of Canterbury.

In 1972 the Athens Academy elected Ramsey as a foreign member.

In the same year the Patriarch Athenagoras fell in his house on the island of Halki and fractured his thigh and died in hospital. His last message to Ramsey told him how he always had before him the chalice which Ramsey gave him. During his last years he felt himself watched by the Turkish government. In 1964 they banned all his publications, in 1971 they finally shut the college at Halki. As the quarrel over Cyprus moved towards the threat of war between Greece and Turkey, the pressure on Greeks in Turkey grew. The government demanded that he excommunicate Archbishop Makarios, the Greek leader in Cyprus. He refused steadily. He said that he could not mix religion with politics. Meanwhile he met suspicion from Greek conservatives for his friendliness to the Pope and the Anglicans and the Lutherans, and some of them were shocked at his desire to persuade Orthodox churches to have organs. A number of the monasteries on Mount Athos declared that by his ecumenical acts he had made himself a heretic. He shocked some Orthodox late in his life by saying that the doctrine of papal infallibility was a private religious opinion and we could agree to differ. By the day of his death more than half the monasteries on Mount Athos did not pray for him in the liturgy, and various monks left Mount Athos because they refused to treat their patriarch as a heretic.

He saw friends and supporters emigrating because they no longer felt secure in Istanbul. His English friends thought that he had lost some of his sparkle. At his death there were only 20,000 Greeks in Istanbul and a few thousand elsewhere in Turkey. The condition of the patriarchate reached its lowest point since the Turks conquered Constantinople in the fifteenth century. And outside Turkey, outside Mount Athos, outside Athens, the reputation of the patriarchate through the world had never been higher.

Ramsey insisted on travelling out for the funeral, which was held at 100 degrees with some of the congregation fainting, and without the presence of the Greek metropolitan whom the Turks would not allow to come. The Archbishop of Canterbury stood next to Cardinal Willebrands, who represented the Pope. Ramsey was asked by the BBC to speak an obituary for Athenagoras. He talked about the warmth of his personality and his courageous attitude to life and said, 'Of all the men I have known, the term ecumenical applied to him above all others.'

The Turks refused to give up their veto on the election of a Christian patriarch and gave the Church only 72 hours in which it must submit three names from which to choose. This was tough. They were still tougher. They struck off, one by one, each of the three names whom the synod proposed. The synod was reduced to no list; and then to a younger candidate so unknown that the government could not object.

Demetrios I was elected, a shy and retiring man with nothing like the range of experience of Athenagoras. During his service of election he told the deputy governor of Istanbul that he would always put himself at the disposal of his government. Later at a press conference he spoke in Turkish and refused to speak Greek, which was his native language. But he also said at his enthronement that he intended to pursue the line towards Christian unity of his 'great predecessor Athenagoras'. The hand of the State lay heavily upon the little Church—still the head of all the Orthodox world. The Patriarch Demetrios survived well, and did well, and grew in stature, and won the respect of the Orthodox world and of Ramsey's successors. But his local flock continued to disappear so that by the end of the 1980s there were only 2,000–4,000 Greeks in his city and people asked, as they had asked before, how the Ecumenical

Patriarchate could survive in Istanbul for more than another ten years.

The hand of the State also lay heavy upon the Greek Church. The year after the death of Athenagoras the colonels forced Archbishop Kotsonis of Athens to resign because he criticized their regime and so justified Ramsey's opinion that this was a good man. Naturally the year after that, when the Turks invaded Cyprus and the colonels fell from power, 51 Greek prelates met in a conference to discuss the separation of Church and State. The new Archbishop of Athens was Serafim, who was elected after the colonels disqualified more than half the electors from voting, but despite this uncomfortable start was recognized by the Churches and held an extraordinary session of the Greek hierarchy to fill twelve of the fourteen sees which the Greek government had kept vacant. He survived into the late 1980s.

3. RUSSIA

If the most influential person in the Eastern Orthodox Church was the Patriarch of Constantinople, the most powerful person was Alexei, the Patriarch of Moscow. He was allowed by Stalin to reconstruct the Church after the terrible pre-war persecution. His Church was much the largest in numbers in the Orthodox Church. And if his government liked to use him in power politics, it was one of the two most powerful governments in the world.

Archbishop Fisher was determined to reduce Russian ignorance of the Anglicans. Almost every year after the war he suggested to Patriarch Alexei that there should be a meeting. In 1955 he achieved a meeting at Lambeth with visiting Russians, Bishop Michael Ramsey of Durham in the chair; and from this the invitation came at last to Fisher, to come himself or to send a mission to Moscow.

The Russians were confused by the Dean of Canterbury, who was not only a Communist but a Stalinist, and the holder of the Stalin peace prize. They recognized that in the dean's person the Church of England had at least one deep-thinking theologian and therefore should be encouraged. They imagined that the freedom of the dean to talk so enthusiastically of Marxism must mean that his archbishop was a fellow-traveller. Lambeth was very surprised when the invitation arrived.

Ramsey, just newly of York, was the obvious person to send. No English bishop knew more about the Russian faith, none had more affection for it. He took with him two bishops and five priests and went to Moscow on 13 July 1956. At each stop someone told him to turn back. At Copenhagen the dean urged him not to go while the Russians behaved so atrociously in the Cold War. At Helsinki a Finn stuck a finger into the stomach of the Bishop of Derby with the cry, 'You are a Communist!' (This was far from the truth.) On the aircraft before Moscow Ramsey had to promise the Russians that he was not gun-running, nor smuggling drugs, nor importing into Russia the horns of steppe-antelopes.

The hosts thought that their guests should see the splendours of Moscow. The morning of 14 July was devoted to the underground system. Ramsey wore a purple cassock and made his party wear cassocks and this caused a sensation among travellers on the Tube. One woman thought that Ramsey was the Pope. One man looked at them with hatred. But the crowd were fascinated and some were reverent. He inspected nearly every station of the clean system.

The big moments were church services. Not many churches were open so the churches were crowded. He set up a numinous feeling of common faith. As he spoke to the people, they could feel his under-standing of their prayers and his affection for them. They listened intently. At times a frisson, almost a shudder, rippled through the church; at times clapping, instantly shushed. 'We are looking for peace together in Christ . . . we pray with you for Russia—that she may become a Christian country'—wave of excitement—'and we ask you to pray with us for England, that she may become a Christian country' —another ripple of excited movement. He would tell that though the English have many customs different from theirs, we worshipped the same Blessed and All-Glorious Trinity, and were baptized, and fed with the body and blood, and honoured the saints, and sang the song of Mary every day at the evening service. At the end there were cries of Thank you, and God bless you, and bouquets of tired gladioli. It sounds little enough in description. But in the rapt atmosphere could be felt a communication of the heart between the Russian and British peoples.

The theologians had to meet. They did not get on at all. In a conference room of a hotel, it was a dogfight where stately dogs stalked round one another and occasionally snapped. Since the beginning of the century when this converse was last possible, the Russians grew more conservative because of the persecution and the British grew more liberal. Some of the Russians were shocked at English heresy, some of the English were shocked at Russian obscurantism. 'Why', asked Professor Osipov ferociously, 'have you not got the *Epistle of Jeremy* in your Bibles?' Ramsey struggled to remember what the *Epistle of Jeremy* is and began to shake with silent laughter. Asked afterwards why he laughed, he said, 'I am laughing because the peace of Christendom hangs upon the existence of a small book about which the Anglicans are hazy.'[2]

And yet, amid these snaps, the meeting was real; because it was not diplomatic they talked about true problems, not without surprise that they could do so. Despite their suspicion that Ramsey was a heretic, they awarded him the degree of doctor of theology, otherwise held only by the Patriarch Alexei, his second in command Nikolai, and the patriarchs of Antioch and Bulgaria.

The third important thing that happened was a friendship with Patriarch Alexei, as important as the friendship with Athenagoras of Constantinople. When Alexei spoke and moved, it conjured up a vision of another world, when tsarist princes and King Edward VII met at Marienbad. It was an old-fashioned aristocratic courtesy: the tsarist bishop from before the first World War, unpretentious, humorous, and considerate, everything about him in exquisite taste. He had seen terrible things; what humiliations and compromises he survived to be where he was, Ramsey did not presume to ask. The English longed for him to write his autobiography and knew that he never could. Here was a sweet-natured old man, with too much experience of the villainy and the courage of humanity and now serene, prayerful, reflective, and warm. Ramsey came away from Russia thinking Alexei's right hand Nikolai to be a good man trying to do his best but too political to be trustworthy. He came away with affection for Alexei.

Ramsey was fitted to make the best impression on the Russians. His religion was otherworldly as was theirs. He understood the life of the monks, which they cared about; he shared their way of worship; and he was a big personality.

On 18 July 1956 he attended the feast of St Sergius at the monastery of Zagorsk. He walked to the cathedral in procession, beneath the white walls and the golden domes, amid a milling crowd of 20,000, wearing cope and mitre, immense and statuesque, and walking with a holy dignity as the people bowed to his right and left. Alexei, looking frail and with a beautiful head, told the people how these visitors came from a far country out of good will to the Russian Church and Russian people and for the honour of St Sergius whose body lies there in a shrine of the side aisle.

The Russians have the custom of kissing the relics of St Sergius. The Church of England has not the custom of kissing the bones of saints.

---

[2] The Epistle of Jeremy is a short piece of the Old Testament Apocrypha; in English Bibles it is the last chapter of Baruch.

Ramsey saw that the people would think them irreverent if they did not. His kissing of the relics was one of the charges against him later made by Ulstermen. Ramsey said that by the tomb of St Sergius he had a sensation that he stood near the heart, not only of the Russian Church, but of the Russian people.

After the liturgy came a vodka-laced banquet where the atheist Commissar of Church affairs, Karpov, paraded his bossiness over the Church and the Archbishop of Tyre and Sidon made a sycophantic speech and Ramsey gave the patriarch two silver candlesticks. Five days later Karpov gave another, and farewell banquet to seven archbishops. The archbishop of Tyre and Sidon made a second sycophantic speech. Ramsey got up. 'I propose a toast to something greater than Russian politics, greater than the Soviet government' (electric silence in the room). 'I propose a toast to the Russian soul.' Next morning he flew back to London.

He was left with the opinion that the Muscovites had a good underground railway; that Communist art and architecture were deplorable; that the godless State had come, when the glorious cathedrals of the Kremlin stood silent as museums. What he most loved and remembered was the people, and how the old spirituality was kept alive among them. About the conference he was amused at the snail's pace at which it moved, and yet late in life he said that it was the best of all the conferences with the Easterners which he had known. *No fudge*, he said. For all the bumping and denunciation and failure to understand, the two sides knocked away at each other honestly, on real issues.

The year after he became Archbishop of Canterbury he was back in Moscow with Alexei. The Berlin Wall was built not long before and all Europe was in tension. This willingness to be friends with the Russians at such a time did not go unnoticed in Europe. The French press nicknamed him the red prelate, but partly they muddled him with his dean. The British Foreign Office advised him not to go. When he insisted on going they took private steps to ensure that his dean was not in Moscow at the same moment. He was the first Archbishop of Canterbury to visit Moscow.

On his first visit, late at night, when the official interpreters had gone, the Russians would say quietly that things were still bad; that they were so much better than they were; that this was irreversible; that they had hope for more and more liberty. On his second visit Ramsey was disappointed to find that this had not happened. Khrushchev stepped up the pressure on the Church. It was nothing like Stalin's earlier days but it could be nasty. Ramsey saw the deputy prime minister, Mikoyan, and Kuroyedov, who was Karpov's successor as Commissar for Church affairs. Their attitudes shocked him. They were bland. They denied everything. He saw that they knew they were telling him what was not true. He said to Kuroyedov, 'You're lying, man, you're lying.' He tried to persuade Mikoyan that there was no necessary antipathy between science and religion and ran into a brick wall. He got only the reply that they were materialists and had no room for religion in their philosophy.

The people he again found moving. He preached, with the aid of incompetent interpreters, to a congregation of 2,500. He was moved to see so many young faces among the crowd. But he soon found that he was less free than in 1956. He saw that the authorities wanted to avoid the popular welcomes which greeted him that year.

Moreover the Metropolitan Nikolai had fallen. The tightrope on which he walked so nimbly collapsed. Some of the Russians thought that he was murdered but no one knew. His successor was a young man, Nikodim. From the first Ramsey and Nikodim could not get on terms. He thought that Nikodim was obviously put in as an agent of the Soviet State. For the next twelve years the mistrust between Ramsey and Nikodim damaged the cause which Ramsey had at heart. With the patriarch the affection was as strong as ever.

On 4 August 1962 Ramsey arrived back at Heathrow. He was tired and met a battery of the press. He said just what he thought and it was not diplomatic. He talked of the heroism of Russian Christians in the midst of intense propaganda against God. He said that his contact with 'rank atheism' was an ordeal and he felt the strain of staying in a Communist society. Someone asked whether a Christian could be a Communist. He said 'No. Communism is definitely an atheistic way of life.'

Afterwards he worried that this speech might hurt the Russian Churches. The chaplains worried too, they thought that he grew emotional because he was tired. There is no evidence that it did harm. The British ambassador in Moscow, Sir Frank Roberts, wrote to say how much good was done by the visit. Ramsey hardly minded various British atheists who complained that he called them rank. But, with his brother Frank in his memory, he could not want them to think that he did not respect honest atheism. So he said that he saw a difference between the atheism which set a high value on conscience and accepted moral principles, and the materialist atheism derived from Karl Marx. Someone wrote to the newspaper to ask why, if a Christian could not be a Communist, the Dean of Canterbury was in office.

It made no difference to Alexei. He saw Ramsey praising the Russian Church. He agreed to come to Lambeth; the first Patriarch of Moscow ever to come to Britain. He came on 25–27 September 1964; he was 86.

He attended a service at Canterbury cathedral and was escorted up the aisle of Westminster abbey under a canopy.[3] He marvelled at the beauty of boys' voices in English choirs. He made a charming speech at dinner. He visited Rab Butler at the Foreign Office, and told him how Ramsey seemed to sing rather than talk, and surprised everyone at the end by saying, 'God bless the Queen!' He avoided the press, and turned aside every question about Russia. Joan Ramsey found him an electric wheel-chair. He hesitated for a minute; then smiled into his beard, pressed the button, and shot away down the corridor of Lambeth Palace, with skirts flowing out behind and chaplains in pursuit. He liked it so much that she got him another to take back to Moscow.

Underneath all was not so well. He brought Nikodim. To the British Nikodim was too busy, and did not want them to know that he was busy. He was under orders to stop comments in the British press on the 'persecution' of the Russian Church. He was under orders to get rid of Metropolitan Anthony Bloom, the best expounder of Russian piety in Britain and revered by many Anglicans as by Orthodox; than whom no one in Britain did more to make the British respect the Russians. But this machination of the subordinate was nothing in comparison with the delight and friendship of his patriarch.

This was the high point of harmony between Canterbury and Moscow. It was never the same again, during Ramsey's tenure of his see.

The cooling had three causes. First, two years later Ramsey visited the Pope in Rome. Many in Moscow regarded the Pope rather as Ian Paisley in Northern Ireland regarded him. Secondly, Alexei went on and on, and got older and older; and power slipped ever more into the hands of Nikodim. Thirdly, Britain and the Soviet Union drew further apart politically. That had a consequence in the Churches.

A series of incidents marked the cooling. At an interview by Canadian journalists in Fredericton (1966) they asked him about the Vietnam war. He said that America entered the war with a sincere motive of resistance to Communist aggression. But now the war achieved nothing. It was urgent to bring it to an end. He deplored American bombing of North Vietnam. He wanted the Americans to start making peace but said that the North Vietnamese must help.

Intelligent Russians might have thought this speech useful to their cause. Probably it reached Moscow in a garbled form. What mattered to them was the first statement—that the Americans were sincere to resist

---

[3] The Ecumenical Patriarch was not under a canopy when he went to the Abbey because you cannot get a canopy over a head of six feet several inches tall.

Communist aggression. Ramsey was surprised to read in the *Journal of the Moscow Patriarchate* (December 1966, p. 62) a nasty attack upon himself by an acquaintance, Archpriest Ivanov, a glum member of the Russian team of 1956. Ivanov talked of the widening gulf between the Archbishop of Canterbury and the rest of Christendom. He accused him of harshness as well as isolation. The protest which went to Moscow was milder than Ramsey felt. If a writer under the authority of Patriarch Alexei abused the head of another Church he ought to get his facts right. The Russians did not apologize.

And now a new person came to disturb the scene. Michael Bourdeaux was fascinated by the Russian Church while he was a student. He got money to study in Moscow. Ramsey recommended him to the Metropolitan Nikolai and asked that he be given access to clergy for conversation and discussion. In Moscow every obstacle was put in Bourdeaux's way, partly by the State, partly by hierarchs too prudent to be kind to a young foreigner. When he came back he made himself an expert. He appeared before the public for the first time in a book of 1965, *Opium of the People*. Alexei protested to Ramsey against its portrait of the Russian Church.

The evidence which Bourdeaux produced began to impress Ramsey. When a Church is under persecution by a State, it is necessary for its leaders to compromise with the State, for the sake of being a legal organization; for only if they are legal can they get the sacraments to the people and help the sick or the young. Then there comes a point, which varies from person to person, where the conscience is asked to compromise too far, and feels that compromise here would corrupt the personality. Ramsey understood and respected this predicament. He did not blame Alexei although he knew that he must compromise to be where he was. But in the later 1960s, with the cooling under Nikodim, and then the Russian tanks in Prague, he studied the evidence of Bourdeaux and began to think that compromise by the hierarchs went further than it should. He had not wanted to speak loudly about persecution in Russia because it would make the job of Alexei more difficult and because it might bring worse persecution on individuals. But now, for him 'the hierarchs' were not an otherworldly Alexei. They were a too worldly Nikodim. Are these Christian bishops compromising with tyranny beyond the limits of Christian compromise? He began to talk freely about persecution in Russia and to ask for prayers for the suffering people. That did not commend him to Moscow.

Nikodim kept telling Ramsey that the Church was not persecuted at all; that this was only a political campaign in the West against the Soviet State; that it was due only to ignorance, and helped to build international tension. The Soviet ambassador in London sent him a book to prove that in Russia religion is completely free.

In 1969 Michael Bourdeaux published another indictment. It was entitled *Patriarch and Prophets*. Nikodim thought this a monstrous book. This could not surprise because it contained evidence that Nikodim was not only talented but odious and unscrupulous. Nikodim said that the book insulted the Patriarch Alexei. Indeed it contained a translation of a document which pictured Alexei as a lovable man too complaisant with villainy.

Then Bourdeaux created a research institute, the Centre for the Study of Religion and Communism. He wanted Ramsey to be its president. The Lambeth advisers were strong against him accepting. Why should he alienate Moscow without necessity? Ramsey accepted to be the president. Probably he would have hesitated longer if Alexei still lived. But Alexei had died at last, aged 93, and the Russians began electing a new patriarch.

In agreeing to be president he made conditions—that the Centre should be neutral in politics and above all should not be thought a spy agency for western governments. He expressed a wish that it should not conduct a witch-hunt about persecution but should record the spiritual renewal in the Eastern Churches.

Russian State, or hierarchs, or both, could not forgive Ramsey for backing Bourdeaux. They displayed extreme coolness by failing to invite the Archbishop of Canterbury to the enthronement of the new Patriarch Pimen, who was the only candidate.

He had come to feel that what mattered were the Russian ordinary people who went to church, and their priests, some of whom he thought of as heroes. He never forgot how close he was to their hearts on his first and freest visit, and how close they were to his.

In 1973 Nikodim was kind to Ramsey's envoy Michael Moore when he went to Leningrad to mend fences and allowed him to give the archbishop's greeting to the congregation. In Moscow Moore called on the Metropolitan Juvenaly, who was the new head of foreign relations, and was jeered at by a squad of teenagers as he went in and it was impossible that the jeers should be spontaneous. Ramsey let Michael Moore do what he could to bring more confidence. But he left it to his two successors to get back a closer amity.

There was one more curious meeting. In 1978 the retired Ramsey hastened across Europe from Durham, and the not retired Nikodim hastened across Europe from Leningrad, to attend the funeral of Pope Paul VI in Rome. They found themselves next to each other in the front row. Ramsey felt a twinge of discomfort.

Nikodim had come a long way since the early years when Ramsey knew him and had his suspicions. They had managed to keep him out of the presidency of the World Council of Churches at Uppsala in 1968, but he was elected seven years later. For he threw himself into the ecumenical movement; and especially into the difficult endeavour to make the Vatican and Moscow less far apart. In Rome at the time of the funeral of the Pope, he knew that he was criticized by many in the West as a politicized clergyman and a compromiser. For in Rome, not knowing the calamity that was to happen, he made privately to a Roman Catholic friend the best or the only defence of compromise with the Russian State. He said 'Do not judge our Church. You do not know what our bishops and priests have suffered—prison, hunger, torture. When the Russian Church teaches a faith which is not that of the gospel and the early Fathers, then you will be able to condemn us.'[4]

Nikodim stayed in Italy for the election of the new Pope John Paul I. On 5 September he was received by the new Pope in his private library and offered the wishes of his patriarch for a long pontificate blessed for the good of the Church. Nikodim had time to receive the Pope's thanks and then slipped off his chair and heaved a deep sigh and died on the carpet. He was only 49 years old. Afterwards it was rumoured that he was poisoned by Russians who loathed Rome. The Vatican knew that many in the West took a low view of him. But their recent experience gave them a contrary opinion. They gave him the benefit of any doubt there might be.

4. THE BALKANS

Except for Greece, all the Balkan States were under Communist rule, were all governed by dictators or a dictatorial politburo, and were all officially against religion. In Albania, which had a large Muslim population as well as a Christian, this led to the most horrible repression of the modern epoch where priests in labour camps were shot for baptizing babies at the plea of their mothers; until Albania pretentiously declared itself the first atheist State in the world. In the other countries the Church which had the worst time was the Roman Catholic; for in the Cold War the Pope declared it impossible to be a Christian and a Communist and so made his people in the Balkans suspect of disloyalty. The Roman Catholics had a much worse time where they were few in number, as in Bulgaria and in most of Romania,

---

[4] *La Croix*, 7 Sept. 1978.

than where they were numerous, as in parts of Yugoslavia. The Protestants, Calvinist or Lutheran, were under heavy pressure or total destruction, except in Hungary where they were numerous, and in the historic German Church inside Romania, where they were much discouraged but not destroyed.

Therefore the only Church which had much chance in the Balkan States was the Orthodox Church. The Orthodox Churches had no outside authority to control them and so were not suspect for being influenced by foreigners; and in their inheritance from the old Turkish rule, they became a part of the nationality and freedom of the peoples against the Muslim Ottoman. This was truest in Romania, where the State had the most noisome of dictators outside Albania, but where nationality and religion were still inseparable in the minds of the people; and under an able Patriarch Justinian, who of necessity compromised but *perhaps* not too much, the Church flourished. In Yugoslavia, where they had in Tito the least barbarian of the Balkan dictators, the Church was associated with Serb nationality and so prospered modestly with not too much need for compromise though with inability to educate or to build churches. Bulgaria had the largest Muslim population outside Albania and for a time the State behaved with a murderous hostility to some of the Christian leaders. But in 1967 an exceptional patriarch, Kiril, achieved a settlement with the State which suddenly was conscious of the utility of the Church as the preserver of national monuments and a lure for tourists. In all the States the pressure continued: against young men going into the priesthood or into a monastery; against the building of new churches or even the repair of old churches if they were not old enough to be historic.

In these tough but not intolerable circumstances, the Church leaders were helped by visits from eminent visitors abroad. If they could persuade the Patriarch Alexei to come from Moscow, for example, that strengthened them in the eyes of their government because outside Yugoslavia the Russians were almost as influential in their State as their own politburo. And if they could persuade the Archbishop of Canterbury to come, and could get permission for him to come, that also helped them in the eyes of their government—for it proved that they were of international interest and concern. And all the Communist States wanted to encourage Peace. They had nightmares about the Americans and their allies in the West as nuclear warmongers. Even a materialist government was willing to put up with an eminent western Church leader who was an advocate of peace and who was not a Roman Catholic. If they knew that Ramsey also said, like the Pope, that a Christian could not be a Communist, it did not matter to them, for they had no Anglicans among their people. The fear that he would encourage disloyalty to the State did not arise, at least not sharply.

Ramsey saw a duty to visit them if he were allowed to do so; and to bring their patriarchs out to Lambeth if they could get leave to come. His first motive was that which took him first to Russia: he could help to draw these fellow-Christians, shut behind their Iron Curtain, out of isolation. His second motive was to help them. He was one of the only people in the West who could show the Marxist governments that the Churches which they so disliked had an international importance.

He saw the need to take care that he did not himself compromise. To fraternize openly with Marxists or their yes-men who dressed up as Christian bishops—if there were such, and his informants thought that there were a few—would lead him into a situation where he would appear to bless an excess of compromise. But it was not his business to conduct an enquiry into the private opinions or action of individuals. He went to share the prayers of a Church. Once he cancelled an invitation when on the point of going. The Patriarch Kiril invited him to Bulgaria in 1968. In that year Russian tanks of the Warsaw Pact overthrew the Czech Spring in Prague and the Bulgarians were members of the Warsaw Pact. Ramsey, who never forgave the Russians for what they then did to the Czechs, cancelled his visit to Bulgaria. He would not be seen even to bless part of a country which so recently shared in a crime. He went to Bulgaria four years later, under a different and weaker patriarch.

Even so, the exiles from these regimes in the West hated it that he went at all. One critic was obsessive and vocal. Pastor Wurmbrand was a Romanian Protestant and in the earlier years of the Marxist revolution Protestants were as badly treated as Roman Catholics. He experienced torture. That Orthodox hierarchs in Romania paraded about in the favour of the State, and by their complaisance gave the State strength with the people, meant to Wurmbrand that they were unchristian by their compromise. Therefore Ramsey, in accepting their hospitality and taking them at face value, shared their guilt. Wurmbrand published in London the absurdity that Ramsey went to Bucharest and attended a eucharist and had no idea that the congregation consisted of agents of the secret police and their wives. He persuaded one or two members of the Church Assembly to take the same line of protest when the Romanian Patriarch Justinian came to Lambeth. Wurmbrand was second only to Ian Paisley as a fanatic abuser of Ramsey, who took no notice.

If the public abuse by exiles was mostly confined to Wurmbrand, that did not mean that Ramsey did not need to take precautions when the patriarchs came to Lambeth. Exiled Serbs in England disliked it that the Patriarch German of Belgrade should come to Lambeth because he got on well with Marshal Tito and so was entangled with a Marxist State. They threatened demonstrations, and Ramsey took the threat seriously enough to cancel the patriarch's visit. He liked the Patriarch German very much and that very year helped to get him elected one of the presidents of the World Council of Churches; it must be said, with the aim of keeping a Russian out—they needed an Orthodox president, and were afraid that if they invited a Russian the Soviet government would try to use him in politics; and they saw that the Russians had a politicized candidate of weight, Nikodim, who was now Metropolitan of Leningrad. German came to England in 1969, and exiled Serbs threatened demonstrations, and Lambeth warned the police, and CID men attended the banquet in dinner jackets hoping to be mistaken for devout laymen.

Such precautions in England, and his uneasy consciousness while on visits in the Balkan States that hidden behind the scenes were more Roman Catholics and Protestants than dared to appear, did not damage Ramsey's pleasure and gratitude for what happened. He met atheist commissars for Church affairs; but someone who in Moscow told Kuroyedov that he was a liar and tried to convert Vice-President Mikoyan, had no hesitation in saying what he liked to little Balkan bureaucrats on plush carpets. In Belgrade he met the Vice-President Rankovic, who achieved eminence as chief of the secret police and the incongruous pair twinkled at each other as if there was never a serious dispute between Christian and Communist; and afterwards Ramsey said only, 'He said nothing of interest.' In Sofia he met the Bulgarian Minister for Church Affairs, Mihajlov, who listed the technological achievements of Bulgaria and said that the Church was a revolutionary society which threw off the Turkish yoke and claimed virtue for the Communist revolution even in the song of birds in the fields. Afterwards Ramsey said only, 'He was not so difficult as Mikoyan.' The States took him seriously. In Yugoslavia Tito lent him his private train, and he shared the headlines with Tito's visit to the Arab Republics, and was mentioned on television, which was the first time such a religious event was mentioned on television since the revolution. His cavalcade round Bulgaria was eleven cars, from sleek black limousines to dilapidated grey saloons, and other cars, even heavy lorries, were hooted and flashed off the road to let them by.

The political sensitivity of this otherworldly archbishop did not sleep. He always talked of Christian truth, whenever he talked. But he knew also that he would help them by talking of two other themes. The first was Peace; for that was one reason why the Communist regimes let him in and it was truly an interest which he shared with the Christians of their countries. At one point (1972) he had a little trouble over this. The Bulgarians drafted the text of a joint communiqué which among agreed things said two things which no one had mentioned—first that they called for a European security conference, and secondly that they backed the World Council policy against racism. Since Ramsey disagreed with the World Council grants to guerrillas, this was awkward. He said that if they put this in the communiqué they must also include a joint undertaking to work against atheism. This, as he well knew, the Bulgarian churchmen dared not do. So the proposal was dropped from the communiqué.

The second theme was Freedom. He could not imply publicly that they lived under regimes where the citizens were not free. But their freedom from the Turkish yoke was part of their sense of nationality, and sometimes the British helped them in gaining that freedom, and their Church was also an agent in the fight for their freedom. He went up the Shipka pass in Bulgaria to visit the high monument where Russians and Bulgarians fell in the fight for Bulgarian liberty and in the memorial church with golden domes they sang a kontakion for the fallen, which echoed beautifully in the crypt, and Ramsey said a prayer for the departed while the State officers looked straight ahead and pretended not to take part. On the way back to Sofia the motorcade stopped, very late, at a restaurant. The Orthodox hosts sang folk-songs, beautifully. The English could not think what folk-songs to sing in return, so Ramsey and the others sang 'Ten Green Bottles hanging on a Wall', which puzzled the Bulgarians.[5]

The British prime minister Gladstone was a hero of the Liberal politician Michael Ramsey. And Gladstone was a hero of the Bulgarians. His denunciation of Turkish massacres of Bulgarians was a key in their struggle for freedom. Therefore the Bulgarians could value this visiting Englishman as a Gladstone of the new age. He went up to the national shrine at Batak, the village which was the chief cause of Gladstone's fury. There in 1876 the Turks used fire and bees to drive the people out of the church to kill them. Ramsey saw bloodstains and again sang a kontakion for the dead and said a prayer. But it was a grim place which seemed never to have recovered. The men of the village stood looking at them sullenly. They did not want nor like visitors.

---

[5] The Bulgarians worried that an English bishop [= Robinson] said that it is all right to be an atheist, and that the Communists used this in propaganda. Next year Patriarch Maxim visited Britain.

In this way he used the connection between religion and nationality in what he said. The story which was most often told happened in Romania. The bishops gave him a banquet. Five years later they still talked of what he said. The words of the speech, as the Romanian bishops reported them, were like those of a speech which we heard before. He held a glass of wine high above his bald head, and said, 'I drink this toast, and I value this wine—not because it is Marxist wine—not because it is Communist wine—but because it is Romanian wine!' After that date any visitor from Britain who claimed association with Michael Ramsey found Romanian prelates willing to be generous in the way of hospitality.

They loved him not only because he cared about world peace, and because he was a Gladstonian, and because he was abundant, and because, as a ribald writer in the *Daily Telegraph* put it, he was a master of the holy hug. They saw that he understood the Orthodox religion. At colleges and seminaries, where they were allowed, he would lecture on the closeness between Anglicanism and Orthodoxy. In Belgrade he made a speech of which one sentence became famous. It was widely reported among them in the form, 'My exterior is Western but my heart is Orthodox.' That may have been the way the interpreter rendered it; for the most authentic version of the utterance seems to be, 'I believe that Anglicanism has an Orthodox soul.' Whatever he said or the interpreter made him say, the sentiment was received with rapturous applause. Unlike any Archbishop of Canterbury before him, he could say such a thing with a total conviction.

The great liturgies were public events. This was important, for in Yugoslavia a little and certainly in Bulgaria, though not in Romania, the Church thought it better for the most part to lie low. At the church of St Spiridon in Bucharest he talked to 2,000 people and outside was mobbed by a crowd of 3,000 which pressed on the doorhandles of his car and threw flowers and struggled to shake his hand. On Sunday morning 11 June 1972 a procession unwonted in the streets of Sofia set off from the Grand Hotel: the archbishop's chaplain in a blue cloak, bearing the crystal cross of Canterbury; the archbishop in cope and mitre, escorted by two Orthodox bishops; the local Anglican chaplain and Michael Moore, dressed in dalmatics; then two more Anglican bishops in cope and mitre. This procession astounded not only the Bulgarian people but a passing bus-load of English tourists. In the cathedral in front of the sacred doors of the screen Patriarch Maxim and the archbishop made speeches and gave presents to each other, the one an icon, the other a sanctuary lamp; and then the procession moved out, the people pressing to touch them, mothers lifting up their babies to kiss the pectoral crosses or rings, and the same in the street, to the clanging of bells. Into Michael Moore's mind came an irresistible comparison of Archbishop Ramsey to the Pied Piper.

From three countries officers of the British embassies reported to the Foreign Office. Their reports varied in description but all agreed on two things. First, that Ramsey's visits strengthened the local Churches in their difficulties with the State; and secondly, that they helped to change for the better the relations between the British and the peoples of these satellite States behind the Iron Curtain.

It was a special time in the relations between the eastern Churches and western Christianity. Not for all Ramsey's life but for all his adult life, eastern Europe was in the shadow of an atheist great power. It believed, officially, that religion is obsolete; that it promotes superstition among the old; that it hinders the education of the young and is bad for them; that materialism is the only philosophy which can help to make a better society; that religion is reactionary in its political effects. The fall of the equally anti-Christian Hitler left Russian power dominant from Estonia to Bulgaria and ensured in every country a Marxist government with the same philosophy and the same attitude towards religion. These governments did not represent the wishes of the majority of the people. Even in Albania, with a government equal in its brutality to those of Hitler or Stalin, but luckily with power over much smaller numbers, the Secretary of the Communist Party complained that despite everything they could do, people went on observing Christian feasts. Whenever the people got a chance of saying what they liked, religion did better— Hungary in 1956 until the new government was overthrown by Russian tanks, Czechoslovakia in 1968 until the new government was overthrown by Russian tanks, Hungary and Poland in the last year or two of Ramsey's time as archbishop because the worst of the Cold War was slowly passing and the governments moderated their policy a little because they preferred not to be hated by the people. The Archbishop of Canterbury was sometimes miserable about what he heard of the Churches in Eastern Europe. But it never occurred to him that the situation could last. Sooner or later justice, and the wishes of humanity, and the religious instincts of humanity, would win their rights.

But meanwhile he could help as much as anyone outside. He could in some countries do more than the Pope. This was partly because eastern hatred of the Vatican was an integral attitude of the Cold War. It was also because there were Roman Catholics open or concealed in all of the eastern States and the Pope was believed to have the power to make them disloyal; whereas Canterbury would make no one disloyal unless it was dangerous to preach that every people has the right to its freedoms.

In Istanbul the pressure of an Islamic people made the weakened ecumenical patriarchs look westwards, like Byzantine emperors under threat from Ottomans of the Middle Ages. In Jerusalem the creation of the state of Israel did not have the same effect upon the Orthodox Church in Palestine but it still made the Orthodox Church open to help from western Christianity. In Romania and in Yugoslavia and in Bulgaria the leaders of the Churches needed help from the West amid their quiet discomforts with their doctrinaire Marxist governments. Near the end of Ramsey's time the mutual sympathies were damaged by arguments over the ordination of women as priests or whether it was possible for the Anglicans to unite with Methodists. Still, it was a time of opportunity. There happened to be an archbishop at Canterbury who valued the Orthodox tradition, studied its classical documents, used its liturgies, respected its monastic ideals, and wanted its insights to be understood and used by the members of his Church, who thereby, he thought, would grow into a fuller understanding of what Catholicity means. And by accident he happened to encounter four patriarchs among the Orthodox with whom he felt a rapport of the heart as well as the mind—Alexei the last of the tsarist bishops, and therefore with an international as well as a Russian mind; Justinian of Bucharest where no one was likely to identify Orthodoxy with pan-Slavism and whose training went back, like that of Alexei, to a wider world; German in Belgrade; and Athenagoras, the most western-minded patriarch, and one of the biggest in personal stature, ever to occupy the ecumenical see.

13

Rome

I. JOHN XXIII

The Italians had demanded a united Italy and that meant demolishing the historic power of the Popes. Mainly because of this Italian drive, the Popes spent nearly a hundred years with the psychology which is against the world and needs to keep itself pure from the world as a sanctuary. When Ramsey became Archbishop of York the Pope was the last who was educated in the atmosphere where the Pope was 'the prisoner of the Vatican'. He still had the mood of the Papacy as a sanctuary with high walls against modern society. That had a good side, in devotion, prayer, otherworldliness, the traditional virtues of Catholicism. It also had a weak side. It made for rigid attitudes against change; refusal to co-operate much with other Christians in common endeavour; reluctance to concede even common prayer with Protestants; a slow adjustment to the pressing intellectual problems of the age.

Pope Pius XII, the Pope of the second World War, died in 1958 while Ramsey was still Archbishop of York. Ramsey was not a natural admirer of Pius XII. Though otherworldly in his faith, he wanted Churches to be open to the world. When Ramsey became an archbishop Pope Pius XII had entered the last years when his health declined and he almost abdicated responsibility about the internal government of the Church and left affairs to the Curia and grew remote. His successor Pope John XXIII threw open the windows of the Vatican to the fresh air. He threw out his arms to the world, towards the Protestants and the Jews and the Communists. He knocked down the high walls which kept the Church away from humanity.

Ramsey was as grateful as the rest of the world. But the difference was marked at Ramsey's enthronement in Canterbury, to which came two representatives of the Russian Orthodox Church, for the first time ever, but no representative of the Roman Catholic Church.

Ramsey welcomed the second Vatican Council and watched its progress with interest and hope. But in under two years after he became the Archbishop of Canterbury, John XXIII decayed into what proved to be his last illness.

In September 1965 two of the Lambeth staff recorded their conviction that Ramsey was less enthusiastic about relations with Rome than his predecessor. At first sight this was astonishing. Fisher was a low churchman, Ramsey an Anglo-Catholic. Fisher had little sympathy or understanding for the prayers, liturgies, mysticisms, and hierarchies of the Roman Catholic Church. Ramsey was a man of Catholic devotion who more than once wanted to be a monk, who loved the daily eucharist, whose prayers were the corona of sacraments, and who cared for the historic descent from the apostles and for a due succession in sees.

Fisher was a cheery man of common sense. He thought the difficulties between the Churches would be blown away if people were sensible instead of bigots. He imagined that nearly everyone was as sensible as himself and we shall solve all this fairly easily if we get together.

Ramsey had no such enthusiasm for going to Rome. He understood, no one better, that the predicaments of the Church could not be solved by sensible men knocking their heads together. And he did not like what happened in England. He did not like the way in which some Roman Catholics tried to make proselytes of devout Anglicans. He specially disliked the rigidity of rules about mixed marriages between Catholics and Protestants; that is, Roman insistence that non-Catholic parents should sign forms promising that the children of the marriage should be brought up Roman Catholic. One of his staff thought that the verb *abominate* was not too strong to describe his feelings. He also abominated the Roman re-baptism of converts, with its uncharitable implication that baptism in his Church was an empty nothing. His first relations with the Archbishop of Westminster were not particularly happy. Early in 1966 there was public scandal about the Roman rules on mixed marriages.

By the time this affair blew up, it was settled that Ramsey should go to Rome. But discomforts before it and like it made him hesitate whether he was sensible to go to Rome as though everything between the two Churches was serene. Bernard Pawley, who represented the Anglicans in Rome, sensed that Ramsey did not wish him to be too prominent, or to take too much initiative. At that time Ramsey did not like it if anyone suggested that Christendom might one day be reunited under the chairmanship of the Pope and that this was the goal towards which these efforts after unity tended.

Moreover the statesman in him saw a snag. He was head of a world-wide communion, which contained in its net every variety of fish;

and some of those fish, in Northern Ireland, in bits of Australia, in bits of North America, were taught to hate or fear the Pope. If the archbishop went to Rome, he would be pursued by protesters. Sordid things might happen like the daubing of graffiti on Canterbury cathedral. Not much like that happened when Fisher went to see John XXIII. Protests happened but they were containable. No one could suspect Fisher of being about to become a Roman Catholic. He exuded Protestantism, robust and foursquare. Ramsey knew that he was not in the same situation. Here was the first disciple of Newman to be Archbishop of Canterbury. He was suspect to some Protestants for his ritual, and for his mysterious high church reputation. If he went to see the Pope, he might diminish hostility between Protestants and Catholics, which was an important thing he could do. But if he went to see the Pope, he would raise worse fears in Belfast, or Sydney, or South Carolina, than ever Fisher could do. Suppose it got around in Londonderry that the Archbishop of Canterbury was to be made a cardinal and that the English Church was nearly Roman Catholic, might that bring bombs and murder into Londonderry streets?

Twice a week or so Bernard Pawley sent him reports out of Rome on the way the Vatican Council went and every two or three months Pawley would go to Lambeth to report personally. Pawley never felt at any of these interviews that Ramsey showed much enthusiasm, or anxiety to act.

Four forces pushed him towards putting away his hesitation and visiting the Pope. The first was, that Fisher did it; was welcomed by a warm-hearted Pope; and the pair of them did nothing but good to Christendom. This example was impossible for Ramsey to avoid. Journalists kept asking him, when are you going to Rome? Whenever asked, he replied that he hoped to go. He could give no other answer.

The second was that some of his best advisers, those who knew Rome best, wanted it to happen and expected it to happen. The third was that the Pope's representative in London, the friendly and unstuffy apostolic delegate Igino Cardinale, came to England in January 1964 and warmed up the air between Lambeth and Westminster. Ramsey was much taken with Cardinale. This made a difference to him.

The fourth was the personality of the two Popes. John XXIII was so ill in December 1962 that the English were afraid that he would die and some reactionary would be elected to succeed him. There was question of Ramsey hurrying to Rome to assure him of the esteem in which he held him, at a week or two's notice. When John XXIII died Ramsey preached a sermon to more than 2,000 people on the way in which that Pope captured the imagination of the world. He got into trouble with some Protestants for this sermon. He was also in trouble for celebrating on behalf of the dead Pope a service which he was alleged to have called a requiem, though he had not called it a requiem. It was held in Lambeth Palace chapel on 11 June 1963, in the presence of some Roman Catholic representatives headed by Lord Longford. This was not much of a trouble, for mostly it was members of the National Union of Protestants picketing the chapel.

2. PAUL VI

Cardinal Montini was elected to be Paul VI in June 1963. He was Ramsey's kind of man. It was true that his career lay in diplomacy whereas Ramsey's lay in teaching. But he was also an intellectual, carrying about with him crates of books. Partly from his Lombard origins and his family at Brescia in North Italy and partly from the influence of a French Catholic philosopher Jacques Maritain, he acquired something of that tradition of humane, European, political liberalism which was also the tradition of Ramsey, and which was to make him the most open-minded of Popes for more than two centuries.

He was a man of the Curia, who understood better than any of his contemporaries how an ecclesiastical bureaucracy works; certainly better than Ramsey who hardly understood it at all; and yet Paul VI had none of the dryness traditionally associated with men in offices, he retained an affection and a charisma. He it was who had to apply the results of the second Vatican Council, with the conception of a renewal of the Church; in going out to humanity, in deepening its spiritual life, in friendship between denominations, in a Christian quest for justice and human rights; a man of tradition but with the sense that tradition is alive and fertile and looks forward as well as back. He was a person of simplicity who ceased wearing the papal tiara and abolished the papal guard of noblemen and simplified ceremonies and stripped papal masses of their sumptuousness and made them less unlike the Lord's Supper. He was capable of a tough authoritarian line if he believed it necessary; of which the two chief demonstrations were his condemnation of birth control when many of his advisers pointed in another direction and his dictatorial removal from his see of the ancient confessor against Marxism, Cardinal Mindszenty, exiled from Hungary, for the sake of the peace and pastoral care of the Balkan Churches. But he was also capable of sudden gestures of a charismatic generosity. In Jerusalem he met the Ecumenical Patriarch Athenagoras and they exchanged the kiss of peace and a few months later Pope and Patriarch joined in issuing a declaration which deplored the mutual anathemas between East and West of nine centuries before and the schism which resulted. In Istanbul he caused a little crisis because he went to visit the great Santa Sophia, for centuries a Christian cathedral and then for centuries a mosque and now a museum, and could not bear only to be a tourist in so historic a place of prayer, and suddenly knelt and said his prayers—to the anger of young Turks who were not allowed to use it for their Muslim prayers. In the Sistine chapel he suddenly knelt before the envoy of the Ecumenical Patriarch and kissed his feet, and shocked his own staff who did not know what to do; and by that act, which in most people would be overdramatic but in him sprang out of the heart, he wiped out centuries of a feeling of humiliation which the Easterners thought they suffered from the pride of Rome. We shall see what a difference to the English archbishop this charismatic generosity was to make.

Moreover Paul had more knowledge of English religion than any of his predecessors. He had a special affection for Ramsey's predecessor St Anselm; he often read in the Venerable Bede; he had a respect, unusual in Italian prelates of those days, for the English religious tradition. 'I have a great affection for your Book of Common Prayer,' he said to a visiting English layman, Sir Gilbert Inglefield, who told him about the Series 2 experimental liturgy in England, 'you must not abandon it. It is very beautiful poetry.' He was a friend of George Bell, the Bishop of Chichester, who helped him towards an understanding of Anglicanism. Since Ramsey was a political liberal by conviction, he would never easily have come to terms with a Pope who stood on the extreme right of European politics. But Paul VI was his sort of Pope.

In 1964 the second Vatican Council agreed its decree on ecumenism. The language of this decree gave the chief place, among Churches separated from Rome, to the Eastern Orthodox Churches. Among the Churches—not called Churches but communions—derived from the Reformation—not quite named the Reformation but named 'what is called the Reformation'—the Anglican Communion (named as such) was elevated to a special place as a Church which preserved much of the structure and traditions of Catholicism. The tone of the decree was freed from the air of telling other Christians all to become Catholic and was drafted in such a way as to encourage ecumenical dialogue. This decree was of the first importance in the history of the modern Church in changing the relations between Rome and the other Churches. And naturally it raised the impetus to send Ramsey to Rome.

Other decisions of the Vatican Council also pleased the Anglicans. The language which it used about the Church, and about the liturgy, was language far easier for Protestants to understand than the language which was used in official Roman Catholic documents for four hundred years. And Michael Ramsey himself added a fourth—not only the decrees on the Church, and on the liturgy, and ecumenism, but the declaration on religious liberty. With this last, the Roman Catholic Church jettisoned the long tradition that toleration was only to be put up with, never accepted as the ideal constitution for a State.

By March 1965 there began to be talk in Rome that the Archbishop of Canterbury would come. But not until near the end of 1965 was it certain that it would happen.

On 18 March 1966 about a hundred demonstrators, wearing black armbands, marched across Lambeth Bridge to the gate of Lambeth Palace. They sang hymns as they went but Ramsey was away. Dr Ian Paisley and four others booked flights to Rome on the same plane. One leapt out on the tarmac at Heathrow and started to shout at Ramsey but Robert Beloe muffled his noise with a large fist. On the flight the archbishop and his party were booked into the small first-class compartment and the door between this and the ordinary seats was guarded. The Paisleyites tried to invade Ramsey's compartment but were thwarted by a detective. At Fiumicino airport both the airline and the Italian police were co-operative. The aircraft opened only the forward door for Ramsey and his party to descend and then let no one else off until Ramsey had had a drink in the VIP lounge (the only time he was known to drink campari) and sped away in a Mercedes limousine provided by the Vatican, with a troupe of outriders on motor cycles who swept him past the red traffic lights. The police refused to allow Paisley and another into the country—under what law or regulation is not known; but they were in trouble with the Italian police over an incident of four years before, when they protested at the presence of observers at the Vatican Council. Nevertheless Paisley achieved publicity at the airport by opening waistcoats in front of the reporters, inside carrying slogans such as 'Archbishop Ramsey traitor to Protestant Britain'. The rump of the demonstrators, whose presence was quite halved by the removal of Paisley, tailed Ramsey in Rome and were tailed by the police and were ejected from the Anglican church of All Saints when Ramsey went to preach there; and were booed by the crowd when they tried to do the same at the other Anglican church of St Paul's. The British press thought all this important.

The visit was made easier by Fisher's previous visit. But the difference between the two visits was marked. The Vatican treated Fisher's visit as unofficial, Ramsey's as official. They always referred to Fisher as 'Dr Fisher'. An observer who saw both events in the Church information service, Colonel Robert Hornby, defined the contrast. Fisher was swept past the Swiss guards by courteous but brisk escorts, and the Vatican allowed no photograph of Fisher with the Pope. Yet the Pope spent 67 minutes with Fisher, which is long for a papal audience. Still the gap between the two meetings felt to Colonel Hornby more like five centuries than five years.

Ramsey stayed as the Pope's guest at the English College. The set of rooms was sumptuously decorated for the English Roman Catholic bishops when they came to the Vatican Council. The students were told that they were not to show an extravagant demonstration of welcome. When his car arrived they broke ranks, crowded round him, and kissed his ring. He shook hands with everyone in the courtyard. The students offered the services of their Rugger Club as a guard against Ulstermen, and the Rector put a notice on the students' board saying that tact and common sense were to be used if they found suspicious characters lurking in the building. The notice said, 'They will probably be wearing "clergyman" but this alone is NOT a sufficient excuse for assaulting anyone.' After lunch Ramsey asked the rector if he might pay a visit to the Blessed Sacrament in the chapel. On the day after, the rector asked him to say the prayer at that visit. He used Archbishop Laud's prayer, 'that we may seriously lay to heart the causes of our unhappy divisions . . .' and this prayer was thenceforth taken into the cycle of prayer used by the English College.[1]

The College of Cardinals gave a reception for him in the Borgia apartments at the Vatican. The great doors were opened for him ceremoniously by guards with halberds, and he stood framed in the doorway, in Anglican choir dress, buckled shoes, scarlet chimere, lawn rochet ironed by his chaplain, velvet Canterbury cap on his head, and on his breast the jewelled crucifix given to him by Patriarch Alexei. The effect was a gasp in the silence. He was led to a chair on a dais from which to receive them. The Pope's Secretary of State, Cardinal Cicognani, turned to John Andrew and said to him, 'What a sight! This place hasn't seen a sight like it since Archbishop Arundel came.' They have long memories in the Vatican, for Thomas Arundel of Canterbury, who by his mother was a Plantagenet and was a bishop from the age of 21, and who amid his dramatic career was lord chancellor and impeached by the House of Commons and banished the land, came to Rome as a fugitive in 1397. Ramsey was not at all a fugitive.

His interest in those parts of Rome that were not people was limited.

[1] Ramsey went to the Anglican Centre, a house of study founded in the Palazzo Doria mainly by John Moorman, and blessed it.

They passed the Coliseum in the car. Someone pointed out to him that this was the Coliseum. He did not look out of the window.

On the morning of 23 March 1966 he met Pope Paul VI in the Sistine chapel for the symbolic, almost sacramental, meeting; where beneath Michelangelo's painting of the Last Judgement they exchanged their messages of greeting, and later they exchanged gifts: the Pope gave Ramsey a fresco of Christ in glory, of the twelfth century, from a church in North Italy, which would be framed and hung in the chapel at Lambeth, and a set of Mansi's edition of all the Catholic Councils; and Ramsey gave the Pope a pectoral cross made by the students of the Canterbury College of Art and a set of his own writings specially bound. Colonel Hornby remembered how Pope John's gift of books to Fisher had to be smuggled to the office of the British minister by Cardinale; whereas it was perfectly impossible to smuggle a fresco and Hornby did not envy the Lambeth chaplain who would have to arrange for its transport.[2] In the formal addresses at the Sistine chapel they were not naïve; Ramsey talked of the goal as a good way ahead, Paul VI talked of the bridge they were building as still rickety (*nondum satis firma*) and under construction. Ramsey pleaded that they should join in persuading the nations to disarm and to modify their insistence on national sovereignty. The Pope included a generous sentence: 'as you cross our threshold, we want you especially to feel that you are not entering the house of strangers, but that this is your home, where you have a right to be.' In the late afternoon they met again, for a private talk in the Pope's library, with only two helpers, John Findlow on one side and Monsignor Willebrands on the other.

Characteristically, Ramsey did not begin the agenda with Church politics, or with friction between the Churches, but with spirituality. He wondered whether the right way forward was through a growing unity in prayer. He raised the possibility that there might be joint retreats. He went on to say that on occasion lay people valued common worship. Paul VI answered this with a sentence which no Pope before him would have spoken: 'This was a sign from God, since the People of God expressed the spirit of God.' They talked of the possibility of common forms of prayer, and a common translation of the Lord's Prayer, and a common translation of the creeds. The Pope said that the two Churches venerated certain saints in common—he mentioned St Augustine of Canterbury, and the Venerable Bede, and Edward the Confessor. He said that he had visited Durham and Canterbury and mentioned St Anselm. Ramsey reminded him how the tomb of Edward

---

[2] Hornby in *Tablet*, 10 Oct. 1970, 974 ff.

the Confessor in Westminster abbey was still a place of pilgrimage for Roman Catholics.

Only then, after the question of common worship, did Ramsey turn to theology. Did there not need to be a joint commission of theologians? The Pope accepted the plan, and they discussed how to start it. This set the Pope off into a digression on the importance of Cardinal Newman's thought for our time. 'I consider Newman one of the greatest spirits of our time. I would like to honour him by publishing his works and spreading his thought.'

Then Ramsey asked about Anglican Orders. Since Leo XIII's bull Apostolicae Curae of 1896 it was official Roman Catholic doctrine that the ordination of Anglican ministers was invalid and that their sacraments were null. The Pope said that he was ready to reopen the study of the subject.

So far all was harmony. Ramsey then raised the points where he was unhappy: the rebaptism of converts; the rigidity over mixed marriages. The Pope gave away little. He said that he would write to Archbishop Heenan of Westminster that there might be no apparent minimizing of Anglican baptisms. He said that the new joint commission (which we now call ARCIC)[3] would be able to treat of marriage; and that meanwhile canonists would work on the problem. He insisted that the Church needed to be strict over the form of marriage. He drew Ramsey's attention to the 'openness' of the documents of the second Vatican Council.

The meeting did not resolve Ramsey's difficulties. The Pope conceded that the gulf over Anglican Orders might be less unbridgeable than was supposed. But this was more important to Ramsey as a sign of charity than as a real concession; for Archbishops of Canterbury were contemptuous of any doctrine that a gulf about Anglican Orders needed to be bridged, and resented the prospect of a commission of canonists weighing up what to them needed no weighing. That in his extreme old age Pope Leo XIII acted unwisely and erroneously made a problem for the Church of Rome, not for the Church of England.

This meeting had a hidden consequence. Ramsey formed more than a respect, he formed an affection for Pope Paul. Personal affections weigh as feathers in the scales of politics. But if we pause and consider when in history an Archbishop of Canterbury was on such terms with a Pope —certainly not with Fisher and John XXIII, though both were jolly

[3] Preparatory commission, Gazzada, N. Italy 1967; Huntercombe, Berkshire, September 1967; Malta, December 1967–January 1968. ARCIC proper 1969; agreed statement on eucharist, Windsor 1971; in the ministry, Canterbury 1973. These agreements were astonishing but not fudged. Naturally they were not welcome to all on either side.

outgoing men—we see that this was a new stage in the history of the Churches since the Reformation.

Ramsey's personality and appearance made a big impression on the Roman people. They thought that he looked like Pope John XXIII.

On the morning of 24 March Pope and archbishop worshipped together at the basilica of St Paul-without-the-walls, the place where, it was supposed, St Paul was buried. A common declaration was read. At the end of the service Pope and archbishop said the blessing together in Latin—'Benedictio Dei Omnipotentis . . .'—with Ramsey visibly moved at joining with the Pope in giving a blessing—and then they exchanged the kiss of peace, and left the church through the west door, walking side by side, with the crowd clapping or cheering according to whether they were British or Italian. When the Pope said goodbye, he gave Ramsey his most generous gift of all. He slipped off the episcopal ring, with its emeralds and diamonds, which was given to him by the city of Milan when he was archbishop there, and put it in Ramsey's palm and Ramsey put it on his finger. No Pope could have said anything louder about that vexing sore over the validity of Anglican Orders. It spoke more loudly than any bull or encyclical. John Andrew, who was consulted beforehand on the manner of the gift and agreed that it should be a surprise to Ramsey, said afterwards, 'this gesture is too daring to be contemplated with equanimity by the Churches'. Some Scottish Roman Catholics were outraged by the action of the Pope—'handing over the very symbol of his authority'. This was not the feeling of many Catholics in Rome itself. After Ramsey died Joan Ramsey gave the ring to Archbishop Runcie so that it should become the permanent property of the see of Canterbury.

Those close to Ramsey said that they had rarely seen him so speechless as after the giving of this ring. 'I felt vividly', he said later, 'that he was giving me a piece of himself.' At the press conference afterwards a reporter asked him, 'Does this mean that Rome is tacitly recognizing the apostolic succession in England?' He replied, 'Not at all; but what it does betoken is the official recognition of the Church of England as an official Church with its rightful ministers. That from Rome means a great deal.'

Before he left Ramsey spent an evening, at his own insistence, with the students at the English College. His happy memory of his student days at Cuddesdon rose to the surface. He said to them, 'Let's have an open forum—no punches pulled!' He told them, 'It takes me back to my own student days, which, I must say, were I to have over again, I would spend at the English College.' They asked him questions about Anglican orders, and his impressions of Rome, and of mixed marriages. They sent him into a gale of laughter when someone asked him, 'What do you consider the most annoying trait shown by English Catholics?' He replied with perfect frankness: 'The natural inferiority complex of any minority group, spiced with a certain—one might call it—bumptiousness'; and the students received his frankness with a burst of good humour. He begged them for prayer in common, whenever possible. That night the Greater Silence, which was the rule of the college, vanished and the students talked about Ramsey and the situation into the small hours.

As he left the college to leave Rome, the students gathered in the courtyard and the rector asked Ramsey for his blessing. He gave it; and then the students cheered him and he threw his Canterbury cap high in the air, with glee on his face.

3. BEC

On the way home Ramsey went to the World Council of Churches at Geneva and presented its secretary Visser t'Hooft with the Lambeth Cross and gave an altarbook to the Ecumenical Centre. He returned to Lambeth Palace amid a tribe of protesters, mostly girls, singing hymns lugubriously in the rain, with a banner which said prematurely, 'Lord Ramsey, Judas of the 20th century'. He slipped in by the side door. His postbag was heavy with letters of protest (Mr Kensit's among them) and letters of gratitude.

In the next year, April 1967, he did what must have pleased Pope Paul. He went to the abbey of Bec in Normandy and lectured on St Anselm and Christian unity. It was the first visit of an Archbishop of Canterbury to France since the Field of the Cloth of Gold in 1520.

This visit was one of Ramsey's happiest occasions. The abbey of Bec, properly the abbey of our Lady of St Hellouin at Bec, was founded before the Norman Conquest and suppressed by the French Revolution. During the time while Normandy and then England were under the single ruler William the Conqueror, it was built up as a good place of education by the Italian Lanfranc, who became Archbishop of Canterbury and sought to reform the Church in England by putting monks from Bec into key posts. Lanfranc was followed as head of the monastic school by another Italian, Anselm of Aosta, who also became (1093) Archbishop of Canterbury and whom Ramsey always regarded as the biggest mind and best archbishop among his predecessors. It was not until the Hundred Years War between England and France that the link between Bec and the Church in England was broken. After the second

World War the buildings, which were a stud-farm and then an army depot, were handed over by the French War Office to the Historical Monuments commission; which in 1948 repaired them and gave them on a long lease to the Olivetan monks. These Olivetan monks under Dom Paul Grammont refounded the abbey, with a community of nuns nearby. Its history led it to conceive of ecumenical work, especially with the Anglicans, as a main vocation.

Ramsey and the abbot immediately struck up a rapport of intensity and happiness. They sang the monastic lauds and vespers by candle-light in the chapel, which was an old stable, and Ramsey laid his cross of Canterbury by the coffin of St Hellouin where the abbot laid his crozier, and was given the Asperges to do round the statue of the blessed Virgin, and in the morning celebrated the Anglican liturgy in the oratory, and was reluctantly persuaded to eat at breakfast porridge laced with Calvados wine to please the monk-cook. At the high mass, in the presence of the Archbishop of Rouen, Ramsey preached a sermon full of historical references to the links between Bec and Canterbury. He was moved by the holiness of the place, and the unaffected brotherliness of the Benedictines. Afterwards he often referred to this visit with gratitude. He went on to Paris and the story reached England that he was seen kneeling before the reserved sacrament in one of the Paris churches and was in tears.[4]

He went again to Bec, this time with Joan, five years after his retirement from the see and this was the visit which the monks particularly remember, for then he talked to them about what St Benedict meant to him personally and of the importance of the monastic tradition in the building of England and of Europe.

Not all was harmony between Rome and Canterbury. Not all that Pope Paul did could please Ramsey, and not all that Ramsey's Church did could please Pope Paul. Among the staff at Lambeth they argued whether the Pope had a truly liberal mind or was only a diplomat who needed to look liberal; and decided that truly this was a mind of openness. In January 1967 there was a brisk exchange of cross letters when Pope Paul was tactless—he ordained sixteen priests from the Beda, a college for training English priests. Five of these were ex-Anglicans. In his address the Pope called for better relations with the Church of England; a failure of timing which at such a moment disturbed Ramsey and even made him ask whether the Church of Rome

---

[4] On this visit he was received by de Gaulle; prayed before the altar in Notre Dame where demonstrators tore up the service sheets; lectured on the Transfiguration. He had met de Gaulle before, at Churchill's funeral.

was serious about dialogue. The Anglicans sometimes wondered whether the Vatican was up to date, as when the Pope suggested to them that the medieval schoolman Duns Scotus and his teaching might make a suitable framework for the dialogue between Anglicans and Roman Catholics.

Pope Paul sent a good message to the Lambeth Conference of 1968. Almost simultaneously he condemned the use of contraception in an encyclical. Cardinal Suenens, the Belgian, begged the Pope to be more open about birth control and warned Ramsey that the Pope had refused his plea. When the encyclical came out, Ramsey issued a statement that there was nothing unchristian about family planning. In a public debate with students at London University, Ramsey said he was very willing to recognize the Pope as chief of a united Church. But he would never be willing to call him head of the Church because Christ alone is head of the Church.

Ramsey was not pleased about the Pope canonizing English martyrs of the reign of Queen Elizabeth I, because in England some of the names had controversial associations. Why should two denominations who were now trying to be friendly, choose this moment to rake up the history that in the Reformation they burnt and killed each other? He steadily argued against it; made his feelings plain to the Pope; advised the Crown, which asked his opinion, not to send a Minister of the Crown to the ceremony but to be content with the British Minister at the Vatican; and himself refused to send a bishop to the ceremony but was content with the director of the Anglican Centre in Rome. If they wanted to do something about the Reformation in this year 1970, why did not they rescind the bull of 1570 which excommunicated Queen Elizabeth?

In the allocution at the ceremony of 25 October 1970 Pope Paul referred to the Anglican Communion as 'our ever-beloved sister', words which he inserted into the bull in his own hand, with the evident intention of weakening any anti-Anglican effect of the canonization.

On his side the Pope was perturbed about happenings among the Anglicans: the growing outspokenness of radical divinity and the ability of the Church of England to tolerate what looked like extreme negations; and secondly the ordination at Hong Kong of two women as priests.

4. THE QUESTION OF A NUNCIO

The Pope was represented in London, since 1938, by a sort of ambassador, called apostolic delegate; with a secret agreement that the British government should have a veto on the person appointed. This was a junior form of representation, and not formally accredited to the government. The equivalent of an ambassador was a papal nuncio. There was a difficulty about having a nuncio in London. Since the Congress of Vienna in 1814 the Pope claimed that the nuncio must have precedence among ambassadors and Catholic states conceded this demand. The British did not see much point in a nuncio and were sure that to give him precedence among ambassadors would cause an unnecessary quarrel. Yet many countries of the British Commonwealth now had diplomatic relations at the level of ambassador and nuncio. It was odd that the British were behind the Commonwealth.

From time to time the Roman Catholic leaders in Britain approached the government on the matter. The Duke of Norfolk raised it in Archbishop Fisher's time. Then Pope John XXIII succeeded and the Roman Catholic laymen felt that they could rely on the new climate of friendliness to Rome among the Churches. Early in Ramsey's time as archbishop they approached the prime minister Macmillan, who approached Ramsey. The British Cabinet considered the question and was divided, with a majority in favour of a nuncio. The arguments in favour were these: the present system is illogical; the present Pope has a character which creates response; it would be helpful in combatting Communism to have this link; and it would please many of the Queen's subjects. It was proposed that the Pope's representative should be an internuncio not a nuncio, then he would not need to have precedence; or they would make an agreement that if he were a nuncio he should not have precedence. All this seemed sufficiently important for Macmillan to come to Lambeth to discuss it. Macmillan had a personal wish to give this recognition in the time of Pope John XXIII and was afraid that Pope John would soon die and would be succeeded by a 'fundamentalist Pope', as the prime minister described the danger.

The difficulty for Ramsey was that he knew that many Roman Catholic leaders in England had no desire for a papal nuncio, whose presence would diminish the independent action of the English Roman Catholic bishops; he also knew that some people in the Vatican preferred to reduce their diplomatic service rather than extend it, for it had a vaguely out-of-date feeling in modern international relations; and he saw that the unofficial channel of an apostolic delegate like his friend Cardinale was more helpful to friendship between the Churches than an official nuncio could be. He thought that the whole idea of nuncios fostered the idea of the Papacy as a triumphalist and sovereign temporal state which was now an anachronism. His man at Foreign Relations, Satterthwaite, was horrified at the British government's idea that if they created formal diplomatic representation with the Vatican they would do it partly with the object of getting more information on Communism. Ramsey's advisers also told him that it was he who would have to bear a lot of odium if this happened. Therefore he ought not to be seen to give Macmillan's plan even tacit approval. Accordingly Ramsey advised Macmillan of these doubts, and Macmillan did nothing more about it except to say that he might raise it again later. 'I confess', said Macmillan, 'to some sense of disappointment.'

Three years later Norman St John Stevas, a Roman Catholic member of the House of Commons, raised it in Parliament; asking whether Britain was not being 'gravely discourteous to the Holy See'. Ramsey was consulted beforehand and took the same view as before. To create ambassadors would put future progress between the Churches into diplomatic channels and they were more likely to get on if they remained as they were. The government accordingly gave a negative response. The situation as it was, they said, was appropriate.

During 1973 various Roman Catholic members of Parliament thought of raising the question in Parliament. They approached Mervyn Stockwood, of Southwark, who raised it with Ramsey. He was still of the same mind. He had no enthusiasm. But he did not want to be a brake upon what another religious denomination wanted if it was true that they wanted it. He preferred now to say that this was nothing to do with the see of Canterbury and to keep out of the argument. He went to see Harold Wilson the prime minister (on the way he got lost for a time somewhere in the House of Lords) and made it plain that he thought most Anglicans would be happy with the change but that he could not speak for the Church of Scotland or the Church of Ireland.

Over a matter of ritual the archbishop did not mind at all. The customs of heralds were conservative by their nature. In the arms of clergymen they only permitted Anglican bishops to have mitres in their arms, on the ground that the State did not recognize any other bishops as true bishops. This was not an ecumenical attitude in the tradition of heraldry. The Roman Catholic bishops of England asked the College of Heraldry if it could be changed. Garter King-of-Arms asked the Archbishop of Canterbury and the Free Churches and the Archbishops of Wales and Armagh. The Archbishop replied delightfully to Garter that he had 'no objection in principle'.

Anglican archbishops had long had good relations with Roman Catholic archbishops, providing the Roman Catholic archbishops presided over sees outside England. In this way Ramsey established an intimate friendship with the Belgian Cardinal Suenens, and they lectured together in New York. In 1966 he received Cardinal Beran, not long after he was released from years of imprisonment by the government of Czechoslovakia, the most anti-Christian of the satellite governments beyond the Iron Curtain (counting Albania as no longer a satellite). He also went to Brussels cathedral to the service for the EEC, and to be the guest of Cardinal Suenens. At the beginning of the sermon Catholic demonstrators let off foul-smelling smoke bombs behind the altar and steel-helmeted riot police hurriedly removed pamphlets distributed to protest against Suenens giving Ramsey permission to celebrate a sacrament in the Roman Catholic cathedral. Ramsey's sermon in Brussels was a remarkable utterance on the place of Christianity in helping to create the idea of Europe and of its place in the future of Europe. At the end of the service the two archbishops, Roman Catholic and Anglican, gave the blessing to the people simultaneously.

The friendship with Cardinal Suenens did not help Ramsey with all the Roman Catholic Church. During the crisis which hit the Catholic Church in 1970–1, through division between the conservative and the radical interpreters of the second Vatican Council, Suenens was seen to possess too open a mind for the ultras. There came a moment when some three-bottle fanatic of orthodoxy defaced his cardinal's coat-of-arms in Rome. The respect between Ramsey and Suenens could not help Ramsey with the Siris of the Roman Church, who mourned that the second Vatican Council ever happened. It made no difference to his friendship with Pope Paul VI.

In these years the old barriers with English Roman Catholic bishops started to break down. Ramsey never thought that Cardinal Heenan was interested in the ecumenical movement at depth. But this idea that Heenan was lukewarm was weakened when Heenan asked Ramsey to preach in Westminster cathedral. There, while demonstrators jostled and bayed outside the west door, Ramsey had a tumultuous ovation from a vast congregation mainly consisting of Roman Catholics who were well aware what this heretical prelate had done for the peace of the Churches, and with a number of young London University students standing on chairs at the back and cheering. Then Cardinal Heenan came to preach at St Paul's cathedral and despite some heckling the occasion was of tolerance and fraternity between Christians. Finally on 7 July 1970 a Roman Catholic mass was celebrated in the precincts of Canterbury cathedral to commemorate the 800th anniversary of the murder of Archbishop Thomas Becket. Police leave was stopped and two people were arrested, and Ian Paisley was expected to appear and boom away; and still it was an occasion of charity and gratitude by both Churches. The two archbishops became personal friends on Christian name terms, Jack and Michael, the first two to be personal friends since 1850 when the first Archbishop of Westminster was made.

And yet Ramsey saw that Heenan was torn inside himself; used to the old certainties and content with them and nervous of where these novelties might take him or his Church. Heenan came to speak at a Church leaders' conference at Selly Oak, Birmingham, in September 1972. The conference disliked what he said and thought that the atmosphere of what he said came from an obsolete world.

5. THE FOCOLARI

Chiara Lubich was from a worker's family in North Italy. She started as a schoolmistress who taught a group of girls in an air-raid shelter during the war. On a pilgrimage to the holy House at Loreto she had an overwhelming conviction of a special vocation, not to a nunnery nor to marriage but to the *focolare* (Italian for fireplace or hearth)—that is, to make a family of God, living and working in the world. At the age of 23 she took a personal vow to be unmarried. She began with a little community at Trent; and at a retreat of the community in 1949 near her home near Trent, she had a vision of the way in which her community ought to go. It was the Focolari, and they were to be groups of Christian love in the world and to look to deepen internal Catholic unity and ecumenical unity among all the Churches. She won the approval of Pope John XXIII. She went to see the Ecumenical Patriarch Athenagoras, and saw him several times, and became one link between him and Pope Paul VI. She went to see several leaders of the World Council, and in Germany a community was founded. In 1966 she came to see Michael Ramsey at Lambeth. Always afterwards she treasured what he said: 'God's finger is in this movement.' The meeting was important to her, and afterwards her Focolarini talked much of it. They were one of the best products of the new ecumenical mood of the age because one of the most gentle and most spiritual.

6. THE FUNERAL OF PAUL VI

Ramsey had a last duty to perform in his retirement. Pope Paul VI died in 1978. The Church of England appointed three representatives for the funeral, headed by Bishop Ellison of London. Nothing would stop Ramsey hurrying to Rome, not to represent his Church but to be a private mourner at the funeral of a valued friend.

About this there was a row in the British newspapers. Ramsey was observed queueing up like the rest of us at London Airport. Why no VIP lounge? Why no special attention? The public imagined that their archbishop always travelled in limousines and first class aircraft and had no idea that once he ran across an airport apron flustered by asinine policemen and once he sat quietly on a suitcase reading at an airport while the travelling world hurried by oblivious and once he helped push a car out of a hole—quite like the rest of us. The Managing Director of the British Airports Authority had to defend himself from the charge of being the worst kind of petty bureaucrat by saying that VIP status was given only to a list provided by the British government and it was clear that ex-primates were not upon the list. Ramsey thought all this a fuss about less than nothing.

The Vatican could not believe that Michael Ramsey came to the funeral as a private mourner and not as a representative of the Church of England. In their eyes he was *the* representative of the Church of England. When the Secretariat for Unity found that Ramsey was coming, nothing would induce them not to treat him as a representative of the Church of England and put him in a very high seat. Bishop Ellison saw at once that his old archbishop and friend of Pope Paul ought to be the leader of the Anglican delegation. So, unexpectedly, he sat in one of the highest of seats; which, by a rueful chance, made him sit next to Metropolitan Nikodim from Leningrad, with whom his last communications had been chilly. The Roman prelates noticed that he wore the ring which Pope Paul VI gave him. They approved.

As he helped some of the Orthodox Churches in their difficulties with the State, and as we shall find him helping the Lutherans behind the Iron Curtain, could he help the Roman Catholics? They were passing through a difficult time during his years, amid the pulls between those who stood for renewal and progress and those who wanted to keep what was strong in the past. In this turmoil they lost something like every tenth priest who was between the ages of 30 and 45. It was the age of student revolution, and the young of the world were against institutions of any kind, and the Roman Church was the most traditional of institutions. On top of that was the unsettlement of the moral debate which affected both Churches. Paul VI and Michael Ramsey were the first heads of their Churches fully to face the more effective and reliable methods of modern family planning. The Pope condemned contraception. But two-thirds of the Roman Catholics in the world did not believe him or accept what he said on this matter, so that though they still respected him much, this increased the tension between institution and the conscience of its people. Even more fundamental for the Churches was the debate about sexual intercourse before marriage. Christianity stood for the sacredness of the family and the care of children. Both Churches were unhesitating in maintaining the rule, no sexual intercourse except in a permanent marriage; though they admitted reluctantly that those who were permanent and committed partners without legal marriage were not like adulterers. But in the United States of 1973, for example, fewer than half the Roman Catholics were willing to condemn premarital intercourse. This difference in moral judgement was a subtle though not to be measured force in separating a Christian people from confidence in leaders who inherited from the New Testament an apostolic authority.

In all this unsettlement of a historic Church, which was partly caused by its system of government but was still more part of a general crisis in Christendom, could Ramsey do anything whatever that would help?

He could help them to respect the Protestant tradition. Perhaps in that he could help more than anyone else, even more than the Secretary of the World Council of Churches. As with all the more spiritual disciples of the Oxford Movement, he could help them to see the extent of the inheritance from Bible and early Church which was shared by both Catholic and Protestant.

History thinks little of personal influences. The fall of the French Empire in the far East caused a vacuum of power in Vietnam which was sure to throw Russia and the United States into tension; and as the States drew apart, so did their Churches. In consequence of the Cold War western Europe came to see its common interest and common culture, and to create a European economic community; and so bring Italy and Britain nearer to each other, politically, than at any time since the Romans ruled them both. And religion was a weighty part of common culture. Individuals fit their times. The cooling of Ramsey towards Moscow hierarchs, and his warming towards Rome were facets of the political and social movements of an age. But individuals still matter.

Fisher was the Archbishop fortunate to be still in office at Canterbury when the Roman Catholic Church elected Pope John XXIII and started throwing down the high walls which divided it from society and the world. But he was only in office for three more years. It was Ramsey who reaped the benefit of this unlooked-for change and needed to cope with the problems which it produced. As he was fortunate in leading his Church during the time of Patriarch Athenagoras of Constantinople and Patriarch Alexei of Moscow, so he was even more fortunate in having in Paul VI a Pope whom he could regard not only with personal admiration but with affection. As John XXIII and Paul VI drew the Church of Rome out of its isolation, so Ramsey was fitted to draw the Church of England out of its insularity. The achievement was big. And if he was fortunate in them they were fortunate in him. He might say rude things about them—their rigidities about mixed marriages, their Victorian anachronism about Anglican orders, their backwardness about family planning, their insistence on a statement of the infallibility of Popes which had no use except to divide the Churches and the infallibility of anybody was not a notion which Ramsey could ever believe. But Catholicism in its broad stream, flowering, devotional, self-sacrificing, proud of history and learning from history, sacramental and sometimes mystical and sometimes contemplative, that he understood and they could see how he understood. They came to regard him, as Athenagoras of Constantinople regarded him, as another patriarch of the Churches.

In 1981 he was for the last time in Rome to preach in the Anglican Church in Rome at Michaelmas. Those who were there said that his utterance showed no sign of failing. A Roman Catholic priest in the audience said that somehow he managed to distil a lifetime of contemplation. He asked for a private audience with Pope John Paul II ('there are things I want to say to him'). The Pope was convalescing from a bullet in his stomach, but received him in his country house at Castel Gandolfo. They had a talk without anyone else there except Bishop Torrella in case interpreting was needed. Afterwards the Pope came out and gave Ramsey a papal medal and Joan a rosary. It is not known what passed but the conversation was not made of silences, for at Ramsey's death the Pope said that he was an outstanding spiritual leader. Cardinal Willebrands used the same word leader but put it stronger. He called him 'one of the great spiritual leaders of our century. His warmth of character, his deep spirituality and his facility for teaching the truths of the faith with simplicity and conviction all made him an outstanding pastor.'[5] Which other Protestant was called by a cardinal one of the outstanding spiritual leaders of the century in which he lived?

[5] Willebrands to Runcie, 27 Apr. 1988.

14

The Protestants

I. THE METHODISTS

Since about 1910 the idea of Christian unity was in the air. Everyone talked about it piously, but not much was done about it except to hold committee meetings; and except in South India, an example which was followed, or attempted to be followed, in other parts of Asia and Africa. It looked shameful that so many words, so many eloquent speeches, and so much jargon, but also such true and genuine feelings, should lead on the international scale to little more than a whimper. But of two Churches in England, with common roots and many common understandings of prayer and Christian life, it really looked as though something should be achieved.

Of all other Churches the Methodists were by history and in spirit the closest to the Anglicans. Their founder John Wesley owed his faith to the Anglican tradition and died as an Anglican priest. They parted from the Anglicans with faults on both sides. But for many decades Methodists believed that they were a group within the Church of England for the encouragement of true Christian lives. Many of their members and ministers used prayers from the Book of Common Prayer, which some Methodists valued more than some Anglicans. They affirmed the creeds and loved the two gospel sacraments. If Anglicans suggested that not all Methodists were sound in the faith, the Methodists would have an easy retort. If Anglicans said that among the Methodists there was a streak of anticlericalism, the Methodists could reply that no one said more unkind things about bishops than some Anglicans. Some of the hymns most treasured by the Anglicans were Wesleyan in origin.

The Anglicans were attractive to the Methodists because of this long-standing sense of kinship, because of their reverent liturgy and their pastoral concern. The Methodists did not mind bishops, because most Methodist Churches in the world had bishops. What they minded was the high Anglican idea of bishops. They were not hostile to establishment but they were used to independence and would not put up with a system where a prime minister chose their bishops.

The Methodists were attractive to the Anglicans because they stood for a simplicity of the Christian way, because of their manifest quality as a Christian community, and because of the long-standing sense of kinship. They were not attractive so far as some of them imbibed the stouter qualities of old dissenting Protestantism, which to Anglicans always looked like dissent for the sake of dissent rather than dissent for the sake of truth.

In a world where ecumenical ideas were full of expectation, it was inevitable that Anglicans and Methodists should turn in hope towards each other. If they, who had such common spirit and such common history and such mutual respect for each other, could not unite as denominations into a single Church, which Churches could? It looked like a test whether the ecumenical movement meant business or gas.

The snag was that both Churches were broad in their adherents. The middle of the Anglicans and the middle of the Methodists—no problem. The left of the Methodists and the right of the Anglicans—poles apart. The Methodist Church contained persons who were stout dissenters and would hardly be willing to unite with any Church which had bishops. The Methodist Church with which the negotiations took place was itself a union, dating from 1932, of three distinct Methodist Churches—the Wesleyans, who were closest to the Anglicans, the United, and the Primitive Methodists. The Primitives contained Quaker influence in their background, and the Quaker disapproval of sacraments passed into some of their members. The Anglican Church contained persons of a stout Catholic spirit who would find it hard to unite with such Protestant persons as Methodists were known to be.

The Anglicans valued the continuity of sacramental life since the days of the apostles; this was symbolized and safeguarded by the apostolic succession of the bishops. It helped them to feel part of a world-wide and Catholic Christendom. For two hundred years the Methodists were happy in their ministry without any bishops. They recognized that for a union of the Churches they would need to accept bishops. But naturally they were determined not to accept bishops in such a way that it would cast doubt on the effectiveness or validity of the work of Methodist ministers during the two centuries when they were not ordained by bishops. This was the practical snag. They were never going to pretend that up to now they were laymen and now, with ordination by a bishop, they were real clergy for the first time.

The question was already under discussion when Ramsey became Archbishop of Canterbury. He had a far better chance of carrying a union successfully than either his predecessor or his successor. Someone had to carry the high Catholic Anglicans into believing that this proposed union with Methodists was a Catholic act and would not destroy a future chance of union with the Eastern Orthodox Church and the Church of Rome. Fisher could not have done this (supposing that he wished to, which he did not) because the Anglo-Catholics knew that he was a Protestant and had no confidence in him as a Catholic. Coggan could not have done this (supposing that he wished to, which he wished ardently) because the Anglo-Catholics knew that he was a Protestant and had no confidence in him as a Catholic. But Ramsey was an Anglo-Catholic theologian and man of Catholic devotion, and was doing more than anyone had ever done to change for the better the relations between the Church of England and the Church of Rome. If he believed in Anglican Methodist unity he had a chance of carrying a goodly number of the Anglo-Catholic party with him; and so making it possible.

At first Ramsey was not outspoken on the matter and watched to see how it would develop. But he was prompted to utterance by a new difficulty for the Church. The Church of England had never had a retired Archbishop of Canterbury who remained in this country and was active after his retirement. The reason was that Archbishops of Canterbury did not retire but went on till death. Archbishop Fisher was the first Archbishop of Canterbury to have long years of life before him when he retired. Though he retired because he was fatigued, he always had energy and did not lose all of it when he retired. He watched a Church about which he cared for so many years and could not bear to keep silent if he thought that it was liable to go astray. The result proved again that a retired archbishop, whether or not he keeps silent, is still a power in the Church.

This argument had the effect of making Ramsey's attitude very plain. This Anglo-Catholic leader and descendant of Newman and lover of Eastern Orthodoxy saw no reason whatever why Anglicans and Methodists should not through charity and mutual concession come together to form a united Church.

This attitude carried with it, he quickly realized, a more resolute attitude to the need for changes in the relation between Church and State. The Methodists had a system of self-government by Conference and were not likely to wish to unite with a Church unless they could preserve the same sort of self-government. Therefore a concession which the Church of England would need to make would be first, the securing of freedom to order its own ways of prayer and to choose its leaders; and second, to convert the ramshackle system of government,

muddled between Parliament and bishops and two separate Convocations and Church Assembly, into some sort of self-governing synod
which could be seen to be sufficiently representative to command the
sort of loyalties in the Church which Conference commanded among
Methodists. If Ramsey had thought these changes wrong in themselves
he would not have been persuaded towards them by the negotiations
with Methodists. But we have already seen that he was persuaded that
this was the way things ought to go.

He showed no sign that he thought these proposed changes were like
the Labours of Hercules. Would prime ministers, or the Queen,
willingly surrender their rights in the choice of Church leaders? And if
the system of Convocations and Church Assembly stopped anything too
new, how should they be cajoled into doing anything so new as to
abolish themselves and turn themselves into a single representative
synod? Some of the ecclesiastical lawyers, and the prime minister's
patronage secretary, thought that all this was asking for the moon.
Ramsey went quietly forward, confident that it would happen because it
was right and because it was sensible; and confident also that the needs
of unity with the Methodists would make the feet-draggers see how
right and how sensible it would be. In his presidential address of 1965
(19 January) to the Convocation of Canterbury, delivered in St
Margaret's Church Westminster, he explained how the Methodists
needed more self-government in the Church of England if they were to
unite with it and that it was important to be seen to use effectively a
system of synodical government in which laity and clergy shared
together.

He had internal scruples because at least once he compared what they
had to do with the process of reforming the canon law under his
predecessor which took years of pregnancy to give birth to a mouse, and
hoped that this was not what the future held. He also asked himself
whether a more efficient system must mean a more bureaucratic system
and hoped that would not be true. 'None of us', he told the Convocation
of Canterbury (14 May 1968), 'wants a centralized bureaucracy, and all
our inclinations are towards travelling light.' He also faced candidly
what he called 'the tradition of complacent separation'. Two Christian
communities went on in the country side by side for a couple of
centuries and they saw no reason to alter and they knew not much about
each other and they did not bother. The presumption would therefore
be against any change which could mean radical reconstruction.

He had another problem; he was bringing much more friendliness
between the Church of England and the Church of Rome. He did not
wish what happened over Methodism to be a set-back to this new-found

friendship. He consulted the Secretariat for Christian Unity at Rome and got the comments of the Roman Catholic theologians on the crucial documents of the scheme for unity between Anglicans and Methodists, especially the service of reconciliation between the two ministries. He also went to a conference with several Roman Catholic leaders in England to assure himself that they were satisfied by the scheme of union, and was happy with what they told him. The proposed united ordinal dropped the word priest and used only the word presbyter. Ramsey thought that this was a mistake. But when he consulted the Roman Catholics he found that they were happy about the wording of the ordinal, and so was content.

In July 1967 the Methodists took a step forward by passing a resolution supporting the plan for unity with the Church of England. The full scheme itself was not published by the negotiating commission until the early days of April 1968. Only a month later there was already a plan for a future continuing Church of England which would have nothing to do with a Church united of Anglicans and Methodists. A few months after that there was a plan for a continuing Methodist Church after union; and though this opposition was not numerous, it was formidable.

Ramsey was not put off. 'This is not to say', he wrote to a Durham friend, 'that I think everything in the Anglican-Methodist scheme is all right, but I do think that moaning and groaning does not help very much . . . The Holy Ghost has not ceased to take a part in Christian decisions and the movement of history.' He confessed that he had a little fear about it. The fear was not that Christianity would be 'watered down'. He was afraid that the union would reinforce the ultra-conservative tendency within Anglicanism.

One of the suffragan bishops in London, Graham Leonard of Willesden, attacked the nature of the scheme. By March 1969 he demanded a share in the endowments of the Church for those who refused to participate in the union. An English diocesan, Cyril Eastaugh, the Bishop of Peterborough, questioned the authority of the bishops to promote such a scheme. He said that the scheme, intended to make union, would make division. He was backed by John Moorman, the Bishop of Ripon, who was the principal Anglican observer at the second Vatican Council and always had at heart the good relations between the Church of England and the Church of Rome. Both the Bishops of Peterborough and Ripon hinted at resignation of their sees if the union went through. The great body of bishops, however, stood solidly with Ramsey. On the Methodist side Franz Hildebrandt, a former refugee from the Nazis, resigned from the Methodist Church because the Methodists wanted the scheme of union, and he was not the only Methodist minister to resign.

The plan was in two stages. First, constitute an Anglican Church and a Methodist Church which could mutually recognize each other's ministries and sacraments and be in full communion; together with a pledge that after some years of growing together (number of years unknown) there should be an act of formal union. The key point of the first stage was a service of reconciliation. After this service the bishops would consecrate some Methodists as bishops and all future Methodist ministers would be ordained by bishops. 'I should have thought', said Ramsey, 'that that was going to be rather a miracle.' In some parts of the Methodist Church the sacrament of holy communion was at times celebrated by laymen. It was agreed that no further licences for such celebrations would be given and so this custom would die out. Confirmation by bishops would come into the Methodist Church but would not be invariable there.

This service of reconciliation proposed thus: that Methodist ministers should kneel before the Archbishop of Canterbury and receive a laying on of hands with prayer. The words asked that each, according to his need, 'might receive' the Spirit. Then the Archbishop and Anglican priests would kneel before the Methodist ministers and receive their laying on of hands; and the Methodists would pray the same words for them.

These were words upon which the assault directed its fire. Were the Methodists being re-ordained or were they not? If it was an ordination to the Anglican ministry, the high Anglicans would be happy. If it was not an ordination to the ministry, but only a commissioning to further pastoral work, the Methodists would be happy. Were the Anglicans being re-ordained or not? If not, they were happy; if it was an extension to their ordination, the Methodists would be happy. Therefore both sides could be happy with the proposal—provided that they understood the words in different senses. Hence the critics used very hard language about this text—muddled, dishonest, an intentional deception, and some worse descriptions. In a letter to *The Times*, Lord Fisher called it 'open double dealing' (21 January 1969).

The opposition among the Anglicans consisted in an alliance between certain though not all Anglo-Catholics and certain though not all evangelicals. The low churchmen thought it wrong to ask Methodists to do any such act as to imply that anything might be wanting to their existing ministry. The high churchmen thought it wrong to ordain people when some of the people being ordained would think it a pretence; and they thought it wrong for priests to go through a form of words which could be taken to imply that anything was wanting in their priesthood. Let no one think this to be horse-trading in ecclesiastical politics. Feelings deep inside the soul were engaged on both sides.

Ramsey movingly explained his position, and defended this service of reconciliation, in a speech to the diocesan conference of the Canterbury diocese (26 October 1968).

I know that I am a priest and a bishop in the historic order, referred to in our prayer book as coming down from the apostles' times. I know that Methodist ministers are ministers of the Word and sacrament used by Christ and they have been for many, many years. I know that their ministry is not identical with the historic episcopate and priesthood, but I am unable to define precisely what the relative value of the two is. I am frankly agnostic about a great deal of the Methodist ministry, knowing that it is not identical with my own, but also being perfectly certain that they are not just laymen. I am frankly agnostic. Is there anything wrong in acknowledging that? I have not invented this agnosticism for the purpose of this service. I have all my life been agnostic about this. Very well then. In this laying on of hands with prayer I would be asking God through his Holy Spirit to give to the Methodist ministers what He knows that they need to make their ministry identical with ours as presbyters and priests in the Church of God. It would be perfectly clear what was being asked for, the equalization of our ministries. What would be undefined and undefinable is the present relative status. For that there is a great deal of room for variety of opinion. You might have your opinions, I might have mine, the Methodist minister might have his, but that doesn't come into the service. The service asks God to be good enough to make our ministries equal, giving to them what grace and authority he knows that we need . . .

What would I mean receiving that laying on of hands? I would mean this. I believe that I am a priest and bishop in the Church of God. Nothing can make me more so. But I do believe that my ministry will have a very new significance and authority as a result of this Anglican–Methodist union, and I pray that God will give me that enrichment and significance through receiving the laying on of hands from the Methodist president and his colleagues.

In his presidential address to the Convocation of Canterbury on 14 January 1969 he warned Convocation against the rejection of the scheme. He said that the service of reconciliation was accused of dishonesty on the ground of double meaning. 'I have done a good many things of doubtful morality, but I am sure that, if I am allowed to share in the service of reconciliation, this will not be one of them.'

The question now was, how would the Church of England accept the scheme? It would not be unanimous. It would not wish to act on a bare majority. What majority was needed to go forward? The two archbishops suggested an 80 per cent majority as the figure which should be sought, with a two-thirds majority in each of the three houses of the Church Assembly—bishops, clergy, and laity. The Methodists were willing to accept this proposal. In January 1969 the Convocations slightly eased the prospects by making the required majority 75 per cent instead of 80 per cent. In June 1969 there should be a referendum among the Anglican clergy whether they were willing to take part in the proposed service of reconciliation to inaugurate stage 1 of the scheme of union. This produced an average majority in favour of 'only' 68.5 per cent.

Was it now sensible to go ahead? They could do no other but try it. In July 1969 it came to the vote by both Churches. The opposition gained two bishops who were committed in favour but believed that the scheme was now too divisive, Bulley of Carlisle and Ronald Williams of Leicester. Ramsey spoke at length in favour of the union. There would be tension and strain if they went forward, there would be more tension and strain if they did not go forward. The Anglicans produced 69 per cent in favour, which they had agreed to call not enough; the Methodists at Birmingham produced 77.4 per cent, which they had agreed to call enough. When Ramsey announced the result of the vote there was a burst of clapping accompanied by cries of shame from the gallery. The *Daily Sketch* produced a vast headline, BOOS AS CHURCH BARS UNITY PLAN. All over the country people in pews had a sense of disappointment.

Ramsey to Eric Kemp (Dean-designate of Worcester, one of the Anglo-Catholic leaders who saw nothing uncatholic in the plan), 11 July 1969:

. . . I see the cause rather in the psychology of fear of change deepening and becoming obsessive and making use of various phenomena as a means of excusing itself, e.g. certain defects in the report, the myth that there was a better alternative, the myth that Rome was antagonistic, and for some the excuse that as Lord Fisher disliked the proposals there must be something fishy about them. When once the psychology of fear became really obsessive it was, I think, beyond the power of argument to help the situation. Now however the fact of the Methodist acceptance at the same moment as our rejection has given a big shock, and I think that the shock may already be beginning to have its effects upon people's attitudes . . .

More Christian worship went on with joint services of Anglicans and Methodists. The Archbishop marked this by holding a joint confirmation service in Canterbury cathedral, conducted by himself and the chairman of the Methodist district sitting side by side. Later that same year the Anglican theological college Queen's College, Birmingham, under its principal John Habgood, became a joint ecumenical college, and the Archbishop of Canterbury was present with the President of the Methodist Conference at its inauguration.

This was nothing like the end. Some observers held that the system was what was responsible—that Convocations and Church Assembly were still separate and cumbersome so that laity did not for the most part hear the clergy debate. It was agreed already that these bodies should merge into a General Synod. This reform came into effect on 6 November 1970, when the Queen attended the opening of the General Synod. And everyone who wanted union with the Methodists hoped that a more effective body for decision would produce a different decision—that meant, a larger majority in favour.

In July 1971 therefore the General Synod, meeting at York, voted in favour of the scheme by 65.3 per cent still with two bishops voting against. Ramsey spoke resolutely but not eloquently in favour. The question then went out to the dioceses, which produced 67.9 per cent in favour (the diocese of London right down, to 42.7 per cent). And in May 1972 the last vote was taken. It produced 65.81 per cent in favour—six bishops now voting against. The scheme was dead.

In the *Church Times* that week Margaret Duggan wrote a moving article to describe the scene. It was a very full house, and full galleries. 'It was the Archbishop of Canterbury's day' . . . 'His two speeches were wholly memorable; and compared with all others who spoke that day, he was in a class so on his own that he made the others look like non-starters . . . On that day the majority regard for him came something close to hero-worship.' People who had only heard him speaking when hesitant on a television interview, were astounded by the power of the personal utterance on a subject about which he cared deeply. Joan Ramsey sat in the gallery and it could be seen that the look on her face was tense as he spoke. Nobody else seemed to have much heart, and no one else scintillated. The controversy was not bitter, but it was boring —the thing had gone on too long. But Ramsey had the last word. 'To reassure us that all would not be entirely lost, he finished by quoting *Godspell*, "Long live God" he cried, "Long live God".'

Two days after the debate the Lord Mayor of London entertained the bishops to dinner at the Mansion House. Ramsey did not let the social occasion make him mince his words. 'It is not the first time that the Methodists have been the leaders of Christianity in this country . . . In these latter years we Anglicans have liked to think of ourselves as being the leaders in the matter of Christian unity. But at the moment we are not—the Methodists' (and he banged the table with his fist)—'it is the Methodists who are the leaders now.'

On 5 October 1972 an important event of English Church history took place, the union between the English Congregationalists and the English Presbyterians into the United Reformed Church. They invited Ramsey to speak in the Central Hall at Westminster and afterwards he walked with Cardinal Heenan in the celebration at the Abbey. The meeting gave Ramsey what an observer described as 'a tumultuous welcome'. He was probably the first Archbishop of Canterbury whom the free churchmen thought about as 'our archbishop', and some of them remembered that he was a Congregationalist in his origins. He made plain to them his conviction that while nobody wanted uniformity in way of worship, somehow or other the heirs of the Prayer Book, and the heirs of the old Congregationalists and Presbyterians who parted from the Church of England at the end of the English Civil War, and the Methodists, were meant in time to be one body of Christians.

This failure to unite with the Methodists, into which Ramsey put so much effort and conviction, was and is held to be the big failure of his life. Certainly it was a failure by the organs of the Church of England. The constitution of the Convocations, ever since they were framed in the Middle Ages, was not designed for this kind of exercise; and when they merged into the General Synod they were still not very suitable agents for what they were trying to do. The Church of England laid down in 1888 and in 1920 conditions for union. The Methodist Church accepted those conditions. Then the Church of England refused to unite with the Methodists. Was the Church of England seriously, and after all, and after such ardent talking, not interested in Christian unity? Were they uninterested in allowing the quality of Methodist life and faith and devotion to flow more freely among themselves?

Or was it just that the scheme proposed by a committee was not a good plan—it asked too many people to do things they would be embarrassed to do or about which they would feel something to be a sham?

Ramsey was blamed from two sides. Some people believed that he entered the argument too late; that while others published pamphlets, the Archbishop of Canterbury was quiet and restrained; that he should have stumped the country, converting his Church to the plan; that if he had given them earlier the muscular leadership which he gave during the last few months of the debate, he might have carried the day. Some people also believed and still believe that it was he and Archbishop Coggan who killed the scheme by demanding an unnecessarily large majority (they alleged) for carrying it out.

But the weightier criticism came from the other side. He was a representative figure to whom all the Church looked. Was it right to commit himself so strenuously to one side of a vehemently argued division within his Church? His old friend Ronald Williams, the Bishop of Leicester, who wanted the scheme but got into trouble for voting against it because it would be too divisive, and who much admired Ramsey, thought in retrospect that this failure to sit above the battle was the one big mistake of his time as Archbishop of Canterbury. Williams noticed in his memory the pain of the episode and how it brought Ramsey into heart-rending relationships with the Methodists, for whom, said Williams, he developed an enormous affection. Williams thought that the biggest mistake of all was to bring the plan forward a second time, after it was rejected in 1969, on the plea that the new General Synod would be more representative.

The historian of these events finds it hard to see how Ramsey could have acted other than he did. So long as the scheme was only in draft, he must be right to sit above the conflict so far as possible, except by making clear how he valued the Methodists. For in the moment when he entered one side of the fray, he would be accused of all sorts of wickedness—of which the worst charge was that he would only promote to bishoprics or deaneries people who thought just as he thought. Someone accused him, for example, of getting Eric Kemp made into the Dean of Worcester not because Kemp was a good Anglican priest and one of the most learned clergymen in England, but because he agreed with Ramsey on Anglican–Methodist unity. Someone else who disagreed with the scheme was sure that he would never get any promotion out of Ramsey and was bitter about it. These outrageous comments were a bit of the suffering which had to be endured by a leader who entered the fray on one side. Therefore it was better to desist from the fray for as long as was possible. The tradition that the Church is fair to all different schools of thought must at all costs be seen to be maintained.

But once the scheme was no longer in draft but was on the map, the idea that the Archbishop of Canterbury could keep his mouth shut was fanciful. His predecessor was not keeping his mouth shut, he kept opening it, and would have done so had he still been in office. It is impossible to imagine Ramsey's hero Archbishop Temple keeping his mouth shut. Archbishop Randall Davidson sounded so judicious that some people might have imagined him sitting comfortably on a fence; but closer examination of a Davidson text would show that this was not true. A century and a quarter before, Archbishop Howley would have spoken with such incoherence that the hearers might have imagined a mind which did not know what it thought; but this also would have been untrue on inspection. Some people said that archbishops were such representative persons that they should never speak out on any subject whatever. Some people said that it is always wrong for an archbishop to be in a controversy. It was not Ramsey's conception of his office that an archbishop is a stuffed dummy girt in brocade and topped by a candle-snuffing hat. He accepted the doctrine that anyone who talks too much loses influence. He refrained from many appeals to say something if he thought that he could achieve nothing by speaking. But his idea of a bishopric was that of an apostolic magisterium, or teaching office to which he was commissioned. If the question of practical union with another Church was not a big question, nothing was big.

In the retrospect of history, his leadership on this point was indispensable to the future morale and good feeling of the Church of England. Some people, whose judgement was to be respected, were against the scheme because they thought it a bad scheme. A majority of people thought that charity, integrity, and ordinary Christian kindness were in favour of going ahead with the scheme; and if their Church rejected it, that lowered their Church in their eyes. But no one could say that their Church did reject it properly, if the ecclesiastical head of the Church was the chief advocate of the scheme. A lot of them took far more notice of what Ramsey told them than of what 35 per cent of the Church Assembly said, for the Church as a whole cared little about the Church Assembly and cared a lot about the Archbishop of Canterbury. Ramsey, though he did not single-handed save the Christian charity of the Church of England, enabled many members of his Church to feel that their Church after all was a Church of Christian charity. If he had to endure acid letters from people abusing him for bringing division into parishes, he could be warmed by the heaps of letters of thanks which flowed into Lambeth from simple Christians all over the country.

More than one student of Michael Ramsey argued that he changed; that the Anglo-Catholic professor of Durham, who wrote most of the report *Catholicity*, the Anglo-Catholic Bishop of Durham who torpedoed loose attempts to get intercommunion with Protestants, had not the same mind as that possessed by the Archbishop of Canterbury when he advocated Methodist union. They noticed that he received communion at a Lutheran mass in Norway, and that he received communion at a Presbyterian celebration at the Churches' leaders' meeting of 1972, though he could (and did) justify it by a resolution of the 1968 Lambeth Conference. They did not suppose that he ceased from his glory in the Eastern Orthodox tradition or in his love of the Catholic faith; but they wondered whether one of two things affected him. Was it the far wider experience of the world and the Church which was brought to him when he became Archbishop of Canterbury? Or was it that his father died in 1954, and his early religion was marked by reaction from a pious Congregationalist father, and so after 1954 he accepted many more of the freedoms of his early Congregationalist tradition? There was no answer to this speculation. But in his old age he was asked about the theory. He thought that there was truth in the idea that his wider experience of the world and the Churches had a subtle effect upon his understanding of Catholicity.

But this was not to be exaggerated. In his first year as Archbishop of Canterbury he gave an address on the third centenary of the Prayer Book. This address is full of gratitude for Cranmer and the English book of prayers, though he also said, to a congregation which included the Queen and the prime minister, that revision was urgent. But at one point it is also full of gratitude for the nonconformist inheritance and what it gave to English religious life, from John Bunyan to the chapels where little folk learn to pray and love the Bible. If in later years he adjusted his mind to experience, it must not be thought that he was ever anything but grateful to the Congregationalist inheritance.

Yet within his heart something changed as a consequence of the vote and the failure. This he never allowed the outside world to see; only the most intimate friends.

When he was Bishop of Durham and was afraid that the Church of England might do something to make itself an uncatholic Church, he wondered whether he ought to resign his see. He asked himself whether he was now in the same situation—had the Church of England, his Church, done something uncatholic by its refusal? When reporters asked him whether he would resign his see because of the failure, they treated it like a prime minister resigning if his party failed to carry a weighty piece of policy in the House of Commons. And when Ramsey replied to the reporters, he treated the question lightly, as though archbishops are not in the situation of prime ministers, and said that he was not the sort of person to give up his job because he could not get what he wanted.

But inside himself the question was painful. He had loved the Church of England—did he now? He valued the Church of England above all for its intellectual integrity and its marriage of that integrity to a Scriptural and a Catholic faith. But had it behaved with intellectual integrity over the Methodists? On reflection he did not think that it had. Suddenly he found himself forced to ask himself again, after so many years of a settled mind, where he stood. What did he believe in? It was odd to be thinking like this when he seemed to have fixed his vocation once for all in the arguments with his brother Frank, and the experiences of Cambridge and Cuddesdon. He seemed to himself to be thrown back upon fundamental Christian truths, bigger and deeper than 'the C. of E.'—to confess again a faith in God the Holy Trinity, and a faith in the Holy Catholic Church as God's creation, and in the necessity that it should have a form as an institution in history. Could he now think that his Church lay within this historic form? He was sure, when he asked himself this question, that he could answer it with a Yes. But what he could no longer answer with a Yes was whether he had an enthusiasm for his Church, whether he could still plead with conviction, or feel, that it was the best of all Churches. It had undermined its claim to be that. And he consoled himself by remembering that Churches ought not to be proud of themselves and that Anglican pride was a little too apparent to members of other Churches.

'What then does one do?', he asked one of the Mirfield community, his long friend and colleague in the work for Catholic unity, Geoffrey Curtis. 'It is very painful. But I think the call is to *stay*, and not to despair; because' the faith in the Triune God and in the Holy Catholic Church 'stand as the essential rock, and because the Church of England has not put itself outside the Catholic Church. So we stay, and serve the Lord painfully and joyfully. What has vanished is the idea that being an Anglican is something to be commended to others as a specially excellent way.'[1]

Four hundred years before, an archbishop had agonized over his faith far more grievously than Michael Ramsey. But since Thomas Cranmer none had seemed to. We cannot be sure, because leaders with disciples have a duty not to show their inner hesitations to those who trust them. Before him Fisher had the certainty of common sense and public school religion. Temple before Fisher had the assurance of a faith structured within a system of Oxford idealist philosophy. Lang's scruples were personal, hardly of faith. Davidson before Lang was the last to be rooted in a whole society which was still reasonably assured about religion. But Ramsey saw no certainty in common sense, and was no philosopher, and was an integrated personality, and grew up in a household where the cleverest young man in England battered at his beliefs. He was, it seems, the first archbishop in modern English history who was made to cling to his assurance of faith. God the creator; God the redeemer, God dwelling among his people—those were his certainties; and the bad weeks of June–July 1972 were a time when he went back to his foundation.

---

[1] Ramsey to Father Geoffrey Curtis, CR 20 June 1972, Borthwick Institute, Mir 14/D11.

2. THE LUTHERANS

Of all the Churches on the Continent of Europe, the Lutherans of Germany and Scandinavia were the most akin to the Methodists.

From his postgraduate studies in Germany Ramsey knew the Lutheran and Reformed Churches of Europe and respected their scholarship and the thought. Then at Amsterdam and other meetings of the World Council of Churches or its committees he was often up against Barth or Schlink in argument. In 1957–8 the Swedish Parliament voted the right of women to be ordained priests. Since the Church of England was in communion with the Church of Sweden, this raised a difficulty with all the Anglo-Catholics, and Ramsey had to study the Scandinavian Lutherans. In the sixties he was forced by the cries about 'religionless Christianity' or a 'demythologized Christianity' to study the Germans Bonhoeffer and Bultmann. But for all his capacity for sympathy, the continental Reformation was not the natural world of an Anglo-Catholic. He could respect their thought and their attitudes but it was hard for him to share them. His reading lay in the Bible and the Fathers and the Easterners and in the old Anglican divines; much less or not at all, in Luther or Calvin or John Knox or Melanchthon. One of his fellow-presidents of the World Council of Churches was the German pastor Martin Niemöller, the tough leader of the German Church resistance against the Nazis. Ramsey admired Niemöller as one of his heroes, for what he suffered under Hitler. But although they were fellow-presidents, he never got to know Niemöller; partly because they were both irregular at going to meetings, and partly because Niemöller had a robust dislike of the idea of an archbishop, and partly because Ramsey had no devotional sympathy with Niemöller's tradition in religious thought. It remained to be seen how an Anglo-Catholic Archbishop of Canterbury, who wholly approved of the ecumenical movement but was not regular in attending those meetings where he was likely to converse with Lutherans, would manage with that important bit of Christendom, who numbered the third largest Christian denomination in the world.

The politics of Europe complicated his life. There was still no peace treaty with Germany after the second World War. Down the middle of historic Germany ran the Wall, the most immoral European sacrament of the aggressions and fears of humanity. Beyond the Wall to the East lay the only large Protestant Church under Marxist and atheist rule. The Wall prohibited the Church from common action with its brothers in the Lutheran Churches of West Germany. It was far from certain that Ramsey would be allowed beyond the Wall. If he only visited Germany this side of the Wall, he was part of the western Cold War alliance against Communism; and at a time when his affection for Patriarch Alexei of Moscow and his friendliness with the Russians did something to make the Cold War less cold.

In 1964 he went to Sweden to attend the eighth centenary of Uppsala cathedral.

In the same year he went to West Germany where he met leaders of the German Evangelical Church and visited the British Army of the Rhine. On 9 November he addressed the synod of the Hanover Church (where the bishop was Lilje, who served so bravely under Hitler) —what do we learn from Luther? The supremacy of Holy Scripture —our salvation is never won by merits or works—the kingship and priesthood of all believers—faith is to be expressed in good works. He said that he was grateful that Anglican–Lutheran conversations had begun. On 10 November 1964, which was the anniversary of the birthday of Martin Luther, he gave the address in St Lawrence's Church in Nuremberg; and said that though not a Lutheran he could share with them in thanking God for great truths to which Luther bore witness and could learn gratefully from him.

The question of going to East Germany was on the map in 1970 but it seemed the wrong thing to do until the State was recognized by the British government. In the autumn of 1970 he received a delegation from East Germany to Britain under Bishop Schönherr of East Berlin.

In September 1970 he received at Lambeth a delegation from the International Synod of the Latvian Lutheran Church. In the following month he received a delegation from the Polish Lutherans in Britain. During 19–24 May 1971 he went to Oslo to celebrate the 900th anniversary of Christianity in the diocese. He was warned to expect a critical reception and hostile questions from the press, but nothing like that happened. He was given dinner by the King of Norway in Oslo Castle and gave an address at the morning centenary service in the old church ruins of St Halvard and afterwards gave the blessing at the high mass in the cathedral and gave a lecture in the university lecture-room where twenty years before he had listened to Emil Brunner lecturing. In Oslo he received the holy communion at the Lutheran liturgy. He justified the act as 'an act anticipatory of the relations of communion which we hope will come before long between our Churches'. Then he flew to Trondheim and visited the national shrine and gave an address there and lectured to the pastors; he went on to Copenhagen 24–27 May. In both Norway and Denmark he was widely reported in the press. Various reporters asked him impromptu questions and he gave free answers—yes, it was possible that the World Council Grants to guerrilla organizations in Africa would be used for military purposes; was pornography bad?—sex in advertising was worse because more subtle.

Afterwards he asked himself and others about the prospects of intercommunion with the Scandinavian Churches. He thought that it could only be achieved if Norway and Denmark took from Sweden the apostolic succession for their bishops—or, putting it more administratively, 'regularized' their bishops. His conversations in Norway showed him that the Norwegians seemed quite happy with the idea. His conversations in Denmark showed him that the Danes were very unhappy with the idea. Some of them said that apostolic succession of bishops was worse than unnecessary, it was evil.

In May 1974 he went at last to East Germany. It was made possible by circumstances outside his control: by the less rigid policy of the West German government towards the East; by the Pope being willing at last to recognize the Polish dioceses in that part of Poland which was formerly in Germany, as true dioceses and not as temporary expedients. That is: a more general acceptance in the West of the new eastern border of Germany, or western frontier of Poland; a partial forgetting that the Poles seized a lot of historic German territory and ejected millions of Germans. This was hard to achieve; but once it was achieved it made it more possible to cross the Wall.

He preached in the cathedral of East Berlin, and made history by being the first Church leader to be received by the East German head of State, Willi Stoph, the man who decided to build the Berlin Wall. As was his way he was perfectly frank. He told Willi Stoph that it was not enough to end the Cold War, that the Cold Peace must be turned into a warm peace, and that ordinary people should be able to travel. The phrase *warm peace* was taken up by the western press and for a few days was famous. He went to Leipzig and admired the singing of the famous choir at St Thomas' church and preached there to a packed congregation. Here occurred one of those unplanned incidents which enchanted Ramsey's followers. To St Thomas's was lately moved the grave of J. S. Bach. Ramsey went over to the stone and laid on it three roses and gave thanks for the gift of Bach's music to mankind; and the three roses moved the vast congregation. He visited Goethe's house in Weimar and walked among curious streets and a few scoffing teenagers and then visited the site of the Buchenwald concentration camp and prayed in the cell of the martyred pastor Paul Schneider, who died after brutal torture by his guards; and put a message in the visitors book which he ended in capitals—CHRIST IS RISEN. Then he went to Martin Luther—to the Wartburg, and Eisenach, and Erfurt; and in the room of the Wartburg Castle where Luther translated the Bible he prayed the famous collect of the 1662 Prayer Book—'Blessed Lord, who has caused all holy Scriptures to be written for our learning, grant that we may in such wise hear them, read, mark, learn, and inwardly digest them, that . . .'. In the Roman Catholic cathedral at Erfurt he presided at an ecumenical service, two Roman Catholic bishops on the one side and two Lutheran bishops on the other; and as he moved to the door at the end the large congregation broke out into applause. He was not naïve about East Germany. He disliked it that children could not receive religious instruction at school; and that there was an anti-Christian rite of confirmation; and that students at the university had to take a course in Marxism; and that no new churches could be built. But he found it different from modern Moscow; a truer freedom for Christian worship within a Communist country. Years later at Ramsey's death the presiding Lutheran bishop in East Germany said that this visit was important in bridging the Wall.

PART 5

——

THE MAN OF GOD

15

The Silences

1. THIS WORLD AND THE OTHER

The impression of Ramsey's personality was striking but seldom formidable. The railway porters and ticket collectors recognized him as he was so recognizable and could be seen warming to his smile and his eyebrows. He had a face which easily burst into hilarity, but though the laugh was vast, and might have come under Dr Samuel Johnson's aspersion on the merriment of clergymen, it did not sound to the listener raucous. One trained observer talked of seeing him in a purple cassock, now chuckling like some jolly monk, now 'solemnly compassionate like a carving of God the Father'.[1] Someone published a collection of comic photographs of him, looking rollicking or quaint, and called it *The Canterbury Pewside Book*. Ramsey was asked privately whether he minded this pulling of his leg and he did not mind in the least. The book was irreverent, but it was dedicated to 'the genial Friar Tuck of a man . . . whose unfailing good humour and generosity of spirit is an example to all Christians and non-Christians alike'.

He was likely to end a sentence, or wait for his own reply to a sentence, or prepare some humorous epigram, or take a space to meditate upon a considered answer to a questioner, by saying, in a decreasing order of decibels, 'Yes . . . yes . . . yes . . . yes'. An interested listener once counted more than twenty yeses in succession. They were pleasant and humorous to hear, they did not embarrass. We have from a visitor to Lambeth Palace a picture of his reception. 'The Archbishop . . . arms held high above his head in a form of greeting . . . He looked so benign as he continued nodding and beaming with his arms still in the air . . . I reached up to his right hand and shook it. "Ah!" he said suddenly, beckoning towards an armchair. "Yes, yes, yes, yes, yes".' When the visitor left, he looked back and Ramsey 'was

[1] David Edwards, in Martin, *Great Christian Centuries*, 8.

smiling, holding his hands together as if in prayer, rocking them gently. One felt good'.[2]

He could repeat phrases often. A small girl explained to him her difficulty in rowing; that she caught a continuous series of crabs and kept being knocked backwards. 'Very natural,' said Ramsey, 'very natural . . . very natural . . . very natural. You need a rhythm . . . you need a rhythm . . . you need a rhythm.' They came in to tell him that a clergyman had died, and that clergyman's career was controversial. Ramsey said, 'Not the beatific vision yet. No. Not the beatific vision yet. No. Not yet.' His bushy eyebrows were mobile. Princess Margaret was once reported to have said, 'He waggled his eyebrows and we could not understand him.' The Queen was alleged to have begged him, during a rehearsal for the coronation, to keep his eyebrows still because they made her smile and she did not wish to smile in the wrong place. Probably such stories were *ben trovato* rather than true, but they were credible.

When Ramsey was Archbishop of York Leonard Woolf published the first volume of his autobiography, and declared that often the faces of dignitaries of the Church of Rome and the Church of England had a sullen malevolence, and said that it was perhaps difficult to reach high office in the law or the Church without becoming a hypocritical and angry old man. This was not the only foolish thing which Woolf wrote but it was probably the most foolish. Ramsey could be cross, even angry; his face could frown, his eyebrows could beetle; but malevolence and Ramsey were opposite ends of the scale of humanity. He could despise folly or illiteracy; he found it hard to forgive illiterate bishops, or woolly-mindedness in bishops. He was the least angry of old men, or of young men either, if by those phrases is meant a person bitter against his time and generation. His confidence in society and the Churches, his wishes for society and the Churches, were realistic, but they were full of hope. He always raised morale.

Leonard Woolf classified the faces of archbishops. Ramsey's face did not fit the category. The square jaw, big lower lip, long mouth, big upper lip, almost gave the impression of three parallel lines, topped by a Roman nose; the long straggling eyebrows coming down at an angle over the eyes, big ears flat to the head, and then the great bald dome above. He talked with both hands out, all fingers together, breast-high but usually going up and down, coming together at points, rising in emphasis to shoulder height and occasionally even to head height, elbows always bent. Sometimes he would make an emphasis by slap-

[2] John Heilpern in *Observer*, 18 Apr. 1971, 25.

ping his knee, or slapping the arm of the chair. Occasionally he would slap with a sudden alarming knock the actual pages of the Bible, or the book in front of him. But mostly when he picked up the Bible he was like the director of an art gallery gloating over the delicacy of his most precious and most newly acquired picture, with an air of ecstasy at the possession mingled with the happiness of searching out the full meaning to be found in it. His unathletic fingers touched the pages with a reverence which had something of the informed care of a collector running his fingers over an old piece of Chinese porcelain; not because it was fragile but because it was unique.

He had no manual co-ordination, and no dexterity. He never picked up anything like anyone else. He would seize a saucer with his first finger uppermost and the thumb on the underside. He could never make his fountain-pen work properly, and when the ink did not flow he would shake it so that walls and carpet and fingers and even cassock could be peppered with the flying stains of ink. But his handwriting was mostly legible if the reader worked at it a little, until in his old age it shrank into script so small that before his friends could read their letter they had to write above some of the words what they thought they might be. At Fiji the lack of dexterity turned into a social disaster. He had to drink a ceremonial draught of coconut liquid in a prescribed ritual way amid a watching group, and however hard they tried to get him to do it right, he could not manage the physical act; and his staff could not rescue the situation by explaining that he could not do it for physical reasons and intended no offence.

The voice range was quiet to loud, deep to high—a higher tone in excitement—each consonant pronounced so that he was audible when soft. It had the touch of sing song which many people smiled at and some found parsonical but which was attractive to listen to and never monotonous on the ear. People rarely slept during his utterances. He was always audible; however big the audience, however bad the acoustics. The voice was clear and high; and the manner of speech was almost like plainsong, which carried to the west door of vast cathedrals without a sense of strain.

Despite his large bodily frame, he existed on a light diet. He was not teetotal, he liked it if there was a visitor and he had a glass of sherry before dinner and a glass of hock with dinner. He never drank spirits. He cared very little about his appearance. It was the chaplain's duty, prompted by Joan, to ensure that the cassock was clean and the hair cut and the lawn ironed before a solemn occasion.

He said late in life, 'I loved to preach—if I felt that they wanted to know. If I got no reaction, I felt depressed. Preaching and talking about

God is a dialogue. It is a giving and receiving.' He was willing to preach the same sermon in different places. A Durham sermon got into four Cambridge colleges in succession. He liked to preach from notes and not a full text. 'The object of notes is to get it into the head beforehand. If I construct sentences I read them and that has led to several disasters. My head and my eyes are not in harmony.' While he was Archbishop of York he came to Cambridge to preach at a university sermon in the evening and at teatime visited his Aunt Lucy, whom many years before he helped to prepare for confirmation. After tea he wrote out a whole mass of paper for an hour and then threw it all into the waste paper basket. Lucy said, 'Do you realise that you have thrown away your sermon?' Ramsey replied, 'Yes. But I have a photographic memory.'

This was not always his method. At the time of the controversy about 'religionless Christianity', which most people thought to be a nonsense-phrase, Ramsey went down to Cambridge to preach a university sermon about it (23 February 1964) and about the name of the German martyr associated with the idea, Dietrich Bonhoeffer. Although the time was 2.30 on a Sunday afternoon the undergraduates turned up to hear him in large numbers. In this sermon it was noticed that he had a large packet of notes, too large for the lectern on the pulpit. It took just over half an hour in delivery. Opinions differed. The regius professor of divinity said that it was a fine sermon. A historian in the congregation ran back over the centuries in his mind and decided that the last Archbishop of Canterbury who could have preached a university sermon of that calibre was Tillotson (1691). A young Jesuit in the gallery went to sleep. The Senior Proctor, who was not an ardent churchgoer but had to be there from his office, said that he found the delivery bad and he had never heard of this German Bottlegruber.

In February 1970 he went to Cambridge again to deliver four sermons in the university church on successive Sundays at 8.30 p.m. The church was full each night, and on the first Sunday he was relayed by an overflow to the Senate House. The vice-chancellor thought the first sermon too long for the material—over 35 minutes—but all the other three were regarded as utterances of excellence; yet it was observed, about the notes which he used, that during his third sermon the lighting of the pulpit went wrong so that he could hardly see the notes at all; and the utterance sometimes stumbled, yet the listeners agreed it to be fine.

Hugh Montefiore, the vicar of the university church at Cambridge during part of Ramsey's time as archbishop, who was concerned to find preachers who could hold the attention of students at the big under-graduate service on Sundays, regarded Ramsey as the best preacher whom he could invite for the purpose. He said, 'They hung on his lips'; and afterwards he was 'brilliant at questions'.

He was valued as a conductor of retreats; not surprisingly. About the silences of a retreat he was humane, for when he conducted a retreat at Cuddesdon he introduced silent croquet into the programme.

We have a portrait of him by someone who attended a retreat which he gave at the retreat house at Pleshey in Essex. He sat in front of the altar of the little chapel with his prayer book and notes on a little stool, but never referred to them. He could quote not just a sentence but long passages from memory—the hymn 'O Strength and Stay', the hazel-nut of the Lady Julian of Norwich, a passage from St Irenaeus out of the second century. The only sign of age was an increased waddle in the gait. He talked on the transfiguration, one of his favourite themes. He occasionally used Greek words to add to a point, but always explained them. It was a biblical, very biblical, indeed evangelical exegesis of the gospel texts. Once he said '*gooder*' and hastily corrected to '*better*' showing that he had not intended the word. Suddenly he would break into poetry—St Peter making shelters on the mountain to make them stay and not melt away like mists on the mountainside—but the line was thrown away, he had no consciousness that it was poetry, there was no sense of rhetoric nor of anything artificial. He would use an occasional startling phrase. The only non-biblical phrase which he used was 'the night of sense—I believe that this phrase of the spiritual writers conveys much truth'. Some of the utterances were memorable—'There are *people* who make God near. This is the most marvellous thing that one human being can do to another.' He conveyed a sense of glory; of closeness to God; and an unearthly sort of comfort from that. When he said a thing was *tremendous* or *exciting* the hearers realized that it was indeed tremendous and exciting. They did not subtract from these words of conventional overstatement.

He thought for himself all the time. He had a closeness of meditation on the passion; almost line by line. He loved the symbolism of St John's gospel. An address on the washing of the feet in St John was full of humour, wreathed in smiles, punctuated with chuckles, radiant with happiness. The address had a total simplicity of idea and construction, yet the simplicity was somehow elaborated without being elaborate. He dwelt on the text with affection, almost with glee. He never hesitated or said 'Er'. He never needed to go back in a sentence to correct the grammar. All flowed in perfect construction of sentences. He once said 'between he and us' and he once used the non-existent verb *ultimatize* to mean, making the State into the end of life.

The addresses were shot through with smiles and amusement without the least detraction from reverence or the least lowering of tone. The amusement relieved the high language and made it sound still higher. The retreat addresses were quite short; probably less than fifteen minutes each. No one could fail to be lifted towards the rest of their soul in God. The last address was on heaven, and was perfect eloquence for the highest of themes—and without notes. He bubbled with ecstasy over the beatific vision. He had so real a sense of the joining with angels and archangels here and now in worship. He ended movingly, 'Thank you so much for letting me join you. Alleluia, Amen.'

Going into breakfast someone smiled at him. He looked at him sourly. He celebrated the holy communion, Rite A, with a profound quiet, and without emphases. He could be heard humming the tune of the hymn when it was played over (this hum was celebrated, it led some people to nickname him Winnie-the-Pooh) and he sang all the verses of the hymn though he had no book in front of him. In the confessional he was affectionate, humane, and wise—accepting an attrait but adding to it with a delicacy and sureness of touch.

Such is the portrait of Ramsey conducting a retreat. A retreat is a time when the personality of the conductor is very exposed to his hearers. All this was at the centre of his personality.

If he sat down at a meal he could make no effort to start a conversation with his neighbour if that neighbour was an adult and unknown to him—if the neighbour was a student it could be different. If he were placed next to another shy person at a meal, the two would sit side by side in silence throughout the meal and the hostess or host would wonder desperately what to do about the situation. There was a rumour that when he was at York the general officer commanding the army in the north came to pay a courtesy call and the conversation came to a total halt. Some people regarded small talk as courtesy and thought that anyone unable to discuss whether it will rain tomorrow was guilty of not making an effort needed by society. Such people were apt to think him inconsiderate or even rude. They did not realize that he did not regard words as an essential means of communicating between human beings.

These silences were more awkward with women than men. Women would sit next to him at a meal and come away afterwards with no sense of rapport whatever. The exception to this rule was widows when their husbands had just died and they needed comfort. He would say nothing or almost nothing, but he would seize her hand and shake it again and again and again, with an inarticulate passing into her of the sincerity and warmth of his fellow-feeling and his pity.

Even people who knew him well found occasions when it was impossible to get him going. Get him going and everyone would have a very good time. He could be very comic in reminiscing. He was most easily got going on some subject that was historical or in part theological. And if his interest was keen, his talk would be like a flame leaping upward. His after-dinner speeches could be brilliant—not quite so funny as Fisher's, which were always a rollicking leg-pull—but a delight to hear, and they sparkled not only with humour and bonhomie but with wit. The hearer was reminded that this was once the undergraduate president of the Cambridge Union. When Dean Matthews of St Paul's attained his ninetieth birthday Ramsey proposed his health in the Jerusalem Chamber and the utterance was agreed by the guests to be perfect of its genre.

He was a man of affections and loyalties. Any colleague who once won his respect would also win something of his affection and that affection stayed ever afterwards. De-la-Noy, the information officer, said about him in his book on Lambeth (p. 35) that he was essentially a lonely and sad man with no close friends apart from his wife. This is a wrong judgement.

Everyone is agreed that he would have been lost without Joan. If he was ill she got into a terrible state, if she was ill he got into a terrible state. One of his staff who worked with him over many years and was intimate with them both said, 'It was one of the closest unions I have ever observed at close quarters, and very moving.' When he came back from some engagement she was always at the door to welcome him and they would walk up the stairs together hand in hand.

No one was less sad as a person. He felt the burden of the world and the Churches. He felt injustice even if it was four thousand miles away, and it was a grief to him. But he threw it all in faith onto his Redeemer whom he saw as a saviour from the world's suffering, and was deep down light in heart; and this lightness kept bubbling up among his friends in laughter and affection and charm and compassion. And there must be quite a number of people still living in the world whose experience proves the contradiction of the dictum that he had no close friends.

Yet there was something about him which gave various people the impression that he was not a man of friends. They saw that he loved God; they saw that he loved Joan; they saw that the pinnacle on which the Church placed him isolated him of necessity. But they also saw that he did not seem to need them. He did not look to his staff, or to the bishops, or to his family, for ordinary company to make him happy. Many of his closest friends were books. A new book would arrive in the post and at once he was at it, and it could take such hold of him that he would not fulfil his next engagement on time. He was a fast reader. He liked sniffing books. He said, 'I always like sniffing books because if you know a book really well, its smell means something to you. Yes, yes. The smell of books is very fascinating.' Once he was asked how in his busy life he found so much time for reading, and he said, 'I approach it like an alcoholic his drink, secretly and often.'

Some of his favourite books he read several times. He liked to come back at a book at certain seasons. A book which once helped him at Easter, for example, might be brought off the shelves again on successive Easters. The journey to holidays at Holne in Devon was accompanied by several packages of books, and after he retired and went by train, a packing case was sent off for delivery.

Most of the books were in English, but apart from his Latin and Greek he read French and German easily. But as he had no ear for language, his spoken German was hard to understand and his spoken French would have made Frenchmen wince if they were not so courteous.

He was very good with other people's dogs. If he stayed in a house and made friends with the dog, the dog was likely to receive a letter afterwards from Ramsey, addressed by name to him on the envelope.

On holidays he and Joan went every year to Holne near Ashburton in Devon, to the oak-timbered Church House Inn (ten bedrooms, ten guineas a week all in, 1961 prices); and every day he went out for a stout walk in a tweedy grey-flecked sports jacket which only just seemed to get round his bulk, and baggy flannel trousers and a tie and a cloth cap and a heavy ash walking stick and a mackintosh slung over his shoulder. The customers noticed that though he did not go into their bar he had a flagon of cider on his table. In the road the local males took off their caps as he passed and the local women curtsied. At times the local anglers brought in a catch for the Ramseys' table. If there was a fête he had three goes for sixpence on the hoop-la and a coconut shy. Holidays were four weeks in August and a week after Christmas and Easter. The people of Dartmoor renamed a footpath upward to the moor Ramsey's Way.[3]

At Lambeth or Canterbury he never went to bed late and never got up very early, and got through quite a lot of reading in bed. From about 7.15 a.m. he would be into the chapel to meditate for half an hour. The morning service (matins, then holy communion—which in the privacy of his 'family' he normally called the eucharist, but if speaking to a high churchman he might call mass) was always at 7.45 a.m. and was celebrated alternately by himself and by one of the chaplains. At Bishopthorpe he always read from the Ronald Knox translation of the

³ *Western Times Gazette*, 7 Sept. 1972.

Bible and he followed this custom at first at Lambeth but then changed to the Jerusalem Bible, and his chaplains found that he read most memorably, often with great humour. The chaplains felt that this round of prayer—'blessed and sensible regimen', said one of them—was what kept him sane under the pressures. As the new liturgies came out they were tried out in the chapel as an experiment. After a new liturgy he would see some absurdity and his comment would have a salty humour. But this could happen with the oldest of liturgies. He went to the low church theological college in London, Oak Hill; and found himself and his chaplain kneeling each end of the altar, north and south. It suddenly came over him that they looked like book-ends, and laughter that was hardly decorous came quickly.

At ritual he was magnificent and reverent and conjured reverence. But he never liked processions. Just occasionally earlier habits recurred, and he could be heard whistling 'Turn back O man' in the middle of a procession while the choir sang a hymn. He enjoyed ritual calamities as long as they did not make for irreverence among the people. At the Christmas Day service in York Minster in 1960, while Dean Milner-White preached on the carol 'I saw three ships come sailing by', Ramsey fidgeted on his archiepiscopal throne and got his feet trapped under the rug; and in full view of the congregation an embarrassed chaplain had to crawl in a heavy blue cloak and release his toes.

Once when he was asked about his own devotion he said this: 'You build up what some writers call an interior castle . . . to be able to have a kind of interior serenity and tranquillity in the midst of all the many storms of life. I find the daily quietness myself most valuable at the time of holy communion.' There was a brisk exchange once with a pert American reporter:

Q. Have you said your prayers this morning?
R. Yes.
Q. What did you say in your prayers?
R. I talked to God.
Q. How long did you talk to God?
R. I talked to God for one minute. But it took me twenty-nine minutes to get there.

Everyone who was near him at times of devotion felt his humility and sense of Presence. Sometimes he could be felt to 'lose himself'; it could happen in the middle of a morning's work, or even in the car on the way to an engagement. He was unusual in that he preferred a silent time of prayer where most other people would have felt a necessity for words.

More than one person, taking new and important work, asked if he might come and pray with him. In each case Ramsey simply sat in silence for half an hour with the other person; not a word was spoken, until at the end Ramsey said, 'Thankyou. That was very helpful'. It is possible that some of the silences which embarrassed the visitor were of this sort. He interviewed Michael Saward for the post of radio and television officer. They sat in armchairs and the interview lasted three-quarters of an hour. A third of the total time was in silence. The candidate found this gruelling.

From time to time he made his confession; with a regularity, either three or four times a year, it cannot now be known which. He never had a single person every time as his confessor. Wherever he found himself at the right time, he looked for a nearby priest. That is, it was not direction or guidance of soul for which he looked. It was the meeting with God in penitence through the sacrament.

The private meetings of any pastor are impossible to record and wrong to record if one could do it. But some evidence exists; usually a little letter of thanks from someone who came to him in turmoil of mind and left with the sensation that he was helped. A single example of these very private communications will suffice. An intelligent man was to marry a devout woman. He had no faith in God but it bothered him that he had no faith in God, and he respected his wife's faith and would like at least to understand it if not to share it. He went to Ramsey at Lambeth; we do not know how often but at least twice, and each time for more than an hour. At first he was surprised by the 'tolerance', that is, respect for the sincere agnostic, which he found. The second time he dreaded to go back to Lambeth because he knew that still he could not say what Ramsey would like to hear. But during the hour or more that he sat with the archbishop, he said that a strange sense of peace came over him and that in many ways he felt closer to God than for a very long time. This experience was not too uncommon. Quite a lot of people who sat for a time with Ramsey, not just for small talk but to discuss something serious to the personality, felt closer to God after the conversation—and after more than the conversation, it was after the experience.

Under Fisher the frock coat and gaiters were still *de rigueur* for bishops. Laymen expected it and did not think their bishop treated them seriously if they appeared in any other costume. Fisher could be fierce in his insistence that the bishops must wear gaiters at bishops' meetings.

Ramsey possessed frock coat and gaiters and in them looked magnificent. The waddle in his walk was grander when his legs were encased in gaiters. When he was Archbishop of Canterbury he wore them at times if they were expected, as when he was enthroned, or in Bermuda. But otherwise he always wore a purple cassock. Even abroad he appeared in a purple cassock and a Canterbury cap. The purple cassock was just as striking to the beholder as the gaiters. If the object was not to be ostentatious it was not a good change. A person who when travelling on the Moscow Tube is mistaken by another passenger for the Pope is evidently not so dressed as to merge unnoticed into the background. But the cassock no longer carried the faint suggestion of Barchester. It was that of a more international and less insular sort of bishop. This was a benefaction to bishops, that single-handed he should destroy their obligation to wear an archaic and expensive costume. The change was quick. Four years after he became archbishop a national newspaper took the trouble to report that the Bishop of London appeared in gaiters. Not everyone thought the change an improvement. Ritualists wondered whether something was lost by what one of them called 'sartorial permissiveness' in bishops. But for Ramsey the change was symbolic of something more. He was not interested in the prelatical or hierarchical or triumphalist type of archbishop. He did not think much of being called My Lord or Your Grace, though he was not so rude as to stop laity or clergy who adopted the old salutation.

The apparently trivial change had two consequences which were unexpected. It made the Church a little less openly hierarchical; and it made some Buckingham Palace garden parties a little more ecclesiastical. If bishops did not wear gaiters, deans and archdeacons were not likely to do so and would not be expected by society to do so. Deans and archdeacons had no other distinguishing marks to show who they were and they looked just like parish clergy. The idea of a 'dignitary' in the Church was weakened.

Someone suggested to the Lord Chamberlain that clergy might be allowed to wear cassocks (if they wished) instead of frock coats at Buckingham Palace garden parties. The Lord Chamberlain consulted Ramsey, who approved. Lord Fisher protested. He said that the alternative to formal dress is a lounge suit and he was afraid of a demarcation between Anglican clergy and ministers of other denominations. But the option remained.

The change made one difference from formality. Gaiters were accompanied by a black hat with a rosette on the hat-band and strings which were the relic of the days when bishops rode horses. The cassock was accompanied by a velvet purple Canterbury cap. Ramsey had a party-trick which meant the expenditure of a velvet cap. If he found himself among a young and cheerful party, he might fling his cap high and let them tumble for it. In Bermuda he broke away from a procession of dignitaries and crossed the square to 200 children and had them after his cap sailing through the air. In the English College at Rome, where the students revelled in him, the cap chase was his farewell. At the college at Maynooth in Ireland the cap was caught by an athletic priest and rammed on the head of the president of the College. And once even the missionaries who came to a garden party at Lambeth Palace scrambled after the cap, which was caught for ever, high in the air, by a camera.

When he began at Lambeth an enormous black limousine transported the archbishop and someone in Australia made it or him a present of streaming flags for its bonnet, which made policemen salute instinctively as its long lines passed. He liked spreading all his books and papers over the back seat. But soon he had a Morris 1000 for shorter journeys. It was thought to be the only chauffeur-driven Morris 1000 in the country. The passenger seat had to be mounted nine inches further back than is normal. The chauffeur preferred driving the larger car, which after a few years he changed to a Ford.

The chauffeur, who was also a sort of butler, Walter Brindle, became one of Ramsey's personal friends. He had chauffered William Temple and Garbett and stayed eighteen years with Ramsey.

Ramsey made it a principle to accept jobs when they were offered to him without enquiring about the stipend or the house in which he and Joan were to live. When he offered someone else a job, it pleased him if the person made no enquiry about stipend before accepting it; though he did not hold it against a candidate who enquired. He had no interest in gardens. His visit to Tresco in the Scilly Islands paid no attention to the flowers. He was not interested by visual beauty, unless it was in church architecture. He loved church music as well as church buildings, and in his study would play records of anthems and plainsong, and this was the third recreation after walking and reading political biographies.

They told him that statistics showed the number of worshippers declining or the number of ordinands inadequate or the church buildings falling down. These glooms made not the least impression. He did not pay the smallest attention to the analysis of contemporary society, or plead that he was the first archbishop to cope with the full force of television and therefore with the reluctance of people to go out and with the decline of every meeting, whether political or theatrical or worshipping. He pleaded no excuse because he thought no excuse to be called for. He simply replied that he went to a university and 1,500 young people turned up to hear him; or that 2,000 young people turned up at Canterbury cathedral; or that all his experience contradicted the idea that Christianity was for the older generation; or that even if people went to church less often the depth in prayer of the generation was manifest. But not all of this was observation. It was inner conviction that God looks after his Church and although we do not know where Christianity is going it will still be doing its work for humanity in a century or two centuries and we can rest in that faith.

This was very good for the morale of the Churches and even of the nation. He was not a doubter. When he looked back he would say to himself that there were three times in his life when he doubted his faith—once at school after the preparation for confirmation, once when his mother was killed, and once when his brother Frank died. His difficulty of faith, after the early battles with his brother, was not doubt that God is, but resentment at what he does. In old age he said, 'Except for an agnostic patch in my teens, I've never doubted the existence of God. But I've sometimes found my faith in him so painful that I would rather have been without it. But that is the Christian way. Since the early tragedies of my life (the deaths of my mother and my brother) I have been as sensitive as anyone can be to suffering—God himself taking on the darkness of alienation. That has made me very wary of any attempt to reconstruct the Christian faith without maintaining the place of the cross of Christ in the redemption of suffering.'

In some respects he was not a layman's archbishop. The academic in him was hard for the layman to follow. At first he was not good on television; and though he gradually grew more comfortable in front of the camera and by the end of his time had mastered the technique, his talk was sometimes, even then, too high or difficult for the average layman or laywoman. Curiously, although he never said 'Er' in private conversation, because his 'Yes yes' was a form of 'Er', that is, a way of pausing while thinking how to go on—the transcript of a television interview with Eamonn Andrews records 25 'Ers' in a total of sixteen answers. For the astringent laymen the manner was against him—'just an old parson', one heard said after some television interview. Gerald Ellison thought that while laymen could understand Fisher and Coggan, they could make neither head nor tail of Ramsey.

But whether they approved of him or not, everyone saw that religion and theology were central to his being; and more, that these two things, religion and theology, which in most people are two distinct things, were in him a unity.

He was still the Liberal politician of his youth. Despite the other-worldliness he was far from taking no interest in politics. He suspected what the Conservative Party did. He tried to like what the Labour Party did but mostly could not manage it. He was always a man of the liberal centre, a little bit more to the left of centre than right. He disliked class distinctions. He warmed towards people who spoke in the accents of the north country. During his retirement he talked to the Durham students' union about the difference between a very spiritual sort of Church which kept away from the world and a very politically minded Church where the life of the spirit decayed; and then argued that each extreme was wrong; and he illustrated this *via media* by the words, the Church of England 'is a sort of perpetual Lib–Lab pact between the two schools of thought'.[4] And he went on to tell students that while the two major parties leap-frogged each other in offering material bribes to the electorate, the Liberal Party always stuck to its ideals. More than fifty years after the Liberal undergraduate leader inspired his party, we can still see him holding to those early-won principles.

In June 1977 the Liberal Party marked its 'centenary' by long sponsored walks and by planting trees and by a service in Westminster abbey. They invited Ramsey to preach the sermon. He took the text of Isaiah 32: 8 from the Authorized Version: 'The liberal man deviseth liberal things; and by liberal things shall he stand'; and the *Liberal News* wisely printed the text as 'The Liberal man . . .' etc. He sang the praise of what the Liberal Party had done for the country though he hinted that he did not like the idea that 1877 was the year when the party was founded; he talked of Gladstone's prophetic power, of Campbell Bannerman, and Asquith 'the last of the Romans', and Lloyd George, less panegyrically, as a zig-zag flash of lightning in the brain. He sang a hymn to the freedoms, of minorities, and of the people, and of the individual to be his true self; and quoted John Stuart Mill and a saying of Maynard Keynes to the Liberal summer school which he heard just before he was an undergraduate, and ended with his conviction that the preservation of freedom needed a foundation in Christian faith.[5]

The refusal to countenance the World Council grants to guerrilla organizations was a sign of something deep in his outlook. He was not a pacifist. He believed it legitimate to go to war in a just cause. He admired Winston Churchill for winning a war. He admired John F. Kennedy for his strength. But he was against the possession by Britain, or by anyone else, of nuclear weapons and doubted whether in a nuclear age a war (which was more than a large police action) could ever be a just war. Because he was not a pacifist he thought that a revolution might in some circumstances be justified. But just as he accepted intellectually the possibility of a just war and doubted whether today any war could be

---

[4] *The Palatinate*, 9 Feb. 1978; a reference owed to Paul Hunt.
[5] *Liberal News*, 14 June 1977, 3.

just, so he accepted the rightfulness of revolution in some circumstances and yet doubted whether in modern conditions of armaments the
result was not more likely to be fearful than good in its outcome. The
heroes for whom he expressed admiration were non-violent men. One
of the reasons for his love of India was his perception how its national
spirit was marked by the mind of Gandhi and the idea of a non-violent
resistance. In South America it was not Camilo Torres whom he
admired, the priest who went out to fight for the oppressed with guns
and was shot down by the army, but Helder Camara, who fought
tyranny by a passive resistance. In South Africa it was not the people
planting bombs who found their way to his heart, but the people who
were ready to suffer for the cause of South African humanity, like
Beyers Naude and Helen Joseph. And this affection for the passive
resisters was something to do with his faith. Christian leaders ought not
to engage in the encouragement of murder, which in a well-armed world
was almost always the alternative to passive resistance. And if it be said
that the passive people let tyrants rampage unchecked, we must have
faith in the providence which rules the world and know that time and
the inward sense of right in the human race will bring them to nothing if
not to destruction. He was the son of a suffragette who contended
strenuously for the rights of her sex but would never countenance the
violence practised by some of her colleagues.

He loved monks and nuns. If they were bad monks or nuns he could
be tough with them. But his ideal of religion was quietness and
retirement. He loved them if they belonged to active orders because
they did so much good, like caring for the old or the poor or the young,
or like conducting retreats or missions or hearing confessions: the
vocation which he called 'caring for the distressed in Christ's name'. He
loved them if they belonged to orders of prayer and contemplation
because he rejoiced in the sense that dotted across the land were little
powerhouses of prayer. When he wanted something badly for the good
of the Church or society he liked to bring it to the attention of the monks
and nuns whom he knew and ask for their prayers. He knew that the
active Church must spend its time not in silence, and was glad that here
and there were oases of silence inside so raucous a world.

He would have liked to see more people feeling the possibility that he
or she had a vocation to be a monk or a nun—because, he said, they are
'no small part of the praying heart of the Church'. He liked to be the
visitor of the community of the Resurrection at Mirfield and on his
visitation to interview all the religious individually. He liked to accept
the invitation to make time to conduct a retreat for the mother superiors
of the nunneries. He liked to visit the nunnery at West Malling, and

helped to consecrate its new chapel, and rejoiced that several communities worked in his diocese of Canterbury. When he had some eminent Catholic or Orthodox visitor, a patriarch or a cardinal, he liked them to go to prayer at West Malling as part of their journey to Canterbury. His own background in the devotion of the Oxford Movement made him grateful for the Cowley community, and at its centenary he gave an address on the work of its founder. It pleased him much that the Church of England had Franciscans and Benedictines, for here his historical affections were touched as well as his otherworldliness.

He insisted on making time in 1973, when he was in France, to visit the ecumenical religious community at Taizé. At first he suspected that the vast publicity which surrounded Taizé was not compatible with the true purposes of a religious community and must be allowed to subside before it found its true way. He had a doubt whether a religious community which was ecumenical was part of no Church rather than all the Churches, in other words, what Christian or apostolic discipline were they under, or in other words, whom ought the prior to obey in a controversy? In November 1972 the Prior Roger Schutz came to Lambeth to address a great crowd of young people at St Paul's cathedral and talked with Ramsey over breakfast and found him as he said 'a Patriarch for the Church of God'. When Ramsey went to Taizé the following year, the place had everything that he loved: a religious community; full of young people questioning and saying their prayers; Catholics and Protestants worshipping together.

If a member of a community discovered that after all he or she had no vocation to be a monk or nun, or some nun discovered that she must leave her order in order to care for an aged mother, and the superior asked for a dispensation to relieve him or her of vows, Ramsey always gave it. But he gave it with a sense of sadness; and he would at times accompany the dispensation with a private letter to the superior full of gratitude for the goodness of God to that community and at its continuing strength.

Certain objects were important to him. The episcopal ring which Pope Paul VI put on his finger at the church of St Paul's outside the Walls became at once his own episcopal ring. He had his previous large amethyst ring, which was given to him by the Fellows of Magdalene College, cleaned and polished and put in the safe, and never took off Paul VI's ring; he cleaned it without taking it off his finger, and was wearing it when he died. An equally important object was a picture. Between school and university he went into a picture shop in Cambridge to find one or two pictures to make the walls of his future undergraduate room less bare. He found a print of the crucifixion by

Perugino and chose it not because it was the crucifixion but because he liked the picture.

It was a picture with a romantic history. It was painted for the confessor of the Borgia Pope who gave it to a church in San Gimignano. When the French revolutionary armies invaded Italy it was mysteriously replaced in the church by a copy, and the original passed for decades into the art market, until a Russian prince Galitzin acquired it for his home in Moscow, so that henceforth it became known as the Galitzin Triptych. Then it passed into the great museum of the Tsar at the Hermitage, from which Stalin's government in need of money put it up for sale, and Andrew Mellon in the United States bought it for himself and then gave it to the National Gallery at Washington, where now it is to be seen. It is the most serene crucifixion ever painted; the figure on the cross looking down with a prayerful care upon Mary and St John, and in the background a towered city by a pleasant harbour with sailing ships, and on each side a high rocky outcrop; on one rocky side St Jerome with a friendly lion, and on the other rocky side St Mary Magdalen with a fair two-handled jar; and all the four people below the cross give the eye a sense of adoration.

Ramsey was not interested in this strange history, and when he acquired the print, did not know that Bolshevists had the original and regarded it only as money, or that when his religious sense fastened upon it America was soon to hold it.

He hung the reproduction over the mantel-piece in his room at Magdalene. Slowly it came to be something more than an ornament. It hung in the same central position in every house or apartment where he lived; so that it hung during his life on nineteen different walls but never, so to speak, changed its place. 'At the time of purchase', he said, 'I thought it a "nice picture". It soon came to be the centre of theology, doxa.'[6] 'It is for me a great picture, because it wonderfully shows a large part of what Christianity means. Christ is seen suffering, suffering terribly; and yet in it there is triumph; because love is transforming it all.'

The pectoral cross which he wore was less important to him than these two objects. The topaz was given to a family in Dover by a refugee fleeing from the French Revolution. He gave it in gratitude for his rescue. The descendants of the rescuers mounted it as a cross and gave it to Ramsey. He liked it but in his retirement rarely wore it and did not regard it with that special affection with which he looked at the ring and the Perugino reproduction.

[6] *doxa* is Greek for glory.

As a speaker, he was regarded by the bishops, who heard him most often, as having on days and off days; on days when he was superlative and off days when he said nothing much. The best of all talks had a historical slant; his strong historical sense united with his affection for the permanent in the universe to make an amalgam of those incompatibles time and eternity. If he gave an address on St Benedict, the founder of western monasticism, in a church dedicated to St Benedict, the effect could be transcendent; all the lasting values of humanity lit up a historical context of a moving and developing society. But these occasions did not need to refer to past time. The secretary-general of the United Nations Dag Hammarsjköld was killed in the Congo trying to stop a murderous civil war and was perhaps murdered himself. Ramsey's address in Westminster abbey on Hammarsjköld (23 October 1961) was a statement of the quest in the modern world for an international amity instead of the old nationalisms and said that history must judge him but meanwhile we could thank God for a servant of humanity. President Kennedy was murdered and Ramsey gave the address in St Paul's cathedral (1 December 1963) and talked of him as symbol of the Christian fight for peace and freedom and aid to hungry peoples.

2. NO RELIGIOUS TRUTH WITHOUT PRAYER

While he was regius professor of divinity at Cambridge it was with his approval that Clare College appointed John Robinson, a promising scholar in the New Testament, as its new young dean. In March 1963 Robinson, by then the suffragan Bishop of Woolwich, and more famous for giving evidence for the defence against those who sought to prove that *Lady Chatterley's Lover* was a book of pornography, published *Honest to God*. The message of the book was at bottom simple and Christian—that people's old conventional image of God (if that was what they had) as a grandfather in the sky kept God out of real life and made Him remote. Yet there must be a basis in God for all the universe, and this basis must be personal, and if the world shrinks from God out there, let them look for God within themselves. In morals nothing is laid down finally except the law of love. And the forms of service in the churches have the danger that they create a private or separate 're-ligious' world which is against the secular world; whereas we have to come to the perception that the secular world is sacred, that is, it is God's world.

There was nothing about these proposals with which informed

Christians could disagree. But some of the language disturbed because it cast doubt or worse upon simple people, or even sophisticated people, who still were helped to think of God out there in the sky even though they knew it to be poetry or parable.

Ramsey expressed himself on the subject in an interview on television (1 April 1963). Here he was positive in praise as well as critical. He said that Robinson was right in trying to find out whether some new mode of God's image might help people outside Christianity. But he was wrong in his negatives—'utterly wrong and misleading to denounce the imagery of God held by Christian men, women and children: imagery that they have got from Jesus himself, the image of God the Father in heaven'. He followed this by writing a little booklet on the subject, which he sent out to various friends for their opinion, and published at the end of April as *Image Old and New*. This booklet attempted to seek out the good things in Robinson's book. He aimed to show that the Church treated new ideas in no obscurantist spirit; and he wanted to help ordinary people whose minds were disturbed by all the press blather that a bishop did not believe in God.

On 7 May Ramsey made a presidential address to the Convocation of Canterbury. He did not in the least regret that Robinson should think original thoughts. The Church had to teach its faith, but obscurantism was as big a danger as heresy. The questions which Robinson discussed were questions which needed to be discussed. What he said he was grieved about was the manner in which Robinson presented his ideas to the public; tentative hesitant ideas in the book, but first presented to the public in a clear and untentative article in a newspaper (*Observer* 17 March 1963) headed 'Our Image of God must go' (naturally a headline suggested by the newspaper, to which Robinson reluctantly consented); an article which appeared to suggest to the world that the idea of a personal God in popular Christianity and in orthodox faith is outmoded. The book was trying to deal with real questions in a way for which Ramsey felt much sympathy. But Robinson's method of doing it only succeeded in disseminating to the country a negative message.

And Robinson had already published his belief in the biblical and Catholic faith and Ramsey said that it was right that he should say this as clearly as he had criticized the presentation of the ideas. After the speech in Convocation, Ramsey and Robinson were observed talking together, each with a glass of champagne, at Mervyn Stockwood's birthday party. Ramsey could be heard saying, 'Up there and in here—yes!'; Robinson could be heard saying, 'The ground of our being'. Clement Attlee was there and could be heard saying laconically, 'Never read the book'.[7]

The controversy was created by the press, which made a bishop notorious because he said that *Lady Chatterley* is a book which some Christians should read, and so were sure that what he said about faith must be daring though it was not. Thus it brought pressure to bear on Ramsey. This pressure came through no fault of Robinson's, except so far as he accepted a headline of which he did not approve and except so far as a bishop might mislead people about his opinions generally if he agreed to be cross-examined in a witness-box about the Christian value of the sexuality in *Lady Chatterley*. Old ladies in the country, archdeacons in the north, assumed that the Church had a bishop who was an atheist and appealed to Ramsey to help them. He did help them.

But a decade later, when he looked back upon the controversy, he thought that his reaction was mistaken. He even confessed to Mervyn Stockwood, who blamed him for being unduly harsh, that his reaction was very harsh and unsympathetic. A reader of the documents after Ramsey's death will find this absurd self-depreciation. He continued to think that the author of *Honest to God* was not profound enough in what he then wrote and that some of his expressions were negative without necessity. But always afterwards he saw Robinson's mind for the Christian mind that it was. Always later he regretted that the doubtful reputation which Robinson gained from *Lady Chatterley* and these events prevented him from receiving the place in the Church which was his due.

On reflection he realized that the hullabaloo was symptomatic of a crisis of faith in the nation and that it needed a treatment different from that of his first reaction. It showed gropings, conscious and unconscious, among many people on the periphery of faith. It needed more understanding than contradiction. It was not just a press hoo-ha. There were people who really were distressed that their image of God was too much like the old gentleman in the sky, and who were helped by the idea that something in their inmost being had transcendent quality. There were other people who knew God as 'the God of the market-place' and wondered whether the 'God of the temple' was the same God. There were people who understood what was meant by a meeting with God at the level of a deep decision or an agony and yet 'felt encumbered by what seemed to be the load of myth and miracle'. 'A world of half-belief and half doubt, of searchings and questionings, was dug up by *Honest to God*.' 'Here was the opportunity to learn from that wistful

[7] Stockwood, *Chanctonbury Ring*, 148.

world which was being uncovered, to understand, to discriminate, and then to try to guide with patience.'[8]

Later he looked back and thought that he was not prepared intellectually for what happened in the sixties. William Temple's death, he said to himself, left a vacuum in the leadership of English religious thought. The young minds went after other sages or pseudo-sages. Paul Tillich, a German exile in America, an unintelligible Hegelian, became the rage. To his dismay Ramsey realized that he had never read Tillich and was not interested in Tillich. At first he had a sensation of floundering. Suddenly he recognized that his tradition of thought—Gore/Hoskyns/ Temple/Ramsey—was not quite able, for all its coherence, to meet the needs of the new time. He struggled to see how it was to be adapted.

During the later years at Lambeth he once said, 'People say that my coming to Lambeth meant the end of me as a theologian. They could not have been more mistaken. If I had stayed at York I would have remained a complacent Tractarian. As it is, coming to Lambeth has forced me to think about a whole lot of new subjects, and I became a theologian.' This was one of those remarks about himself which anyone could see to have a very small truth. It is not possible to believe that he was ever a *complacent* Tractarian, or that he was ever not a theologian, since the day that he argued with a brother.

Ramsey was a professional. Whenever he reviewed an academic book, which was often, the review was informed, level-headed, clear, and sometimes it contributed fresh thinking to the theme of the book. But if we are to ask what was his intellectual contribution, and what English-speaking Christianity owed him most, it would not be so much in the books of technical studies but the large area where divinity passes into prayer and religious experience, that area which is commonly known as spirituality. The certainty in his faith could be felt even by many who did not know him well. His sense of an immediacy in God could be felt especially by those who came to know him well. And yet he came of such a family that he must have sympathy for the doubter and the sceptic and the hesitant. A man with certainty and yet a man with an open mind—that was not so common a contribution to religious thinking or experience and made him special. 'People ask me if I have ever felt like losing my faith. No: my faith is part of me. But faith isn't a state of easy and calm security. It is an adventure of ceaseless battling with troubles: a peace of mind and serenity indeed, but a costly peace and serenity in the midst of conflict.'[9]

[8] Cf. *Canterbury Pilgrim*, 3–5.
[9] Duggan, *Through the Year with Michael Ramsey* (1975), 15.

In a generation where the world lost its way in religion, he was an anchor; but not the kind of anchor which pulls against freedom of the mind; the guardian of what is best in the past, but not because it is the past; rather the guardian of the past so that it can be powerful in the changing future and adapt itself to that future. An observer of the religious climate of that age said that Ramsey's soft and sometimes sing-song voice 'reassured many churchmen that, whatever else the Church of England may have lost, it has not lost its soul'.[10]

During his time as archbishop he published more books than any archbishop since Thomas Cranmer in the sixteenth century. But this is misleading. It was not possible for him to find time to do original work. What he published were his addresses or his lectures, whether separately or in collections. Twice he published little books on controversial subjects of that moment; and the motive for these was twofold; first because the Church needed guidance in an unsettlement; and second, because he needed to think it out for himself in order to be able to give sound guidance. He never lost the hope that one day he would have time, in his retirement, to write again a fundamental book. But he never expected while archbishop to do more than write small books or to print addresses or lectures.

When he retired from his see in 1974, Margaret Duggan produced a book called *Through the Year with Michael Ramsey*. It contained a short passage from Ramsey for each day of the calendar year. No one can use this book without being helped in their religion. That says two remarkable things about Ramsey. First, it suggests that if the best of him is to be found in extracts, rather than in some big book of theology, the best of him is in the soul ruminating, thinking about the impact of Christ upon the world and upon the guidance of God and the prayerful life. Secondly it suggests that characteristic which we have met already —the ability to sum up a body of thinking in some telling phrase with an insight that he could usually make clear to the simplest person.

The book of his retirement which sold more copies than all his other books put together, and so proved that it was what the world wanted, was called *Be Still and Know*. It was a conviction of his heart that stillness and silence are of supreme importance in the Christian life. In the book the theme recurs that the Christian world is suffering from the neglect of silence and stillness. He presented prayer not as an isolated religious exercise but as one part of a many-sided converse between the soul and its Maker, with the beauty of nature, or the events of history, or the stirrings of conscience, or the inspiration in the writings or words

---

[10] David Edwards in Martin, *Great Christian Centuries*, 13.

of men and women, as other parts of the same converse. And he represented prayer as no withdrawal from the caring for humanity but as the force behind it—'the prayer with beautiful buildings and lovely music must be a prayer which also speaks from places where men and women work, or lack work, and are sad, and hungry, suffer and die' (pp. 13–14). It was characteristic of him that he should see the heart of the New Testament upon prayer to be St John chapter 17, with the idea of glory as its climax. The only book by himself which he quoted was the book on the Transfiguration which is all about glory; and one of his chapters in *Be Still* is about the Transfiguration. He commended the Jesus-Prayer familiar to the Eastern Orthodox Church, with its ceaseless quiet repetition of 'Lord Jesus Christ, Son of the living God, have mercy upon me, a sinner'; and his inference from this takes us for a moment into the hidden place of his own practice of prayer:

The repetition, many times and many times, is found to quieten the distracting parts of our personalities and to keep us wonderfully subdued and concentrated, and as we repeat the words again and again we bring into our heart the many people and needs about whom we really want to pray. As the words proceed the heart has the people on it one by one.

The text proves something very private about Ramsey; how he drew on the Eastern Orthodox tradition for his sense of continuous prayer and how that sense of continuous prayer was inseparable from a steady prayer on behalf of all the people for whom he felt a need to pray, people who were not just classes of people but were individuals, passing one by one through his mind. The book also proves that his private prayer centred upon the eucharist; that he liked to draw into his partly wordless contemplation biblical texts, especially from the psalms or the gospels; and among the psalms, especially psalm 119, with what he called its 'rolling cadences'. He was moved to write about the mystical tradition in Christianity, and to quote the medieval English mystics: *The Cloud of Unknowing* (the author of which, contrary to the common opinion, he believed to be a woman) and Richard Rolle of Hampole and Walter Hilton as well as the Lady Julian of Norwich; and then the Counter-Reformation mystics St Teresa of Avila and St John of the Cross. Ramsey never wrote more heartfelt prose than in the later part of this little book about prayer. It will remain a classic of Christian devotion.

The book also proved that he stood where he did about private confession. He taught that every Christian is free not to use private confession. But he lamented that during the last two decades of his life the practice had declined; partly because other ways of counselling were

376   *The Man of God*

freely available, but partly because the sense of sin was less lively.
'Sacramental confession can be a meeting with Jesus as wonderful and
decisive as meeting him in Holy Communion' (p. 108).

In one other place of the book he turned for help to the Eastern
Orthodox Church: on the communion of saints. From his early knowledge of the East during his thirties and forties he often thought about
heaven and the beatific vision. 'When the western Christian experiences
the worship of the Eastern Orthodox Church he is likely to feel how
vivid is the sense of union between heaven and earth.' Those who knew
him well thought that during his last years, as he contemplated the
theme and lived it out, this sense of heaven and of the communion of the
saints gained refinement or even a rapture.

16

The Quiet Years

I. RETIREMENT

During the late sixties there was talk of introducing a retiring age for the clergy. Everyone else except judges, almost, had a retiring age; and people knew of parishes, just a few but enough to be offensive, where the parish priest went on and on although he was past work and might even be on the verge of senility. The special difficulty with the clergy was that they were asked to give a solemn undertaking, that their vocation would be for life—were we going to ask the clergy to take their ordination vows till they were only 65? In addition they were not well paid, and this was tolerable because they were given for their life a free house. What would be the consequence if suddenly, at 65 or 70, they had to make provision for a new home to house themselves and their wife and perhaps some children? And there were those, like Guy, the Bishop of Gloucester, who said that compulsory retirement would make the Church lose some of its best people while they were still at their best. He asked what would have happened to the Church of Rome if under a rule of compulsory retirement they had been unable to elect Pope John XXIII?

The clergy retirement measure of 1975 provided that clergy should vacate office on the day of their seventieth birthday. Naturally this could not apply to those already in office, for legislation could not be retrospective. Therefore it did not apply to Ramsey. Before the new measure was law, he knew that he would retire on or before the 'compulsory' day even though it was not compulsory for him; partly to set a good example, and partly because he began to tire, and partly because he thought that the Church entered times when it needed a younger man. But he had the less hesitation in this resolve in that he was a professor *manqué*. There were things which he wished leisure to do. His original intention was to retire in the middle of 1974, a few months before his seventieth birthday. 'My brain is beginning to be very

tired—and while I can do six things at once, I cannot now do twelve
things at once, which my job requires'.[1]

The effect of the retirement measure, which Ramsey did not need to
obey, meant that he retired younger than any other archbishop had ever
retired. The three who retired before him were 80, 77 and 74. He was
likely to have a longer time of retirement than any ex-archbishop. The
prospect pleased him. There was much which he wanted to do. In the
Argentine that summer of 1974 he was asked by the journalists what he
meant to do with his time, and he said that he wanted time to read, and
write, and travel, and give lectures. 'I don't mean ever to retire from the
fight.' They asked him what he planned to read and he said (for he was
in South America) that he wanted to read the works of Dom Helder
Camara; and that he would go back to his old love among the Greek and
Latin classics, to Homer and to Vergil; and that he would read some
moderns for whom he wanted time, like T. S. Eliot and C. S. Lewis.
This last is interesting for neither of these writers would naturally be in
rapport with Ramsey's thinking. There is no evidence that he ever did
read the works of Dom Helder Camara. He found that retirement
brought him too many other things that needed doing.

He already had a vision of what he wanted to write. Two books, at
least. The first on the Holy Spirit; for he was interested by the
charismatic movement of that day and the truths in Catholic tradition
for which it stood. 'I also have a dream that I might write a comprehensive exposition of Christian doctrine which would hold together
traditional values and some understanding of all the contemporary
commotions and new trends.' Not much was afterwards heard of
this dream.

Archbishops of Canterbury who retired in the twentieth century
without exception became peers—Lord Davidson, Lord Lang, Lord
Fisher. Since 1905 an outgoing archbishop had to die of gout in office in
order not to be a peer. As early as 1969 Ramsey was asked about this and
felt that to him something was incongruous about a peerage and he
doubted whether he would accept one on his retirement. When he knew
that he was retiring, he decided to refuse a peerage if it was offered. His
motives for refusing, as he privately expressed them to himself, were
first that he thought peerages could be justified only if the peer did some
work—that is, the peerage is not an honour but a function—and he
could not see himself in his retirement attending the House of Lords, at
least not often enough to do the job well; and second, that he wanted to
kill the idea that an ex-archbishop continues to be a parliamentary

[1] Ramsey to Donald Harris, Palm Sunday 1973.

statesman. This was what he said privately. But it does not convince, because no one in Britain thought that ex-archbishops were parliamentary statesmen. And we may attribute something to the nonconformist childhood—avoid unnecessary grandeur. He did not mention this motive but we can hardly doubt that it played a part.

But when early in 1974 he wrote to Edward Heath, the prime minister, to tell him that he would retire on his seventieth birthday in November that year, Heath took him 'unawares' by offering him a life peerage. Then he knew that experience had given him an affection for the House of Lords and what it could do, and he realized that it would give him pleasure still to be a member, and he fancied that he might on occasion be thereby enabled to play some little part. But the scruples remained. He consulted Launcelot Fleming, the Dean of Windsor. Fleming was sure that he ought to accept it; and said that if he had repugnance to being called Lord Ramsey that was not a necessary part of a peerage and he could be called Bishop Ramsey. 'I think', said Fleming, 'that Joan must be so used to being called Lady Ramsey that she won't mind accepting that style of address.'

Still not without a scruple, he accepted the peerage, and to himself justified the consent as the acceptance of work and not honour. To enquirers he said that he had no intention of becoming again the Liberal politician of his young days, and that he cared nothing about the corridors of pomp and power, but that to refuse would seem like contracting out of the secular world, and to be a member of Parliament still would be an opportunity for occasional service. After his retirement he did attend the House of Lords a few times but within a few months ceased to attend altogether because he wanted to be doing his real thing, and eventually asked to be on the list of those peers who are excused from attendance.

His first feeling was against being called Lord Ramsey. Even when he was told that the Queen approved the conferring upon him of the dignity of a life baron, he pleaded that the word *dignity* be removed from the notice; and it was. Once when he was a little nonconformist boy at school, he and another boy went out to tea and there was a bishop also as a guest. His friend told him that he must call the bishop My Lord. When little Ramsey refused to call the bishop My Lord because he did not think this compatible with his nonconformity, his friend kicked him on the shins under the table.[2] This memory remained, that long ago he was a boy-martyr for a non-title.

[2] For the historical record, the boy who had such zeal for the customary courtesies due to bishops was André Tait. He was killed commanding a destroyer flotilla in the Atlantic. Ramsey retained a happy memory of him. He was the grandson of a bishop.

It is probable that once a man is an archbishop he cannot stop being archbishopized, any more than he can stop being most reverend, and Fisher became on his writing paper Archbishop Lord Fisher of Lambeth. Actually many people called Ramsey Lord Ramsey because that was what they wanted to call him. But he himself followed Dean Fleming's suggestion and preferred to be called Bishop Ramsey. It did not work universally. His correspondence with *Who's Who* and Crockford's Clerical Directory and SPCK, to make them break their rules about titles, was awkward. Not many people could remember to call him Bishop Ramsey. Joan became Lady Ramsey because people wanted to call her that and not to have used the title would have been more ostentatious instead of less. Within a few years Ramsey accepted the situation and did not mind heading his letters 'From Lord Ramsey of Canterbury'. He said, 'The title Lord had advantages in some contexts, especially when outside Church circles—some little mark of distinction was helpful.' In old age he still had occasional scruples whether he did right to accept the peerage.

He had a final duty; to advise the prime minister on whom he thought should succeed him. We have seen what complications this duty led to when he himself succeeded Fisher. It was equally complicated now. Perhaps it was more complicated, because the system of consultation among the bishops and dioceses was so far advanced, and the General Synod felt that it had a right to be consulted. Never were consultations so wide in the history of episcopal appointments in England. Still, whatever the breadth of the consultations, Ramsey had a duty to tell the prime minister his opinion.

There was an obvious person, Donald Coggan, the Archbishop of York; because Archbishops of York are obvious and because he was a good man and no one can deny that Archbishops of Canterbury ought to be good men. But the new retiring age gave a new problem. If the new archbishop, unlike Ramsey, would be forced to retire at the age of 70, the age of appointment became much more important in order that he might have a length of tenure in which he could make his mark. Donald Coggan was 65. Ramsey believed that in the tension of that age the Church needed a younger person who would have more years than five.

During the argument which we saw about the filling of the see of London, he wondered whether Runcie of St Albans might be such a younger person. For a time he wondered about Ian Ramsey of Durham but even before Ian Ramsey died Michael Ramsey formed the impression that it could not be right to have someone who wore himself out in such a whirlwind. But now he came to think that John Howe, the Secretary-General of the Anglican Communion, would be the right person. No one knew more about the Anglican Communion as a whole, and this part of the work was more and more prominent, not least because of what Fisher and Ramsey both did. Howe, who was said to have climbed almost every mountain in Scotland, was a pupil of Ramsey's when he was a professor at Durham and Ramsey knew that Howe understood theology, a quality which was important to him. By the early spring of 1974 the press got hold of the idea that Ramsey wanted John Howe as his successor; and understood that this was because of the weight which he attached to the Anglican Communion. Only, as one journalist recorded in comparing Howe with Coggan and Trevor Huddleston, the Church of England does not have to be told who Coggan and Huddleston are.

So, after anxiety, he recommended to Heath, and then, when Heath's government fell, to Harold Wilson, that Howe should be his successor. But the Queen and the prime minister saw that Donald Coggan was more of a national figure among the English bishops and people than was Howe. It was good judgement.

The business of retiring took ceremonies. The Queen thanked Ramsey for all the help and encouragement which he had given to her family. She gave him luncheon and the Royal Victorian Chain; and when he came back to Lambeth he was bubbling and waving his hands about and saying, 'I've got an honour! I've got an honour!' He thanked his staff at Lambeth and gave presents. Harold Wilson gave him a farewell party at 10 Downing Street and pulled his leg in a speech and Ramsey pulled Wilson's leg in retort. The bishops gave him a dinner at New College, Oxford. In reply to the toast (they all wondered, said Ronald Williams, the Bishop of Leicester, whether it would be one of his nights on or one of his nights off) he said that he dreamt that he was in heaven at a sherry party given by former archbishops. One by one they all came up to talk to him—and they each said something which was in the character of the man's memory. Cranmer, who wrote the Prayer Book, said to him, 'Ramsey, I don't think much of series 3'. And at the end a little man came up, 'whom I immediately recognized as Anselm. When we met we embraced each other because here I felt there was a man who was primarily a don, who tried to say his prayers and who cared nothing for the pomp and glory of his position.' The bishops saw that in this portrait of St Anselm he spoke a portrait of his own ideal for himself.

Almost simultaneously was opened a school with his name; a comprehensive in Camberwell, henceforth the Archbishop Ramsey School. The Convocation of Canterbury expressed its gratitude by giving him (and Joan who was in the gallery) a standing ovation. The press was full of kindly epithets; the most enigmatic and the most photogenic archbishop of the century, genial, ambling, shambling, optimistic, outspoken, intriguing, fatherly, the answer to a cartoonist's silent prayer, of a simple way of life and of transparent integrity.

Meanwhile the porter at Lambeth coped with mountains of mail. He said, 'He's very popular, you know.' The popularity was not new but the quality was not one of which he thought highly. In 1970 the broadcast programme *The World At One* ran a competition among the listeners, for Man of the Year. The result was perplexing. It was 1. Edward Heath. 2. Enoch Powell. 3. Archbishop Ramsey. 4. Harold Wilson. 5. Mrs Braddock. 6. Prince Charles. Ninth came Winnie Mandela and eleventh Mary Whitehouse.

Moving out of a series of large tied houses to the size of house in which most people live is painful in the way of getting rid of vast sideboards for which there is no room or oddments which the owner has forgotten he ever possessed and are now discovered in a cupboard. In a windy marquee at Canterbury an auctioneer got rid of a lot of things which they could not take with them, in what the *Daily Mail* called a glorified jumble sale. It began with five feather pillows and ended with a towel airer going for 50p. Some of the things he was given on his tours and the proceeds from all these went to charity. An African ceremonial skin drum went for £15, a long monkey skin coat tattered at the edges for £30, a mounted waterbuck's head £19; altogether £10,500 and a bit more.

2. CUDDESDON AGAIN

First he moved to the old vicarage at Cuddesdon, a charming little stone house with apple trees in the garden, which they designed six years before as a place of retirement. They found it with woodworm but did a lot to put it to rights, including turning four little rooms into two spacious rooms, and putting steel girders into the ceiling. He loved his short time as a student there, and associated it with a religious ideal, and hoped to be useful as a teacher to promising ordinands.

This was not the opinion of his advisers. His chief of staff at Lambeth, Geoffrey Tiarks, thought that the village was too isolated for what he and Joan planned to do, and warned the Bishop of Oxford that in his opinion they would not stay long there. Robert Runcie, who knew Cuddesdon well for he had been the principal of the college, had the same doubt whether it could work.

At first all was well. The students of the college needed him as an adviser or confessor and he felt welcomed in both college and village. He recaptured his old feelings at the services in the beautiful village church. He enjoyed taking part in the weekly seminar of the students on Christian doctrine, where he preferred to stay silent and then to give a sort of summing up at the end. He rejoiced to discover that they now had the daily sacrament even in vacations, which they had not done in his time. And the kind Audrey Heaton, who came with them from Lambeth to keep house, thought at first that she did not mind how far or how often she drove them in the car, so that the isolation was not a problem.

But things began to be troubling. To settle was more difficult than he expected.

First, a busy person had to remake his life. He imagined that he would easily return to be a sort of professor—read, write, lecture. He had plenty of invitations to lecture and he wrote. But he meant to write a big and fundamental book as professors are supposed to do; on the Holy Spirit, he thought, which needed a new enquiry and new presentation. Before long he realized that he had fallen out of the academic world for too long; that too much had been written while he was busy in pastoral care; that he would never catch up; that the only books which he would succeed in writing were small books, of his personal insights. He asked the principal of the college for a list of recent scholarly books about the New Testament and meant to read them systematically but never made the time to do so. He hoped that these smaller books which he wrote would be no less valuable than a big book, and might help more people because more people could afford to buy them. Still, this was an adjustment of his plans which he had not expected.

Secondly, he failed to remember the rule that if later in life someone returns to an idyll of his youth, it seldom works, both because in the meanwhile the place has changed and because the someone has changed. Like so many others he had Cuddesdon framed in an aura from the past. But all such colleges were hurdling over the age of student revolution and unsettlement. The Cuddesdon of 1974 had continuity with the Cuddesdon of 1928 and yet was a different place with different students. The students, or many of them, he enjoyed. But the mood of the place was strange to him and not what he remembered. It was a case of the peril of going back to an old affection. He expected Cuddesdon to be the Cuddesdon of 1928; which was impossible.

This was true in the realm of Christian thought. The sixties produced much radical Christian thinking and could not leave theological colleges unaffected. The principal of the college, Leslie Houlden, was on the radical side of New Testament studies. Ramsey was not used to this, and it did not fit his idea of the Cuddesdon which he remembered. The contemporary mood of the College was not quite adapted to his kind of teaching. It was, he thought, a presentation of Christian faith which he regarded as thin. He consoled himself by remembering that he must expect to find himself a back number.

But there was another reason for the discomfort. He was bad at saying no to invitations. People kept asking him to preach or to lecture or to give a retreat or to conduct a refresher course for clergy or to visit a university and be a one-man brains trust; and these seemed so much less than what he was used to that at first he did not realize how many they were and how much time they took. These engagements took the more time because now he had no staff officers to plan them and coping with engagement books and diaries bothered him. He left a trail round the universities and religious communities and retreat houses. The bedroom which he occupied at the chaplaincy of one university bore a placard, 'Bishop Ramsey lived here'. As on his journeys round the world, he would be asked to plant trees in England as a memento of his visit. The leaves of the *acer brilliantissimum* which he planted in the churchyard of Little St Mary's at Cambridge are beautiful as these lines are written.

This very active life produced the problem which the Lambeth chief of staff predicted: the need to travel from a spot whence travel was not easy. Audrey Heaton would drive them anywhere; but soon the combination of functions as chauffeur, housekeeper, shopper began to tell on her.

Then in 1975 the powers that be amalgamated Ripon College, Oxford with Cuddesdon and called it Ripon College, Cuddesdon and put it at Cuddesdon. The old tradition of Ripon was of English Modernism, which the undergraduate Ramsey learned to think of as superficial even when it was clever; though in young Ramsey's day the attitudes of Ripon College were much more negative than they were in 1975, by which time it had become central in Anglicanism. Naturally in this union of colleges the one tradition affected the other. The old traditions of worship continued. The trouble turned out to be, not the marriage of different ways of thought or ways of worship, but the more intangible friction in the union of a group of persons living in their old buildings and another group of persons with different habits who moved into that building as a corporate entity. This was a normal human awkwardness. But it made life in the college rather uncomfortable in certain non-physical ways for a year or two; and the year or two happened to be while Ramsey resided.

Moreover, quite soon, a moral question came in. Whether it was the atmosphere of the age, or whether it was the liberal tradition of openmindedness about a more conventional morality, or whether it was a very few of the people who happened to be there, the moral right or wrong of homosexual relations in ordinands and priests started to be argued with emotion; and in this argument several students came to consult Ramsey. He found that he did not like being involved as an outsider in this predicament.

Yet when he wrote a letter to the Bishop of Oxford to tell him that they were to move, he said how much happiness they had had while at Cuddesdon. After he went away, he rejoiced to see the revival of the college as it settled down properly to the union.

The most spectacular engagement of this time was when he preached for the centenary of the Liberal Party at Whitsun 1977 in Westminster abbey; Jeremy Thorpe being his host. Or perhaps, even more spectacular, was a visit to the Pontifical University of Salamanca in Spain where he received an honorary doctorate and read a paper to an Anglican–Roman Catholic conference and was allowed to celebrate the sacrament at the tomb of St Teresa in the convent church of Alba. He kissed the relics of the saint and then peered at the nuns through the enclosed grill, which must have surprised them. At 11 p.m. he said that he was going to bed, very tired. At midnight they found him glued to a television set, watching a bull fight.

The Spanish doctorate had magnificent ceremonies. He was wrapped in a splendid white silk cape with lace cuffs. Then the cardinal put his doctor's ring on his finger and a black octagonal biretta with a white tassel-cum-fringe on his head. Then Ramsey gave an allocution on theology and unity. He swore to uphold the traditions of the Church, though fortunately no one specified what those traditions were. The ceremony ended with the kiss of peace and the singing of 'Gaudeamus Igitur'.

But under this magnificence lay something important. Because of the Spanish civil war and its aftermath, and because of the mind of General Franco, the Spanish Church was the most reactionary of all the Catholic Churches. It found it hard to accept the second Vatican Council. Then the dictator at last died. The Spanish had suffered such agony in the past from a divided nation that they were nervous what would happen. A month after Michael Ramsey came to Salamanca, a general election was due, the first to be held in Spain for forty years—most of the Spaniards had no idea what a general election was like and what it could produce; and a Church, so linked to the old political right wing, had reason to wonder what was going to happen. What was certain was that the Spanish Church needed to open its eyes to the outside world; that is, for the first time to look for ecumenical contact. They decided to start with the Church of England. They did not expect to get Ramsey to Salamanca but they would not have sent the invitation to the Archbishop of Canterbury if Ramsey had not done what he had done. He did not disappoint them.

Still, he realized that he had far more time 'at home'. He began to write. Just before his retirement he published a book with a perfectly appropriate title, *Canterbury Pilgrim*. This was a collection of his addresses, but few had been published before. Some people value this as the best book he ever published.

3. NASHOTAH HOUSE

This was originally a small mission station to the Indians in Wisconsin. It became a seminary of the episcopal Church of America. It stands in beautiful grounds by two lakes, not far from Milwaukee. It is of the Catholic tradition, and had nearly a hundred students on a three-year course. On Ramsey's tour of the United States during 1967 he was invited to receive an honorary degree there and sent John Andrew to investigate. Andrew reported that it was very like Cuddesdon. Both Ramseys fell in love with the place and said how they wanted to come for a longer time when they retired.

Nashotah House became the most considerable work of his retirement. He spent six periods there in all, all of six weeks except one in 1978 when he spent three months as professor of systematic theology while the professor was away. They lived in the cloister in a small apartment which was designed and built for them, and after a little time the students called it Lambeth West. They were part of the worshipping and social life of the community. He found the chapel numinous for his prayers. He liked the library and took lively interest in its additions, and always had a carrel reserved for him, and spent part of each morning at it. The students took him and Joan to see baseball at the County Stadium in Milwaukee but, said an observer, 'Bishop Ramsey was not really enthusiastic about baseball'. He was hardly able to watch the match because the screen announced that he was present and thereafter there was a queue for his autograph. On many evenings they had supper with married students in their quarters. On many afternoons he would take a student walking round the lake (a walk of an hour and a half). They made friends among staff and students. He steadily refused to enter into controversy. He brought student tears when on Maundy Thursday he preached a sermon on the humility of Jesus and then knelt to wash the feet of twelve people. The visit in September 1979 coincided with the fiftieth anniversary of his ordination to the priesthood. The community laid on an affectionate celebration of the event both in chapel and at a feast, with old boys returning and a little presentation.

Nashotah House did for him what he had expected from Cuddesdon, and he gave Nashotah House what he had hoped to be able to give to Cuddesdon, and which Cuddesdon by the passage of time could not quite do or receive. Ramsey always looked back on Nashotah House as a halcyon time and as the most important part of his retirement; a quiet and beautiful place, half like a monastery, with a regular round of ordered prayer and praise; where his teaching quality was used on those subjects about which he cared most; and his pastoral quality was used by individuals; and where the atmosphere was young, and forward-looking. They valued him as he valued them. In the month after he died the trustees decided to build accommodation for married students and their families, about which they knew that he and Joan were much concerned. It was to be named Ramsey Hall.

If ever Nashotah House is relegated to an obscure corner of American history, it will need to be remembered that for a few years it gave a monastery to one who revered the monk's life, a professor's chair and a library to a professor *manqué*, and a haven of retreat to a lover of contemplation.

4. DURHAM AGAIN

During the Lent term of 1976 he went to Durham to give lectures in pastoral care. Both the Ramseys had their affection for Durham rekindled and they thought it a good idea to move there. They bought a house at 50 South Street, Durham, with a splendid view over the river towards the castle and the west end of the cathedral. They moved there in May 1977.

Roland Walls met him in the station. Ramsey was wearing a Durham miners' cap. He asked Ramsey whether he liked being back in Durham. 'Yes yes I like Durham, I like Durham, but there's only one snag. We've landed in what I think they call a charismatic parish—yes charismatic—and I don't like it.' 'What don't you like?' 'All that hugging just when you want to say your prayers before holy communion—I don't like it and I've taken two avoiding actions—one successful and the other unsuccessful.' 'What was the unsuccessful one?' 'I stayed kneeling, but an impertinent young man tapped me on the head and said "Peace be with you".' 'What was the successful one?' 'I go to the cathedral for the quiet early morning service—yes—the quiet service' —his train began to move and his friend pushed him in and shut the door.

The Ramseys found next winter that the house had a disadvantage. He and she liked to walk nearly every morning to the early sacrament in the cathedral, and three times in a month he celebrated the sacrament himself on dates which he chose. This meant a steep hill down and a steep hill up; and in winter the surface could be icy. They stayed in that house for over a year. But then a house belonging to the dean and chapter came up in 16 South Bailey, just under the east end of the cathedral, and this was far better for a man who liked to be at the cathedral early in the mornings. Even so in winter snow he could be seen inching his way along on Joan's arm. He told his friends that much the best place for him to die was just by Durham cathedral and the Durham University library.

He ruefully noticed his status of guru *passé* by the circumstance that at Evanston (Seabury-Western Seminary) far fewer students came to hear his lectures than when he gave the course of lectures there nineteen years before. Even at home they noticed less power in his speaking. He made a speech at a dinner of the Nikaean Club in London in 1981 and the guests saw that it had little of the old vim. He began to be a bit more unpredictable when conducting the service—non-plussing a choir by singing Cranmer when they were supposed to be singing series 3, or getting into an embranglement in the middle of a prayer—'by whom . . . with whom . . . in whom . . . about whom . . . from whom . . .' until the server pointed out the place in the book. Yet sometimes the old power and magic were there in profusion. Some people who heard him preach on All Saints Day 1982, and other people who heard him give a lecture in 1983 on the centenary-and-a-half of the Oxford Movement, thought the utterances as good as anything they had ever heard him do.

Meanwhile he was in demand to conduct retreats. No one should fail to remember how onerous and how exhausting the work of a retreat conductor can be. During the ten years from his retirement from the see he conducted twenty-five retreats, which averages between two and three a year. Often he was near his roots; frequently visiting Cambridge, living in Durham, conducting devotion at Cuddesdon. One of the visits to Cambridge was unusual. He and Billy Graham occupied two parallel pulpits in Great St Mary's (February 1981) and discussed with each other. They were supposed to argue but mostly they seemed to agree. Unlike what would have happened in some other countries most of the audience of students was more interested to hear Ramsey than Graham.

There was something very mellow about the years of retirement at Durham and York. As the years passed, and people looked back, they realized what he had done. When he was in office they criticized him for warmongering at Rhodesia, or for not being Mary Whitehouse, or for resisting tight immigration bills, or for being donnish on television. Now they saw the stature and what he did for all the Churches and for England. In Durham he had a wide acquaintance of every social class. He was relaxed. The idea that he had no small talk did not occur to the Durham folk.

Outside Durham honours continued to come his way; an honorary fellowship at more than one college, an honorary fellowship of the British Academy for his services to scholarship—'a remarkable climax' —he replied in his letter of thanks to the President, 'for a rather BACKWARD BOY'. When the chancellorship of Cambridge University fell vacant in 1975 Sir Denys Page, the Master of Jesus, who was a humane agnostic, led a campaign to get Lord Ramsey made the Chancellor as the best of the Cambridge graduates for the post; but in the event the Duke of Edinburgh became Chancellor. Occasionally he spoke of his numerous honorary degrees. 'I accept doctorates of divinity as inevitable, doctorates of law as part of the system, but I rejoice in two or three doctorates of literature because I pretend that they are given me as a writer of English prose.'

Pope John Paul II came to visit Canterbury Cathedral in May 1982. He went along the line of Anglican bishops kissing them. The congregation was silent during the rite. But when he came to Ramsey and kissed him, there was an outburst of clapping. One of the newspapers commented on this kiss that they embraced so long that it was like two lizards who have been happily married for forty years. Another observer (Valerie Pitt) said that 'the pair of them ought to have been framed—or put in a glass case—as a sample of the Creator's imaginative art'.

Not that Ramsey was yet without enemies. On 30 January 1980 he wrote a letter to *The Times* against torture in Chile; and in the *Daily Telegraph* Peter Simple scourged him, 'Recent archbishops, foolish when in office, get more foolish when they retire. They acquire an extra layer of density', etc. (*The Times*, 4 February 1980; *Telegraph*, 8 February 1980).

He would not comment on the affairs of the Church. But naturally he meditated about the Church. He remembered the past as fun and they seemed to him to have less fun nowadays. He wanted ordinands to have the old training in theology and the Bible and Church history and thought courses like psychology a poor substitute. He had a critical opinion of the more radical theologians—their theology, not their persons. He thought they did not teach enough; they were so busy exploring that they forgot to tell people how to marry their religious life to the Christian creed.

During these years his friends had the sensation that somehow he was nearer to God. It was not that he was on the point of death. He was as humorous as ever, his mind could be as quick as ever, he was hardly more absent-minded. He still had a historical sense and all his interest in his favourite parts of history. When he walked to a pulpit he waddled a little more, and in the pulpit he felt for words a little more, and he accepted very few invitations to speak. He was still inclined to assume that his audience knew more than some of them did. 'I am sure', he told a very ordinary congregation (1980), 'that you all think that Anselm of Bec was the greatest of the Archbishops of Canterbury.' But something about him gave those who knew him the sensation that even more than before he walked with God. And this was felt by people who did not know him well. It could be felt by a meeting. He went to Cambridge to talk to the John Mason Neale Society on one of his favourite subjects, Anglican–Orthodox relations; and the students were fascinated by the old man who so revelled in his theme, and who could represent the grandeur and glory of the Orthodox tradition more easily than he could represent the Anglican, and who could so mingle delicious touches of humour with an otherworldliness which might be felt to be impracticable but had a stature and a sweep of apprehension. And if it could be felt by a meeting, it could be felt still more by a congregation. At the chapel of another college in Cambridge (1982) he celebrated the sacrament for a large congregation of the young; with big bald head right down over the book, voice soft but reaching to every corner; one of the congregation said that he was so moved that he wanted to dance in the aisle.

He started to dwell on the past, as old people do. He remembered with horror the year 1965, when Lord Dilhorne and Lord Kilmuir held him up to scorn before the nation over homosexuality and capital punishment, and when almost every newspaper in England pilloried him as a warmonger for his attitude over Rhodesia. He fed his horror by going to read *The Times* for 1965 and did not like at all what he read.

Their domestic difficulties began to hit them. The housekeeper at Lambeth, Audrey Heaton, looked after them at Cuddesdon and in Durham. But in April 1983 she damaged her leg in an accident and had to give up. Looking after themselves was not easy as eyes started to fail. But to stay in the house at Durham was an experience for a visitor. One visitor who was ordained by Ramsey while he was at Canterbury stayed in South Bailey and found it strange to be brought tea in bed in the morning by an ex-primate in the untidiest of all pyjamas and felt the quiet and godliness of the house; for after he left he wrote in his diary, 'It has been like a country house weekend with saints'. They walked together along the towpath at Durham—or rather the young priest walked while Ramsey tottered—and the younger told the older how he had lost the sense of a personal God and asked what was he to do, and came away reinspired.

David Paton visited him and said when he left that perhaps they would not meet again in this life. Ramsey said, 'It is not necessary to visit in order to be present.' Paton asked him what he did when he was not talking or writing but just doing nothing. Ramsey said, 'I think of my friends.'

Suddenly Joan's life, with her partial blindness, was much more difficult. They kept worrying whether they ought to move house, as their infirmities grew. They began to think where to go. He was keener to go than she, for he could see the problems of her blindness better than she could feel them.

In February 1984 they decided to move to a sunny house at the village of Greatham near Hartlepool, but then decided not to. The sight of all four eyes began to fail. Ramsey had cataract operations at Sunderland in July and September 1985 but they were not successful. He was using a very powerful magnifying glass to make out print, word by word. For a man whose life was prayer and reading, the difficulty of sight made a suffering. He did not complain.

Then John Habgood, the Archbishop of York, offered them a ground floor flat in Ramsey's old home at Bishopthorpe.

Before they moved there they suffered a small calamity. On 3 August 1986 both the Ramseys were being driven in Durham and at the roundabout just outside the peninsula, where cars come whizzing from unexpected angles, their car was hit by another car, with severe jolting. Neither of the Ramseys was badly injured, but both suffered from shock and both felt after their recovery that they were older. He began to suffer from fits of dizziness.

5. PORTRAITS

While he was retired at Durham he had his portrait painted for the last time.

When he was a new Bishop of Durham, his sister in law Lettice Ramsey, who since Frank's death set up a photography business in Cambridge, took a formal portrait of Ramsey, not in robes but in a cassock and wearing his pectoral cross. Lettice's daughter gave this photograph to the National Portrait Gallery in 1988.

While he was Bishop of Durham there was not time to organize any portrait of him.

In 1958 the Honourable George Bruce painted him for Bishopthorpe. The painting hangs there still, and is liked, and by a strange series of events was the first of three portraits of Ramsey by Bruce. They struck up a friendship; which was sealed when Bruce persuaded him to try painting on his holiday in Devon and produced the paints and found that he came back with nine watercolours. One of these watercolours has quite the misty magic of Dartmoor and George Bruce took it away and framed it and Joan Ramsey kept it. But Ramsey did not persist in this refreshment on holiday, it took time, and he preferred to spend his time walking and reading.

Peter Greenham, RA, painted Ramsey for Lambeth (1964). Ramsey sat in a room at the top of a tower, almost in silence. Every now and then Greenham heard what at first he thought was the passing of an underground train but it turned out to be Ramsey humming a hymn tune.

Durham now wanted a portrait and because Ramsey liked the portrait which Bruce did for Bishopthorpe, Bruce painted him for the diocese of Durham (1965). This now hangs in Auckland Castle.

In 1965 Ruskin Spear painted him for Magdalene College, Cambridge. Ramsey went to Ruskin Spear's studio in the West End. Spear said: 'He came down the path in a curious way,—blessing everything—it sanctified the occasion.' When sitting he hummed soft hymn tunes. This portrait made Ramsey look like a beery medieval friar. It was the portrait which the Fellows of Magdalene moved out of their hall just when the Rhodesian quarrel was hot and Ramsey was unpopular in the national press. The undergraduates believed that the Fellows moved it because they were afraid of someone bedaubing it. Actually, their reason had nothing to do with Rhodesia but it was only that Ramsey's Aunt Lucy, who lived in Cambridge, told them that she could not bear it. Later it moved back into the college hall, where it now hangs. Because Ruskin Spear was slowly accepted as a leading portrait-painter of our time, whatever the element of humour which he did not eschew, this Magdalene portrait started to be illustrated in books on the work of Ruskin Spear. This portrait was not in robes but just in the purple cassock of which the colour caused such comment.

Lambeth wanted another portrait. Roy Strong was then the head of the National Portrait Gallery and recommended Guy Roddon for the work. Roddon painted Ramsey during the winter of 1969–70; fifteen sittings; a seated archbishop, wearing the white and gold damask cope which was made for his enthronement as Archbishop of York. This portrait was hung for public exhibition in the National Portrait Gallery for three weeks of May 1970. On the first day of public exhibition (6 May) the *Daily Telegraph* reproduced it. Underneath was a headline which said that the picture was deplorable, though the editor excused himself by putting the word deplorable into inverted commas. The experienced art critic Terence Mulally used this as a text to assault the fashion in portrait painting in that generation, for he called the picture 'a painful reminder of our age'.

The picture hung in the corridor at Lambeth Palace for a number of years but eventually people came to think that still another portrait was needed for Lambeth.

The *Readers Digest* for June 1971 decided to have an article on Archbishop Ramsey and asked John Worsley for a portrait of him to include in that number. There was no time for sittings. So Worsley worked from some twenty-five photographs and was forced to finish it within four days. It is a portrait of Ramsey, profile leftwards, in purple cassock and with pectoral cross and looking upward towards heaven. It hangs in John Worsley's studio.

In the autumn of 1981, seven years after his retirement from the see of Canterbury, Ramsey sat for his portrait again. This was because most people at Lambeth except Joan did not think that the Roddon portrait did him justice. Ramsey himself did not mind it, he thought that it made him look jolly and bibulous. They eventually persuaded Joan that another ought to hang in Lambeth. Ramsey was asked whom he wanted to paint him now. 'Yes, yes, I shall have George Bruce to paint me because he does not frighten me.' Thus Bruce painted his third portrait. It is dated 1982, puzzlingly to those who do not know the circumstances, and hangs now in the archbishop's main corridor at Lambeth between the portraits of Archbishop Fisher and Archbishop Coggan. Not everyone was pleased. But when Ramsey and Joan were afterwards asked which was their favourite portrait of Ramsey, they replied that it was this by Bruce. George Bruce also described how Ramsey used to hum hymn tunes during the sittings. Bruce specially remembered 'Turn back O man'. He also remembered doo-di-doo, di-doo-di-da, in iambics or hexameters or pentameters.

In 1981 the National Portrait Gallery said that they wanted to have a portrait of Lord Ramsey in their collection and asked if he would consent to sit. He consented and Julia Sorrell, whose father had taught Ruskin Spear, came up to Durham to do the painting. He sat for this during the winter months of 1981–2. She alarmed him by asking for a large number of sittings and with self-sacrifice he agreed to 'twenty sittings before Christmas and a dozen more in January', but that was far more sittings than he had ever been asked for before. The artist had nightmares before she arrived because she was told that he was so intellectual. He found the sittings to be exhausting and the company of the artist to be fun. She found herself racking her brains for something to say after a silence of ten minutes or so. But he did not like people who talked all the time when he sat. Sometimes she could hear him murmuring to himself, she thought it might be that he was counting up to a hundred; sometimes he just hummed. Once he hummed the nursery rhyme 'Girls and Boys come out to play'. Occasionally he quietly started to sing a hymn. At first she found the sudden laughter unnerving. She found the conversation when it did occur fascinating. She noticed the unusual thing that although he waggled his eyebrows in company, he never did so when sitting for his portrait. She noticed how small and delicate and tapering his hands were in proportion to his towering frame. She noticed that whenever he looked at Joan a look of affection came into the face. She preferred to go on painting for two hours but found that after one hour he began to wriggle too much. She told a friend, 'If anyone could convert me to fervent Christianity it is him, he is so inspiring and talks sense.' She told her mother, 'One feels a great awe emanating from him and one feels no desire to say a harsh word.' The portrait is of him in a purple cassock. Behind on the shelves can be seen books, and a few of the titles are discernible: the Acts of Convocation 1921 onwards, Norman Sykes's *Man as Churchman*, the *History of the English Church*, edited by Hunt and Stephens in eight volumes, etc. The portrait went to the National Portrait Gallery at the beginning of February 1982. When Ramsey died the director placed the portrait for a time in the place of honour at the head of the entrance stairs where it attracted favourable attention from the visiting public.

Ripon College, Cuddesdon possesses a green bronze bust of Ramsey by John Doubleday, given by A. A. Gates, formerly of Wadham College, who was an enthusiast for Doubleday's work and an admirer of Ramsey and who also gave Wadham College its posthumous statue of the former Warden of Wadham, Maurice Bowra. The bust was not done for Cuddesdon College. For this bust, Ramsey was a reluctant sitter. The bust was presented to Cuddesdon College in June 1974. It stands in the college library. At first it was not fastened and from time to time students getting into bed found there Bishop Ramsey's head.

At almost the same time the sculptor Barbara Kulik was asked by Simpson, of the Council of Christians and Jews, to do a bust of Lord Ramsey. He did not sit for her but she worked from photographs. The figure is full length. The press reported it as the portrait of an athlete about to run a race or enter the boxing ring, though still wearing a pectoral cross. It is now in Hampstead.

6. YORK AGAIN

They moved to York at the end of August 1986. Through the window of his dining-room he could see across the courtyard and when the sun was right could see his own (Bruce) portrait hanging within the archbishop's part of the house; which amused and pleased him. The flat at Bishop-thorpe suited them almost perfectly: on the ground floor, with room for the necessary books, shops nearby for Joan, chapel of the house across the court for Ramsey, kindness of the Archbishop of York's wife, walks available in the garden, ease with which friends passing North to South or the other way could drop off at York station and take a taxi to see them. His only regret was that the service in the chapel each weekday morning was morning prayer instead of the sacrament.

He shed some books in Durham, and in York got rid of a lot more books to Blackwell's of Oxford. His handwriting was now so shaky or crabbed that it became very hard to read. He kept a little collection of books which he described as part pious and part biographical. It pleased him that in each of his two universities, Cambridge and Durham, was founded a Ramsey Society. In Durham the name Ramsey commemorated both Michael and Ian, the physically big and the physically little, in Cambridge just Michael. Both societies were for theological discussion. He did not quite know what to make of this. 'Any standing as a guru which I might ever have had is now very much a thing of the past.'

On 21 May 1987 his old friend Reggie Cant died in a York nursing home. Cant taught in Durham while Ramsey was professor there, and helped him with his book on Frederick Denison Maurice, and later was a canon of York Minster. Ramsey regarded him as a close friend and admired him as the best type of Anglican priest of the high church tradition; humane, learned, dedicated, caring, and a master of the English tradition of spirituality. He insisted on going to York minster for Cant's funeral. There another friend of Cant saw the procession and described it:

I had not realized how great a grief was Cant's death until I saw Michael Ramsey being helped along the choir aisle in the minster—like a great ruined crag—looking indeed like Rodin's great statue of Balzac—(mutatis mutandis —it's the rocklike sense of presence)—and thought of those two good old men sitting together when Michael went to visit Reggie—one of them too blind to see much and the other unable to walk or to speak. I could have howled like a dog—which would not have been well seen in the minster.

Ramsey was moved by Cant's funeral. It pleased him that the requiem was identical with that drawn up by Edward Lord Halifax for his own requiem in 1959, a requiem where Cant, and Ramsey as Archbishop of York, were both present. Cant had lingered for many months, and it was time that he should go. Ramsey thought the service full of hope. And he was touched as he reflected upon his own predicament—nearly blind, and with dizziness, and with a half-blind wife, and needing to move into a home where he would be under care, and struggling to keep full of faith and of cheerfulness; and in this mood he found two paragraphs written by Cant, which the dean and chapter of York printed on the sheet for the funeral. Cant wrote them in *The Churchman's Companion:*

. . . Death itself does not frighten me so much as the thought of a long and feeble old age. The litany in the Prayer Book prays that we may be delivered from sudden death, but it means sudden and unprepared, and we are not meant to want to linger . . . More difficult is to learn to hand over to God one's willingness to be old and feeble, to enter a second childhood in which one loses all one's adult dignity, and is stripped of all one's painfully acquired knowledge, and has to begin all over again, at the mercy of other people . . .

My bodily life will be finished, and it will be a relief if the body is worn out, and the purpose of my life will have been achieved, and I shall be with God . . . I shall see him face to face. It will not be pleasant, for my sins will have spoiled my taste for him. But I believe that he wills to cleanse me in the saving death of Jesus, and I know that I will to receive his cleansing love here, and there; now, and then. Through his mercy I believe that I shall achieve my true end for which I was born, and towards which all my prayer and daily life have been pointing, the enjoyment of God for ever in communion with the blessed company of all faithful people.

Ramsey found this quotation, in his circumstances, *inspired*.

By July 1987 they saw that they could not stay at Bishopthorpe. To prepare a meal took Joan a long time groping for pots. In the summer of 1987 Ramsey had a slight stroke in the bath at Bishopthorpe. At first it was not recognized to be a stroke. His fits of dizziness made him tumble over. He appeared with a black eye because he fell—'I was thinking', he said, 'of higher things'. Their doctor said that they must move to a place where they would get nursing care. A considerate Church would have found them a little house and put in a nurse. They had no feeling of this kind.

7. THE END AT OXFORD

They were promised a room at St John's Home, attached to the All Saints Sisters in Cowley on the south-eastern edge of Oxford. Until the rooms at St John's Home were free ('Two people', he wrote, 'who were expected to die have not succeeded in doing so but the Mother goes on using optimistic language') they lived for six weeks in the deanery at Christ Church, aided by the dean and his wife, Eric and Rachel Heaton.

In St John's they had a comfortable bedroom; and just along the passage a sitting room, with two chairs and two little desks and two little bookcases. On the door were their names thus, Bishop and Lady Ramsey. In one of the bookcases he had a selection of devotional books, in the other the twentieth-century volumes of the Dictionary of National Biography, and a very few historical works, especially the Life of Asquith. He made out print with a magnifying glass, and the oculist in Oxford thought that he might be able to create some very powerful spectacles which would partially restore the ability to read, so they were not without hope. They gathered their news from the headlines, which was not an informative mode of keeping up with the world. It was a trial to him that he could not visit Blackwell's the bookshop because his movements were so unsure. On the wall were Perugino, and Eric Milner-White, and William Temple and himself at Bishopthorpe, and the Patriarch Alexei, and himself and Pope Paul VI, and himself with Billy Graham at Cambridge; and the crucifix from Africa.

Ramsey was glad to be back where there was a daily eucharist. He felt it a big loss that he dare not celebrate the sacrament himself. He did not look well. He kept getting fits of giddiness. He could walk or totter along the passage with the aid of a stick. He preferred not to take anyone's offered arm—'other people's balance seems to upset my balance'. Visitors were important to him. He loved them especially if they were young. A group of old Durham undergraduates, now ordinands at St Stephen's House in Oxford—a college of which in 1987 he thought highly whereas forty years before he thought it a wretched narrow seminary—came to tea with him and quite excited his affections and his memories and his hope for the future. When there were no visitors he sank back into passivity in his chair.

He would like to reminisce, gently, of what it was like as a regius professor, or how long it took him to get the atmosphere of the House of Lords, or how appalling were the tensions in the days of the debates over Rhodesia and homosexuality. Or he would speak of the importance of Nashotah House to him in the earlier years of retirement, or of the way in which the Church of England was going in 1987; but amusedly and with hope. He sat fidgeting with the ring as he talked.

On Sunday mornings his barber and friend Dennis Pratley took them both to the service at the parish church of Cowley St John. He refused to sit at the front 'because that might make me look important' and he refused to sit at the back 'because that might seem like trying to look unimportant'. It was faintly tense, getting him physically up to the communion rail, between Joan as supporter on one side and Dennis Pratley on the other. After service they joined the party in the church hall, and chairs were placed, and two queues formed to talk, and in the queue, to his pleasure, some students.

Just before Christmas 1987 he attended his last dinner-party. It was fitting that it was held at the House of St Gregory and St Macrina in Oxford, which is dedicated to better understanding between the Orthodox and Anglican Churches.

He preached his last sermon, to the sisterhood in the chapel of All Saints, on Christmas Day 1987. The superior hesitated to ask him to preach because she wondered if anyone would hear what he said. But every word was audible. Each time he said *glory* it came out as a shout. He started to recite a few lines of a poem by Studdert Kennedy and forgot some of the words so he substituted dum-dum, dum-dum, dum-dum, and not many people noticed. About the same time he wrote his last paragraphs for print; a preface to a history of the convent.

His health visibly declined further. A young Muslim from Bangladesh, who kept the post office across the road where he used to buy stamps, came to visit him, and asked him how long he had been ordained. He said, 'Nearly sixty years'. The young man said, 'That's a very long friendship'; and Ramsey repeated the phrase more than once, savouring its memory and smiling. In the middle of April 1988 he caught bronchial pneumonia. The strain upon his system was too severe. Even in these last hours or especially in these last hours the lines from Izaak Walton spoke the truth about him—

> Of this blest man, let this just praise be given,
> Heaven was in him, before he was in heaven.

He died peacefully, still cherished by Joan, still with his sense of glory, in the early hours of 23 April 1988. He was 83. He died still wearing the ring which he received from Pope Paul VI by the church of St Paul outside the Walls.

It would please him that at his funeral in Canterbury cathedral on 4 May 1988 the choir sang to the Slavonic tone the great Russian Kontakion of the departed, as the coffin was carried down the nave towards its last rest.

During the year before he died he was consulted about what he would like for a memorial stone, and where he would like it. As early as 1974 the Dean of Canterbury asked him about it. He said, 'I should like to be not far from William Temple.' Temple's remains and stone lie in the cloister of Canterbury cathedral.

Accordingly, in the year before he died, there was discussion with the Dean and the Archdeacon of Canterbury how best to carry out these wishes. To be buried near William Temple it was necessary to be cremated because of the rules about space. He preferred not to be cremated but accepted that this was necessary. After various ideas were put forward, it was agreed that the inscription should be made by Kindersley, that master in the art of epigraphy. The perfect quotation was chosen for the end of the inscription, from the Greek Father of the second century, St Irenaeus.

With Thanksgiving
Pray for the soul of
Arthur Michael Ramsey
1904–1988
Archbishop of Canterbury
1961–1974
Scholar Priest and Friend

*

The Glory of God is the living man;
And the life of man is the Vision of God.

APPENDIX 1

The Travels as Archbishop

The extent of his journeys as the most travelled Archbishop of Canterbury till then should be recorded.

As Archbishop of York: Moscow 1956, United States 1959, Central Africa, Sierra Leone, Ghana 1960.

As Archbishop of Canterbury:

1961   New Delhi, World Council Meeting. Elected one of the presidents.

He stayed with the High Commissioner; visited the Cambridge Mission to Delhi and made a pilgrimage barefoot to Gandhi's memorial; talked at St John's College, Agra; visited leper work in Calcutta and Bishop's College.

At Delhi he told the Secretary of WCC Visser t'Hooft that as President he did not want to be 'embroiled' in the administration of WCC but would like to help on 'theological matters'. He also said to him that he found the ecumenical movement now much more mature (i.e. than at Evanston).

1962   Istanbul and Athens; Moscow; United States.

1963   Belgium—Louvain; Toronto—Anglican Congress.

Utterances of Ramsey at Toronto won attention.

 1. MRI = Mutual Responsibility and Interdependence—a long-winded way of saying that the Anglican Churches across the world should care for each other—was given a touch of inspiration by Ramsey saying, 'The Church which lives to itself will die to itself'. When they asked where he got this quotation he begged them to read the second Epistle to the Corinthians.

 2. He wanted to get away from the idea that the European Churches were always the givers and the African or Asiatic or Latin American Churches always the receivers. Since Evanston and New Delhi and his travels in Asia and Africa he realized what the younger Churches had to give to the older Churches. At Toronto he put this dramatically, by saying that Asia and Africa should send missionaries to help convert the English. This got headlines.

 3. For the first time he publicly asked for the study by the clergy of the tradition of Christian spirituality and mysticism. This got no headlines.

1964   Sweden (eighth centenary of Uppsala cathedral); West Germany (including the British Army on the Rhine); address at Nuremberg on Martin Luther's birthday.

1965   Nigeria, Honolulu, Fiji, New Zealand, Australia, Mauritius, and Madagascar.

1966   Rome—meeting with the Pope. Geneva, to visit World Council. Jerusalem to be a pilgrim and to preside over the Anglican Consultative

Body; Belgrade; Canada, all the dioceses. This Canadian tour he enjoyed very much but it was too packed, and he came back tired, and henceforth tours were planned more leisurely. At Vancouver he got into trouble for more critical remarks about Billy Graham's methods, though by now they were friends.

1967   Abbey of Bec in Normandy, and Paris. USA—several ecumenical services—Chicago, St Louis, Little Rock, Las Vegas, San Francisco, Seattle (General Convention), Milwaukee (first visit to Nashotah House), New York—preached in cathedral, lectured at Union and General Seminaries.

1968   Bermuda; Uppsala (meeting of World Council of Churches, his last as one of its presidents. It was full of revolutionary youth whom he liked, and noisy political jargon which he disliked. He was followed about by some hostile demonstrators but they were side-tracked by the press officer).

1969   West Indies, Nassau, Puerto Rico, Belize, Jamaica, Antigua, Bermuda.

1970   United States. Joint Lectures with Cardinal Suenens in New York. South Africa, Uganda.

1971   Oslo (900th anniversary of religion in Norway), Denmark. Canada (three lectures Trinity College, Toronto; 75th anniversary of Roman Catholic diocese of Ottawa, preached in RC cathedral to 3,000). Limuru, in Kenya.

1972   United States. He took part in a conference of three days at the Trinity Institute, New York, on the subject of the charismatic Christ. He preached in the Roman Catholic cathedral of St Patrick as well as the Episcopalian cathedral.
        Bulgaria.

1973   France: Sens and Lyons; Taizé.
        Belgium, four days: he was the head of a British Churches delegation which went to a special service for the European Economic Community in Brussels cathedral. He stayed with his friend Cardinal Suenens and celebrated the sacrament in Cardinal Mercier's chapel within Brussels cathedral. In his address he said that a Christian Europe was a Europe which looked to the needs of other continents with poverty and hunger. 'Let it be a Europe in which God is honoured and worshipped, a Europe in which men and women ask God's forgiveness for their sins, a Europe in which the family is held sacred. Let it be a Europe in which the divine image in every man and woman is reverenced, a Europe in which the love of money and of material things is not supreme, a Europe which knows that beyond the sovereignty of States there is the sovereignty of the righteous God.'
        Far East, Singapore, South Korea.

This last, of four weeks, included a visit to the Church of South India in the year of its silver jubilee, that is, the cathedral of Madras where the bishop was still his old ecumenical friend Lesslie Newbigin. He loved India because of the historic connection between Britain and India; because it is so religious a country; because he admired the ideals of Gandhi to whose tomb he went barefoot on the visit of 1961; and because the Church of South India, lately recognized as in full communion with the Church of England, was a symbol for him of the better hopes for unity among Christians.

He went on to South-East Asia where the dioceses were still under the jurisdiction of the Archbishop of Canterbury; this included Singapore, Malaysia, Sarawak, Brunel, and Sabah; two days in Hong Kong. In Manila the Cardinal sliced a mango for him, and he greeted the small Philippine Episcopal Church, which was part of the Anglican Communion, and the large Philippine Independent Church, which was in communion with the Anglicans. Then to South Korea, also under his jurisdiction; and finally two days in Japan.

1974   South America, East Germany.

APPENDIX 2

Honorary Degrees

I. MICHAEL RAMSEY'S DEGREES

It is not easy to track all Ramsey's honorary degrees. They included at least the following: DD: Durham (1951); Cambridge (1957); Edinburgh (1957); and then Hull, Leeds, London, Manchester, Keele, Columbia (1962); General Theological Seminary, New York (1962); Trinity College and Wycliffe College, Toronto; Huron College, Virginia Theological Seminary (1962); University of King's College, Halifax, Nova Scotia; Pacific Lutheran University (1967); Episcopal Theological School at Cambridge, Massachusetts (1967) where he was photographed trying on the Boston Red Sox baseball cap which the students gave him; Institut Catholique at Paris; Salamanca (but we have seen that the Salamanca degree was originally intended for Donald Coggan).

Doctor of Laws: Oxford (1960); Occidental College, Los Angeles (1962); University of Canterbury, New Zealand (1965); Kent (1966); Nashotah House (1967) (this was unique in that it was a doctorate of canon law; and charming that he should have accepted, when we remember his indifference to the reform of the canon law of the Church of England).

Doctor of Letters: Newfoundland (1966); Keele; Woodstock College, New York (a Jesuit theological seminary—this was 1970, jointly with Cardinal Suenens). That list includes twenty-four institutions. If universities in the full sense only are counted, it makes fourteen.

He had to refuse the offer of an honorary doctorate at the university of Sierra Leone because he could not be there at the time; similarly for the university of Notre Dame (hon. Doctor of Laws proposed) and Drury College, Springfield, Illinois. The historic university of Louvain was tragically divided into two by the national problem of language between Flemish and Walloon. Both universities agreed to unite in awarding him an honorary doctorate. But they could not agree on a common ceremony so the plan fell through. This was when he went to Brussels in 1973 for the sermon on the EEC.

The general idea of universities would be to award a doctorate of divinity for contributions to religious studies or religious life; a doctorate of laws for a contribution to the state or society; and a doctorate of letters for a contribution to thought or literature or history.

In 1962 he was elected an Honorary Master of the Bench of the Inner Temple. In 1974 he was elected Honorary Fellow of Merton College, Oxford, where he had been ex officio the Visitor. He was elected an Honorary Fellow of

Selwyn College, Cambridge, where he had served on its Council 1950–2. He was long an Honorary Fellow of his own college Magdalene.

2. LAMBETH DEGREES

His own use of the archbishop's right to award Lambeth degrees he used sparingly. Until 1923–4 the older universities gave all bishops who were their graduates a DD degree. Then they stopped doing so, except for the archbishops and their own bishops of Oxford and Ely. Since bishops were by convention Dr So-and-So, Archbishop Davidson stepped into the breach with Lambeth DD degrees for all new bishops. This custom continued to the end of Archbishop Fisher's time and Fisher thought it a good one. It had the demerit that the bishop so honoured had to pay some £35 in legal fees. Fisher started to persuade the Church Commissioners to pay these fees. All was not quite well. Loyd of St Albans refused the Lambeth degree because he disliked the system.

Ramsey with his academic background thought that it was cheapening the DD degree if the archbishop awarded more of such degrees than both the ancient universities put together; and since the gown and hood worn by those honoured with a Lambeth degree were by long custom the gown and hood of the archbishop's university, he could not bear the idea that he should be distributing more Cambridge hoods and gowns than the university itself. He decided that if he continued the custom he would have to invent a special hood for the Lambeth degree. (Fisher had already considered this possibility and received legal advice that nothing in law stood in the way.) However, as soon as Ramsey became archbishop he stopped the custom; not without a little grief. He even needed to modify his plan a little, especially with the primates of provinces overseas, where the degrees were very much valued. Cf. Ramsey to Eric Abbott, 30 January 1967. 'I do not regard Lambeth Degrees as rewards for service to the Church, even for intellectually distinguished service . . . Were I to yield to that concept there would be a good many lay persons commended to me for such an award. I want before I die to let it be completely clear that my doctorates have a distinctly academic character and go to the sort of people who would have obtained doctorates from a university were it not that their circumstances put them outside the usual academic cursus.' One award of a Lambeth degree was special. Reginald Somerset Ward, priest from 1904, was a man of prayer and little known but dedicated his long life to the quiet direction of souls. At times now his mind was muddled, and he could not travel to Lambeth to receive the degree. The archbishop motored down to Farncombe to confer the degree and Somerset Ward well understood what happened (30 April 1962).

He was not able to award a Lambeth degree to the great South African enemy of apartheid Beyers Naude because the recipients must take an oath of allegiance and therefore must be British subjects. But the recipients did not need to be Anglican and it delighted him to be able to award a degree to John Huxtable, the Congregationalist leader, by then Moderator of the United Church.

Note on Archbishop Ramsey and the Non-Christian Religions

In a broadcast television appearance (1971) where he was open to questions, Archbishop Ramsey was asked about other religions. He said, 'Other religions contain a great deal of truth and have to be reverenced. The light that lighteth every man. There is something unique in Christianity, and that is God coming in Jesus. And there is something universal that gathers up all that is true in other religions.'

His relations with the leaders of the Jewish faith were always happy. Archbishop of Canterbury to Chief Rabbi (Dr Israel Brodie) 17 September 1962: 'Remembering that Friday is the Jewish New Year's Day I am venturing to write to you with my warmest good wishes, and my brotherly greetings to you and to the Jewish Community. I need say no more than how thankful I am, and my fellow-Christians with me, for all that your Community does for God and for Righteousness in this country, and how much I pray that brotherhood and tolerance may prevail in the service of what is true and right.' He congratulated Jakobovits on his election as Chief Rabbi.

When the Israeli athletes were so brutally assassinated at the Munich Olympics, Ramsey was in the United States; but when he flew home, he gave a memorial address in the church of St James, Piccadilly. It was a purely Christian address but the mere fact that he gave it caused fierce correspondents to accuse him of being anti-Arab. Incredible though it sounds now, the first meeting between an Archbishop of Canterbury and a Chief Rabbi happened on 27 February 1972. In July 1974 he opened the Soviet Jewry exhibition. At this time he was accused by the Arabs of being pro-Jewish and anti-Arab because in the tension in Palestine he refused to appoint an Arab to be Anglican Bishop in Jerusalem and played for time by putting the ex-Bishop of London, Stopford, temporarily in charge. Some of the Anglican Arabs therefore abused Ramsey as a 'racialist'. Nevertheless his relations with the Jewish people were a little complicated because he wanted Jerusalem to remain, at least religiously, an international city; and criticized its ugly new buildings put up by the Israeli authorities after the Six-Day War.

When Ramsey was in India for the Delhi Assembly he went barefoot to the tomb of Gandhi. 'We who are Christians proclaim that Christ is the perfect and final revelation of God . . . At the same time we reverence the divine image in every man, and believe that the divine light has shone in good men of other religions and wherever that light shines we know that we are on sacred ground', *Canterbury Pilgrim*, p. 137, his address in St Paul's, 30 January 1969.

He remembered how Gandhi specially loved the hymns 'Lead kindly light' and 'When I survey', made non-violence his ideal, put simplicity of life before wealth and comfort, put the things of the spirit before material things, 'made the cause of the poor and the outcast his own and sealed it all by a martyr's death'.

The World Congress of Faiths was a body with respectable Anglican clergymen among its officers. Ramsey would have nothing to do with it. In 1969 they invited him to be present—not to preach at—an All Faiths service at the West London synagogue and he refused. In the following year Edward Carpenter, who was President of the Congress, asked the Archbishop to take part in a meeting at the Central Hall Westminster with a view to promoting 'the high view of man for which the great faiths of the world stand'. Ramsey explained to Carpenter why he could not happily take part in such a meeting.

I recognize that the Christian doctrine of the light that lighteth every man demands a reverence for other faiths as being in various ways expressions of the divine wisdom, and I think it right to give practical expression to this reverence for them. On the other hand I do not believe that 'religion' is a kind of banner under which we should all unite as if it contained the essence of what is good versus 'irreligion' as its opposite. Not all religion is good . . . So far from regarding religion as a uniting banner, I believe that some rationalistic and non-religious modes of thought are as relevant as some religions are. I cannot subscribe to the view that 'religion' itself contains a high view of man and the hope for the future . . . I am ready to join with anyone in the assertion of human rights and belief in the dignity of man, and for this purpose to join with those whose view of man is not specifically Christian or theistic. But this is not achieved by making 'religion' the slogan, as for this purpose many scientific humanists and non-religious persons have. I would join in a human rights platform, but not on the basis of 'religion'. . . .

Edward Carpenter was disturbed by this argument and wrote a long letter to plead for the opposite view. The archbishop was still uncompromising. 'My misgivings are about presenting a platform of "religion" as the way forward for humanity as I am not really sure what it is.' On 17 December 1969 he met Carpenter and Lord Sorensen to talk about it.

He was willing to commemorate for the Sikhs their spiritual hero Gur Nanak—a great teacher of mankind—6 November 1969 at a dinner.

On 29 April 1970 he visited the Hindu temple at Golders Green; and the Shri Sai-Baba Hindu Centre in connection with it; and spoke and dined. It was reported amusedly that at the meeting he sat on a chair borrowed from the nearby Unitarian church.

He welcomed the exiled Dalai Lama at Lambeth.

In 1972 the Board of Governors of the Church Commissioners, with the archbishop presiding, rescinded an earlier decision to make a redundant church in Wakefield available to the Muslims for use as a mosque. The chairman of the meeting was totally opposed. Afterwards he expressed his disagreement with the decision, at a question and answer session in Norwich cathedral.

He welcomed at Lambeth (1) Swami Venkatesananda 3 August 1972, whom he asked to explain to him Yoga and the length of training and told him that it was important to promote spirituality in all by all means; and when the Swami asked for his blessing he gave it. (2) Swami Shree Pramukh the leader of the Shree Swaminaryan faith within Hinduism, summer 1974.

Select Bibliography

(Place of publication London unless stated otherwise)

WORKS BY A. M. RAMSEY

The Gospel and the Catholic Church, 1936; second edition, 1956.

The Resurrection of Christ: An Essay in Biblical Theology, 1945; revised edition 1961; with different subtitle *A Study of the Event and its meaning for Christian Faith*, and with an added bibliography. There was a French translation.

The Church of England and the Eastern Orthodox Church: Why their Unity is important, 1946.

Catholicity: A Study in the Conflict of Christian Traditions in the West, 1947. Ramsey was the principal drafter and chairman of the group responsible but Dom Gregory Dix, the Anglican Benedictine, certainly drafted part.

The Glory of God and the Transfiguration of Christ, 1949 (French translation 1965). There was a revised English edition 1967, with a new preface about the changed setting in which Biblical theology now works; a number of errors were corrected and the bibliography was omitted.

F. D. Maurice and the Conflicts of Modern Theology, 1951. These were the Maurice Memorial Lectures at King's College, London, in Lent 1948.

Durham Essays and Addresses, 1956.

From Gore to Temple: The Development of Anglican Theology between Lux Mundi and the Second World War 1889–1939, 1960. These were the Hale Memorial lectures at Seabury-Western Theological Seminary for 1959. As the Americans were less familiar with the Englishmen Gore and Temple, and more likely to think from the title that the book was about primitive anthropology, the American edition was entitled *An Era in Anglican Theology*, New York, 1960.

Introducing the Christian Faith, 1961. A printing of addresses given from notes at a mission to Oxford University, 1960, and also at Oxford, 1953, Cambridge 1954, Trinity College Dublin, 1961. Revised edition 1970.

Image Old and New, 1963. The first considered reply to John Robinson's *Honest to God*. Only 15 pages but beautifully written. In this connection H. W. Bartsch published at Hamburg a discussion on *Honest to God* in which Ramsey took part; published under the title *Ehrlich gegenüber Gott*, which was an accurate mistranslation of Robinson's title, which indeed was impossible to convey in German.

Canterbury Essays and Addresses, 1964.

Sacred and Secular: A Study in the other worldly and this-worldly aspects of Christianity (Holland Lectures for 1964), 1965.

Rome and Canterbury (public lecture at Dublin, 23 June 1967), 1967.

God, Christ and the World: A Study in Contemporary Theology, 1969. This, though short, is a weighty book in the development of Ramsey's thought. From 1936 (*The Gospel and the Catholic Church*) to 1961 (*From Gore to Temple*) his mind moved in the same pattern and tradition of modern Christian thinking. His basis was very strong and continued still to guide his thinking, but in the middle sixties he asked himself what we can learn if anything from the more radical theologians (Bonhoeffer, Bultmann, Harvey Cox, the Death of God writers, Teilhard de Chardin). Whereas once he drew on Hoskyns, Temple, Maurice, he now also drew on Hans Urs von Balthasar, Karl Rahner, Arthur Vogel, and Macquarrie. It is a wider air of American and European divinity.

Freedom, Faith and the Future, 1970. Four addresses given at Great St Mary's Church, Cambridge.

The Future of the Christian Church (with L. J. Suenens), 1971 (New York edition 1970).

The Christian Priest Today, 1972 (revised edition considerably altered 1985). This is dedicated to the clergy whom he ordained in his three dioceses 1952–72 and consists almost entirely of the charges which he gave them on the eve of their ordinations. The 1972 edition had German and Italian translation. On this theme he also gave a preface to a republication in 1958 of Hensley Henson's *Ad Clerum*, which contained Henson's Charges to the clergy whom he ordained.

The Charismatic Christ, New York, 1973, London, 1974. Three lectures out of six in the book; what is right and what at times is perilous about the charismatic movement; about the musical *Godspell*, and about *Jesus Christ Superstar*. The lectures were given at the Trinity Institute, New York, in January 1972.

Canterbury Pilgrim, 1974 (collected essays, mostly unpublished before).

Come Holy Spirit (with L. J. Suenens), New York, 1976 (papers delivered in New York, 1974).

Holy Spirit, 1977. Spanish translation, Salamanca, 1979 (*Espíritù Santo*).

Jesus and the Living Past, Oxford, 1980. This was originally the Henson Lectures at Oxford University, on 'History and Contemporary Christianity'; these were never published. He deposited copies in the Bodleian library and then used the substance in the Hale lectures at Evanston in October 1978. This is still the old biblical theologian of *The Gospel and the Catholic Church* or *The Transfiguration*; still with the conviction that to be a theologian it is indispensable to be a person of prayer, critical of theologians who said that you could not take a theology out of its cultural context, because great teaching has the power of reaching out across the frontiers of culture; and therefore radical changes in presentation or interpretation do not prevent an underlying identity in the faith that is believed and the gospel that is preached; and he did not think that the Incarnation could be for Christians a dispensable concept.

Be Still and Know, 1982.

For a selective list of Ramsey's published articles see James Dunkley (to whom I owe indispensable help) in *Nashotah Review*, vol. 16, no. 3. Ramsey republished many of the best of them in *Durham Essays and Addresses* or in *Canterbury Essays and Addresses* or in *Canterbury Pilgrim*. But there are articles especially in *Sobornost'* which he did not republish.

Two anthologies of Ramsey's writings are excellently done:

DUGGAN, MONICA, *Through the Year with Michael Ramsey*, 1975—devotional readings for each day of the calendar year.
KENDALL, LORNA, *Gateway To God*, 1988. (Brief selected citations by theme; it appeared within four days of Ramsey's death).

WORKS BY OTHER AUTHORS

BEESON, TREVOR, *The Church in Crisis*, 1973.
BOURDEAUX, M., *Patriarch and Prophets*, 1969.
BUCHANAN C. O., *et al.*, *Growing into Unity*, 1970 (the best critique of the Anglican-Methodist Unity scheme. Interestingly they began the book with a quotation from MR, *The Gospel and the Catholic Church*).
BUSCH, EBERHARD, *Karl Barth*, Engl. trans., 1975.
CARPENTER, E., *Cantuar*, 1971, rev. ed. 1988.
CHADWICK, O., *Hensley Henson*, Oxford, 1983.
CLEMENTS, K. W., *Lovers of Discord*, 1988.
CORNWALL, P., *One Step is Enough*, 1986.
CRADDOCK, P., ed., *Recollections of the Cambridge Union, 1815–1939*, 1953. This is an introduction by Craddock for the period in which the presidents are dead and then reminiscences by several distinguished presidents of the early twentieth century, including (on pp. 124 ff) MR.
CURTIS, P., *A Hawk among the Sparrows* (a Life of Austin Farrer), 1985.
DE-LA-NOY, M., *A Day in the Life of God*, Derby, 1971.
Duggan, M., *Runcie*, 1983.
EDWARDS, D. L., *Ian Ramsey, Bishop of Durham*, Oxford, 1973.
——, *Leaders of the Church of England*, rev. ed. 1978.
EDWARDS, DONALD, *The Two Worlds of Donald Edwards*, London, 1970.
FOUILLOUX, E., *Les Catholiques et l'unité chrétienne du XIXe au XXe siècle*, Paris, 1972.
GRAHAM, A. A. K., *A History of Lincoln Theological College*, Lincoln, 1974.
GRUBB, K., *Crypts of Power*, 1971.
HALL, CLARENCE, 'Canterbury Pilgrim Archbishop', in Readers Digest, vol. 98 (June 1971), pp. 39ff.
HAMILTON, E., *Cardinal Suenens*, 1975.
HARRIS, RONALD, *Memory-Soft the Air*, Edinburgh, 1987.

HASTINGS, A., *A History of English Christianity 1920–1985*, 2nd edition 1987.

HENDERSON, R. J., *A History of King's College Choir School*, Cambridge, 1981.

HERBERT, IVOR, *The Way to the Top*, 1969.

HEUSTON, R. F. V., *Lives of the Lord Chancellors 1940–1970*, Oxford, 1987.

HOLTBY, ROBERT, *Robert Wright Stopford*, 1988.

HOPKINS, GORDON, *Memories*, Durham, 1989.

HOWARTH, T., *Cambridge between the Wars*, 1978.

HOWE, JOHN, *Highways and Hedges: Anglicanism and the Universal Church*, Toronto, 1985.

JASPER, R. C. D., *George Bell*, 1967.

KEYNES, M., *Essays in Biography*, 1972.

LEECH, KENNETH, 'The Real Archbishop: a Profile of Michael Ramsey' in *The Christian Century*, vol. 103, no. 9, 12 March 1986.

LLOYD, ROGER, *The Church of England 1900–1965*, 1966.

MARTIN, CHRISTOPHER ed., *The Great Christian Centuries to Come*, 1974.

MELLOR, D. H., *'Better than the Stars'. A Portrait of Frank Ramsey*. BBC 1978.

NAMIER, J., *Louis Namier*, London, 1971.

Nashotah Review, vol. 16, no. 3, Autumn 1976: *Essays in Honor of Michael Ramsey*. Nashotah House, 1978.

National Committee of Commonwealth Immigrants. Reports 1967–8.

NEWSOME, D., *On the Edge of Paradise. A. C. Benson: the Diarist*, 1980.

PARE P. N., and DONALD HARRIS, *Eric Milner-White*, 1965. (MR wrote an epilogue).

PAUL, L., *A Church by Daylight*, 1973.

PAWLEY, B. and M., *Rome and Canterbury through four Centuries*, rev. ed. 1981.

PAWLEY, M., *Donald Coggan*, 1987.

PEART-BINNS, J. S., *Ambrose Reeves*, London, 1973.

——, *Eric Treacy*, 1980.

——, *Defender of the Church of England: The Life of Bishop R. R. Williams*, Oxford, 1984.

——, *Archbishop Joost De Blank*, 1987.

——, *Wand of London*, 1987.

——, *Graham Leonard*, 1988.

POPE, FRED, *The Canterbury Pewside Book*, 1966. This was a book of straightforward photographs which were made occasionally though mildly comic by irrelevant captions underneath and by a red gargantuan archiepiscopal laugh on the front cover. There are among them good pictures of Joan Ramsey and also of the Patriarch Alexei of Moscow.

PURCELL, W., *Fisher of Lambeth*, 1969.

SIMMS, GEORGE, 'Thoughts after Lambeth' in *Studies* (1968), 345 ff. This is so far the best short survey of the general mood in the Conference of 1968. It prints one of MR's two important speeches at the Conference, a speech not published elsewhere.

SIMPSON, J. B., *The Hundredth Archbishop of Canterbury*, New York, 1962. (MR annotated his copy with important glosses).

—— and E. M. STORY, *The Long Shadow of Lambeth X*, 1969.

SMYTH, CHARLES, *Cyril Forster Garbett*, 1959.

STEPHENSON, A. M. G., *Anglicanism and the Lambeth Conferences*, 1978.

STOCKWOOD, M., *Chanctonbury Ring*, 1982.

TEMPLE, W., *Christian Faith and Life*, 1931.

TIBBATTS, GEORGE, *John How*, Oxford, 1983.

VIDLER, A. R., *Twentieth Century Defenders of the Faith*, 1965.

VISSER T'HOOFT, W. A., *Memoirs*, Engl. trans. 1988.

WAKEFIELD, GORDON, *Crucifixion-Resurrection*, 1981 (on Hoskyns. A book which MR valued and to which he wrote a foreword); 'Michael Ramsey: a Theological Appraisal', in *Theology* (Nov. 1988).

WELSBY, P. A., *A History of the Church of England 1945–1980*, Oxford, 1984.

WILKINSON, P., *Memoir of Eric Milner-White*, Cambridge, 1963.

Index

Index

OXFORD

MORE OXFORD PAPERBACKS

Details of a selection of other Oxford Paperbacks follow. A complete list of Oxford Paperbacks, including The World's Classics, Twentieth-Century Classics, OPUS, Past Masters, Oxford Authors, Oxford Shakespeare, and Oxford Paperback Reference, is available in the UK from the General Publicity Department, Oxford University Press (RS), Walton Street, Oxford, OX2 6DP.

In the USA, complete lists are available from the Paperbacks Marketing Manager, Oxford University Press, 200 Madison Avenue, New York, NY 10016.

Oxford Paperbacks are available from all good bookshops. In case of difficulty, customers in the UK can order direct from Oxford University Press Bookshop, 116 High Street, Oxford, Freepost, OX1 4BR, enclosing full payment. Please add 10 per cent of the published price for postage and packing.

RELIGION AND THEOLOGY
IN OXFORD PAPERBACKS

Oxford Paperbacks offers incisive studies of the philosophies and ceremonies of the world's major religions, including Christianity, Judaism, Islam, Buddhism, and Hinduism.

A HISTORY OF HERESY
David Christie-Murray

'Heresy, a cynic might say, is the opinion held by a minority of men which the majority declares unacceptable and is strong enough to punish.'

What is heresy? Who were the great heretics and what did they believe? Why might those originally condemned as heretics come to be regarded as martyrs and cherished as saints?

Heretics, those who dissent from orthodox Christian belief, have existed at all times since the Christian Church was founded and the first Christians became themselves heretics within Judaism. From earliest times too, politics, orthodoxy, and heresy have been inextricably entwined—to be a heretic was often to be a traitor and punishable by death at the stake—and heresy deserves to be placed against the background of political and social developments which shaped it.

This book is a vivid combination of narrative and comment which succeeds in both re-creating historical events and elucidating the most important—and most disputed—doctrines and philosophies.

Also in Oxford Paperbacks:

Christianity in the West 1400–1700   John Bossy
John Henry Newman: A Biography   Ian Ker
Islam: The Straight Path   John L. Esposito

ART AND ARCHITECTURE IN
OXFORD PAPERBACKS

Oxford Paperbacks offers a growing list of art and architecture books, ranging from Michael Baxandall on Renaissance Italy to George Melly on pop art and from Anthony Blunt on art theory to Bram Dijkstra on fin-de-siècle 'erotic' art.

ENGLISH PARISH CHURCHES AS
WORKS OF ART
Alec Clifton-Taylor

In the course of his life Alec Clifton-Taylor visited thousands of churches and recorded his observations and opinions on their merits. The result, in this book, is not a dry analysis of the chronological evolution of churches and their styles, but a revealing tour of the parish church with the greatest emphasis on aesthetic value.

As all those who got to know him through his television appearances will agree, Alec Clifton-Taylor was the ideal guide to architecture—deeply knowledgeable and enthusiastic in his responses. His first book, *The Pattern of English Building*, is regarded as a classic and his popular BBC television series, *Six English Towns*, and its sequels, claimed a wide audience.

'"What a church!" writes Alec Clifton-Taylor of Walpole St Peter in Norfolk . . . "an unforgettable experience" . . . [Mr Clifton-Taylor] was one of the most individual, civilized, and lovable historians I have ever met.' Patrick Nuttgens, *Times Higher Educational Supplement*

Also in Oxford Paperbacks:

Painting and Experience in 15th-century Italy
Michael Baxandall
American Buildings and their Architects: The Colonial and Neo-Classical Styles   William H. Pierson
Vision and Design   Roger Fry
Revolt into Style   George Melly

PAST MASTERS

General Editor: Keith Thomas

The people whose ideas have made history . . .

'One begins to wonder whether any intelligent person can afford not to possess the whole series.' *Expository Times*

JESUS

Humphrey Carpenter

Jesus wrote no books, but the influence of his life and teaching has been immeasurable. Humphrey Carpenter's account of Jesus is written from the standpoint of an historian coming fresh to the subject without religious preconceptions. And no previous knowledge of Jesus or the Bible on the reader's part is assumed.

How reliable are the Christian 'Gospels' as an account of what Jesus did or said? How different were his ideas from those of his contemporaries? What did Jesus think of himself? Humphrey Carpenter begins his answer to these questions with a survey and evaluation of the evidence on which our knowledge of Jesus is based. He then examines his teaching in some detail, and reveals the perhaps unexpected way in which his message can be said to be original. In conclusion he asks to what extent Jesus's teaching has been followed by the Christian Churches that have claimed to represent him since his death.

'Carpenter's *Jesus* is about as objective as possible, while giving every justifiable emphasis to the real and persistent forcefulness of the moral teaching of this charismatic personality.' Kathleen Nott, *The Times*

'an excellent, straightforward presentation of up-to-date scholarship' David L. Edwards, *Church Times*

Also available in Past Masters:

PAST MASTERS

General Editor: Keith Thomas

The *Past Masters* series offers students and general readers alike concise introductions to the lives and works
of the world's greatest literary figures, composers,
philosophers, religious leaders, scientists, and social and
political thinkers.

'Put end to end, this series will constitute a noble encyclopaedia of the history of ideas.' Mary Warnock

HOBBES

Richard Tuck

Thomas Hobbes (1588–1679) was the first great English political philosopher, and his book *Leviathan* was one of the first
truly modern works of philosophy. He has long had the reputation of being a pessimistic atheist, who saw human nature
as inevitably evil, and who proposed a totalitarian state to
subdue human failings. In this new study, Richard Tuck shows
that while Hobbes may indeed have been an atheist, he was
far from pessimistic about human nature, nor did he advocate
totalitarianism. By locating him against the context of his age,
Dr Tuck reveals Hobbs to have been passionately concerned
with the refutation of scepticism in both science and ethics,
and to have developed a theory of knowledge which rivalled
that of Descartes in its importance for the formation of modern
philosophy.

Also available in Past Masters:

POLITICS IN OXFORD PAPERBACKS

Oxford Paperbacks offers incisive and provocative studies of the political ideologies and institutions that have shaped the modern world since 1945.

GOD SAVE ULSTER!

The Religion and Politics of Paisleyism

Steve Bruce

Ian Paisley in the only modern Western leader to have founded his own Church and political party, and his enduring popularity and success mirror the complicated issues which continue to plague Northern Ireland. This book is the first serious analysis of his religious and political careers and a unique insight into Unionist politics and religion in Northern Ireland today.

Since it was founded in 1951, the Free Presbyterian Church of Ulster has grown steadily; it now comprises some 14,000 members in fifty congregations in Ulster and ten branches overseas. The Democratic Unionist Party, formed in 1971, now speaks for about half of the Unionist voters in Northern Ireland, and the personal standing of the man who leads both these movements was confirmed in 1979 when Ian R. K. Paisley received more votes than any other member of the European Parliament. While not neglecting Paisley's 'charismatic' qualities, Steve Bruce argues that the key to his success has been his ability to embody and represent traditional evangelical Protestantism and traditional Ulster Unionism.

'original and profound . . . I cannot praise this book too highly.'
Bernard Crick, *New Society*

Also in Oxford Paperbacks:

Freedom Under Thatcher   Keith Ewing and Conor Gearty
Strong Leadership   Graham Little
The Thatcher Effect   Dennis Kavanagh and Anthony Seldon

PAST MASTERS

General Editor: Keith Thomas

Past Masters is a series of concise and authoritative introductions to the life and works of men and women whose ideas still influence the way we think today.

'Put end to end, this series will constitute a noble encyclopaedia of the history of ideas.' Mary Warnock

SHAKESPEARE

Germaine Greer

'At the core of a coherent social structure as he viewed it lay marriage, which for Shakespeare is no mere comic convention but a crucial and complex ideal. He rejected the stereotype of the passive, sexless, unresponsive female and its inevitable concommitant, the misogynist conviction that all women were whores at heart. Instead he created a series of female characters who were both passionate and pure, who gave their hearts spontaneously into the keeping of the men they loved and remained true to the bargain in the face of tremendous odds.'

Germaine Greer's short book on Shakespeare brings a completely new eye to a subject about whom more has been written than on any other English figure. She is especially concerned with discovering why Shakespeare 'was and is a popular artist', who remains a central figure in English cultural life four centuries after his death.

'eminently trenchant and sensible . . . a genuine exploration in its own right' John Bayley, *Listener*

'the clearest and simplest explanation of Shakespeare's thought I have yet read' Auberon Waugh, *Daily Mail*

Also available in Past Masters:

Paine   Mark Philp
Dante   George Holmes
The Buddha   Michael Carrithers
Confucius   Raymond Dawson

HISTORY IN OXFORD PAPERBACKS

Oxford Paperbacks offers a comprehensive list of books on British history, ranging from Frank Stenton's *Anglo-Saxon England* to John Guy's *Tudor England*, and from Christopher Hill's *A Turbulent, Seditious, and Factious People* to Kenneth O. Morgan's *Labour in Power: 1945– 1951*.

TUDOR ENGLAND

John Guy

Tudor England is a compelling account of political and religious developments from the advent of the Tudors in the 1460s to the death of Elizabeth I in 1603.

Following Henry VII's capture of the Crown at Bosworth in 1485, Tudor England witnessed far-reaching changes in government and the Reformation of the Church under Henry VIII, Edward VI, Mary, and Elizabeth; that story is enriched here with character studies of the monarchs and politicians that bring to life their personalities as well as their policies.

Authoritative, clearly argued, and crisply written, this comprehensive book will be indispensable to anyone interested in the Tudor Age.

'lucid, scholarly, remarkably accomplished . . . an excellent overview' *Sunday Times*

'the first comprehensive history of Tudor England for more than thirty years' Patrick Collinson, *Observer*

Also in Oxford Paperbacks:

John Calvin William J. Bouwsma
Early Modern France 1515–1715 Robin Briggs
The Spanish Armada Felipe Fernández-Armesto
Time in History G. J. Whitrow

HISTORY IN OXFORD PAPERBACKS

Oxford Paperbacks' superb history list offers books on a wide range of topics from ancient to modern times, whether general period studies or assessments of particular events, movements, or personalities.

THE STRUGGLE FOR
THE MASTERY OF EUROPE 1848–1918

A. J. P. Taylor

The fall of Metternich in the revolutions of 1848 heralded an era of unprecedented nationalism in Europe, culminating in the collapse of the Hapsburg, Romanov, and Hohenzollern dynasties at the end of the First World War. In the intervening seventy years the boundaries of Europe changed dramatically from those established at Vienna in 1815. Cavour championed the cause of *Risorgimento* in Italy; Bismarck's three wars brought about the unification of Germany; Serbia and Bulgaria gained their independence courtesy of the decline of Turkey— 'the sick man of Europe'; while the great powers scrambled for places in the sun in Africa. However, with America's entry into the war and President Wilson's adherence to idealistic internationalist principles, Europe ceased to be the centre of the world, although its problems, still primarily revolving around nationalist aspirations, were to smash the Treaty of Versailles and plunge the world into war once more.

A. J. P. Taylor has drawn the material for his account of this turbulent period from the many volumes of diplomatic documents which have been published in the five major European languages. By using vivid language and forceful characterization, he has produced a book that is as much a work of literature as a contribution to scientific history.

'One of the glories of twentieth-century writing.' *Observer*

Also in Oxford Paperbacks:

Portrait of an Age: Victorian England   G. M. Young
Germany 1866–1945   Gorden A. Craig
The Russian Revolution 1917–1932   Sheila Fitzpatrick
France 1848–1945   Theodore Zeldin

ILLUSTRATED HISTORIES IN
OXFORD PAPERBACKS

Lavishly illustrated with over 200 full colour and black and white photographs, and written by leading academics, Oxford Paperbacks' illuminating histories provide superb introductions to a wide range of political, cultural, and social topics.

THE OXFORD ILLUSTRATED HISTORY
OF ENGLISH LITERATURE

Edited by Pat Rogers

Britain possesses a literary heritage which is almost unrivalled in the Western world. In this volume, the richness, diversity, and continuity of that tradition are explored by a group of Britain's foremost literary scholars.

Chapter by chapter the authors trace the history of English literature, from its first stirrings in Anglo-Saxon poetry to the present day. At its heart towers the figure of Shakespeare, who is accorded a special chapter to himself. Other major figures such as Chaucer, Milton, Donne, Wordsworth, Dickens, Eliot, and Auden are treated in depth, and the story is brought up to date with discussion of living authors such as Seamus Heaney and Edward Bond.

'[a] lovely volume . . . put in your thumb and pull out plums' Michael Foot

'scholarly and enthusiastic people have written inspiring essays that induce an eagerness in their readers to return to the writers they admire' *Economist*

Other illustrated histories in Oxford Paperbacks:

The Oxford Illustrated History of Britain
The Oxford Illustrated History of Medieval Europe

OPUS

General Editors: Christopher Butler,
Robert Evans, Alan Ryan

A HISTORY OF WESTERN PHILOSOPHY

This series of OPUS books offers a comprehensive and up-to-date survey of the history of philosophical ideas from earliest times. Its aim is not only to set those ideas in their immediate cultural context, but also to focus on their value and relevance to twentieth-century thinking.

CLASSICAL THOUGHT

Terence Irwin

Spanning over a thousand years from Homer to Saint Augustine, *Classical Thought* encompasses a vast range of material, in succinct style, while remaining clear and lucid even to those with no philosophical or Classical background.

The major philosophers and philosophical schools are examined—the Presocratics, Socrates, Plato, Aristotle, Stoicism, Epicureanism, Neoplatonism; but other important thinkers, such as Greek tragedians, historians, medical writers, and early Christian writers, are also discussed. The emphasis is naturally on questions of philosophical interest (although the literary and historical background to Classical philosophy is not ignored), and again the scope is broad—ethics, the theory of knowledge, philosophy of mind, philosophical theology. All this is presented in a fully integrated, highly readable text which covers many of the most important areas of ancient thought and in which stress is laid on the variety and continuity of philosophical thinking after Aristotle.

Also available in the History of Western Philosophy series:

The Rationalists   John Cottingham
Continental Philosophy since 1750   Robert C. Solomon
The Empiricists   R. S. Woolhouse

HISTORY IN OXFORD PAPERBACKS

As the Oxford Paperbacks' history list grows, so does the range of periods it covers, from the Pharaohs to Anglo-Saxon England, and from Early Modern France to the Second World War.

EGYPT AFTER THE PHARAOHS

Alan K. Bowman

The thousand years between Alexander the Great's invasion in 332 BC and the Arab conquest in AD 642 was a period of enormous change and vitality in the history of Egypt. The Hellenistic era under the powerful Ptolemies ended with the defeat of Antony and Cleopatra in 30 BC, and Egypt became a province of Rome.

Throughout the millenium, however, many of the customs and belief of old Egypt survived, adapting themselves to the new rulers, who were in turn influenced by Egyptian culture. The heritage of the Egypt of the Pharaohs remained a vital force in the history of the land until the coming of Islam.

A vast collection of papyrus texts has survived from this period recording not only the great events but the everyday letters, lawsuits, accounts, and appeals of ordinary Egyptians. From these texts and from the evidence of archaeology, Dr Bowman draws together the Egyptian, Greek, and Roman strands of the story, presenting a masterly survey of the history, economy, and social life of Egypt in this thousand year span.

'eminently readable . . . should be studied by anyone who is seeking details of everyday life in the Roman period' *British Archaeological News*

Also in Oxford Paperbacks:

A History of the Vikings Gwyn Jones
A Turbulent, Seditious, and Factious People Christopher Hill
The Duel in European History V. G. Kiernan